STUDIES IN CHRISTIAN HISTORY AND THOUGHT

Imputation and Impartation

Union with Christ in American Reformed Theology

STUDIES IN CHRISTIAN HISTORY AND THOUGHT

A full listing of titles in this series
appears at the end of this book

STUDIES IN CHRISTIAN HISTORY AND THOUGHT

Imputation and Impartation

Union with Christ in American Reformed Theology

William B. Evans

WIPF & STOCK · Eugene, Oregon

Wipf and Stock Publishers
199 W 8th Ave, Suite 3
Eugene, OR 97401

Imputation and Impartation
Union with Christ in American Reformed Theology
By Evans, William B.
Copyright©2008 Paternoster
ISBN 13: 978-1-60608-478-6
Publication date 2/11/2009
Previously published by Paternoster, 2008

"This Edition Published by Wipf and Stock Publishers by arrangement with Paternoster"

STUDIES IN CHRISTIAN HISTORY AND THOUGHT

Series Preface

This series complements the specialist series of *Studies in Evangelical History and Thought* and *Studies in Baptist History and Thought* for which Paternoster is becoming increasingly well known by offering works that cover the wider field of Christian history and thought. It encompasses accounts of Christian witness at various periods, studies of individual Christians and movements, and works which concern the relations of church and society through history, and the history of Christian thought.

The series includes monographs, revised dissertations and theses, and collections of papers by individuals and groups. As well as 'free standing' volumes, works on particular running themes are being commissioned; authors will be engaged for these from around the world and from a variety of Christian traditions.

A high academic standard combined with lively writing will commend the volumes in this series both to scholars and to a wider readership.

Series Editors

Alan P.F. Sell, Visiting Professor at Acadia University Divinity College, Nova Scotia, Canada

David Bebbington, Professor of History, University of Stirling, Stirling, Scotland, UK

Clyde Binfield, Professor Emeritus in History, University of Sheffield, UK

Gerald Bray, Anglican Professor of Divinity, Beeson Divinity School, Samford University, Birmingham, Alabama, USA

Grayson Carter, Associate Professor of Church History, Fuller Theological Seminary SW, Phoenix, Arizona, USA

To Fay, Andrew, and Rebecca

Contents

Acknowledgements	xiii
Introduction	1

Part I: Prologue

Chapter 1 John Calvin: Influence and Ambiguity	7
The Centrality of Union with Christ for Calvin	7
Calvin's Doctrine of *Unio* in Recent Scholarship	8
The Nature of Union with Christ	14
Union by Faith and the Holy Spirit	14
Union with Christ through Word and Sacrament	17
UNION WITH CHRIST IN BAPTISM	17
UNION WITH CHRIST IN THE LORD'S SUPPER	19
"Substantial" Union with Christ	23
Union with Christ and Applied Soteriology	29
Sanctification through Union with Christ	29
Justification through Union with Christ	30
JUSTIFICATION AS FORENSIC AND SYNTHETIC	31
THE RELATION OF JUSTIFICATION AND UNION WITH CHRIST	32
The Structure of Calvin's Soteriology	38
Chapter 2 Reformed Orthodoxy and Union with Christ	43
Reformed Orthodoxy and Scholastic Method	44
Reformed Orthodoxy and the Loci Method	45
Reformed Orthodoxy and Resurgent Aristotelianism	46
Reformed Orthodoxy and the *Ordo Salutis*	52
Federal Theology and the Bifurcation of Union	57
Federal Theology and "Extrinsic Legalism"	59
The Scottish Federal Reconceptualization of Union with Christ	65
The Influence of Pietism	75

Devotional Communion with Christ	76
Puritans and the Sacraments	78
Conclusion: The Federal Orthodoxy Dilemma	81

Part II: The New England Trajectory: Imputation Eclipsed

Chapter 3 Jonathan Edwards on Salvation and Union with Christ — 87

Edwards and the Reformed Tradition	87
The Philosophical Context of Edwards' Thought	89
The Religious Context of Edwards' Thought	92
Edwards on the Nature of Union with Christ	95
The Human Perspective—Faith as Union with Christ	96
The Divine Perspective—Union with God	97
Edwards on Applied Soteriology	100
Justification by Faith	101
Imputation and Original Sin	104
The Relation of Justification and Sanctification	107
Summary—Edwards on Union with Christ	111

Chapter 4 Later New England Thought: Samuel Hopkins and Timothy Dwight — 113

Samuel Hopkins	114
Hopkins' Contribution to New England Theology	115
Hopkins on Applied Soteriology and Union with Christ	122
Summary	129
The Rational Evangelicalism of Timothy Dwight	130
Dwight's Relation to Earlier New England Thought	131
Dwight on Applied Soteriology and Union with Christ	134
Conclusions and Observations	136

Part III: The Mercersburg Soteriology

Chapter 5 John W. Nevin and Organic Union with Christ — 141

Biography	141
The Mercersburg Theology	146
German Influences on the Mercersburg Theology	147

IDEALIST ONTOLOGY AND EPISTEMOLOGY	148
ORGANIC VIEWS OF HISTORY	149
CHRISTOCENTRIC APPROACHES TO THEOLOGY	150
THE MEDIATING THEOLOGIANS	152
Nevin's Theological Method	155
The Nature of Union with Christ	158
Union with Christ and Applied Soteriology	168
Sanctification in Christ	168
Justification in Christ	169
Union with Christ and the Sacraments	175
Interpretive Questions and Observations	181
Summary and Conclusions	183

Part IV: The Princeton Defense of Imputation

Chapter 6 The Federal Theology of Charles Hodge	**187**
Biography	188
The Method and Context of Hodge's Theology	189
Scottish Common Sense Realism	189
Religious Experience	193
The Reformed Tradition	194
The Problem of Solidarity—The Defense of Imputation	195
Original Sin and the Solidarity with Adam	196
Soteriology and Solidarity with Christ	202
Applied Soteriology—The *Ordo Salutis*	208
Applied Soteriology—Justification	211
Ecclesiology and the Sacraments	215
Chapter 7 The Later Federal Textbook Tradition:	
A. A. Hodge and Louis Berkhof	**229**
A. A. Hodge	229
Louis Berkhof	233
Conclusions Regarding the Princeton Federal Trajectory	235

Part V: Epilogue

Chapter 8 Subsequent Developments — 241
The Academic Tradition — 241
Evangelical Theology — 254

Chapter 9 Retrospect and Prospect — 259
Retrospective Observations — 259
Prospect — 261
  A Spiritual and Eschatological Realism — 262
  A Concrete and Christocentric Soteriology — 264
  Benefits of a Revisioned Reformed Soteriology — 266

Bibliography — 269

Index — 293

Acknowledgements

Interest in the theme of Union with Christ and its role in Reformed theology was stimulated for this writer over twenty years ago now by two professors at Westminster Theological Seminary in Philadelphia—Sinclair B. Ferguson and Richard B. Gaffin, Jr. This volume, in truth, is an attempt to provide historical context for contemporary Reformed and Evangelical discussions of applied soteriology. Such historical context is particularly needful today, as questions regarding the doctrine of justification, imputation, and the relationship of justification and sanctification have a new and pressing saliency in the contemporary context.

Volumes such as this do not appear without the support and encouragement of others. This work has its origins in a 1996 dissertation completed for the History of Christian Thought program at Vanderbilt University. The chair of the doctoral committee, Eugene TeSelle, was unfailingly helpful, prompt and incisive in his reading of chapters, and extraordinarily knowledgeable. One could not ask for a better *Doktorvater*. The author found in the Graduate Department of Religion at Vanderbilt University a congenial and supportive community of scholarship. In addition to professors such as John R. Fitzmier, Eugene TeSelle, and Peter Hodgson, fellow GDR students John H. Dawson, John S. Mason, Lawrence R. Rast, and Douglas A. Sweeney were sources of encouragement. Of course, historical studies of this sort require extensive library support, and the staffs of the Vanderbilt University Divinity Library and, more recently, the Erskine College and Theological Seminary Library were eager to acquire needed research materials.

The administration of Erskine College has in various ways encouraged the completion of this book. The two College Deans under whom the author has served, James W. Gettys, Jr. and Donald V. Weatherman, have supported faculty research and writing activity, and a sabbatical in the Spring of 2005 provided concentrated time for work on editorial revisions to the dissertation. Also to be mentioned are the students in the "Christian Theology" course at Erskine College, many of whom have come to recognize and reflect deeply on the importance of the theme of union with Christ for their own understanding of salvation.

The staff of Paternoster, particularly Jeremy Mudditt, Robin Parry, and Anthony Cross, has been thoroughly competent, courteous, and helpful with the myriad of details that comprise such a project. Their extensive publication program continues to provide a substantial service to the church.

Penultimately, thanks are due those who have read the dissertation in its original form and encouraged its publication as a monograph. Along the way, Mark A. Noll read the manuscript with care and provided incisive comments and suggestions. John S. Mason and Rob Roy McGregor shared insights on certain translation matters. Any errors in this volume are, of course, imputable only to the author.

Lastly, special thanks are due the author's family. My wife Fay and my children Andrew and Rebecca have witnessed this project from its inception. Their unfailing love, patience, and support have been an ongoing example of grace and favor. It is to them that this book is rightly dedicated.

William B. Evans
Erskine College
Due West, South Carolina, USA
Christmas 2007

Introduction

Over twenty years ago now, this writer encountered Charles Hodge's review of Mercersburg theologian John W. Nevin's *The Mystical Presence*. In that review, the Calvinist stalwart of Old Princeton Seminary took Nevin and his doctrine of the sacraments and union with Christ to task as incompatible with the Reformed faith in its purity. More surprising was Hodge's treatment of Calvin in the same review. After dismissing the doctrine of union with Christ evident in Calvin's view of the sacraments as a case of pandering to Lutheran interests, Hodge went on to allege that Calvin's doctrine lay in conflict with a fundamental principle of the Reformation itself—the doctrine of justification by grace through faith.[1]

The irony of nineteenth-century America's arch-Calvinist pillorying Calvin himself for subverting a central principle of the Reformation is obvious. Further study and research uncovered a surprising amount of controversy within the nineteenth-century American Reformed community over the nature of union with Christ and over related matters having to do with applied soteriology, or the application of salvation to the Christian. This book is an attempt to place those controversies within the larger context of the development of the Reformed tradition itself.

The Centrality of Union with Christ in Reformed Theology

The centrality of "union with Christ" as an organizing motif in Reformed soteriology has long been recognized. In his compendium of classical Reformed theologians, Heinrich Heppe, the nineteenth-century German historian of dogma, wrote: "At the root of the whole doctrine of the appropriation of salvation lies the doctrine of *insitio* or *insertio in Christum*, through which we live in him and he in us. So the dogmaticians discuss it with special emphasis."[2] More recently, Emil Brunner has termed union with Christ "the center of all Calvinistic thought."[3] Indeed, some have argued with good reason that this Reformed emphasis upon union with Christ stands in marked contrast with the Lutheran tradition, which takes the doctrine of justification by faith as its point of departure when discussing the application of redemption.[4]

Despite the centrality of this motif, it has received relatively little scholarly

---

[1] See Charles Hodge, "Doctrine of the Reformed Church on the Lord's Supper," *The Biblical Repertory and Princeton Review* 20 (1848), 229-230, 253-254.

[2] Heinrich Heppe, *Reformed Dogmatics*, ed. Ernst Bizer, trans. G. T. Thomson (London: George Allen & Unwin, 1950), 511.

[3] Emil Brunner, *Vom Werk des Heiligen Geistes* (Zurich: Zwingli Verlag, 1935), 38.

[4] See e.g., Mathias Schneckenburger, *Vergleichende Darstellung des Lutherischen und Reformirten Lehrbegriffs*, 2 vols. (Stuttgart: J. B. Metzler, 1855), I:182-225.

attention. Calvin's view of the theme and of its place in the larger soteriological context has received considerable scrutiny, but with little resulting consensus. With regard to the period after Calvin, while the motif is repeatedly recognized as important and even crucial, it has generally been treated only incidentally in the context of sacramental studies, studies of Puritan piety or in examinations of the federal theology which arose after Calvin and which was enshrined in later Reformed confessional documents such as the Westminster Confession and Catechisms.

The formal centrality of union with Christ underscores the significance of the theme. Many Reformed theologians from Calvin onward have attempted to subsume all of applied soteriology (acceptance with God and transformation of life) under the rubric "union with Christ." But this formal agreement should not be allowed to mask fundamental and pervasive disagreements among prominent representatives of the tradition regarding the substance and implications of the theme. For this reason, this work will often refer to "union with Christ" as a "motif" or "theme" rather than a "doctrine." We will see that a number of divergent conceptions of "union with Christ" have competed for recognition within the tradition.

Scope of the Study

The bulk of this work focuses on American Reformed thought from Jonathan Edwards through the nineteenth century. Although the theme was certainly discussed elsewhere (the intriguing suggestions of John McLeod Campbell [1800-1872] in Scotland come to mind), it was in America that the conceptual possibilities of the theme were most fully explored. This, of course, was a period of doctrinal crisis for the Reformed churches generally. For American Reformed thinkers in particular, it was a period of soteriological crisis as the older federal theology, which still found ardent and articulate supporters, was challenged by formulations both old and new. During this period there was intense conflict over topics which had traditionally been treated under the rubric "union with Christ"—the nature and mechanism of the imputation of the merits of Christ to the Christian, the relationship of justification to sanctification in the *ordo salutis*, the precise character of the *unio Christi*, and so forth.

We find in American Reformed thought of this period a community of inquiry as well. There was a good deal of spirited debate and interaction among American theologians on these matters; this was a time when, in the memorable words of Mark Noll, "Calvinists got down to the serious business of beating up on each other."[5] This community of inquiry should not, however, be viewed as provincial in outlook. In addition to being well-versed in the Reformed

---

[5] Mark A. Noll, *America's God: From Jonathan Edwards to Abraham Lincoln* (New York: Oxford, 2002), 262.

tradition, a number of the theologians to be examined kept abreast of the latest developments in British and continental theological scholarship. Indeed, certain developments cannot be understood apart from these influences.

Attention to both the pre- and post-history of the theme of union with Christ is also needful here. Because the exact nature of Calvin's own thought became a matter of intense debate during the nineteenth century, the views of this magisterial Reformer are examined in detail. Similarly, because federal theology figures so prominently in the nineteenth-century controversies, the origins and character of the federal theology associated with Reformed scholasticism is also treated. In addition, these developments have continued to exert influence in Reformed and Evangelical circles down to the present, and so the latter portion of this work explores twentieth-century developments and contemporary implications. Here particular attention is paid to influential Continental and British theologians (Herrmann, Barth, Torrance), the Biblical Theology movement, the Dutch-American theologian Lewis B. Smedes, and developments in twentieth-century Evangelical theology.

Method of the Study

This study will involve the isolation and examination of a number of trajectories in American Reformed thought—the New England Calvinism of Jonathan Edwards and his successors, the Mercersburg Theology of John Williamson Nevin, and the Princeton theology of Charles Hodge. Each of these treats the theme of union with Christ in a distinctive fashion. The use of the term *trajectories* points to the developmental dynamic which characterizes any vital theological movement, no matter how much it may claim merely to repristinate the past. The term *trajectories* also implies that, amidst change and development, we may discern a unity of concern or approach which is characteristic of a particular trajectory. In the examination of these trajectories, particular attention will be given to the public documents, the "school-texts," which shaped the thought of generations of ministers and individual Reformed Christians. As much as possible, the authors of these texts will be allowed to speak for themselves.

Finally, in a study of this sort there is sometimes a temptation to rush too quickly to value judgments. More than a few earlier studies dealing with these matters have tended to present later doctrinal developments as lamentable declensions from an alleged earlier purity (Calvin is sometimes viewed as Paradise, with Reformed scholastic orthodoxy as the Fall). It is important that doctrinal developments be understood in their context. Even when a doctrinal move later turns out to be unfortunate, it was generally not without reason or logic in its immediate context, and an understanding of the rationale for it may shed considerable light on the dynamics of doctrinal development within the Reformed tradition.

PART I

PROLOGUE

CHAPTER 1

John Calvin: Influence and Ambiguity

Though this book explores the views of a group of theologians often called "Calvinists," it is not simply about John Calvin's doctrine of union with Christ—an implication of contemporary scholarship is that continuity between the views of Calvin and his Reformed successors must be demonstrated rather than assumed. Nevertheless, the influence of the Genevan Reformer is rarely far from the surface of subsequent Reformed discussions of this motif and related matters. Calvin bequeathed to his Reformed successors both a formal terminological legacy *and* a set of conceptual difficulties. While subsequent Reformed thought departed from Calvin at numerous points, these departures themselves were nevertheless set within a terminological framework which derives largely from Calvin.[1] For these reasons, it is necessary to examine carefully both Calvin's doctrinal formulations and the varying evaluations of them.

The Centrality of Union with Christ for Calvin

Any discussion of Calvin's soteriology, or doctrine of salvation, should begin where the Reformer himself does—with the pregnant opening passage from Book III of the *Institutes*. Here the Reformer calls attention to the believer's union with Christ prior to any discussion of the benefits which Christ brings to those united with him. Justification, sanctification, adoption, and glorification cannot be abstracted from the believer's union with Christ. Indeed, there is a certain priority to union with Christ, and this priority points to the importance and necessity of this union.

> How do we receive those benefits which the Father bestowed on his only begotten Son—not for Christ's own private use, but that he might enrich poor and needy men? First, we must understand that as long as Christ remains outside of us, and

---

[1] Of course, any comprehensive history of the Reformed tradition must take into account the contributions of the Zurich theologians Zwingli and Bullinger, as well as others such as Bucer, Musculus and Vermigli. These others, however, did not accord the theme of *unio Christi* the same prominence as Calvin (e.g., Zwingli and Bullinger) or they looked to Calvin for inspiration at this point (e.g., Peter Martyr Vermigli).

we are separated from him, all that he has suffered and done for the salvation of the human race remains useless and of no value for us.[2]

While recent Calvin scholarship has for the most part rejected the notion that Calvin's theology can be described as a logical system controlled by a "central dogma," the relative prominence of the union with Christ motif in the Calvin corpus has led some to suggest that union with Christ may still be identified as a theme of crucial significance for interpreting Calvin's theology in general. Charles Partee, for example, writes,

> Without denying or minimizing the importance and excellence of various other ways of approaching Calvin's thought, this essay has attempted to suggest the breadth and depth of doctrine of "union with Christ" as the central mystery of Calvin's thinking about every other doctrine and with the expectation that it is a useful and comprehensive way of introducing and surveying Calvin's theology. Such a claim has the advantage of suggesting a theological rather than a philosophical basis for the description of Calvin's thought.[3]

Calvin uses quite a number of expressions—"union (*unio*) with Christ," "communion (*communio*) with Christ," "engrafting (*insitio*) into Christ," "participation (*participatio*) with Christ," and so on—to denote the believer's union and solidarity with Christ. He speaks of a relationship of the greatest intimacy, and yet the precise character of the union and, just as important, the nature of the relationship between this union and the benefits of salvation, have remained topics of keen debate.

Calvin's Doctrine of *Unio* in Recent Scholarship

While summaries of modern scholarship on Calvin's doctrine of union with

---

[2] John Calvin, *Institutes of the Christian Religion*, ed. John T. McNeill, trans. Ford Lewis Battles (Philadelphia: Westminster Press, 1960), III.1.1.

English translations of selections from Calvin's Old Testament commentaries are from *The Commentaries of John Calvin* (Edinburgh: Calvin Translation Society, 1844-1856; reprint, Grand Rapids: Eerdmans, 1948-1950). English translations of Calvin's New Testament commentaries are from *Calvin's New Testament Commentaries*, ed. D. W. Torrance and T. F. Torrance, 12 vols. (Edinburgh: Oliver and Boyd, 1959-72).

[3] Charles Partee, "Calvin's Central Dogma Again," *The Sixteenth Century Journal* 18:2 (1987): 198. See also Tjarko Stadtland, *Rechtfertigung und Heiligung bei Calvin* (Neukirchen-Vluyn: Neukirchener Verlag, 1972), 118.

The prominence of the application of redemption within Calvin's larger theological schema is noted by B. B. Warfield: "The fundamental interest of Calvin as a theologian lay, as is clear, in the region broadly designated soteriological. Perhaps we may go further and add that, within this broad field, his interest was most intense in the application to the sinful soul of the salvation wrought out by Christ." Benjamin Breckinridge Warfield, *Calvin and Augustine* (Philadelphia: Presbyterian and Reformed, 1956), 484.

Christ and its relation to justification and sanctification are available elsewhere,[4] it is interesting to note that treatments of this complex of issues tend to fall into one of several distinct approaches. This situation is due primarily to the fact that Calvin combines a vigorous insistence on a "synthetic" doctrine of forensic justification by faith, involving the imputation of the alien righteousness of Christ to the believer, with a soteriological structure in which justification and sanctification both appear to flow from union with Christ through the Holy Spirit.[5] In a programmatic section of the *Institutes* to which we will return, Calvin writes,

> By partaking of him, we principally receive a double grace: namely, that being reconciled to God through Christ's blamelessness, we may have in heaven instead of a Judge a gracious Father; and secondly, that sanctified by Christ's Spirit we may cultivate blamelessness and purity of life.[6]

This combination of factors—with its extrinsic and intrinsic elements—has been the cause of considerable perplexity, and the majority of Calvin interpreters tend to place controlling emphasis either on forensic justification and imputation on the one hand or on the intrinsic nature of the union and the impartation of the life of Christ to the believer on the other.

There are, first of all, those who claim to detect an inner contradiction between forensic justification and Calvin's doctrine of union with Christ. Mathias Schneckenburger, the nineteenth-century Lutheran historian of dogma, echoed an older Lutheran polemic against the Reformed view by arguing that Reformed theology construes union with Christ as the necessary condition of justification, while Lutherans view union with Christ as the effect of justification. From this, Schneckenburger concludes that for the Lutherans, justification is a "synthetic" declaration, while for the Reformed it is "analytic."[7] In short, the Lutheran tradition views justification as a divine declaration of forensic righteousness of the *sinner* (a declaration based solely on the work of Christ), while the Reformed tradition views justification as a divine declaration of righteousness based on the actual righteousness of the believer (i.e., through union with Christ the sinner is actually made righteous, and on the basis of that transforming union is also proleptically declared to be

---

[4]See, e.g., Wilhelm Kolfhaus, *Christusgemeinschaft bei Johannes Calvin* (Neukirchen: Kreis Moers, 1939), 11-23; Werner Krusche, *Das Wirken des Heiligen Geistes nach Calvin* (Göttingen: Vandenhoeck & Ruprecht, 1957), 265-275; Stadtland, *Rechtfertigung und Heiligung*, 21-26; Cornelis P. Venema, "The Twofold Nature of the Gospel in Calvin's Theology: The *duplex gratia dei* and the Interpretation of Calvin's Theology" (Ph.D. diss.: Princeton Theological Seminary, 1985), 16-34, 217-224. The analysis in this section is in part dependent on the typology suggested by Venema.

[5]On the distinction between analytic and synthetic justification, see G. C. Berkouwer, *Faith and Justification*, trans. Lewis B. Smedes (Grand Rapids: Eerdmans, 1954), 15-16.

[6]Calvin, *Inst.* III.11.1.

[7]Schneckenburger, *Vergleichende Darstellung*, I:195-96; II:15.

righteous in anticipation of that moral transformation).

Willy Lüttge's extensive study of Calvin's doctrine of justification differs from Schneckenburger in that he recognized the presence of a forensic and synthetic doctrine of imputation in Calvin, but also found a tension between two mutually exclusive views of justification and union with Christ articulated side by side in the *Institutes*.[8] On the one hand, in dependence upon passages where Calvin describes justification as flowing from union with Christ, Lüttge claims to discover in Calvin a conception of subjective justification involving consciousness of the forgiveness of sins effected by spiritual union with Christ. On the other hand, Lüttge also finds another, incompatible doctrine of justification involving a "pure forensic conception" of the positive imputation of the righteousness of Christ to the Christian.[9] In seeking to reconcile this apparent contradiction, Lüttge argues that the "pure forensic conception" (involving the imputation of Christ's righteousness to the Christian) is formally asserted by Calvin but has, in actuality, no real place in Calvin's thought and must be subordinated to a conception of justification as the result of the renewal of life through union with Christ.[10]

W. E. Stuermann tries more diligently than Lüttge to reconcile the various elements of Calvin's theology; he effectively rejects Lüttge's contention that a tension exists between justification conceived as the forgiveness of sins and justification construed as the imputation of the righteousness of Christ. But he too finally concludes that there is a conflict between the purely forensic doctrine of justification and the doctrine of union with Christ. Stuermann argues that the imputation of Christ's righteousness occurs *through* mystical union, but that this union is construed (at least when justification is in view) in such a way as not immediately to threaten the purely forensic character of justification. In short, justification can be said to occur through union with Christ because the relation in question is not an actual union at all but merely an indwelling of the Christian by Christ, an indwelling to which the believer contributes nothing and is entirely passive.[11] Nevertheless, Stuermann finally concludes that this notion of "union" does not accord with the active and personal character of faith and with the effect of the Holy Spirit within the believer which Calvin describes elsewhere. In other words, the idea of forensic imputation through spiritual union with Christ is, in the final analysis, incoherent.[12]

While Schneckenberger, Lüttge, and Stuermann differ on many details, they agree that there is a fundamental incompatibility between Calvin's doctrine of justification as a forensic and synthetic imputation on the one hand, and his

---

[8]Willy Lüttge, *Die Rechtfertigungslehre Calvins und ihre Bedeutung für seine Frömmigkeit* (Berlin: Reuther & Reichard, 1909), 41-51.

[9]See ibid., 43, 44.

[10]See ibid., 48.

[11]See Walter E. Stuermann, *A Critical Study of Calvin's Concept of Faith* (Tulsa, Okla., Privately printed, 1952), 192-193.

[12]See ibid., 385.

treatment of justification as an outworking of union with Christ on the other. C. P. Venema phrases the perceived difficulty well:

> There is a tension, so it is argued, between Calvin's treatment of justification in terms of imputation—a juridical category, denoting a new relation of acceptance before God—and his claim that this is made possible by, or is one aspect of, one's union with Christ, the other being regeneration or repentance. If justification depends upon union with Christ, it cannot be wholly defined in juridical categories.[13]

Such a line of interpretation constitutes either a challenge to Calvin's adherence to what has been termed the "principle of Protestantism"—the doctrine of forensic justification—(Schneckenburger) or an explicit accusation that Calvin's theology at this point is incoherent (Lüttge, Stuermann), and a variety of scholars have responded by asserting the essential continuity of Calvin's doctrine of union with Christ with the doctrine of forensic justification.

Replying to Schneckenburger, Albrecht Ritschl argued that Calvin's concern in highlighting union with Christ is to call attention to the way the Christian becomes *conscious* of his or her justification through the merits and work of Christ.[14] This consciousness of justification (i.e., assurance of divine favor) occurs, according to Ritschl, only in the corporate context of the church, and the special role accorded by Calvin to union with Christ is intended to call attention to the *ecclesial* context of assurance: "For Calvin's *unio mystica* indicates the individual's membership in the Church as the condition under which he becomes conscious within himself of justification through Christ's obedience."[15] In this way, Ritschl moves the discussion from the realm of a causal or instrumental function of union with Christ in the objective application of salvation to the corporate context of the individual's subjective experience of justification: "For *unio cum Christo* is assumed to be not the sufficient cause but the *conditio sine qua non* of the justification that is experienced."[16]

Other interpreters of Calvin who see no conflict between forensic justification and union with Christ, however, have not been content to maintain that union with Christ has to do simply with the consciousness of justification. E. Doumergue argues that those, such as Lüttge, who posit a contradiction

---

[13] Venema, "Twofold Nature of the Gospel," 21.

[14] Albrecht Ritschl, *A Critical History of the Christian Doctrine of Justification and Reconciliation*, trans. John S. Black (Edinburgh: Edmonston and Douglas, 1872), 185: "And yet Calvin's doctrinal delineation...is determined precisely by a chief regard to the original reformation phenomenon of the subjective consciousness of justification. The order of the themes and the mode of their treatment in the *Institutio religionis Christianae* (third edition, 1559), is dominated by the inquiry after the antecedents which must have existed without and within the Subject, in order that he may become conscious of justification through Christ alone."

[15] Ibid., 186.

[16] Ibid., 192.

between union with Christ and forensic justification fail to distinguish between the ground or cause of justification and the means of its application to the believer.[17] Doumergue's work is also significant in that he is almost alone in raising, if only in passing, the question of the *mode* or *means* of forensic imputation. As we shall see, the majority of interpreters appear to assume that Calvin's forensic and synthetic doctrine of justification must involve what later came to be termed "immediate imputation"—a mode of imputation implemented simply by an act of the divine will without regard for any personal connection between the parties involved.

A third approach to this larger matter is evident in those interpreters who profess to find no conflict between union with Christ and forensic justification, but who also deny any internal relationship between the two.[18] Two important characteristics of this approach require mention here. First, union with Christ is framed in extrinsic terms. For example, S. P. Dee understands Calvin virtually to identify faith with *unio Christi*. In an often-quoted statement, he asserts that in distinguishing faith and *unio mystica*, Calvin makes only a "logical distinction."[19] Cornelis P. Venema asserts that for Calvin the relationship involved in *unio mystica* "remains a union at the level of a personal relationship and encounter."[20] Second, these interpreters insist that the relationship between union with Christ and forensic justification must be construed in noncausal terms. In an influential passage, Kolfhaus writes, "Justification and union do not stand in a causal relationship with one another, but designate one and the same divine act, in which there is no talk of a before or after."[21] In this way,

---

[17]Émil Doumergue, *Jean Calvin, les hommes et les choses de son temps*, 7 vols. (Lausanne: Georges Bridel, 1899-1928), IV:275: "Thus there is a *cause* and a *means*. The cause of our justification is the sacrifice of Christ, whose righteousness is imputed to us.—The means, by which this righteousness which is imputed to us becomes ours, is the mystical union with Christ, a union which results in our sanctification. Where is the contradiction?" (Ainsi il y a une *cause* et un *moyen*. La cause de notre justification est le sacrifice du Christ, dont la justice nous est imputée.—Le moyen, par lequel cette justice qui nous est imputée devient nôtre, c'est l'union mystique avec le Christ, union dont le résultat est de nous régénérer. Où est la contradiction?)

[18]See Simon Pieter Dee, *Het Geloofsbegrip van Calvijn* (Kampen: J. H. Kok, 1918); W. Kolfhaus, *Christusgemeinschaft bei Johannes Calvin*; Werner Krusche, *Wirken des Heiligen Geistes*; François Wendel, *Calvin: Origins and Development of His Religious Thought*, trans. Philip Mairet (New York: Harper and Row, 1963); Venema, "Twofold Nature of the Gospel." See especially the helpful discussion of this general approach in Venema, "Twofold Nature of the Gospel," 22, 222-23.

[19]Dee, *Geloofsbegrip van Calvijn*, 190.

[20]Venema, "Twofold Nature of the Gospel," 120; see also pp. 222-23.

[21]Kolfhaus, *Christusgemeinschaft*, 60: "Rechtfertigung und Einpflanzung stehen nicht in einem Kausalverhältnis zueinander, sondern bezeichnen eine und dieselbe Tat Gottes, bei der von einem Vorher oder Nachher keine Rede ist." See also pp. 72-73. In a similar vein, Wendel, *Calvin*, 258, asserts: "But this imputation is made possible only by our union with the Christ and because we become at that same moment members of his body, although the union with Christ cannot be regarded as the cause of the imputation

justification and union with Christ are seen as inevitably concomitant in the plan of salvation but not as internally related. Rather, both point beyond themselves to the saving activity of God.

If this is the case, however, Calvin's assertions that union with Christ is the bond uniting justification and sanctification[22] cannot be taken at face value; some other principle of unity must be found. Pursuing the suggestions of Kolfhaus and Wendel to the effect that justification, sanctification, and union with Christ point beyond themselves to the saving activity of God, C. P. Venema, in what is doubtless the most complete presentation of this approach, finds the principle of the inseparability of justification and sanctification, not in union with Christ, but in the action of the triune God. Venema writes, "The unity or integral relation between these two aspects of the *duplex gratia dei* is ultimately rooted in their common foundation in the singular and gracious action toward us of the Father, Son, and Spirit."[23]

If some have asserted that Calvin compromises the doctrine of forensic justification by making justification dependent on spiritual union with Christ (and, by extension, on the moral transformation that comes with it), others have argued that Calvin's soteriology does not meaningfully relate the forensic and the transformatory at all. Hermann Bauke argued that Calvin's formal approach to theology in general may be characterized in terms of a *complexio oppositorum* in which incompatible theological elements derived from Scripture are dialectically juxtaposed without any organic unity being achieved. In particular, Bauke treated union with Christ in connection with an alleged dialectic of religion and morality, arguing that Calvin achieves no unified presentation of the matter.[24] Betraying a somewhat similar interpretive tendency, Alexandre Ganoczy has argued that Calvin's theology is characterized by a dialectical bent which affects both theological form and the content.[25] Contending that Calvin's thought at these points was shaped by his study of law and by the nominalist philosophy, Ganoczy traces the substantive dialectic to Calvin's conception of the disjunction between the divine and the human.[26] According to Ganoczy, this disjunctive divine-human dialectic

---

of righteousness. Imputation and union with Christ are, rather, two inseparable aspects of one and the same divine grace: the one is not possible without the other." On this, see Venema, "Twofold Nature of the Gospel," 22, 222-23.

[22]See, e.g., *Inst.* III.11.1; III.16.1; IV.17.11.

[23]Venema, "Twofold Nature of the Gospel," 248. See also Stadtland, *Rechtfertigung und Heiligung*, 131.

[24]Hermann Bauke, *Die Problem der Theologie Calvins* (Leipzig: J. C. Hinrich'scher Buchhandlung, 1922), 11-19, 76-79.

[25]Alexandre Ganoczy, *Calvin. Théologien de l'eglise et du ministère*, Unam Sanctum XLVIII (Paris: Editions du Cerf, 1964), 59. This analysis of Bauke and Ganoczy is largely dependent on the discussions in Venema, "Twofold Nature of the Gospel," 6-11, 20, 28-29.

[26]Alexandre Ganoczy, *The Young Calvin*, trans. David Foxgrover and Wade Provo (Philadelphia: Westminster, 1987), 187.

conditions Calvin's understanding of the relationship of justification, sanctification, and union with Christ. Justification, on the one hand, has to do with a completely extrinsic forensic declaration of righteousness by God. Sanctification, on the other hand, has to do with ontological transformation involving the activity of the human person, and there is no mediating element or point of contact (such as spiritual union with Christ) between the two.[27]

This brief and selective survey of Calvin scholarship regarding the relationship of justification, sanctification, and union with Christ underscores an extraordinary lack of consensus on a matter that most agree is central to Calvin's soteriology. The sheer variety of conflicting opinions—that Calvin's view of union with Christ is inconsistent with the doctrine of forensic justification or that his theology is hopelessly incoherent at this point, that it is fully developed and quite coherent, and finally that it is disjunctive to a fault— implicitly poses several important questions: Is it possible that the conceptual apparatus utilized in many discussions has been unduly influenced by the framework of later Reformed thought? Also, might Calvin's soteriology be clear in broad outline but incomplete at certain points (particularly from the standpoint of later doctrinal development) and thus ambiguous?

The Nature of Union with Christ

Union by Faith and the Holy Spirit

Even a cursory reading of the *Institutio* reveals that Calvin's approach to the believer's union with Christ is tied to two central considerations—the work of the Holy Spirit and the faith of the believer. What is objectively given by the Holy Spirit must be subjectively received in faith. The balance between these two elements enabled Calvin to avoid the Scylla of subjectivism associated with some forms of Pietism and extreme Puritanism on the one hand, and the Charybdis of objectivism best illustrated by an *ex opere operato* conception of sacramental efficacy on the other.[28]

Calvin begins his treatment of applied soteriology in the *Institutes* with a discussion of the role and ministry of the Holy Spirit, for "the Holy Spirit is the bond by which Christ effectually unites us to himself."[29] While noting that the Christian is united with Christ by faith, Calvin temporarily passes over the issue

---

[27]See Ganoczy, *Calvin*, 86, 100, 105, 109.

[28]On Calvin's dialectic of subjectivity and objectivity see David Willis, "Calvin's Use of Substantia" in *Calvinus Ecclesiae Genevensis Custos*, ed. Wilhelm H. Neuser (New York: P. Lang, 1984), 295. Willis writes: "In contemporary language we would have to use something like the following to capture the almost tautological character of Calvin's insistence that Christ is really present in his humanity and his divinity spiritually: The Spirit is the objective reality by which the objective God-man Jesus Christ is objectively present and becomes subjectively received by those in whom faith has been objectively given by the Word and Spirit."

[29]*Inst.* III.1.1.

of faith in order to discuss the source from which faith stems.

> It is true that we obtain this by faith. Yet since we see that not all indiscriminately embrace that communion with Christ which is offered through the gospel, reason itself teaches us to climb higher and to examine into the secret energy of the Spirit, by which we come to enjoy Christ and all his benefits.[30]

Calvin stresses the close redemptive-historical connection between Christ and the Spirit. Christ has been "endowed with the Holy Spirit in a special way: that is, to separate us from the world and to gather us unto the hope of the eternal inheritance."[31] Thus, the union between Christ and the believer is "spiritual," and it is useless to look elsewhere for the source or means of communion with Christ: "He unites himself to us by the Spirit alone. By the grace and power of the same Spirit we are made his members, to keep us under himself and in turn to possess him."[32]

Although Calvin attributes the reception of Christ and all his benefits to the ministry of the Holy Spirit, he focuses especially upon the Spirit's role in inducing faith, because "faith is the principal work of the Holy Spirit."[33] In addition, while faith is something which the Holy Spirit instills in the human being, and therefore something in which the Christian actively participates, Calvin is quick to state that faith itself is not meritorious nor an element which compels God to accept the sinner. Faith derives its crucial character entirely from its object—the person of Jesus Christ. The faith which saves is that which ingrafts into Christ, for "it does not reconcile us to God at all unless it joins us to Christ."[34]

The experience of faith is also, for Calvin, the means whereby the Christian comes to knowledge and assurance of union with Christ through the Spirit. Apart from faithful reliance upon Christ, union with Christ is incomprehensible.[35] Assurance of salvation is therefore closely connected by Calvin with union with Christ through faith. Crucial at this point is Calvin's metaphor of Christ as the "mirror" of the Christian's election:

> But if we have been chosen in him, we shall not find assurance of our election in ourselves; and not even in God the Father, if we conceive him as severed from his Son. Christ, then, is the mirror wherein we must, and without self-deception may,

---

[30]Ibid.
[31]Ibid., III.1.2.
[32]Ibid., III.1.3.
[33]Ibid., III.1.4.
[34]Ibid., III.2.30.
[35]*Comm.* John 14:20: "For the drift of these words is that we cannot know by idle speculation what is the sacred and mystic union between us and Him and again between Him and the Father, but that the only way to know it is when He pours his life into us by the secret efficacy of the Spirit. And this is the experience of faith, which I mentioned just now."

contemplate our own election. For since it is into his body the Father has destined those to be engrafted whom he has willed from eternity to be his own, that he may hold as sons all whom he acknowledges to be among his members, we have a sufficiently clear and firm testimony that we have been inscribed in the book of life [cf. Rev. 21:27] if we are in communion with Christ.[36]

Of considerable importance is the precise relationship of faith and union with Christ. Though some understand Calvin virtually to identify the exercise of faith with union with Christ, Calvin regards faith as the instrumental means of union with Christ rather than the union itself. "For even though the apostle teaches that "Christ dwells in our hearts through faith" [Eph. 3:17, cf. Vg.], no one will interpret this indwelling to be faith, but all feel that he is there expressing a remarkable effect of faith, for through this believers gain Christ abiding in them."[37]

Similarly, Calvin rejects with equal vigor any reduction of union with Christ to the working of the Holy Spirit: "Moreover, I am not satisfied with those persons who, recognizing that we have some communion with Christ, when they would show what it is, make us partakers of the Spirit only, omitting mention of flesh and blood."[38]

---

[36]*Inst.* III.24.5. Because of Calvin's definition of the faith as "a firm and certain knowledge of God's benevolence toward us" (*Inst.* III.2.7) and statements implying that the essence of saving faith includes assurance of salvation (e.g., *Inst.* III.2.16; *Comm.* on 2 Cor. 13:5), some have concluded that later Reformed scholasticism differs from Calvin in distinguishing between faith and assurance and in moving from a view of faith as knowledge to a voluntaristic conception of faith. See e.g., R. T. Kendall, *Calvin and English Calvinism to 1649* (New York: Oxford. 1979); M. Charles Bell, *Calvin and Scottish Theology* (Edinburgh: Handsel Press, 1985), 22-26. Others rightly point to qualifying statements by Calvin where he notes that many Christians do not enjoy full assurance of salvation (e.g., *Inst.* III.2.4, 15), and argue that the differences between Calvin and later Reformed scholasticism are more apparent than real. See, e.g., A. N. S. Lane, "Calvin's Doctrine of Assurance," *Vox Evangelica* 11 (1979): 32-54; Joel R. Beeke, *Assurance of Faith: Calvin, English Calvinism, and the Dutch Second Reformation* (New York: Peter Lang, 1991), 47-104.

[37]*Inst.* IV.17.5. Krusche, *Wirken des Heiligen Geistes*, 270, argues that Calvin insists on a formal distinction between faith and *unio* only as a "safeguard against an intellectualistic misunderstanding of the knowledge of faith as a bare cognition" (Sicherung vor einem intellektualistischen Mißverständnis der Glaubenserkenntnis als einer nuda cognition). But this fails to reckon with the fact that Calvin consistently asserts the distinction between faith and union in contexts where a misunderstanding of faith as bare cognition is not at all at issue. As we will see below, Calvin was forced to clarify his position on this matter particularly in connection with the Eucharistic debates with Lutheran opponents.

[38]*Inst.* IV.17.7. Ironically, some nineteenth-century federal theologians would later adopt a position similar to the one Calvin criticizes here.

Union with Christ through Word and Sacrament

It was in the context of sacramental debates, particularly involving the presence of Christ in the Lord's Supper, that Calvin was forced to clarify his understanding of the nature of the believer's union with Christ. Furthermore, any treatment of this topic must recognize that Calvin did not view the union brought about in the sacrament as different in kind from the believer's union with Christ through the ministry of the Word. He writes, "Therefore, let it be regarded as a settled principle that the sacraments have the same office as the Word of God: to offer and set forth Christ to us, and in him the treasures of heavenly grace. But they avail and profit nothing unless received in faith."[39]

The sacraments are not superfluous for Calvin, although certain interpreters have argued that, because Calvin posits no special sacramental grace, the logic of his position renders them so.[40] Rather, the sacraments were given by God as visible signs accompanying the Word because of human ignorance and weakness. Calvin writes:

> By this means God provides first for our ignorance and dullness, then for our weakness. Yet properly speaking, it is not so much needed to confirm his Sacred Word as to establish us in faith in it. For God's truth is of itself firm and sure enough, and it cannot receive better confirmation from any other source than from itself. But as our faith is slight and feeble unless it be propped up on all sides and sustained by every means, it trembles, wavers, totters, and at last gives way. Here our merciful Lord, according to his infinite kindness, so tempers himself to our capacity that, since we are creatures who always creep on the ground, cleave to the flesh, and, do not think about or even conceive of anything spiritual, he condescends to lead us to himself even by these earthly elements, and to set before us in the flesh a mirror of spiritual blessings.[41]

UNION WITH CHRIST IN BAPTISM

Calvin defines baptism as "the sign of initiation by which we are received into the society of the church, in order that, engrafted into Christ, we may be reckoned among God's children."[42] Baptism bestows a threefold benefit upon the believer, for it is a token of cleansing for the whole life, a token of mortification and renewal in Christ, and a token of union with Christ.[43] The third is of particular interest for this study.

At the outset, it should be stressed that Calvin views the sacrament of baptism as a real and objectively efficacious means of uniting the believer with

---

[39] Ibid., IV.14.17.
[40] See, e.g., Kilian McDonnell, *John Calvin, the Church, and the Eucharist* (Princeton: Princeton University Press, 1967), 378-79.
[41] *Inst.* IV.14.3.
[42] Ibid., IV.15.11.
[43] Ibid., IV.1-6.

Christ. It is the "sign of initiation" which "engrafts us to Christ." But Calvin is equally insistent that the efficacy of the sacrament is not derived from the mere administration of water in an *ex opere operato* fashion. Given Calvin's emphasis upon the role of faith and the Holy Spirit noted above, it is not surprising to find these themes stressed here as well.

> We must hold, therefore, that there is a mutual relation between faith and the sacraments, and hence, that the sacraments are effective through faith. Man's unworthiness does not detract anything from them, for they always retain their nature. Baptism is the laver of regeneration, although the whole world should be incredulous: (Tit. iii.5:) the Supper of Christ is the communication of his body and blood, (I Cor. x.16) although there were not a spark of faith in the world: but we do not perceive the grace which is offered to us; and although spiritual things always remain the same, yet we do not obtain their effect, nor perceive their value, unless we are cautious that our want of faith should not profane what God has consecrated to our salvation.[44]

The grace communicated in baptism is not simply psychological. While baptism is given to strengthen faith, baptism is not a bare sign, and to be united with Christ in baptism is not simply to believe in Christ. The point Calvin wishes to make is that the grace of baptism and the faith of the recipient are inseparable: "Yet it is not my intention to weaken the force of baptism by not joining reality and truth to the sign, in so far as God works through outward means. But from this sacrament, as from all others, we obtain only as much as we receive in faith."[45] Because of this complex of divine action and human response, Calvin maintains that the efficacy of baptism may be, and often is, experienced long after the moment of administration, and he points to his own experience by way of example.[46] In the same way, Calvin holds that the efficacy of baptism, tied as it is to the continuing ministry of the Holy Spirit and the exercise of faith, is available throughout the entire lifetime of the believer.[47]

---

[44]*Comm.* Ezekiel 20:20.

[45]*Inst.* IV.15.15.

[46]Calvin, *Inst.* IV.15.17, writes: "Now our opponents ask us what faith came to us during some years after our baptism. This they do to prove our baptism void, since it is not sanctified to us except when the word of promise is accepted in faith. To this question we reply that we indeed, being blind and unbelieving, for a long time did not grasp the promise that had been given us in baptism; yet that promise, since it was of God, ever remained fixed and firm and trustworthy." Cf. the similar teaching in *Westminster Confession of Faith*, 28:6. On this, see William B. Evans, "'Really Exhibited and Conferred...in His Appointed Time': Baptism and the New Reformed Sacramentalism," *Presbyterion: Covenant Seminary Review* 31/2 (Fall 2005): 72-88.

[47]Ibid., IV.15.3.

UNION WITH CHRIST IN THE LORD'S SUPPER

In his exposition of baptism, Calvin was more concerned to explain the nature and meaning of the sacrament itself than the nature of the union with Christ effected thereby. In the case of the Lord's Supper, however, he was forced to grapple not only with the question of Christ's presence to the Christian in the Supper, but also with the larger question of the nature and character of the believer's union with Christ. In this regard, Calvin was caught between two opposing forces—the theological successors of Zwingli at Zurich, with whom Calvin was eventually able to reach an accommodation, and the stricter successors of Luther, with whom Calvin battled to his dying day. The irony of this situation is that Calvin himself felt that Luther was closer to the truth of the matter than Zwingli,[48] and he had initialed his agreement with the Lutheran confessional standard, the Augsburg Confession.

As the Jesuit scholar Joseph Tylenda has rightly observed, "Calvin is one with the other Christian communions in teaching a presence of Christ's body and blood in the Lord's Supper."[49] We move now to a consideration of Calvin's teaching on the union which the Christian has with Christ in the Eucharist. As we might expect, the familiar Calvinian themes of the importance of faith and the work of the Holy Spirit again occur. Yet the mere strengthening of faith is not the final end of the sacrament. Faith is to be strengthened that Christ himself might be received.

Calvin often asserted that in the Supper the believer has a "substantial" union with Christ.[50] By this Calvin means, at very least, that the Christian partakes of Christ himself in the sacrament. The Supper is not a bare or empty sign, and in asserting this Calvin argues that the very honor and veracity of God are at stake.

> For unless a man means to call God a deceiver, he would never dare assert that an empty symbol is set forth by him. Therefore, if the Lord truly represents the participation in his body through the breaking of bread, there ought not to be the least doubt that he truly presents and shows his body. And the godly ought by all means to keep this rule: whenever they see symbols appointed by the Lord, to think and be persuaded that the truth of the thing signified is surely present there.[51]

---

[48]See Wendel, *Calvin*, 232-234.

[49]Joseph Tylenda, "Calvin and Christ's Presence in the Supper—True or Real?" *Scottish Journal of Theology* 27 (1974): 65.

[50]See *Inst.* IV.17.19; and John Calvin, *Theological Treatises*, ed. and trans. J. K. S. Reid (Philadelphia: Westminster, 1954), 264. See also the further discussion of this issue below.

[51]*Inst.* IV.17.10. On Calvin's theory of sacramental sign as instrumentally communicating that which it signifies, see Brian A. Gerrish, "Sign and Reality: The Lord's Supper in the Reformed Confessions" in *The Old Protestantism and the New* (Edinburgh: T. & T. Clark, 1982), 122-23.

Calvin goes on to reject four misunderstandings of Christ's presence in the Supper. He opposes, first of all, the theological successors of Zwingli, some of whom equated the exercise of faith with the reception of Christ in the Supper: "But here is the difference between my words and theirs: for them to eat is only to believe; I say that we eat Christ's flesh in believing, because it is made ours by faith, and that this eating is the result and effect of faith."[52] Second, Calvin also emphatically distances himself from those who hold that to receive Christ is simply to experience the work of the Holy Spirit: "Moreover, I am not satisfied with those persons who, recognizing that we have some communion with Christ, when they would show what it is, make us partakers of the Spirit only, omitting mention of flesh and blood."[53] Third, Calvin further clarifies his position by noting that the believer's union with Christ goes beyond the mere reception of the benefits of Christ's work. Answering the Lutheran controversialist Tileman Heshusius, he writes, "Equally futile is he when he says that I keep talking only of fruit and efficacy. Everywhere I assert a substantial communion, and discard only a local presence and the figment of an immensity of flesh."[54] Finally, replying again to Heshusius, Calvin goes further in specifying the nature of the Christian's union with Christ by asserting that the union involves the incarnate humanity of Christ, as well as his deity: "When he represents me as substituting merit and benefit for flesh and blood, and shortly afterwards adds that I acknowledge no other presence in the Supper than that of the deity, my writings, without a word from me, refute the impudent calumny."[55]

The christological dimension of Calvin's doctrine of *unio Christi* assumes particular importance at this point. A central concern here is the necessity of the believer's communion with the flesh of Christ, with his incarnate humanity, for "salvation and life are to be sought from the flesh of Christ in which he sanctified himself, and in which he consecrates Baptism and the Supper."[56] Crucial here is Calvin's view of the flesh of Christ as the channel through which all salvation grace flows: "For as the eternal Word of God is the fountain of life, so His Flesh is a channel to pour out to us the life which resides intrinsically, as they say, in His divinity. In this sense it is called life-giving, because it communicates to us a life that it borrows from elsewhere."[57] Finally,

---

[52] *Inst.* IV.17.5.

[53] Ibid., IV.17.7.

[54] Calvin, *Theological Treatises*, 287.

[55] Ibid., 307-8.

[56] Ibid., 308.

[57] *Comm.* on John 6:51. Regarding Calvin's stress on the reception of Christ's incarnate humanity, see Ronald S. Wallace, *Calvin's Doctrine of Word and Sacrament* (Grand Rapids: Eerdmans, 1957), 145-49; E. David Willis, *Calvin's Catholic Christology* (Leiden: Brill, 1966), 78-100.

Christ's mediatorial humanity functions in at least two ways for Calvin. First, the humanity of Christ acts as a "channel" for the power and life which are integral to Christ in his divinity. This first function appears to relate primarily to the transforming aspects

in what we may take to be his final word on the matter, Calvin writes: "It would be extreme madness to recognize no communion with the flesh and blood of the Lord, which the apostle declares to be so great that he prefers to marvel at it rather than to explain it."[58]

In reading Calvin's frank confession on this matter we should not, however, assume that he taught a local presence of Christ's body and blood in the elements themselves, as if Christ's body and blood are physically chewed and swallowed in the sacrament. Calvin brings two fundamental christological assumptions to this matter.

> Let us never (I say) allow these two limitations to be taken away from us: (1) Let nothing be withdrawn from Christ's heavenly glory—as happens when he is brought under the corruptible elements of this world, or bound to any earthy creatures. (2) Let nothing inappropriate to human nature be ascribed to his body, as happens when it is said to be infinite or to be put in a number of places at once.[59]

In the controversial literature, Calvin places special emphasis upon the latter concern, the integrity of the humanity of Christ: "It is plain from Scripture that the body of Christ is finite, and has its own dimensions. Geometry did not teach us this; but we will not allow what the Holy Spirit taught by the apostles to be wrested from us."[60]

A further crucial factor for Calvin was the ascension of Christ. That Christ has ascended in glory to the right hand of the Father and is no longer present on earth in the manner of his earthly ministry has implications (if the integrity of his humanity is to be maintained) for the mode of Christ's presence in the Supper, and hence for the nature of the believer's union with Christ.[61]

> For as we do not doubt that Christ's body is limited by the general characteristics common to all human bodies, and is contained in heaven (where it was once for all received) until Christ returns in judgement [Acts 3:21], so we deem it utterly unlawful to draw it back under these corruptible elements or to imagine it to be present everywhere.[62]

---

of salvation (i.e., sanctification). Second, communion with the humanity of Christ is crucial because it was particularly as a human being that Christ offered his atoning sacrifice for sin. This second function relates primarily to the forensic benefits of salvation (i.e., justification).

[58]*Inst.* IV.17.9.
[59]Ibid., IV.17.12.
[60]Calvin, *Theological Treatises*, 311.
[61]Calvin interpreted the Ascension literally as involving a change in locality while Lutheran interpreters tended to view it as a transition from a physical presence on earth to a mode of existence unbounded by spatial limitations (as their doctrine of ubiquity demanded). See Wendel, *Calvin*, 347-48.
[62]*Inst.* IV.17.12.

Thus the issue, for Calvin, resolves down to the mode of Christ's presence. A local presence in the elements was objectionable to Calvin in part because the integrity of Christ's humanity would be compromised. To hold, with the strict Lutherans, that Christ's physical body participated in the attributes of deity to the extent that it became ubiquitous was, for Calvin, to imply that Christ's humanity had ceased to be truly human.

Calvin advanced a further objection to the notion of a local presence. When Christ's presence is understood locally, as in the case of both Roman Catholic transubstantiation and Lutheran consubstantiation, it becomes virtually impossible to restrict communion to the believing community. The notion that the unbeliever received Christ in the Supper together with the believer was problematic in that it proved too much. On the one hand, such a view implied that Christ's flesh is not vivifying, and on the other hand it indicated that Christ may be separated from the regenerating work of the Holy Spirit.[63]

Against the memorialism of Zwingli on the one hand and the spatial/local objectivism of the Roman Catholics and High Lutherans on the other, Calvin asserted a true but spiritual communion with Christ, particularly with the incarnate humanity.[64] By "spiritual," Calvin does not mean that the believer's communion with Christ is somehow less than true and actual. Rather, the communion is accomplished by the powerful work of the Holy Spirit. Calvin writes,

> Even though it seems unbelievable that Christ's flesh, separated from us by such great distance, penetrates to us, so that it becomes our food, let us remember how far the secret power of the Holy Spirit towers above all our senses, and how foolish it is to wish to measure his immeasurableness by our measure. What, then, our mind does not comprehend, let faith conceive: that the Spirit truly unites things separated in space.[65]

For Calvin, the consecrated elements are important, not in themselves, but as they direct the believer's faith toward heaven where Christ's saving humanity exists at the right hand of the Father. In dependence upon Eph. 2:5-6, he preferred to speak of the believer's true reception of Christ as a matter of the heart being lifted up to heaven.

> But if we are lifted up to heaven with our eyes and minds, to seek Christ there in the glory of his Kingdom, as the symbols invite us to him in his wholeness, so

---

[63]See Calvin, *Theological Treatises*, 273, 321.

[64]Tylenda, "Calvin and Christ's Presence," 65-75, points out that because the term "real presence" (*praesentia realis*) was closely associated with the notion of a local presence in the elements, Calvin preferred to speak of a "true presence" (*veram praesentium*) instead.

[65]*Inst.* IV.17.10.

under the symbol of bread we shall be fed by his body, and under the symbol of wine we shall separately drink his blood, to enjoy him at last in his wholeness.[66]

This lifting up of the heart is not mere psychology, however, for the "Spirit unites" what is separated by distance. In keeping with this emphasis, Calvin continued to utilize the *Sursum Corda* of the Roman Mass in the Strasbourg and Genevan Reformed liturgies,[67] and he characterizes advocates of a local presence of Christ in the eucharistic elements as those who "refuse to lift up their hearts."[68]

"Substantial" Union with Christ

Given Calvin's forceful rejection of theories which reduced the Christian's union with Christ to simply the exercise of faith, the experience of the work of the Holy Spirit, or the reception of the benefits of salvation, together with his stress upon the importance of the reception of the incarnate humanity of Christ by the believer, it is apparent that Calvin has in mind a relationship of great intimacy. His rejection of local presence explanations of the Supper renders it a matter of considerable conceptual complexity as well.

Particularly striking is Calvin's habitual use, noted briefly above, of the term "substance" (*substantia*) to describe the nature of the believer's union with Christ. Throughout his career, and in a wide variety of contexts and settings—exegetical, controversial, and liturgical—Calvin insists that believers partake of Christ's "substance."[69] But these forthright passages must be evaluated over against other statements by the Reformer which appear to place severe limits on the "substantial" communion involved. For example, in the *Consensus Tigurinus* of 1549, an agreement between Bullinger and Calvin which cemented ties between the successors of Zwingli and the Genevan church, Calvin writes:

---

[66] Ibid., IV.17.18.

[67] See Bard Thompson, ed., *Liturgies of the Western Church* (Philadelphia: Fortress Press, 1961), 207.

[68] Calvin, *Theological Treatises*, 275-76.

[69] See, e.g., Calvin, *Theological Treatises*, 264, 287; *Inst.* III.2.24; IV.17.19; *Comm.* on Eph. 5:30; Thompson, *Liturgies*, 207. D. Willis, "Calvin's Use of Substantia," documents Calvin's extensive and insistent use throughout his career of the term *substantia* to denote the believer's union with Christ in the Supper.

Wendel, *Calvin*, 236-38, contends that Calvin avoided use of terms such as *substantia* to describe the believer's union with Christ after the Osiandrian controversy of 1550-52, and the retention of such language in the 1559 *Institutio* is ascribed by Wendel to Calvin's "inadvertence." In point of fact, some of Calvin's most emphatic statements regarding the believer's reception of Christ's "substance" are found in Calvin's reply to the Lutheran controversialist Tileman Heshusius, "The True Partaking of the Flesh and Blood of Christ in the Holy Supper" (1561). See Calvin, *Theological Treatises*, 258-324.

> When it is said that Christ, by our eating of his flesh and drinking of his blood, which are here figured, feeds our souls through faith by the agency of the Holy Spirit, we are not to understand it as if any mingling or transfusion of substance took place, but that we draw life from the flesh once offered in sacrifice and the blood shed in expiation.[70]

Similar statements are found in Calvin's polemic against Andreas Osiander (1498-1552), who opposed the doctrine of forensic justification taught by Melanchthon. Osiander argued that Melanchthon taught a formal imputation of Christ's righteousness without due recognition of the common life of the believer in Christ. Such a bare imputation was viewed by Osiander as no more than a legal fiction, and in opposition to this Osiander propounded a view of justification as the communication of essential righteousness. For Osiander, justification is not merely declarative; it renders one actually righteous. Osiander also addressed the means whereby this impartation of righteousness was to be accomplished. Christ's humanity was deemed insufficient to this task and so he argued that God's righteousness, in the form of "divine substance," indwells the believer. The effect of this "mixture of substances" was to render the believer actually and completely righteous. In response, Calvin rejected Osiander's notion of a "gross mingling of Christ with believers."[71] While recognizing their mutual concern with the *unio Christi*, Calvin repudiated Osiander's notion of essential union:

> He says we are one with Christ. We agree. But we deny that Christ's essence [*essentiam*] is mixed with our own...Then he [Osiander] throws in a mixture of substances [*substantialem*] by which God—transfusing himself into us, as it were—makes us part of himself. For the fact that it comes about through the power of the Holy Spirit that we grow together with Christ, and he becomes our Head and we his members, he reckons of almost no importance.[72]

Thus there is an apparent difficulty posed by these texts. On the one hand, Calvin staunchly affirms, in a wide variety of contexts, that the believer is united with the "substance" of Christ. On the other hand, Calvin on more than one occasion denies that "Christ's essence is mixed with our own," and such passages are often cited by those who maintain that Calvin's doctrine of union remains, in the final analysis, extrinsic and thus compatible with forensic

---

[70] John Calvin, *Tracts and Treatises*, 3 vol., trans. Henry Beveridge (Grand Rapids: Eerdmans, 1958), 2:219. Care must be taken in interpreting this document because of its compromise nature. John T. McNeill, *The History and Character of Calvinism* (New York: Oxford, 1954), 199, writes: "The reader of the Consensus will perhaps conclude that Calvin accepted phrases that he would not have chosen and that Bullinger drove a hard bargain. Nevertheless, the spiritual presence of Christ in the Eucharist was affirmed." Interpretive questions surrounding the *Consensus Tigurinus* were to be a factor in the nineteenth-century American eucharistic debates.
[71] *Inst.* III.11.10.
[72] Ibid., III.11.5.

justification.[73] In evaluating these texts, two broad sets of considerations must be addressed. First, there is the matter of the precise nature of Calvin's polemic against Osiander. A second crucial consideration involves the problem of Calvin's use of language—in particular, his use of the terms *substantia* and *essentia*.

Calvin's response to Osiander focused upon two particular areas of concern. First, Calvin combatted Osiander's implicitly docetic soteriology by affirming the importance of Christ's mediatorial work, especially the mediatorial humanity of Christ. We have already seen that Calvin viewed the flesh, or incarnate humanity of Christ, as the channel through which the power of his divinity flows to the believer. In this context, Calvin affirms that Christ's sacrificial and mediatorial work was accomplished primarily in his incarnate humanity and that the benefits of that sacrificial work are received through union with that humanity. Here Calvin argues that

> we are justified in Christ, in so far as he was made an atoning sacrifice for us: something that does not comport with his divine nature. For this reason also, when Christ would seal the righteousness and salvation that he has brought us, he sets forth a sure pledge of it in his own flesh. Now he calls himself "the bread of life" [John 6:48], but, in explaining how, he adds that "his flesh is truly meat, and his blood truly drink" [John 6:55]. This method of teaching is perceived in the sacraments; even though they direct our faith to the whole Christ and not to a half-Christ, they teach that the matter both of righteousness and of salvation resides in his flesh; not that as mere man he justifies or quickens by himself, but because it pleased God to reveal in the mediator what was hidden and incomprehensible in himself. Accordingly, I usually say that Christ is, as it were, a fountain, open to us from which we may draw what otherwise would lie unprofitably hidden in that deep and secret spring, which comes forth to us in the person of the Mediator.[74]

Implicit here is the close association Calvin posits of Christ's person and work. Later in the *Institutes*, Calvin declares that the "substance of the sacrament" is "Christ with his death and resurrection."[75] For Calvin, "substantial" communion with Christ involves not only the reception of Christ's body and blood, but the benefits of Christ's work as well.[76]

In summary then, Calvin's polemic against Osiander should not be

---

[73]See Venema, "Twofold Nature of the Gospel," 223-36; and Kolfhaus, *Christusgemeinschaft*, 27-28.

[74]*Inst.* III.11.9.

[75]Ibid., IV.17.11.

[76]The fact that Calvin closely associates person and work in this way is clear; what is at this point not so clear is a conceptual framework within which such assertions may be deemed coherent. In other words, how is it that communion with body and blood (ostensibly an ontological reality) carries with it the reception of forensic benefits grounded in historical acts. This matter is of crucial importance for the problem of imputation and its modality.

construed as directed against a "substantial communion" with Christ *per se*, but rather against substantial communion of a certain kind—a substantial communion involving the unmediated compounding or "mixture" of the divine and the human. Over against Osiander's notion of the reception of unmediated divine "substance," Calvin sets the mediated reception of the divine-human Christ (together with his work) through substantial communion with Christ's incarnate humanity. In words describing the eucharistic theology of Calvin's successor Theodore Beza, but equally applicable to Calvin, Jill Raitt writes: "According to Christ's total being as the *Word* incarnate, there can be no direct participation. According to Christ's nature as man, there can be participation in his very substance."[77] That is to say, we have here a thoroughgoing opposition to mysticism, at least in the technical sense of an absorption of the human person into the divine.[78]

A second matter to be considered when evaluating the apparent tension between Calvin's strong affirmations of substantial communion on the one hand, and his apparent denials of it on the other, has to do with the meanings he ascribes to terms such as *substantia*.[79] Even in the eucharistic context, Calvin uses the term *substantia* in a number of different senses—sometimes in its scholastic Aristotelian sense as the union of form and matter (denoting a local presence),[80] and sometimes in reference to what may cautiously be termed a spiritually-qualified substance (denoting a real but non-local presence).

Calvin's perspective becomes more clear when we realize that, for the Reformer, the mere reception of the physical material of Christ's body and blood is soteriologically irrelevant if those natural materials are abstracted from Christ's very being. Calvin viewed the crucial center of Christ's vicarious humanity as something much more profound than material substance abstractly considered. Calvin writes:

> When I say that the flesh and blood of Christ are substantially offered and exhibited to us in the Supper, I at the same time explain the mode, namely, that the flesh of Christ becomes vivifying to us, inasmuch as Christ, by the

---

[77] Jill Raitt, *The Eucharistic Theology of Theodore Beza: Development of the Reformed Doctrine*, AAR Studies in Religion 4 (Atlanta: Scholars Press, 1972), 47.

[78] On this, see Calvin, *Comm.* 2 Pet. 1:4; Wilhelm Niesel, *The Theology of Calvin*, trans. Harold Knight (Philadelphia: Westminster, 1956), 126.

[79] Literature on this includes Wendel, *Calvin*, 236-37, 341-43; Helmut Gollwitzer, *Coena Domini* (Munich: Chr. Kaiser Verlag, 1937), 117-133; E. D. Willis, "Calvin's Use of Substantia," 289-301.

Wendel, *Calvin*, 342, is no doubt correct in his observation that Calvin's equivocal use of the term in eucharistic debates "helped to give an appearance of ambiguity to his doctrine which his adversaries were prompt to exploit." Calvin's lack of clarity in using the term *substantia* is further explored in Jill Raitt, "Calvin's Use of Persona," in *Calvinus Ecclesiae Genevensis Custos*, ed. Wilhelm H. Neuser (Frankfurt am Main: Peter Lang, 1984), 273-75.

[80] Article 23 of the *Consensus Tigurinus* quoted above is no doubt an example of this.

incomprehensible virtue of his Spirit, transfers his own proper life into us from the substance of his flesh, so that he himself lives in us, and his life is common to us.[81]

Thus, for Calvin, the spiritual substance of Christ's humanity received in the Supper is not an issue (to put the matter anachronistically) of physical molecules but of the animating force or life from which the molecules themselves come. Here the religious genius of Calvin is apparent. He recognized that the Supper is, first and foremost, spiritual food for the soul. Yet the body and blood of Christ (physically considered) could not provide spiritual nourishment unless they were endowed with magical characteristics. This was precisely the problem inherent in all the local-presence theories Calvin combatted—the physical presence of body and blood was abstracted from Christ's mediatorial life. Of this fundamental misunderstanding the medieval scholastic discussions regarding the effects of ingesting the host upon a church mouse were the almost inevitable result. Only as the substance of Christ was understood as the very life of Christ was a true feeding of the soul upon Christ conceivable without resort to magical gimmickry.[82]

From this, however, a crucial question emerges. When Calvin speaks of the substantial union of the believer with Christ, does he make an *ontological* statement? As has been evident in the survey of scholarship, those who construe Calvin's conception of union with Christ in primarily extrinsic terms have been reluctant to concede this point, arguing that Calvin's conception of union is framed in solely personalistic terms or in terms of the reception of the benefits of Christ's work (or both). There are, however, strong reasons for finally concluding that Calvin intends his "substance" language in an ontological sense. His contention that the incarnate humanity of Christ functions as a channel for the reception of the power of Christ's deity and that union with the substance of the humanity of Christ is therefore necessary seems to demand that *substantia* be taken as a reference to ontological reality. Similarly, Calvin's insistent refusal to reduce union with Christ to a "virtual" communion involving only the reception of the benefits of salvation, to the action of faith, or to the reception of the Holy Spirit seems to demand an ontological referent for *substantia*. Finally, when Calvin does speak of substantial union, he does not, for the most part, utilize personalistic terminology, even though such vocabulary was available to him.

Calvin does not, however, use the term *substantia* in a way that strictly corresponds to any formal philosophical ontology. E. D. Willis, one of the few recent scholars to recognize the fully ontological character of Calvin's formulation at this point, observes:

---

[81]Calvin, *Theological Treatises*, 267.
[82]See G. C. Berkouwer, *The Sacraments*, trans. Hugo Bekker (Grand Rapids: Eerdmans, 1969), 228.

Calvin is not beginning with a general category—substance—of which Christ and our life in Christ are instances. *The* substance of the eucharist is the fundamental ontological fact, Christ himself. That is not a non-ontological statement; it is an ontological statement which forces into a subordinate position ancillary philosophical elucidations.[83]

The primarily theological, rather than philosophical, nature of Calvin's affirmations here is underscored by his refusal to offer speculative "scientific" explanations for what he believed was clearly affirmed, if not clearly explained, by Scripture.

Now if anyone should ask me how this takes place, I shall not be ashamed to confess that it is a secret too lofty for either my mind to comprehend or my word to declare. And, to speak more plainly, I rather experience than understand it. Therefore, I here embrace without controversy the truth of God in which I may safely rest. He declares his flesh the food of my soul, his blood its drink [John 6:53ff.]. I offer my soul to him to be fed with such food. In his Sacred Supper he bids me take, eat, and drink his body and blood under the symbols of bread and wine. I do not doubt that he himself truly presents them, and that I receive them.[84]

In summary then, Calvin's doctrine of union with Christ, as expounded in Books III and IV of the *Institutio* and clarified in the context of eucharistic debates, affirms nothing less than the reception by the believer of the substance, the very being, of the incarnate Christ. This union is the *impartation* of the life of the risen Christ to the believer, albeit in a manner which does not diminish

---

[83]Willis, "Calvin's Use of Substantia," 300. On p. 299 Willis notes: "For one of the strengths of Calvin's eucharistic doctrine is that he *does* use substance in expressing the eucharistic presence of Christ. Another strength is the *way* he uses it: he uses it critically as a theological term—not primarily, perhaps not at all, as a consciously philosophical term. Some may prefer that he had been more precise philosophically by identifying several senses which the term had been given in its varied history, and defending his own particular use of it—as was the custom with those who developed considerable chapters of *distinctiones* in their *summae*. But, in any event, Calvin here is philosophically eclectic."

If Calvin's formulations are to be identified with a particular philosophical system, they appear to have some affinity with the Platonism of the Renaissance revival. Such an identification is strongly argued by McDonnell, *John Calvin*, 32-39, who interprets Calvin's doctrine of union with Christ in terms of the Platonic concept of participation. More cautiously, Charles Partee, *Calvin and Classical Philosophy* (Leiden: E. J. Brill, 1977), 114-15, while conceding that Calvin is, in the broad sense, a "Platonist," argues that Plato's notion of participation did not have "any *direct* influence on Calvin's doctrine of the church and sacraments. The only similarity between Calvin and Plato on participation appears to be the word."

[84]*Inst.* IV.17.32. A reluctance to go beyond what he perceived to be the clear teaching of Scripture is a persistent feature of Calvin's theological methodology. Cf. *Inst.* Pref. Add. 4; I.14.4.

the personal individuality of both Christ and the individual believer.

Union with Christ and Applied Soteriology

According to Calvin, as noted earlier, this "substantial" union with Christ by faith and the Holy Spirit issues in a "double grace" involving both justification and sanctification.[85] Calvin's treatment of these two elements is intriguing, however, for in the *Institutes* he discusses sanctification or regeneration prior to justification.[86] This order of treatment may have stemmed in part, as W. Niesel argues, from a desire to forestall Roman Catholic objections that the Reformation doctrine of forensic justification by grace through faith rendered good works superfluous, but F. Wendel is doubtless correct in contending that Calvin was following what he considered to be a proper pedagogical sequence.[87]

Sanctification through Union with Christ

For Calvin, regeneration or sanctification is characterized by repentance and consists of "mortification of the flesh" and "vivification of the spirit."[88] Moreover, both these aspects of regeneration occur by virtue of the believer's union with Christ.

> Both things happen to us by participation in Christ [Utrunque ex Christi participatione nobis contingit]. For if we truly partake in his death "our old man is crucified by his power, and the old man perishes" [Rom. 6:6 p.], that the corruption or original nature may no longer thrive. If we share in his resurrection, through it we are raised up into newness of life to correspond with the righteousness of God. Therefore, in a word, I interpret repentance as regeneration,

---

[85] See ibid., III.11.1.

[86] As Wendel, *Calvin*, 242, notes, Calvin uses the terms "regeneration" *(regeneratio)* and "sanctification" *(sanctificatio)* interchangeably. "Regeneration" refers to the transformational aspect of salvation and it is necessary to note the contrast of Calvin's usage with that of later Reformed Orthodoxy, which increasingly used the term "regeneration" as a technical term for the initial quickening by the Spirit from which faith stems. The Orthodox usage reflects the concern for an *ordo salutis*—a distinctly post-Calvinian development, as will be shown below.

[87] See Niesel, *Theology of Calvin*, 130-31; Wendel, *Calvin*, 233-34. See also Calvin, *Inst*. III.3.1. Calvin's pedagogical strategy is more extensively analyzed by Venema, "Twofold Nature of the Gospel," 190-98, who shows that Calvin's pedagogical motive is twofold. First, when regeneration is correctly understood (i.e., as progressive and incomplete in this life) it is apparent that regeneration cannot contribute to forensic justification. Second, the order of treatment chosen serves to highlight the inseparability of justification and regeneration.

[88] *Inst*. III.3.8.

whose sole end is to restore in us the image of God that had been disfigured and all but obliterated through Adam's transgression.[89]

The fact that the "old man" has been crucified with Christ and the new raised with Christ does not imply for Calvin that the believer is to achieve a state of sinless perfection in this life. For the Christian, "sin ceases only to reign, it does not also cease to dwell in them."[90] The Christian life is a constant and ongoing challenge for believers as they "practice repentance throughout their lives and know that this warfare will end only at death."[91] Also, this regeneration or sanctification only occurs by virtue of the believer's being implanted in Christ. This union is, for Calvin, the means whereby the believer is sanctified, and the dynamic, ongoing character of sanctification corresponds to the dynamic, ongoing character of the spiritual union from which it results. Thus Calvin speaks of how the believer's union with Christ grows deeper and more extensive over time: "Not only does he cleave to us by an invisible bond of fellowship, but with a wonderful communion, day by day, he grows more and more into one body with us, until he becomes completely one with us."[92]

In conclusion, then, the process of sanctification is seen by Calvin as resulting from the dynamic and progressive union of the believer with Christ. As the life of Christ is imparted to the believer through union, the Christian is progressively conformed to the image of Christ by the mortification of the "old man" and the vivification of the new.

Justification through Union with Christ

The fact that Calvin treats justification after sanctification should not be taken to imply any diminution of the importance of the doctrine. Like Luther, Calvin viewed the doctrine of justification as having a certain priority, particularly in terms of the importance of a correct understanding of forensic justification for the life and health of the church. What was for Luther the "article of the standing or falling of the church" was for Calvin the "main hinge upon which religion turns."[93] The fact, as was evident in the preceding survey of scholarship, that the precise relation of Calvin's conception of union with Christ to the doctrine of justification has been a vexed question is an indication

---

[89] Ibid., III.3.9.

[90] Ibid., III.3.11.

[91] Ibid., III.3.9. Studies of Calvin's doctrine of the Christian life include W. Kolfhaus, *Vom Christlichen Leben Nach Johannes Calvin* (Neukirchen: Kreis Moers, 1949); R. S. Wallace, *Calvin's Doctrine of the Christian Life* (Edinburgh: Oliver and Boyd, 1959); John H. Leith, *John Calvin's Doctrine of the Christian Life* (Louisville, Ky.: Westminster/John Knox, 1989).

[92] *Inst.* III.2.24.

[93] Ibid., III.11.1. On the centrality of the doctrine of justification for Luther, see Paul Althaus, *The Theology of Martin Luther*, trans. Robert C. Schultz (Philadelphia: Fortress Press, 1966), 224-27.

of the central role that the doctrine of justification has continued to play for the nineteenth and twentieth-century heirs of the Reformation.

JUSTIFICATION AS FORENSIC AND SYNTHETIC

Justification, according to Calvin, has both a positive and a negative aspect. Negatively, the believer's sins are not charged to his or her account; positively, the righteousness of Christ is imputed, or credited, to the believer. These two aspects are reflected in Calvin's brief definition of justification found in the *Institutes*: "Therefore, we explain justification simply as the acceptance with which God receives us into his favor as righteousness men. And we say that it consists in the remission of sins and the imputation of Christ's righteousness."[94]

The Reformer is careful to emphasize that Christ's righteousness is imputed to the individual and is not to be thought of as an essential righteousness proper to the justified Christian: "man is not righteous in himself but because the righteousness of Christ is communicated to him by imputation—something worth carefully noting."[95] Calvin was forced to fight battles over this issue on two fronts. On the one hand, he stood with Luther against Rome in affirming that justification is a judicial declaration of righteous standing before God solely on the basis of the alien, imputed righteousness of Christ. On the other hand, Calvin also opposed Osiander's theory of essential righteousness attained by the infusion of Christ's deity, and hence his righteousness, into the Christian.

In contrast to sanctification, which is progressive and not completed until the life hereafter, righteous standing before God in justification is fully realized when the believer is united with Christ. Were it not so, the Christian could have no peace of conscience before God.

> But because it is well known by experience that the traces of sin always remain in the righteous, their justification must be very different from reformation into newness of life [cf. Rom. 6:4]. For God so begins this second point in his elect, and progresses in it gradually, and sometimes slowly, throughout life, that they are always liable to the judgment of death before his tribunal. But he does not justify in part but liberally, so that they may appear in heaven as if endowed with the purity of Christ. No portion of righteousness sets our consciences at peace

---

[94] *Inst*. III.11.2. Echoing W. Lüttge, Brian G. Armstrong, *Calvinism and the Amyraut Heresy* (Madison, Wis.: Univ. of Wisconsin Press, 1969), 226, argues that, for Calvin, the theme of justification involves primarily the forgiveness of sins. It is more plausible, however, to view Calvin's references to justification as the forgiveness of sins (omitting reference to the imputation of the righteousness of Christ) as a form of theological "shorthand." Venema, "Twofold Nature of the Gospel," 141, notes that Calvin sometimes omits reference to forgiveness and refers to justification in terms of positive imputation alone (e.g., *Comm*. Rom. 4:3). Cf. *Inst*. III.11.4: "Moreover, in the fourth chapter of Romans he [Paul] first calls justification 'imputation of righteousness.' And he does not hesitate to include within it forgiveness of sins."

[95] Ibid., III.11.23.

until it has been determined that we are pleasing to God, because we are entirely righteous before him.[96]

This immediate and complete justification of the believer in union with Christ is the foundation for the believer's capacity to please God through good works. Although the good works of the faithful are still tainted by sin, the justification of the believer is seen by Calvin as applying not just to the person of the Christian but to his or her works as well.

> For unless the justification of faith remains whole and unbroken, the uncleanness of works will be uncovered. Moreover, it is no absurdity that man is so justified by faith that not only is he himself righteous but his works are also accounted righteous above their worth.[97]

Thus Calvin's doctrine of justification is resoundingly forensic and synthetic—being grounded entirely in the work of Christ and involving the forgiveness of sins and the imputation of the righteousness of Christ through faith to the Christian, even though the Christian remains in this life to some extent a sinner.

THE RELATION OF JUSTIFICATION AND UNION WITH CHRIST

We have already seen that union with Christ is, for Calvin, nothing less than the impartation of the very life of the incarnate Christ to the believer. We have seen, as well, that Calvin at times posits an internal relationship between union and justification, as if union with Christ is necessary to and, in some sense, a cause of justification.[98] As we noted above, the difficulties involved in reconciling Calvin's doctrine of forensic justification with his doctrine of union with Christ have led to a variety of interpretive proposals in which a crucial element of controversy involves the question of the relationship between union with Christ and justification. In addressing this question, careful attention must be given to two elements of Calvin's presentation of the doctrine of justification—the precise character of Calvin's argument for the inseparability of justification and regeneration and the nature of the mode of imputation involved in the attribution of the righteousness of Christ to the believer.

Calvin's argument for the inseparability of justification and sanctification is articulated as part of his polemic against those opponents who contended that the doctrine of forensic justification abolished the necessity of good works and encouraged license. Here Calvin argues from the source of the benefits of salvation, namely, Christ himself. Citing 1 Cor. 1:30, the Reformer points to the person of Christ as the guarantee of the inseparability of forensic justification

---

[96]Ibid., III.11.11.

[97]Ibid., III.17.9. On this "double justification" see Alfred Göhler, *Calvins Lehre von der Heiligung* (Munich: Chr. Kaiser Verlag, 1934), 93-96; Wendel, *Calvin*, 260-263; Venema, "Twofold Nature of the Gospel," 236-248.

[98]See, e.g., *Inst.* III.1.1; III.11.1.; III.15.5-6.

and renewal of life. Here the "everlasting and indissoluble bond" uniting justification and sanctification is nothing other than the person of Christ himself.[99] Calvin then explains:

> Although we may distinguish them, Christ contains both of them inseparably in himself. Do you wish, then, to attain righteousness in Christ? You must first possess Christ; but you cannot possess him without being made partaker in his sanctification, because he cannot be divided into pieces [I Cor. 1:13]. Since, therefore, it is solely by expending himself that the Lord gives us these benefits to enjoy, he bestows both of them at the same time, the one never without the other. Thus it is clear how true it is that we are justified not without works yet not through works, since in our sharing in Christ, which justifies us, sanctification is just as much included as righteousness.[100]

We must ask, however, just what the phrase "divided into pieces" meant to Calvin. Elsewhere, Calvin defines this as the separation of Christ from the Holy Spirit in the application of salvation.

> Those in whom the Spirit does not reign do not belong to Christ; therefore those who serve the flesh are not Christians, for those who separate Christ from his Spirit make Him like a dead image or a corpse. We must always bear in mind the counsel of the apostle, that free remission of sins cannot be separated from the Spirit of regeneration. This would be, as it were, to rend Christ asunder.[101]

Further exploration of this point is necessary, however. Is it Calvin's intent in this reference to Christ and the Holy Spirit merely to refer to the sphere of divine or trinitarian unity of action in general?[102] Such an explanation is inadequate for two reasons. First, it fails to account for Calvin's stress upon the importance of union with the flesh, or incarnate humanity, of Christ (through the power of the Holy Spirit) as crucial for both justification and sanctification.

---

[99]*Inst.* III.16.1.

[100]Ibid., III.16.1.

[101]*Comm.* Rom. 8:9; cf. *Comm.* Rom. 8:13. Though Calvin sometimes particularly associates sanctification and the work of the Holy Spirit (e.g., *Comm.* Col. 1:22: "Christ is made to us righteousness and sanctification...The former we obtain by free acceptance, the latter by the gift of the Holy Spirit."), we seriously misconstrue Calvin's argument if we conclude that he here distinguishes between a completely extrinsic justification and a sanctification by the internal working of the Spirit. Elsewhere Calvin underscores the role of the Spirit in justification as well as sanctification (*Comm.* Rom. 6:2: "Indeed, we are justified for this very purpose, that we may afterwards worship God in purity of life. Christ washes us by His blood, and renders God propitious to us by His expiation, by making us partakers of His Spirit, who renews us to a holy life."). Calvin's point is that an attempt to separate Christ and his Spirit along the lines of justification and sanctification is sure evidence of a defective or "mutilated faith" (*Comm.* Rom. 8:13).

[102]Such is the argument of Kolfhaus, Wendel, and Venema noted above.

Second, it fails to account for the fact that, in speaking of Christ and the Holy Spirit as the bond of justification and sanctification, Calvin refers to a specifically redemptive-historical phenomenon (in which the divine-human mediatorial Christ is made accessible through the power of the Spirit) rather than to the divine action in general. Commenting on 1 Cor. 15:45, Calvin writes: "But we must take note that Christ was also a living soul like ourselves, but over and above His soul, the Spirit of the Lord was poured out upon Him, that by the power of the Spirit He might rise from the dead, and raise up others."[103]

We may summarize Calvin's view in this way: the bond uniting justification and sanctification is the mediatorial person of Christ together with the Holy Spirit with whom Christ has been endowed. The nature and implications of this argument are often overlooked. Calvin is not simply contending that justification and sanctification are concomitant in the economy of salvation and therefore inseparable. Rather, the Reformer argues that the forensic and transforming benefits of salvation are inseparable because both are communicated to the believer in the same way through union with the mediatorial person of Christ by the power of the Holy Spirit.

A second matter requiring detailed examination is Calvin's view of the mode of the imputation of Christ's righteousness to the believer. This is, in fact, a matter that has been largely overlooked by recent scholarship.[104] Many appear to assume that synthetic-forensic justification by imputation must involve a completely extrinsic relationship between the persons involved. Any implication of imputation by means of mystical union is thought to threaten the purely forensic character of justification. Unfortunately, much recent discussion of soteriological imputation in Calvin seems to have assumed the seventeenth-century distinction between "mediate" and "immediate" imputation which arose out of the Amyraldian controversy.[105] Because the theory of mediate

---

[103] *Comm.* I Cor. 15:45. The temporal association of this soteriological combination of Christ and the Holy Spirit with the resurrection of Christ is also significant.

Venema's broader emphasis ("Twofold Nature of the Gospel," 212, 248) upon the trinitarian context of the application of redemption in Calvin is illuminating. See also Alexandre Ganoczy, "Observations on Calvin's Trinitarian Doctrine of Grace," in *Probing the Reformed Tradition: Historical Studies in Honor of Edward A. Dowey, Jr.*, ed. Elsie Anne McKee and Brian G. Armstrong (Louisville: Westminster/John Knox, 1989), 96-107.

[104] As noted above, Doumergue is one of the few to raise the matter, and then only in passing.

[105] See chap. 2 below. The French Reformed theologian Josué de la Place (Placaeus) distinguished between the two modes of imputation in the context of controversy over the doctrine of original sin. By "mediate imputation," Placaeus meant that the sin of Adam is imputed to his posterity through the sinful human nature inherited from Adam. Human beings are accounted guilty of the sin of Adam in that they are in fact sinful. "Immediate imputation," on the other hand, involves the imputation of Adam's sin to human beings by an act of divine will, irrespective of actual participation in the sinful

imputation involves an intrinsic relationship between Adam and his posterity (participation in a sinful human nature) and an analytic judgement (human beings are treated as sinful because they are), it has been assumed that synthetic-forensic justification by imputation must of necessity be "immediate" as to its mode. Thus it is argued that Calvin's doctrine of forensic justification entails an immediate juridical divine declaration imputing the righteousness of Christ to the believer apart from any other relationship which may obtain between the Savior and the saved.

While the outlines of Calvin's doctrine of forensic justification by the imputation of the righteousness of Christ to the believer are fairly clear, the use of *imputatio* in a forensic soteriological sense was a development occurring within Calvin's lifetime.[106] Before the Reformation period, the notion of imputation was used primarily in connection with explanations of the reckoning of Adam's sin to humanity in general. Only with Luther and Melanchthon does the notion of the forensic imputation of the alien righteousness of Christ emerge. Given the novelty of the idea in its sixteenth-century context, one must take care not to project later conceptions back onto this early period. There are, in fact, a number of considerations which indicate that Calvin's understanding of the forensic imputation of Christ's righteousness to the believer does not conform to the later notion of immediate imputation.

In the first place, justification, according to Calvin, is not merely an abstract divine declaration with no implication of personal relationship. Calvin writes: "We do not, therefore, contemplate him outside ourselves from afar in order that his righteousness may be imputed to us but because we put on Christ and are engrafted into his body—in short, because he deigns to make us one with him."[107] Here the christocentrism of Calvin's doctrine of justification is apparent. Justification involves not simply what God has done through Christ in the past, as integral as the sacrifice of Christ is to the doctrine, but also communion with the person of the living Christ.

---

nature of Adam. See Benjamin B. Warfield, "Imputation" in *Biblical and Theological Studies*, ed. Samuel G. Craig (Philadelphia: Presbyterian and Reformed, 1968), 262-69; George P. Hutchinson, *The Problem of Original Sin in American Presbyterian Theology* (Philadelphia: Presbyterian and Reformed, 1972), 10-11; George Park Fisher, "The Augustinian and Federal Theories of Original Sin Compared," in *Discussions in History and Theology* (New York: Charles Scribner's Sons, 1880), 384-94.

[106]Alister E. McGrath, *Iustitia Dei: A History of the Christian Doctrine of Justification*, 2 vols. (Cambridge: Cambridge University Press, 1986), II:2: "The most accurate description of the doctrines of justification associated with the Reformed and Lutheran churches from 1530 onward is that they represent a radically new interpretation of the Pauline concept of "imputed righteousness" set within an Augustinian framework."

[107]*Inst*. III.11.10. McGrath, *Iustitia Dei*, II:37, correctly notes: "Calvin speaks of the believer being 'grafted into Christ,' so that the concept of *incorporation* becomes central to his understanding of justification."

At this point a dialectic of *in nobis* and *extra nos* thinking is evident.[108] On the one hand, the sacrificial work of Christ is accomplished outside the believer.[109] In addition, the believer, although fully justified, is not made fully righteous in this life.[110] In both these senses, the justification of the believer is to be found only *extra nos*. On the other hand, as Calvin so pointedly remarks at the beginning of Book III of the *Institutio*, "as long as Christ remains outside of us...all that he has suffered and done for the salvation of the human race remains useless and of no value to us."[111] Whatever questions have been raised subsequently, it should be apparent that Calvin himself detected no contradiction here. Subjective incorporation and objective substitution are not mutually exclusive categories for Calvin.[112]

The christological dimension of justification is further evident in Calvin's use of "infusion" language in the context of justification. Indeed, imputation and the infusion of Christ's life are, for Calvin, functionally identical if conceptually distinct.

> The only fulfillment he [Paul] alludes to [in Rom. 8:3-4] is that which we obtain through imputation. For in such a way does the Lord Christ share his righteousness with us that, in some wonderful manner, he pours [*transfundat*] into us enough of his power [*vim*] to meet the judgment of God.[113]

An implication of Calvin's Christological doctrine of justification is his emphasis upon the life and economy of faith. Because the believer is justified through union with Christ and is united with Christ by faith and the Holy Spirit, the means of grace (which strengthen faith) are likewise involved in Calvin's

---

[108]See Willem van't Spijker, "'*Extra Nos*' and '*In Nobis*' by Calvin in a Pneumatological Light," in *Calvin and the Holy Spirit*, ed. by Peter De Klerk (Grand Rapids: Calvin Studies Society, 1989), 39-62.

[109]*Inst*. III.11.4.

[110]Ibid., III.11.23: "You see that our righteousness is not in us but in Christ, that we possess it only because we are partakers in Christ; indeed, with him we possess all its riches."

[111]Ibid., III.1.1.

[112]See Paul Van Buren, *Christ in Our Place* (Grand Rapids: Eerdmans, 1957), 97; Krusche, *Wirken des Heiligen Geistes*, 274.

[113]*Inst*. III.11.23. Cf. IV.17.32; *Comm.* on John 14:20; Eph 5:31. Here we note some formal tension between Calvin and the later Reformed textbook tradition, which is often critical of notions of "infused grace" (*gratia infusa*) in the context of justification. The difference should not be overemphasized, however, as the later Reformed scholastic writers direct their polemic against the infusion of a "quality of justice" as the analytic ground of justification, a notion which Calvin clearly does not teach. More recent Reformed discussions have unfortunately tended to conflate the notion personal communion through the infusion of the life of Christ with the infusion of gracious "habits" or qualities of righteousness. See Paul Ramsey, "Infused Virtues in Edwardsean and Calvinistic Context," in *Ethical Writings, vol. 8, The Works of Jonathan Edwards* (New Haven: Yale University Press, 1989), 739-750.

doctrine of justification: "For we know that justification is lodged in Christ alone, and that it is communicated to us no less by the preaching of the gospel than by the seal of the sacrament, and without the latter can stand unimpaired."[114] Here Calvin, in contrast to later Reformed scholasticism, conceives of the forensic imputation of Christ's righteousness in dynamic and relational terms rather than as a static and punctiliar divine declaration. Arguing against the Roman Catholic doctrine of the forgiveness of sins prior to baptism, Calvin contends that a continual justification is necessary.

> Therefore, God does not, as many stupidly believe, once for all reckon to us as righteousness that forgiveness of sins concerning which we have spoken in order that, having obtained pardon for our past life, we may afterward seek righteousness in the law; this would be only to lead us into false hope, to laugh at us, and mock us. For since no perfection can come to us so long as we are clothed in this flesh, and the law moreover announces death and judgment to all who do not maintain perfect righteousness in works, it will always have grounds for accusing and condemning us unless, on the contrary, God's mercy counters it, and by continual forgiveness of sins repeatedly acquits us.[115]

Taking into account Calvin's teaching on the christological nature of the reception of justification, his use of infusion language in connection with imputation, and his teaching on the continual reception of justification through the means of grace, we must conclude that Calvin's view of the mode of the soteriological imputation of the righteousness of Christ to the believer conforms to neither of the later views which came to be characterized as "mediate" and "immediate." It is not "mediate" because the righteousness of Christ is not imputed on the basis of participation in Christ's sinlessness as a moral quality, or proleptically on the basis of the personal transformation which will finally result. On the other hand, it is not "immediate" because the righteousness of Christ is not imputed without regard for any realistic personal union between Christ and the believer, as would be the case with immediate

---

[114]*Inst.* IV.14.14.

[115]Ibid., III.14.10. We should not conclude from this continual reception of the grace of justification through union with Christ that the justification which is received is incomplete. Calvin insists that the justification which is continually received through union with Christ renders the believer fully acceptable to God. See ibid., III.11.11.

This notion of a continual reception of justification stands in considerable tension with the later Reformed *ordo salutis*, in which justification is a punctiliar divine declaratory act which logically and temporally precedes sanctification and the other benefits of salvation. On the development of the *ordo salutis* schema in Reformed scholasticism, see chap. 2 below.

Although Ganoczy, *Calvin,* 105, claims to detect an *ordo salutis* in Calvin, others rightly dispute this. See Venema, "Twofold Nature of the Gospel," 28-29, 157-58, 207; C. Grafland, "Hat Calvin einen ordo salutis gelehrt," in *Calvinus Ecclesiae Genevensis Custos,* ed. Wilhelm H. Neuser (Frankfurt am Main: Verlag Peter Lang, 1984), 221-244.

imputation. Rather, the imputed righteousness of justification is mediated through the realistic and personal union which obtains between Christ and the believer. This union issues, in turn, in the double grace (*duplex gratia*) of justification and regeneration.[116]

The Structure of Calvin's Soteriology

Having examined Calvin's teaching on union with Christ and the relationship of union with Christ to the forensic and transforming benefits of salvation—particularly his argument for the inseparability of justification and regeneration and his view that both justification and regeneration are mediated through an ongoing personal and realistic union with Christ—several conclusions emerge. First, Calvin accords a *causal* priority to union with Christ. In that both justification and sanctification are communicated through union with Christ to the believer, union with Christ may be described (in this carefully circumscribed sense) as the instrumental basis of both justification and sanctification (to be distinguished, of course, from the meritorious basis or ground of justification).[117]

Second, Calvin does not relate the forensic and transforming benefits of

---

[116] It is sometimes argued that Calvin was influenced by the nominalist theology of the *via moderna*. In particular, his doctrine of forensic justification by the imputation of an alien righteousness is said to betray nominalist influence. See Ganoczy, *Calvin*, 99; Stephen Strehle, *Calvinism, Federalism, and Scholasticism: A Study of the Reformed Doctrine of Covenant* (New York: Peter Lang, 1988), 81.

While Calvin's more general relationship to the *via moderna* is complex, it is precisely here that Calvin demonstrates his independence from nominalist influence. In the case of both original sin and soteriological imputation, Calvin is not content with a purely nominal and extrinsic imputation without regard for any personal relationship.

[117] Such a conclusion is implied, though not directly stated, in Calvin's discussion of the four "causes" of justification. Appropriating Aristotelian terminology, Calvin writes (*Inst*. III.14.17): "The philosophers postulate four kinds of causes to be observed in the outworking of things. If we look at these, however, we will find that, as far as the establishment of our salvation is concerned, none of them has anything to do with works. For Scripture everywhere proclaims that the efficient cause of our obtaining eternal life is the mercy of the Heavenly Father and his freely given love toward us. Surely the material cause is Christ, with his obedience, through which he acquired righteousness for us. What shall we say is the formal or instrumental cause but faith? ...As for the final cause, the apostle testifies that it consists both in the proof of divine justice and in the praise of God's goodness."

As Calvin notes in *Inst*. III.11.7, "faith of itself does not possess the power of justifying, but only in so far as it receives Christ." In other words, faith is the instrumental cause only in that it apprehends the material cause of justification—Christ himself. Thus the constituent parts of Calvin's doctrine of union with Christ—the person of Christ, faith, the work of the Holy Spirit—are thoroughly implicated with the language of causality in connection with justification.

salvation directly (a move which would inevitably compromise the integrity of either or both), but indirectly *through* union with Christ. Both justification and sanctification are subsumed under a more comprehensive reality—union with Christ. In this way Calvin avoids the problems of making justification dependent upon sanctification (and thus robbing justification of its synthetic character) or of making sanctification a mere response to justification (thus rendering sanctification ultimately superfluous).[118]

There are, nevertheless, certain difficulties in Calvin's doctrine of union with Christ and its relation to applied soteriology. Not all of these problems are of the same magnitude, but all were significant for the future development of Reformed theology. We earlier noted the philosophically eclectic character of Calvin's use of the term *substantia*. No doubt reflecting the humanist reaction of his day against Aristotelian categories, Calvin's usage here continues to be an asset for theology today in that his formulations are not tied to a particular philosophical ontology current in the sixteenth century. On the other hand, Calvin's philosophical eclecticism was soon to be viewed as imprecise or worse as the successors of Luther and Calvin increasingly turned to the use of scholastic philosophical categories in their codification and defense of Reformation doctrine. The danger here was that the substance of Calvin's position would perish together with his particular formulation of it. As we shall see, both in fact happened.

A second area of difficulty—actually a complex of difficulties—arises precisely where the secondary scholarship on Calvin's soteriology has been most divided. As we noted earlier, those who have understood Calvin to teach that justification is communicated to the believer through union with Christ have tended to argue that his doctrine of forensic justification is compromised thereby, while those who maintain the integrity of forensic justification tend to construe union with Christ in extrinsic terms. A difficulty facing the Calvin interpreter at this point is that the Reformer's view of union with Christ and soteriology in general involves a matrix of realistic, personal, and forensic categories. This is not to argue that such a combination is necessarily wrong or impossible, but rather that some explanation of the mechanism whereby the forensic may be mediated by a personal and ontological union is needed. This Calvin did not provide.

Related to this are difficulties posed by Calvin's stress upon the importance of union with the incarnate humanity of Christ. Calvin clearly assumes that Christ's mediatorial work and the benefits accruing from it are received through union with the "substance" of the humanity of Christ, a factor accounting in part for the richness of Calvin's sacramental theology. Yet how, we might ask,

---

[118]McGrath, *Iustitia Dei*, II:37, writes: "Calvin relates them [justification and sanctification] on the basis of the believer's *insitio in Christum*. Justification and sanctification are aspects of the believer's new life in Christ, and just as one receives the whole Christ, and not a part of him, through faith, so any separation of these two soteriological elements—which Calvin refers to as *les deux principales grâces*—is inconceivable."

is the sacrificial work of Christ (with its forensic implications and benefits) so related to Christ's person such that to receive the one is to receive the other? Again, the difficulty is not so much that Calvin's view is demonstrably wrong as that it is incomplete.

The later development of Reformed soteriology may be viewed in terms of varying responses to the influence of and the aporias inherent in Calvin's doctrine of union with Christ. Inheriting a terminological schema from Calvin which treated all of applied soteriology under the rubric "union with Christ," later Reformed theologians nevertheless modified the inherited tradition at numerous points within the context of that formal structure. One response was to explore further the nature of Christ's work and its forensic implications for his person. In this way the connection (which Calvin assumed but did not explain) between Christ's person and the forensic benefits accruing from his work could be strengthened. In particular, during the period between Calvin and the rise of full-fledged federal theology we see increased attention being paid particularly to the resurrection of Christ as a forensic soteriological act with particular relevance for the doctrine of justification.

Another response to the difficulties posed by Calvin's doctrine was that of federal theology, an approach which achieved overwhelming dominance in British and American Reformed circles prior to the nineteenth century. Here the formal priority of "union with Christ" is maintained, but the substance of Calvin's doctrine is significantly modified. Through an *ordo salutis* schema, justification and sanctification were related in a logical sequence which assured the priority of justification. Furthermore, the doctrine of union with Christ was modified to fit the *ordo salutis* in that there was an increasing tendency to speak of what were in fact two fundamentally different kinds of union—federal (i.e., legal) and spiritual.[119] This formulation, while it safeguarded the forensic

---

[119]Though this is not his typical mode of expression, on one occasion at least, in a 1555 letter to Peter Martyr Vermigli, Calvin does speak of a "second communion" (*secundam communicationem*) with Christ. Calvin writes: "Now I come to the second communion, which for me is the fruit and effect of the first. For after Christ has subdued us by the inner working of the Spirit and united us with his body, according to the Spirit's power he reveals this by enriching us with his gifts." (Iam venio ad secundam communicationem, quae illius prioris mihi fructus est ac effectus. Nam postquam Christus interiore spiritus virtute sibi nos devinxit atque univit in corpus suum, secumdam spiritus virtutem exserit donis suis nos locupletando.) *Ioannis Calvini Opera quae supersunt Omnia*, ed. G. Baum and others, 59 vols., *Corpus Reformatorum*, vols. 29-87 (Brunsvigae: Schwetschke, 1863-1900), 15:723. An English translation of the letter to which Calvin responds is found in J. C. McLelland and G. E. Duffield, eds., *The Life, Early Letters and Eucharistic Writings of Peter Martyr*, The Courtenay Library of Reformation Classics 5 (Abingdon, England: Sutton Courtenay Press, 1989), 343-48, where Peter Martyr distinguishes an incarnational union with all human beings and a spiritual union with the elect.

Some have sought to make this isolated reference the programmatic basis for understanding the relationship of justification, sanctification, and union with Christ in

and synthetic character of justification, had the effect of dissolving the bond of unity Calvin maintained between justification and sanctification and rendering the relation between the two increasingly problematic.

The soteriological dualism inherent in the federal theology in turn spawned reactions in other directions. For some, the answer was to return to Calvin. Hence there were attempts to reformulate the substance of Calvin's position in what were thought to be more modern terms. Another reaction to the difficulties of the federal theology was the entire rejection of the notion of soteriological imputation. It is to this fascinating history that we now turn.

Calvin. See, e.g., Dennis E. Tamburello, *Union with Christ*, 86-90, 101, 107. Tamburello writes (p. 86): "Calvin actually speaks of a twofold communion with Christ, which corresponds to the twofold grace of justification and sanctification." As further evidence, Tamburello cites Calvin's *Comm.* on Gal. 2:20, where Calvin writes, "Christ lives in us in two ways...The first relates to regeneration, the second to the free acceptance of righteousness."

Two comments may be made here. First of all, the distinction Calvin draws in the letter to Peter Martyr is between the secret union by the power of the Holy Spirit whereby the believer is made one body with Christ on the one hand, and the manifestation of the fruits of that inner union in the Christian life on the other. This is not at all the later federal theology distinction of an extrinsic legal union and a spiritual sanctifying union. Second, we have already seen that the structure of Calvin's soteriology utilizes *unio* as the bond uniting the *duplex gratia* of justification and sanctification. That is to say, if Calvin indeed did posit two distinct and separate unions corresponding to the *duplex gratia*, then much of what he says elsewhere on the subject is incoherent.

CHAPTER 2

Reformed Orthodoxy and Union with Christ

Moving from Calvin and the Reformation period to the period of Reformed orthodoxy, the interpreter is faced with a number of important historiographical challenges, many of which relate broadly to the question of continuity between Reformation and post-Reformation thought. Figuring prominently in the debate regarding continuity is the question of the definition of Reformed "orthodoxy" or "scholasticism." The fact that these two terms are often used as synonyms illustrates the way that many define post-Reformation Reformed thought primarily in terms of its appropriation of scholastic method and philosophy. In a definition that has proven influential, Brian Armstrong has described Protestant scholasticism in terms of a commitment to syllogistic reasoning and Aristotelian philosophy, an according to reason "at least equal standing with faith in theology," a belief in the adequacy of dogmatic formulations to express adequately the content of scriptural revelation, and a tendency toward metaphysical speculation in which the doctrine of sovereign divine decrees assumes foundational importance in the theological system.[1]

Against Armstrong and others, R. A. Muller has denied that the theological content of post-Reformation Reformed thought involves a necessary commitment to Aristotelian ontology or a preoccupation with the doctrine of the divine decrees as foundational, and he has defined Reformed scholasticism in almost exclusively methodological terms. Muller then distinguishes between "orthodoxy" (right teaching) and "scholasticism" (a term denoting "the technical and academic side of this process of the institutionalization and professionalization of Protestant doctrine").[2]

While recognizing that theological method and content are often closely intertwined, it is useful to follow Muller in distinguishing between "scholasticism" and "orthodoxy" in the context of post-Reformation Reformed thought. The definitional debate has itself served to underscore the problem of

---

[1] Armstrong, *Calvinism and the Amyraut Heresy*, 32. This "Aristotelianizing" process is often thought to begin with Calvin's successor Theodore Beza. See ibid., 37-42; Walter Kickel, *Vernunft und Offenbarung bei Theodor Beza* (Neukirchen-Vluyn: Neukirchener Verlag, 1967).

[2] Richard A. Muller, *Post-Reformation Reformed Dogmatics*, 4 vols., 2nd ed. (Grand Rapids: Baker, 2003), I:33-34.

the sources of post-Reformation Reformed thought. We will see that Reformed theologians of this period drew not only upon the first and second-generation Reformers such as Calvin, but also upon influences that can be broadly termed "scholastic" and "pietist." Thus, the term "Reformed orthodoxy," as utilized in this chapter, will refer to the dynamic confluence of Reformation, scholastic, and pietist influences.

An additional problem facing the modern interpreter is the sheer geographical and temporal scope of the phenomenon we call "Reformed orthodoxy." It was, first of all, an international movement involving a host of theologians from the old world and the new, each reflecting a variety of influences.[3] In addition, this international movement must be treated diachronically as well. The vital period of Reformed orthodoxy is often described as stretching from the death of Calvin to the end of the seventeenth century—a period of roughly a century and a half, but the formulations of Reformed orthodoxy continued to exercise profound influence during the nineteenth century and beyond.[4] For these reasons it is important that post-Reformation Reformed thought not be treated as a monolith, and that attention be paid to historical development.

Given the scope of the subject material, the treatment of the theme of union with Christ in Reformed orthodoxy will of necessity be both broader and less detailed than the analysis of Calvin. We will examine certain developments in theological content and method which are crucial to Reformed conceptions of *unio Christi*. Here we include in particular the rise of scholastic method, the advent of *ordo salutis* schemas, the development of federal theology, and the influence of pietist concerns.

Reformed Orthodoxy and Scholastic Method

A cursory comparison of the dogmatic works of Reformation-era thinkers such as Calvin and Bucer with later Reformed works reveals a number of important differences. There is, first of all, a shift from a discursive model, best typified by Calvin's *Institutes*, with its structure loosely based on the trinitarian creedal formula and its frequent, prolix, and sometimes vituperative excursuses, to a

---

[3]For surveys of international Calvinism, see McNeill, *History and Character of Calvinism*; John H. Bratt, ed., *The Rise and Development of Calvinism* (Grand Rapids: Eerdmans, 1959); W. Stanford Reid, ed., *John Calvin: His Influence on the Western World* (Grand Rapids: Zondervan, 1982); Menna Prestwich, ed., *International Calvinism, 1541-1715* (New York: Oxford University Press, 1985).

[4]One can argue that the formulations of Protestant orthodoxy should continue to exercise influence today. See Paul Tillich, *A History of Christian Thought*, ed. Carl E. Braaten (New York: Simon and Schuster 1972), 307. Tillich suggests that "all later Protestant theology becomes a bit vague and is suspended in the air if it is not related to the classic formulation of Reformation theology in Protestant Orthodoxy. The vagueness of much theological thinking in modern Protestantism stems from this lack of knowledge of Protestant Orthodoxy."

more concise and tightly structured model.⁵ Most theologies of the Orthodox period utilize the so-called "*loci* method" or the method of "commonplaces" (of which Melanchthon's *Loci Communes* [1521] was the first of a long line) in which each theological topic is treated with relative completeness and in some intentional order. Also, in striking comparison to the philosophical eclecticism of Calvin and others of his generation, one notes an increasing tendency on the part of orthodox theologians toward philosophical precision—a precision that owed a great deal to the metaphysics and ontology of Aristotle. Taken as a whole, these developments point to an intense concern for theological method on the part of the successors of Calvin.⁶

Reformed Orthodoxy and the Loci Method

The mode of presentation governing the theology of the orthodox period owed much to the revolution in rhetoric and dialectic associated initially with the work of the Dutch humanist Rudolph Agricola (1444-1485) and effectively popularized by Peter Ramus (1515-1572).⁷ Convinced that Aristotle's logic and dialectic were cumbersome, Agricola devised a "place-logic" in which the traditional Aristotelian categories and stress upon predication were deemphasized in favor of the identification of "topics" or *loci*. As Agricola's rhetoric-based "place-logic" displaced the older medieval dialectic, the form of written theology changed as well and the *loci theologici* became the preferred format among both Protestants and Roman Catholics.⁸

This trend continues in the work of Agricola's successor, the French Protestant Peter Ramus. Here the term *method* first assumed a prominence it enjoyed for much of the period of Protestant orthodoxy. In short, the Ramist method consisted in the identification of axioms and in their arrangement, moving from the general to the specific. Ramus wrote, "Method is

---

⁵See Muller, *Reformed Dogmatics*, I:60-66. On Calvin's method, B. A. Gerrish, *Grace and Gratitude: The Eucharistic Theology of John Calvin* (Minneapolis: Fortress Press, 1993), 19, writes: "Calvin's strong sense of logical connection...invites the reader to anticipate thematic links between one doctrine and another and to grasp the part always in relation to the whole, not dissecting the work into relatively self-contained topics or *loci communes*."

⁶Perry Miller, *The New England Mind: The Seventeenth Century* (Cambridge, Mass.: Harvard University Press, 1939), 95, writes: "The great difference between Calvin and the so-called Calvinists of the seventeenth century is symbolized by the vast importance they attached to one word, "method." Systematic organization of the creed had indeed been of great concern to Calvin, but never the obsession it was to his followers."

⁷On the influence of Ramus, see Walter J. Ong, *Ramus: Method, and the Decay of Dialogue* (Cambridge, Mass.: Harvard University Press, 1958); Wilbur S. Howell, *Logic and Rhetoric in England, 1500-1700* (Princeton, N.J.: Princeton University Press, 1956), 146-281; and Donald K. McKim, *Ramism in William Perkins' Theology* (New York: Peter Lang, 1987).

⁸See Ong, *Ramus*, 92-112.

arrangement, by which among many things the first in respect to conspicuousness is put in the first place, the second in the second, the third in the third, and so on. This term refers to every discipline and every dispute."[9] This identification and arrangement often took the form of dichotomies, which were then often diagrammed and presented visually by means of elaborate charts intended to convey the larger perspective.[10]

It is important to note the effect of the "place-logic" movement in general and Ramism in particular upon Reformed orthodoxy. Its effect was especially felt in the mode of presentation, but an inevitable relationship between form and content must also be recognized. As the elements of a theological system were split up according to the place-logic of Agricola and Ramus, the interrelationships between the various elements often became obscured, and the assumption tended to be that each element could be adequately treated in a discrete fashion (i.e., without reference to relationships that might be obscured by the schematization of Ramist logic).[11] As Richard Muller observes, the "systematic effect of the *locus* method was to bar the way to the use of overarching motifs in the system and to emphasize the integrity of the topics."[12] The theme of union with Christ is precisely such an "overarching motif" which transcends and unites the *loci* of justification and sanctification in the theology of Calvin.

Reformed Orthodoxy and Resurgent Aristotelianism

Despite the great respect accorded Calvin, the Reformed orthodox were not content simply to recapitulate his formulations.[13] Encumbered with the tasks of

---

[9]Peter Ramus, *Dialectiqve de Peirre de la Ramee* (Paris: André Wechel, 1555), 119, trans. and quoted in Howell, *Logic and Rhetoric*, 152.

[10]Examples of such Ramist charts are found in William Ames, *The Marrow of Theology*, trans. John Eusden (Boston: Pilgrim Press, 1968), 71-73; and Miller, *Seventeenth Century*, 126.

[11]See Howell, *Logic and Rhetoric*, 163.

[12]Muller, *Reformed Dogmatics*, I:188.

[13]On the history and role of Calvin's *Institutio* in the Reformed churches, see Benjamin B. Warfield, "On the Literary History of Calvin's Institutes," in *Institutes of the Christian Religion by John Calvin*, 2 vols., trans. John Allen, (Philadelphia: Presbyterian Board of Christian Education, 1936), I:v-lvi; John Platt, *Reformed Thought and Scholasticism* (Leiden: E. J. Brill, 1982), 34-46.

A key indication of Calvin's continuing popularity was the frequent translation and retranslation, abridgment, and republication of his *Institutio* for popular and academic audiences during the latter sixteenth and seventeenth centuries. To be sure, Calvin was not the only authority for the orthodox, and textbooks by William Ames, Petrus van Mastricht, and others were eventually to eclipse the *Institutio*. But, by reputation at least, the Genevan Reformer remained first among equals. Furthermore, criticism of Calvin by the orthodox Reformed was muted and confined for the most part to exegetical differences over the interpretation of Scripture. Fundamental theological criticism of

articulating basic Reformation doctrine, establishing church orders, and defending the nascent Protestant communities against Roman Catholic threats, the reformers had little time for leisured reflection and they left many items of unfinished business.[14] First and foremost among these matters was a precise accounting of the relationship of divine grace to the human being and to human agency in salvation—in the parlance of an earlier age, the relationship of "nature and grace." Culminating in the work of Thomas Aquinas, the Medieval period had seen the progressive erection of a theoretical edifice in which divine agency and human activity were reconciled in ways that sought to preserve the priority of divine grace together with the integrity and freedom of the human person. Central to this synthesis were an understanding of the psychological faculties derived in part from the *De Anima* of Aristotle, and a view of divine grace which distinguished between uncreated and created grace.[15]

Developed by Bonaventure, Albertus Magnus, and Thomas Aquinas, the distinction between created and uncreated grace was crucial in a number of ways to the Aristotelian-Thomistic soteriological synthesis.[16] In distinguishing between the action of the triune God (uncreated grace) upon the human person and the appropriation of that action in new human capabilities or gracious habits (created grace), the medieval theologians were able simultaneously to assert a certain priority of divine grace in salvation, to account for the real change that divine grace effects in the human being, and to develop a theory of justification as the result of both prior divine grace and meritorious human action.

In describing how created grace becomes inherent in a human being, the psychological notion of *habitus* receives considerable attention by Thomas Aquinas.[17] According to Thomas, gracious "habits" or qualities are infused by divine action into the human soul and become integral to it. These gracious habits in turn serve to perfect the faculties of the soul in such a way that good works are freely chosen by the human being, thus meriting justification.[18]

Calvin, of the sort commonly leveled by leading nineteenth-century "Calvinists" such as William Cunningham, Charles Hodge, and Robert L. Dabney, was rare in this period.

[14] See Miller, *Seventeenth Century*, 93-94.

[15] On the medieval faculty psychology as it was appropriated by Reformed thinkers, see Miller, *Seventeenth Century*, 239-79; Charles Lloyd Cohen, *God's Caress: The Psychology of Puritan Religious Experience* (New York: Oxford, 1986), 25-46; J. Rodney Fulcher, "Puritans and the Passions: The Faculty Psychology in American Puritanism," *Journal of the History of the Behavioral Sciences* 9 (1973): 123-39.

[16] For an account of the twelfth-century emergence of this distinction, see McGrath, *Iustitia Dei*, I:100-109.

[17] See, e.g., Thomas Aquinas, *Basic Writings of St. Thomas Aquinas*, 2 vols., ed. Anton C. Pegis (New York: Random House, 1945), II:366-411 (*Summa Theologica* I-II: Q. 49-54). See also F. C. Copleston, *Aquinas* (New York: Penguin Books, 1955), 214-219; Sang Hyun Lee, *The Philosophical Theology of Jonathan Edwards* (Princeton, N.J. Princeton University Press, 1988), 15-22.

[18] Regarding free will as a necessary condition for the accrual of merit, see Thomas

Although this Thomistic synthesis of nature and grace in general, and the idea of the infusion of supernatural habits in particular, was challenged during the later Middle ages by Nominalists of the *Via Moderna*, it was still very much alive during the Reformation period. It was this Thomistic soteriological complex of created grace in the form of *habitus*, free will, and merit which aroused the ire of Luther and Calvin. As John Platt notes,

> The issue of nature and grace lay at the heart of the Reformers protest against the contemporary scholastic theology. The medieval schoolmen had a positive view of the relationship, "Grace presupposes nature," and although the latter was not considered adequate in itself but required supplementing, nonetheless "grace does not abolish nature but perfects it."...In fact the Reformers' crucial message was the abolition of the grace-nature framework in favour of that of grace alone.[19]

Luther's repudiation of the medieval nature-grace dialectic in favor of *sola gratia* was emphatic. His initial rejection of the *habitus* synthesis was doubtless due to his background in the neo-Augustinian *Via Moderna*, but his antipathy to the Thomistic construction was confirmed and strengthened by the doctrine of justification by grace through faith. Instead of created grace in the form of *habitus*, Luther stressed the uncreated grace of the indwelling Holy Spirit.[20] On this issue, Calvin differed little in substance from his older colleague. While accepting the conventional psychology of his time,[21] he made no theological use of the *habitus* notion and he vigorously inveighed against the medieval scholastic nature-grace synthesis and its correlates of graciously assisted free will and meritorious human action as it had been passed on from Peter Lombard and Thomas Aquinas. Calvin wrote:

> We are not dividing the credit for good works between God and man, as the Sophists do, but we are preserving it whole, complete, and unimpaired for the Lord. To man we assign only this: that he pollutes and contaminates by his impurity those very things which were good.[22]

While motivated by the desire to highlight the priority of grace and safeguard the gratuity of justification, this tendency of Luther and Calvin to frame the soteriological question in monergistic terms left critical questions unanswered.[23] In particular, questions regarding the role of the human being in salvation, and the nature of the positive change that salvation imparts to human nature had been ignored. Soon after Luther's death, the Lutheran communion

---

Aquinas, *Basic Writings*, II:1023-1025 (*Summa Theologica* I-II, Q. 113, art. 3).

[19]Platt, *Reformed Thought and Scholasticism*, 4.

[20]See McGrath, *Iustitia Dei*, I:154; Althaus, *Theology of Martin Luther*, 122.

[21]See Calvin, *Inst.* I.15.6.

[22]Calvin, *Inst.* III.15.3; cf. III.15.7.

[23]Miller, *Seventeenth Century*, 94, observes that the thought of the Reformers' successors "was determined as much by the questions which Luther and Calvin did not solve as by those which they did."

was torn by a series of disputes having to do with the relationship of the divine and the human in salvation. Though not entirely without controversy, the Reformed successors of Calvin moved quickly to give a more complete account of the human role in salvation by appropriating much of the conceptual apparatus of medieval psychology and asserting their own Protestant version of the medieval synthesis of nature and grace.[24]

Seeking more fully to explain the relationship between the divine and human, the change which grace effects in the human person, and at the same time to guarantee the gratuity of justification, late sixteenth century Reformed thinkers such as Peter Martyr Vermigli and Jerome Zanchi returned to the *habitus* construction of the Thomistic synthesis and began to describe the change of the human person in sanctification in terms of the infusion of gracious supernatural habits.[25] The importance of this development should not be underestimated. With the adoption of Thomistic nature-grace categories, the components of Reformed soteriology were being framed in terms that differed significantly from those used by the first and second-generation Reformers.

Given the close relation of justification and sanctification in the Calvinistic context of union with Christ by faith and the Holy Spirit, it was inevitable that the relationship of the human act of faith to divine grace would require further explanation. Was the human act of faith, the instrumental cause of union with Christ and justification, simply the result of direct divine action or was faith to be seen as the result of a prior change effected by divine grace? The first option appeared to depict the human being as a mere pawn, while the second might seem to compromise the gratuity of justification by positing a real change in the human being prior to justification. In dealing with this difficulty, Reformed theologians turned to the scholastic distinction between habit and act.

Crucial to this development was the work of Girolamo Zanchi, who, like Peter Martyr, had been trained in the context of the Italian Thomistic revival.[26] While denying that justifying grace involves the impartation of a quality to the soul, Zanchi nevertheless extends the language of created grace in the form of

---

[24] The revival of Thomism among Reformed scholastic theologians has been explored in some detail by John Patrick Donnelly in his *Calvinism and Scholasticism in Vermigli's Doctrine of Man and Grace* (Leiden: Brill, 1976); and "Calvinist Thomism," *Viator: Medieval and Renaissance Studies* 7 (1976): 441-455. See also, Richard A. Muller, *God, Creation, and Providence in the Thought of Jacob Arminius* (Grand Rapids: Baker, 1991), 31-51.

[25] See Donnelly, "Calvinist Thomism," 42-44; *Calvinism and Scholasticism*, 156; Marvin W. Anderson, "Peter Martyr on Romans," *Scottish Journal of Theology* 26 (1973): 408.

[26] On Zanchi (Zanchius), see Otto Gründler, *Die Gotteslehre Girolami Zanchis und ihre bedeutung für seine Lehre von der Prädestination* (Neukirchen: Neukirchener Verlag, 1965). See also Norman Shepherd, "Zanchius on Saving Faith," *Westminster Theological Journal* 36 (1973-74): 31-47; and J. P. Donnelly, "Calvinist Thomism," 444-453.

infused habits or virtues to the doctrine of faith.[27] This allowed Zanchi to stress both the genuine and the lasting character of the change effected in the human being by divine grace. In addition, in distinguishing between the act and the habit of faith, Zanchi carefully reserves the instrumental appropriation of justification for the act of faith, thus preserving both the real change effected by grace and the appropriation of a completely gracious and gratuitous justification through the (nonmeritorious) act of faith.[28] Thus it was that for the Reformed tradition generally—in Britain and America as well as on the Continent—the phenomenon of faith itself quickly came to be construed in terms of the scholastic distinction of habit and act.[29] On this theory, the act of faith (which instrumentally unites the believer with Christ) cannot be construed as the meritorious cause of justification because it results from the infusion of the habit of faith.

The subsequent history of this Reformed scholastic synthesis of nature and grace indicates, however, that the solution was not entirely satisfactory. While institutionally successful in that it provided a defensible school-text position, it was nevertheless repeatedly challenged—usually because it was thought to undermine the doctrine of gratuitous justification by grace through faith. A striking, indeed almost paradigmatic, example of such dissent is found in the work of Puritan theologian John Cotton (1584-1652). In the context of the Antinomian Controversy of 1636-38 in Massachusetts, Cotton undermined the Reformed scholastic nature-grace schema by denying any instrumental function in justification to the act of faith on the grounds that such a view made justification the result of a work (the act of faith).[30] Instead, justification is communicated to the believer though regeneration and union with Christ (which is seen as including the habit of faith).[31] But even the infusion of gracious habits, involving as it did a genuine change for the better in the human

---

[27] See Donnelly, "Calvinist Thomism," 451-52; Shepherd, "Zanchius on Saving Faith," 33-34.

[28] See Gründler, *Gotteslehre*, 53-60.

[29] See, e.g., "The Canons of the Synod of Dordt," (III-IV, Art. 11; Rejectio Errorum VI) in Philip Schaff, *The Creeds of Christendom*, 3 vols., 6th ed. (New York: Harper and Brothers, 1931), III:566, 569-570. On the use of the habit/act construction in Puritan theology, see William K. B. Stoever, *'A Faire and Easie Way to Heaven': Covenant Theology and Antinomianism in Early Massachusetts* (Middletown, Conn.: Wesleyan University Press, 1978), 41-44, 170-74; Cohen, *God's Caress*, 75-110.

In contrast to earlier Reformed theology of Calvin, which used the term "regeneration" (*regeneratio*) as a synonym for the progressive renovation of the soul, or sanctification, Reformed scholasticism uses the term for the initial infusion of gracious habits or principles into the soul.

[30] See John Cotton, "Mr. Cotton's Rejoynder," in *The Antinomian Controversy, 1636-1638*, 2nd ed., ed. David D. Hall (Durham, N.C.: Duke University Press, 1990), 97-98. See also Stoever, 41-44.

[31] John Cotton, "The Way of Congregational Churches Cleared," in Hall, *Antinomian Controversy*, 401.

being, could be seen as compromising the gratuity of justification, and so Cotton, while formally retaining the habit/act distinction, redefined *habitus* as the constant reception by the human being of the saving activity of the Spirit. In so doing, he effectively undercut the whole idea of created grace.[32]

Even modifications such as Cotton's did not fully succeed in allaying the fears of some Reformed who were zealous to safeguard the gratuity of justification. The mere temporal proximity of either the act of faith or the infusion of the *habitus* of faith to justification was viewed by some as a threat to the gratuity of justification. In an effort further to erect a wall of separation between justification and sanctification, and so to avoid even a hint that the impartation of new life in Christ might be implicated in the imputation of Christ's righteousness to be believer, a small but persistent group of Reformed thinkers, often dismissed as "antinomian," taught various forms of justification from eternity.[33] The key to a correct understanding of the relationship between justification and sanctification, they thought, was not so much to be found in scholastic distinctions of habit and act as in a particular sequence of the *ordo salutis*, a topic to which we will turn in the next section.

Another effect of the use of scholastic categories in the context of Reformed soteriology must be briefly noted in this context. As the conceptual apparatus and terminology applied to the problem of grace became increasingly technical, the concerns of Calvin—particularly his focus on union with the incarnate humanity or *substantia* of Christ—were to some extent eclipsed. With the talk of "created graces" and the infusion of "gracious habits," it was both difficult and increasingly unnecessary to reconcile these categories with the language

---

[32]This is evident in the following passage where the habit is defined entirely in negative terms: "For the very Habit and gift of Faith is of an Emptying Nature, emptying the soule of all confidence in it self and in the Creature, and so leaving and constituting the soule as an empty vessell, empty of it owne worth, and goodnesse, but full of Christ." "Peter Bulkeley and John Cotton: On Union With Christ," in Hall, *Antinomian Controversy*, 44. Cotton's reluctance to give up the "habit/act" terminology was probably due to the fact that the Synod of Dordt had enshrined the distinction.

Stoever correctly notes the difference between Cotton and his ministerial opponents on this issue—the New England elders advocating the Reformed scholastic dialectic of nature and grace, and Cotton opposing it. Stoever goes on, however, to attribute Cotton's views to a subcurrent of English religious radicalism which had nothing to do with Reformed theology. See Stoever, *Faire and Easie Way*, 164-65; Stoever, "Nature, Grace and John Cotton: The Theological Dimension in the New England Antinomian Controversy," *Church History* 44 (1975): 22-33. One can argue, however, that Cotton's rejection of the scholastic nature/grace dialectic was in some sense a return to Calvin and the first generation reformers.

[33]See Beeke, *Assurance of Faith*, 303; John von Rohr, *The Covenant of Grace in Puritan Thought* (Atlanta: Scholars Press, 1986), 97-98. Recent dogmatic appraisals of justification from eternity are found in Louis Berkhof, *Systematic Theology*, (Grand Rapids: Eerdmans, 1941), 517-520; Berkouwer, *Faith and Justification*, 143-168.

and ideas of the first-generation Reformers.[34]

Reformed Orthodoxy and the *Ordo Salutis*

General and more technical usages of the term *ordo salutis* ("order of salvation") should be distinguished. It sometimes denotes the application of redemption in general, but a more technical usage of the term is evident as it is applied to the Reformed theology of the generations following Calvin.[35] Here attention was closely focused upon the sequence and relationship between the various events and elements comprising the individual's experience of salvation (election, calling, regeneration, justification, sanctification, adoption, glorification, etc.).

Pastoral theology, rather than dogmatic theological concerns, provided the earliest impetus toward *ordo salutis* thinking. In a theological context emphasizing the priority of divine grace and the gratuity of divine election, Reformed pastors were inevitably confronted by those who had difficulty obtaining assurance of salvation. Confident on biblical and theological grounds that the elect would indeed be brought to final salvation, and that they would persevere in faith and godliness in this life,[36] the post-Reformation Reformed theologians gave increasing weight to discerning the marks of grace in professing Christians. They argued that because the various elements of salvation are bound together as by an unbreakable chain (the image of a "chain" or *catena* is common), the believer who discerns one or more elements may

---

[34] The incompatibility is particularly evident when we recognize that the Reformed scholastic doctrine of union with Christ was to some extent framed in terms of created habitual graces. Considerable dissonance was generated when the scholastic stress upon habitual created grace (supernaturally infused yet integral to the human soul) was juxtaposed with Calvin's notion of union with the substance of Christ's living incarnate humanity. Any identification of the infused habitual virtues with the *substantia* of Christ's humanity would present an ontological dilemma in that the personal integrity of both Christ and the believer would be threatened.

[35] For example, B. B. Warfield (*Calvin and Augustine*, 484) wrote of Calvin that "his interest was most intense in the application to the sinful soul of the salvation wrought out by Christ,—in a word in what is technically known as the *ordo salutis*."

Two developments, however, differentiate the later Protestant scholastic use of the *ordo salutis* concept. First, together with the Protestant Reformation, a marked distinction was drawn between justification and sanctification. Second, there was the ever-increasing tendency in Protestant orthodoxy to view the event of justification as a point in time, together with a keen concern with the *time* of that justification. In this more specific and defined sense, Berkhof, *Systematic Theology*, 417, correctly notes that the "doctrine of the order of salvation is a fruit of the Reformation. Hardly any semblance of it is found in the works of the [medieval] Scholastics." We saw in the first chapter above that Calvin did not utilize an *ordo salutis* in this more specific and technical sense.

[36] Rom. 8:29-30 was usually cited.

with confidence conclude that he or she holds title to the whole.[37] Thus it was this complex of divine sovereignty and *ordo salutis* which grounded the Reformed orthodox search for assurance of salvation via a *syllogismus practicus*, an approach concisely summarized by the Swiss Reformed orthodox theologian Johannes Wollebius (1586-1629):

> In examining our election by logic it is necessary to proceed from the means of carrying out the decree itself, making a beginning from our sanctification.
> The argument is as follows: Whoever knows that he has the gift of sanctification [in se sentit donum], by which we die to sin and live to righteousness, is justified, called, or endued with true faith, and elect. But I know [sentio] this by the grace of God; therefore, I am justified, called, and elect.[38]

But theological tools forged for one purpose may have other uses as well, and such was the case with the early Reformed "chain of salvation," as a theological movement committed to the gratuity of forensic justification began to use these conceptual tools systematically to isolate the divine decree of justification from the renewal of life (i.e., sanctification). Notions of logical and temporal order and sequence soon became integral to orthodox presentations of the application of redemption and a rough consensus emerged within the Reformed community consisting of divine initiation (election, calling, regeneration[39]), followed by the forensic benefits of salvation (justification and adoption), followed then by the elements involving personal transformation (sanctification and glorification).[40]

This *ordo salutis* provided a framework for addressing certain matters where ambiguity remained in the thought of Calvin and the Reformers—furnishing a context for discussions of the relation of created and uncreated grace, and delineating the precise character of the relationship between justification and sanctification. On the other hand, anomalies just as clearly remained in Reformed presentations of soteriology. The relationship of regeneration to a gratuitous justification is one such area of persistent difficulty. C. A. Briggs writes:

---

[37] This assurance-driven use of the *ordo salutis* theme is present in Reformed theology as early as Beza. See Beeke, *Assurance of Faith*, 84-85. On William Perkins' usage of this theme, see Richard A. Muller, "Perkins' *A Golden Chaine*: Predestinarian System or Schematized *Ordo Salutis*?," *Sixteenth Century Journal* 9 (1978): 69-81.

[38] Johannes Wollebius, *Compendium Theologiae Christianae*, IV.2.15, in *Reformed Dogmatics: J. Wollebius, G. Voetius, F. Turretin*, ed. and trans. John W. Beardslee III (New York: Oxford University Press, 1965), 53. See Stoever, *Faire and Easie Way*, 126.

[39] Regeneration was usually construed to involve the infusion of the habit of faith. The term *regeneratio*, while used by Calvin as a virtual synonym for sanctification, quickly came to be used in Reformed orthodoxy for the initial transition from spiritual death to spiritual life, i.e., in the sense of "quickening."

[40] While there was a majority concensus regarding the basic order of divine initiation, forensic benefits, and transforming benefits, there was considerable room for diversity as to details.

The Protestant theologians have always been troubled where exactly to put regeneration in the order of salvation. There can be no justification without faith; and, according to the Synod of Dort, no faith without regeneration; therefore logically regeneration should precede justification. But then the question arises: Can a man be regenerated before he is justified?...If faith is *infused* in regeneration, as the Synod of Dort teaches, then human salvation is begun by infusion and not by a declaratory act of God in justification. If regeneration is an infusion, why so much polemic against the Roman Catholic view that justification is a process of infusion?[41]

Another point of difficulty, less obvious perhaps, but of considerable importance, is the relationship between the *ordo salutis* framework and the theme of union with Christ. Here there appears to be a fundamental incompatibility between an organic view of salvation as in principle communicated *in toto* and at once (though not fully realized at once) through a spiritual union with Christ (e.g., Calvin), and the Reformed orthodox view of salvation as applied in a series of temporally or logically successive acts.[42] Either all the benefits of salvation reside in Christ and are communicated to the believer through spiritual union with him, or they are communicated through a series of successive and discrete acts, the coherence and unity of which can only be grounded in divine intention and sovereignty (i.e., in theology proper rather than christology).

The difficulty posed by this inherent incompatibility between the organicism of spiritual union with Christ and the discrete sequentialism of the *ordo salutis* played a significant role in the subsequent development of Protestant theology—both Reformed and Lutheran. In both traditions, whose primary founders had strongly stressed the centrality of *unio Christi*, the *ordo salutis*

---

[41]Charles Augustus Briggs, *Theological Symbolics* (New York: Charles Scribner's Sons, 1914), 369. For example, Herman Witsius, *The Economy of the Covenants between God and Man: Comprehending a Complete Body of Divinity*, 2 vols., trans. William Crookshank (London: R. Baynes, 1822), I:395, concedes that sanctification in some sense precedes justification. Much the same argument is urged by James Orr, *The Progress of Dogma* (Grand Rapids: Eerdmans, 1952), 272-274. In view of this difficulty, moves toward eternalizing the decree of justification become understandable, despite the friction created with the biblical materials.

[42]Richard B. Gaffin, Jr., *Resurrection and Redemption* (Phillipsburg, N.J.: Presbyterian and Reformed, 1987), 138-139, poses this dilemma well: "If at the point of inception this union is prior (and therefore involves the posession in the inner man of all that Christ is as resurrected), what need is there for the other acts? Conversely, if the other acts are in some sense prior, is not union improperly subordinated and its biblical significance severely attenuated, to say the least? The structure and problematics of the traditional *ordo salutis* prohibits making an unequivocal statement concerning that on which Paul stakes everything in the application of redemption, namely union with the resurrected Christ." A similar point is made with respect to Lutheran orthodoxy by Werner Elert, *The Structure of Lutheranism*, trans. Walter A. Hansen (St. Louis: Concordia Publishing House, 1962), 154.

framework came to dominate soteriological thinking, and in both traditions the theme of *unio Christi* underwent certain modifications to render it compatible with an *ordo salutis* schema.

At least two solutions to the problem were possible. The approach chosen by Lutheran orthodoxy was to give up the use of spiritual union with Christ as an overarching and unifying category of salvation. Here, spiritual union with Christ was disengaged from any positive relationship to justification and treated as a subsidiary moment in the *ordo salutis*.[43] The other solution (adopted in general by Reformed orthodoxy) was to maintain the formal umbrella function of union with Christ while, at the same time, revising it along lines compatible with the *ordo salutis* structure.

Crucial here was an increasing tendency to speak of *unio* in at least two different senses—on the one hand there was a legal or federal union, on the other a spiritual or vital union. In essence, the Reformed conception of union with Christ was bifurcated along the line of division between the forensic or legal benefits of salvation (i.e., justification) and the transforming benefits (i.e., sanctification). The price paid for this, of course, was that the principle binding justification and sanctification together, so crucial to Calvin, became purely formal. In reality, when the Reformed orthodox spoke of a "federal union" with Christ, they were in actuality speaking of the doctrine of justification as conditioned by the Reformed *ordo salutis*.[44] Likewise, when they referred to a "spiritual union," what was really being described was sanctification. But before this could occur, it was necessary for the conceptual apparatus of federal theology to be developed, and it is to this important matter that we will turn in the next section.

Before examining the rise of the federal theology, however, it is interesting to note that the adoption of an *ordo salutis* framework was perhaps not a

---

[43] While Lutheran theologians evidence some diversity on the doctrine of the "mystical union," the tendency for Lutheran orthodox dogmaticians such as Johann Quenstedt (1617-1685) and David Hollaz (1646-1713) is to place it after calling and justification in the *ordo*. On this see Heinrich Schmid, *The Doctrinal Theology of the Evangelical Lutheran Church*, 3rd ed. rev., trans. Charles A. Hay and Henry E. Jacobs (Minneapolis: Augsburg Publishing House, 1961), 480-486; Elert, *Structure of Lutheranism*, 154-176; Geerhardus Vos, "Doctrine of the Covenant in Reformed Theology," in *Redemptive History and Biblical Interpretation: The Shorter Writings of Geerhardus Vos*, ed. by Richard B. Gaffin, Jr. (Phillipsburg, N.J.: Presbyterian and Reformed, 1980), 256-257.

[44] This criticism is perhaps suggested by R. B. Gaffin's contention that Reformed theology "has tended to equivocate on the notion of union with Christ" (*Resurrection and Redemption*, 139 n. 11). Other recent criticisms of the *ordo salutis* framework include Karl Barth, *Church Dogmatics*, 4 vols., ed. G. W. Bromiley and T. F. Torrance, (Edinburgh: T. & T. Clark, 1936-1969), IV/2:499-511; Otto Weber, *Foundations of Dogmatics*, 2 vols., trans. Darrell L. Guder Grand Rapids: Eerdmans, 1981), II:336-338; Berkouwer, *Faith and Justification*, 25-36; Anthony A. Hoekema, *Saved by Grace* (Grand Rapids: Eerdmans, 1989), 11-27.

foregone conclusion. Shortly after the death of Calvin, there were attempts further to integrate the theme of union with Christ with the believer's justification on the one hand, and the work of Christ on the other, by appeal to a forensic justification of Christ himself at his resurrection.[45] The earliest effort along these lines appears to have been made by the Heidelberg theologian Caspar Olevianus, who together with Zacharius Ursinus composed the Heidelberg Catechism. As noted in the previous chapter, Calvin insisted that communion with the person of Christ (particularly the incarnate humanity of Christ) was necessary for the reception of the benefits of salvation, but the Genevan reformer never explained the how forensic categories of justification and the personal and realistic categories of union fit together. Olevianus' solution to this difficulty was to understand the resurrection of Christ as Christ's own forensic justification, a divine declaration of just standing which applies first of all to Christ himself, and secondarily to the believer in union with Christ. Paraphrasing Olevianus' proposal, H. Heppe writes:

> this first exaltation of Christ (i.e., the resurrection)...is itself a practical declaring righteous of all those who are aroused to faith in Christ. Just as by giving the Son to death the Father actually condemned all our sins in him, the Father also by raising Christ up form the dead, acquitted Christ of our sin-guilt and us in Christ (Olevian, pp. 76-77). So Christ's resurrection is our righteousness, because God further regards us in the perfection in which Christ rose. Whereas the Father regarded us previously in the dying Son as sinners, He sees us now in the resurrected Son as righteous; or rather; whereas previously He regarded the Son in our sins as a sinner, He regards Him now, and us in Him, as the person which He is, and which He is not for Himself but for us (Olevian, p. 80).[46]

This focus upon a forensic justification of Christ did not negate the need for faith on the part of the individual Christian. Care was taken to distinguish the eternal divine intent to justify the elect, the justification of Christ, the actualization of that justification in the individual believer, and the subjective assurance of that justification by the Christian. The English Puritan William Ames (1576-1633) wrote:

> The judgment was, first, conceived in the mind of God in a decree of justification. Gal. 3:8, "The Scripture, foreseeing that God would justify the Gentiles by faith." Second, it was pronounced in Christ our head as he rose from the dead. 2 Cor. 5:19, "God was in Christ reconciling the world to himself, not imputing their sins to them." Third, it is pronounced in actuality upon that first relationship which is created when faith is born. Rom. 8:1, "There is therefore no condemnation to

---

[45]Treatments of this development include Ritschl, *Critical History*, 267-274; Schneckenburger, *Vergleichende Darstellung*, II:63-70; Heppe, *Reformed Dogmatics*, 498-500.

[46]Heppe, *Reformed Dogmatics*, 498-99. See also Geerhardus Vos, "Doctrine of the Covenant," 249. On the forensic character of this christological justification, see Witsius, *Economy of the Covenants*, I:392; cf. I:275.

those who are in Christ Jesus." Fourth, it is expressly pronounced by the spirit of God witnessing to our spirits our reconciliation with God. Rom. 5:5, "The love of God is shed abroad in our hearts by the Holy Spirit which has been given to us." This testimony of the spirit is not properly justification itself, but rather an actual perceiving of what has been given before as if in a reflected act of faith.[47]

In this way, then, the connection between the person and work of Christ (with whom the believer is united) and the forensic benefits of salvation is strengthened and the role of union with Christ is to a considerable extent clarified.[48] On this understanding, Christ is indeed "clothed with his benefits." The justification of the Christian is not merely "on the basis of" or "made possible by" the work of Christ in an abstract sense; rather, the believer's justification resides concretely in the person of Christ as the justified one and is appropriated through union with Christ.

Given the attractiveness of this proposal, it is not surprising that this notion of Christ's justification gained considerable currency, particularly among continental Reformed orthodox divines in Germany and the Netherlands.[49] Quite striking, given the degree of interaction between Reformed divines in England and the continent, however, is the almost total absence of this idea among English-speaking Reformed theologians, particularly after William Ames.[50] This turn of events was in part due to the fact that, as we noted above, the theme of spiritual union with Christ mediating all of salvation does not sit comfortably in the *ordo salutis* context that was being increasingly codified. In addition, the very notion of union with Christ underwent changes in the context of the Reformed federal theology, and these changes rendered unnecessary the idea of Christ's resurrection justification, albeit at some cost.

Federal Theology and the Bifurcation of Union

Nothing was to exert greater influence upon the shape of later Reformed theology than the so-called "federal theology."[51] Given the broad impact of the

---

[47]Ames, *Marrow of Theology*, 161.

[48]Ritschl, *Critical History*, 268, notes that "the Reformed divines, by their view of the exaltation of Christ, have established a closer and stricter connection between Christ's merit and justification than has been done by the Lutherans."

[49]These include Olevianus, Polanus, Ames, Heidegger, Lampe, Witsius, and van Mastricht. See Schneckenburger, *Vergleichende Darstellung*, II:66; Ritschl, *Critical History*, 269.

[50]Regarding this eclipse, Gaffin, *Resurrection and Redemption*, 123 n. 147, observes that "this point was better grasped by the earlier Reformed theologians than subsequently."

[51]The term "federal" derives from the Latin *foedus*, meaning "covenant," "compact," or "contract." Surveys of Reformed federal theology include T. M. Lindsay, "The Covenant Theology," *British and Foreign Evangelical Review* 28 (1879): 521-537; William Adams Brown, "Covenant Theology," in *Encyclopaedia of Religion and Ethics*,

covenant theme on Reformed views of creation, the work of Christ, the application of redemption, the sacraments, and assurance of salvation, William Klempa is doubtless correct in contending that the theology of the covenant represents the "most influential development in Reformed thought after Calvin's death."[52]

Despite its prominence in Scripture (particularly in the Old Testament and in the Epistle to the Hebrews), Christian theology prior to the Reformation makes little use of the covenant theme. During the patristic period, it receives some mention in Irenaeus and Augustine, and it was later revived in the *pactum* theory of late medieval nominalism.[53] While the idea of covenant played a modest but significant role in the theology of Calvin,[54] it assumed considerably more prominence in Reformed circles as the sixteenth century wore on, and it was in the context of Reformed orthodoxy that the covenant achieved an unprecedented centrality and importance. Geerhardus Vos effectively captures the importance of the covenant theme for Reformed thinkers:

> At present there is general agreement that the doctrine of the covenants is a peculiarly Reformed doctrine. It emerged in Reformed theology where it was assured of a permanent place and in a way that has also remained confined within these bounds...With full force it lays hold of theological thinking, which in many cases it bends in a distinctive direction.[55]

The last sentence above anticipates a crucial topic for this study—the effects of the federal theology upon the theme of union with Christ, but before the

---

ed. James Hastings (New York: Charles Scribner's Sons, 1924-27), IV:216-224; Vos, "Doctrine of the Covenant"; Barth, *Church Dogmatics*, IV/1:54-66; John Murray, "Covenant Theology," in *The Encyclopedia of Christianity*, ed. Philip E. Hughes (Marshalltown, Del.: National Foundation for Christian Education, 1972), III:199-216; William Klempa, "The Concept of the Covenant in Sixteenth- and Seventeenth-Century Continental and British Reformed Theology," in *Major Themes in the Reformed Tradition*, ed. Donald K. McKim (Grand Rapids: Eerdmans, 1992), 94-107.

[52]Klempa, "Concept of the Covenant," 94.

[53]On early church uses of the covenant theme, see Brown, "Covenant Theology," 219; Paul Helm, "Calvin and the Covenant: Unity and Continuity," *The Evangelical Quarterly* 55 (1983): 73. For a survey of medieval use of the covenant theme, see Strehle, *Calvinism, Federalism, and Scholasticism*, 6-82.

[54]The covenant motif functions theologically in Calvin's identification of the sacraments as signs and seals of the covenant, and in his defense of infant baptism. Calvin also places particular stress upon the essential unity of the covenant of grace, despite differing modes of administration, throughout the Old and New Testament eras. See *Inst.* II.10.1-5, 8; IV.16.2-16. See also Everett H. Emerson, "Calvin and Covenant Theology," *Church History* 25 (1956): 136-44; Elton M. Eenigenburg, "The Place of the Covenant in Calvin's Thinking," *Reformed Review* 10 (1957): 1-22; Anthony A. Hoekema, "The Covenant of Grace in Calvin's Teaching," *Calvin Theological Journal* 2 (1967): 133-161; Helm, "Calvin and the Covenant," 65-81.

[55]Vos, "Doctrine of the Covenant," 234.

impact of the federal theology on the conceptualization of union with Christ can be addressed, we must examine a complex of issues having to do with the alleged "legalism" of federal theology—the conditionality of the covenant of grace and the issue of "contractualism," and the question of a "federal" or "legal" union with Christ.

Federal Theology and "Extrinsic Legalism"

The issue of covenant conditionality was raised in powerful fashion for modern scholarship by Perry Miller. According to Miller, preeminently it is the doctrine of the covenant which sets Puritanism apart from Calvin and the earlier Reformed tradition, and which thus constitutes the "marrow of Puritan divinity." He contends that "Calvin made hardly any mention of the covenant,"[56] and that the covenant theme arose as an attempt to circumscribe the actions of a transcendent and inscrutable God within well defined limits and so to provide a ground for assurance of salvation and a foundation for ethical exhortation.

It is at this point that Miller's conception of the covenant of grace as a conditional contract is most evident. By fulfilling the conditions of the covenant (i.e., faith and obedience), a person could, in essence, lay legal claim to salvation.

> The union with God...is a definite legal status, based on a *quid pro quo*, an "if I believe" necessitating a "you have to save me." God's will is originally free to pick and choose in any fashion, but once the covenant is drawn up, He no longer acts without a reason, He does not appear to man as a brutal or capricious tyrant. He is bound by certain commitments; He is compelled to play the game of salvation according to certain rules.[57]

Miller argued, furthermore, that on the basis of the conditional covenant even those apparently without any experience of divine grace could be exhorted to covenant obedience and to "prepare" themselves by diligent attention to the means of grace, with the expectation, indeed the guarantee, that God would then respond appropriately.[58] This conception of the covenant then led inevitably to a "spiritual commercialism" and to an undermining of the sovereignty of God in which the effects of original sin were depreciated and innate human capacity elevated in ways quite foreign to Calvin.[59]

Though Miller's presentation of federal theology has been justly challenged at several points,[60] his argument regarding the origin and social rootedness of

---

[56] Perry Miller, *Errand into the Wilderness* (Cambridge, Mass.: Harvard University Press, 1956), 60; see also Miller, *Seventeenth Century*, 365-397.
[57] Miller, *Errand*, 71. See also *Seventeenth Century*, 382-389.
[58] Miller, *Errand*, 85-87.
[59] See Miller, *Seventeenth Century*, 389; *Errand*, 74-82.
[60] Miller's contention that Calvin had little interest in the covenant was rightly

the covenant theology has been more durable and is echoed by later scholarship. Miller writes:

> [T]he federal theology was essentially part of a universal tendency in European thought to change social relationships from status to contract...it was one expression of late Renaissance speculation, which was moving in general away from the ideas of feudalism, from the belief that society must be modeled upon an eternally fixed hierarchy to the theories of constitutional limitation and voluntary origins, to the protection of individual rights and the shattering of sumptuary economic regulations. There can be no doubt that these theologians inserted the federal idea into the very substance of divinity, that they changed the relation even of God to man from necessity to contract, largely because contractualism was becoming increasingly congenial to the age and in particular to Puritans.[61]

Another influential approach was proposed by Leonard Trinterud.[62] Rather than viewing Calvin and the first generation of Reformers as uninterested in the covenant theme, as had Miller, Trinterud identified two different strains of covenant teaching within the Reformed tradition—one associated with William Tyndale, Ulrich Zwingli, and the Rhineland Reformed theologians on the continent; the other linked with Calvin and the Genevan Reformation. The first view involved a "conditional covenant" or "law-covenant scheme" in which "all of God's promises are conditional."[63] Here the covenant is seen primarily

---

challenged by Everett H. Emerson, "Calvin and Covenant Theology," 136-144; and George M. Marsden, "Perry Miller's Rehabilitation of the Puritans: A Critique," *Church History* 39 (1970): 101-104. Norman Pettit, *The Heart Prepared* (New Haven: Yale University Press, 1966), has opposed Miller's argument that covenantal obedience and preparation really served as a *quid pro quo* that required God to act in a certain way. Miller's assertion that the federal theology undermined divine sovereignty and exalted human ability in a way verging on Arminianism has been undercut by William K. B. Stoever, *Faire and Easie Way*, who demonstrates that the federal theology involved a complex dialectic of nature and grace which balanced divine initiative and human response. Finally, Miller's purely contractual interpretation of the federal theology covenant of grace is opposed by scholars such as Michael McGiffert and John von Rohr, who find instead a dialectic of the unconditional and the conditional. See Michael McGiffert, "The Problem of the Covenant in Puritan Thought: Peter Bulkeley's Gospel-Covenant," *New England Historical and Genealogical Register* 130 (1976): 107-129; John von Rohr, "Covenant and Assurance in Early English Puritanism," *Church History* 34 (1965): 195-203; and *Covenant of Grace in Puritan Thought*, 53-85.

[61]Miller, *Seventeenth Century*, 399. Miller's basic thesis that the emerging contractual economy gave great impetus to the federal theology has been echoed in modified form more recently in David Zaret, *The Heavenly Contract: Ideology and Organization in Pre-Revolutionary Puritanism* (Chicago: University of Chicago Press, 1985), 163-174.

[62]Leonard J. Trinterud, "The Origins of Puritanism," *Church History* 20 (1951): 37-57.

[63]Ibid., 39.

as a contract. The second view, associated with Calvin, views the covenant as unilateral in nature—as a divine promise to human beings "which obligates God to fulfill." Rather than being a contract, such a covenant is better understood as an unconditional "testament."[64] More recently, J. Wayne Baker has provided the most extensive recent defenses of this general perspective stemming from Trinterud.[65] Baker calls particular attention to the role of Bullinger in the formation of the conditional covenant trajectory, and he argues that the differences over covenant conditionality between Calvin and Bullinger reflect their differing stances on predestination—Calvin holding to a double decree and Bullinger affirming single predestination.[66]

The Trinterud thesis in its various forms has been increasingly challenged, however, with regard to its depiction of both the Genevan and Zurich/Rhineland perspectives. On the one hand, there are those who note that Calvin, despite his allegedly unconditional, unilateral and testamentary view of covenant, often affirms the presence of conditions, particularly the condition of faith, within the context of covenant administration.[67] On the other, it has also been observed that while Zwingli and Bullinger emphasize the importance of the human covenantal response, they also stress that the human exercise of faith and obedience is itself a gift of God. Lyle Bierma calls attention to the strict predestinarian context of Zwingli's doctrine of the covenant, in which human faith and obedience are but the "signs of election," and to Bullinger's clear statements in the Second Helvetic Confession affirming that faith and obedience are divine gifts given to the elect.[68]

Surveys of subsequent Reformed thought have tended to support the conclusion that covenant conditionality and unconditionality are not mutually exclusive polar opposites. While the conditionality or unconditionality of the covenant became a topic of controversy in seventeenth-century British Reformed circles, the differences should not be overemphasized. There seems

---

[64]Ibid., 45.

[65]J. Wayne Baker, *Heinrich Bullinger and the Covenant: The Other Reformed Tradition* (Athens, Oh.: Ohio University Press, 1980); J. Wayne Baker and Charles S. McCoy, *Fountainhead of Federalism: Heinrich Bullinger and the Covenantal Tradition* (Louisville: Westminster/John Knox, 1991). For critical surveys of this approach, see Lyle D. Bierma, "Federal Theology in the Sixteenth Century: Two Traditions?" *Westminster Theological Journal* 45 (1983): 304-310; von Rohr, *Covenant of Grace in Puritan Thought*, 22-27.

[66]Baker, *Bullinger and the Covenant*, 193-198. According to Baker, the single predestinarian schema allowed more space for human effort, and thus more room for real covenant conditions.

[67]See, e.g., Eenigenburg, "Place of the Covenant in Calvin's Thinking"; Hoekema, "Covenant of Grace in Calvin's Teaching"; Carl W. Bogue, *Jonathan Edwards and the Covenant of Grace* (Cherry Hill, N.J.: Mack, 1975), 57-60; Bierma, "Federal Theology," 313-316. See also Tony Lane, "The Quest for the Historical Calvin," *Evangelical Quarterly* 55 (1983): 106-107.

[68]Bierma, "Federal Theology," 310-313.

to have been a general consensus that the covenant of grace is both conditional and unconditional, though the precise nuances of this dialectic were debated endlessly. John Murray, in a helpful survey of Reformed views on this matter, comes to the following conclusions:

> (1) No theologian within the Reformed camp took the position that, in the saving provisions of which the Covenant of Grace is the administration, the thought of condition is to be completely eliminated. Those who were most jealous for the unconditional character of the covenant as an administration of grace to men were insistent that for Christ as the Mediator of the covenant there were conditions which had to be fulfilled. It was customary for those holding this position to appeal to Christ's fulfilment of the conditions as a reason, if not the main reason, why the covenant, as it respects men, is without condition. (2) Those who maintained the conditional nature of the covenant were jealous at the same time to maintain that the fulfilment of the conditions on the part of men was wholly of God's grace. There was no thought of the covenant as contingent upon human autonomy or as deriving any of its ingredients from a contribution which man in the exercise of his own free will supplied... (3) The dispute was to a large extent focused upon the relation which faith, repentance, obedience, and perseverance sustained to the covenant. None held that the covenant relation obtained or that its grace could be enjoyed apart from those responses on the part of the person in covenant fellowship with God.[69]

We conclude, therefore, that a rigid distinction between a testamentary, unilateral, and unconditional covenant schema on the one hand, and a contractual, bilateral, and conditional covenant on the other, does not fit the evidence, and that conclusions based upon such an alleged distinction are questionable. In their articulation of a federal theology involving a dialectic of the conditional and unconditional, the Reformed orthodox divines were importing a tension already present in the biblical materials. Even as the divine covenant promises to the Old Testament patriarchs and to Israel contained both conditional and unconditional elements, so these elements were imported by the orthodox Reformed theologians precisely because of their concern to be biblical.[70]

We have undertaken this brief historiographical survey because some have alleged that the federal theology itself gave rise to a purely legal and extrinsic conception of union with Christ. This argument has been made most forcefully by the Scottish theologians Thomas F. Torrance and James B. Torrance and their students.[71] T. F. Torrance began by drawing a marked distinction between

---

[69]Murray, "Covenant Theology," 208-209. See also pp. 206-212.

[70]See, e.g., Gen. 12:2-3; 17:2-14; Lev. 26:44-45; Deut. 4:30-31; 7:8-10. The biblical origins of the Puritan federalists' covenant theory are emphasized by Marsden, "Miller's Rehabilitation," 99-100; and Von Rohr, *Covenant of Grace*, 30.

[71]Thomas F. Torrance, *The School of Faith: The Catechisms of the Reformed Church* (London: James Clark, 1959), xi-cxxvi; James B. Torrance, "Covenant or Contract?: A Study of the Theological Background of Worship in Seventeenth-Century Scotland,"

the early Reformed efforts of figures such as Calvin in Geneva and John Craig (c. 1512-1600) of Scotland on the one hand, and the federal theology represented by the Westminster Confession and Catechisms on the other. Later Reformed theology had reversed, he argued, the relationship between union with Christ and the benefits of salvation.

> The Westminster Catechisms, however, did set forth their instruction in accordance with their basic teaching that it is through partaking of the benefits of Christ that we partake of Christ, whereas the earlier Catechisms taught that it is through partaking of Christ Himself that we partake of His benefits.[72]

Torrance coupled his attempt to recover the priority of union with Christ with a suspicion of any theological formulation smacking of "conditions." Here he rejects any distinction between the incarnational or "carnal" union of Christ with all humanity and a spiritual union with the redeemed, the "idea that is taught also by Protestants in their doctrine of a union with Christ which is effected by faith or by conversion through which alone what Christ has done for us becomes real for us." This would "lead to a doctrine of man's co-operation in his own salvation; and so involve a doctrine of conditional grace."[73] The answer to this problem, Torrance asserted, was the recognition of a singular, incarnational union of Christ with all humanity—a union in which the eternal Logos "entered into an ontological relationship with all men in the assumption of our human flesh."[74] Recognizing the implications of this, Torrance does not shrink from affirming an implicit universalism.[75]

Echoing T. F. Torrance's view of Christ's universal headship over creation, and his concerns regarding conditional grace, J. B. Torrance gives further

---

Scottish Journal of Theology 23 (1970): 51-76; "The Covenant Concept in Scottish Theology and Politics and Its Legacy," *Scottish Journal of Theology* 34 (1981): 225-243; "The Incarnation and Limited Atonement," *Evangelical Quarterly* 15 (1983): 83-94; "Calvin and Puritanism in England and Scotland—Some Basic Concepts in the Development of 'Federal Theology,'" in *Calvinus Reformator: His Contribution to Theology, Church, and Society* (Potchefstroom, S.A.: Potchefstroom University, 1982), 264-287.

See also Holmes Rolston III, "Responsible Man in Reformed Theology: Calvin versus the Westminster Confession," *Scottish Journal of Theology* 23 (1970): 129-156; Bell, *Calvin and Scottish Theology*.

[72]Torrance, *School of Faith*, xlii.
[73]Ibid, cvii.
[74]Ibid., cxii.
[75]Ibid., cxvii. Curiously, Torrance insists that this is Calvin's view as well. That this is not the teaching of Calvin, at least in Books III and IV of the *Institutes*, is evident from the opening sentences of Book III, which illustrate his concern for the subjective application of redemption through union with Christ. Torrance's preoccupation with an incarnational union with all humanity seems to owe more to the Origenist tradition as mediated through the Cappadocian Fathers, and to certain Scottish theologians such as Thomas Erskine of Linlathen.

attention to the relation between federal theology and the doctrine of union with Christ, particularly in the context of Scottish theology. For our purposes, three of his general observations require mention. According to Torrance, "first and foremost, the whole federal scheme is built upon the deepseated *confusion between a covenant and a contract*, a failure to recognize that the God and Father of our Lord Jesus Christ is a Covenant-God and not a contract-God."[76] A further fundamental difficulty with federal theology has to do with its particularism, as expressed in the doctrines of double predestination and limited atonement. This particularism, the commitment to which assumes the role of a "major premise" in a deductively Aristotelian system,[77] issues, he argues, in a nature-grace dualism in which all "men stand related to God...under natural law and exposed to the sanctions of the law" while only "the elect are related to God through Christ as Mediator."[78] Finally, an important result of these emphases, according to Torrance, is the deemphasis of union with Christ in Reformed soteriology and its replacement by a purely legal mode of relationship.

> The emphasis of doctrine is no longer on the Incarnation, on Christ's solidarity with all men, but almost exclusively on His Work on behalf of the elect, His passive obedience on the Cross for the sins of believers, with whom he stands related, not in terms of incarnational oneness but of *foedus*, of contract. The result was a loss of the older emphasis on "Union with Christ our Head" which is replaced by a more judicial interpretation of faith.[79]

Some of the problems associated with this thesis are evident from the discussions earlier in this chapter, and they need not be enlarged upon here.[80]

---

[76]Torrance, "Covenant or Contract," implicates Reformed theologians as early as Ursinus in this alleged contractual legalism. As we have already seen, similar conditional language is present in Calvin as well.

[77]Torrance, "Limited Atonement," 88.

[78]Torrance, "Covenant or Contract," 67. Here the terms "nature" and "grace" refer to the covenants of works and of grace, rather than to the earlier Roman Catholic schema.

[79]Ibid., 68. This "replacement thesis" (the contention that Calvin's alleged idea of spiritual/incarnational union was replaced by a notion of legal union) has been sharpened and further developed by M. Charles Bell in a useful analysis of Scottish Reformed theology as related to the doctrine of assurance (some conclusions of which we find ourselves in marked disagreement). Building in large measure on the work of J. B. Torrance, and echoing the themes of covenant conditionality and particularity, Bell, *Calvin and Scottish Theology*, 9, argues that for the seventeenth-century Scottish federal theologians, "Our covenant relationship with God, and our union with Christ too often ceased to be viewed as a real, dynamic participation in the life of Christ, and was instead seen to be a *legal* union. Acting in faith meant pleading the legal implications of a legal union with Christ before the bar of heaven." Bell goes on specifically to implicate Scottish theologians Samuel Rutherford (1600-1661), William Guthrie (1620-1665), and David Dickson (1583-1663) in this process (pp. 79, 84-85, 93).

[80]We have seen, first of all, that no Reformed theologians of the period completely

Despite its weaknesses, what we may term the Torrance "replacement thesis" does important service in pointing to a significant reconceptualization of the doctrine of union with Christ under the auspices of federal theology. Furthermore, while their understanding of the precise nature of this reconceptualization is flawed, and their attempt to implicate all of federal theology in the charge of "legalism" misses the mark, advocates of the "replacement thesis" have rightly called attention to the role of Scottish theologians in this development.

The Scottish Federal Reconceptualization of Union with Christ

The theme of the Christian's union with Christ was destined to remain prominent in Scottish Presbyterianism. John Knox, the Reformer of Scotland who had studied in Calvin's Geneva, accorded the motif much the same place as had his esteemed teacher.[81] After Knox, the theme was carried forward by a series of gifted Scots clergy, whose literary remains were to influence Scottish religious life for generations. John Craig's Catechism (1581), widely used throughout the Kirk, describes union with Christ in staunchly Calvinian terms. In this union "we are made flesh of His flesh and bone of His bone," and "we are made partakers of all His graces and merits."[82] Robert Bruce's sermons on the Lord's Supper (1589), translated numerous times from the original Scots into English, served as a vigorous defense of the Calvinistic doctrine of the real presence.[83] As we shall see below, the theme of union with Christ retained considerable prominence in the thought of much-published theologians of the so-called "second Reformation" in Scotland—Samuel Rutherford (1600-1661), William Guthrie (1620-1665), and their colleagues.[84] Later still, the theme is

---

did away with "conditions," in the sense of human action (such as the exercise of faith) necessary as part of the economy of salvation. Even those of suspect orthodoxy who were dubbed "antinomian" recognized the necessity of human response. Second, the doctrine of limited or definite atonement is hardly the invention of Aristotelianized Reformed scholasticism. It can be traced from Augustine to Lombard. On this point, see W. Robert Godfrey, "Reformed Thought on the Extent of the Atonement to 1618," *Westminster Theological Journal* 37 (1974-75): 133-71.

[81] Bell, *Calvin and Scottish Theology*, 65, writes: "The concept of union with Christ is perhaps the key to Knox's theology...Very important is the way in which Knox holds together justification and sanctification as benefits conferred only in Christ." See also James S. McEwen, *The Faith of John Knox* (Richmond: John Knox, 1961), 56-59, 113-114; Richard L. Greaves, *Theology and Revolution in the Scottish Reformation: Studies in the Thought of John Knox* (Grand Rapids: Christian University Press, 1980), 86-110.

[82] "Craig's Catechism," in *The School of Faith*, ed. Thomas F. Torrance (London: James Clarke, 1959), 124. See also Bell, *Calvin and Scottish Theology*, 48-52.

[83] Robert Bruce, *The Mystery of the Lord's Supper*, ed. Thomas F. Torrance (London: James Clarke, 1958).

[84] On the Scottish "Second Reformation," see John MacLeod, *Scottish Theology, In Relation to Church History Since the Reformation* (Edinburgh: Publications Committee

highlighted in the work of Thomas Boston (1677-1732), whose *Human Nature in Its Fourfold State* (1720) was exceedingly influential.[85]

The Scottish commitment to the theme of *unio Christi* was matched, in fact exceeded, by the Scottish fascination with the theme of covenant, and the interaction of these two themes was to impact profoundly on the way that union with Christ was conceptualized. The Scottish interest in the covenant theme was not a merely theological affair, as even prior to the Reformation there was a long-standing tradition of individuals and groups "banding" together by contractual agreement for a common purpose, often mutual protection.[86] It is no surprise, then, that the covenant motif was readily adapted to Scottish religious life. Just as they had earlier banded together for protection against brigands, so Scots covenanted together to protect the Scottish Kirk against the incursions of the crown in the National Covenant (1638) and the Solemn League and Covenant (1643). And neither is it any surprise that the federal theology then emerging on the continent should find ready and eager acceptance in late sixteenth-century Scotland. Particularly important in this process was Robert Rollock (1555-1599), who as Principal of Edinburgh University and Moderator of the Scottish Kirk did much to popularize bi-covenantal federalism in Scotland.[87] In this context, the logic of Reformed federal orthodoxy was soon inexorably to push the conceptualization of union with Christ in a particular direction, a process that culminated in new formulations by theologians of the Scottish second Reformation that differed in fundamental ways from those of Calvin.

At least one crucial characteristic of federal theology was inherited from Calvin himself, however. As we have already seen, the Genevan Reformer stressed the unity of the covenant of grace in both the Old and New Testament dispensations, affirming that "the covenant made with all the patriarchs is so much like ours in substance and reality that the two are actually one and the same."[88] Calvin goes on to affirm that "they [Old Testament saints] knew Christ as Mediator, through whom they were joined to God and were to share in his promises."[89] While acknowledging differences in "mode of dispensation," the emphasis for Calvin clearly falls on the substantial continuity of the covenant and of the signs of covenant—the sacraments.[90] But Calvin's

---

of the Free Church of Scotland, 1943), 66-102.

[85] Thomas Boston, *Human Nature in Its Fourfold State* (Edinburgh: Banner of Truth, 1964 [reprint ed.]), 253-320.

[86] See John Lumsden, *The Covenants of Scotland* (Paisley: A. Gardner, 1914); George D. Henderson, "The Idea of the Covenant in Scotland," *Evangelical Quarterly* 27 (1955): 2-14; S. A. Burrell, "The Covenant Idea as a Revolutionary Symbol: Scotland, 1596-1637," *Church History* 27 (1958): 338-350; Greaves, *Theology and Revolution*, 120-122.

[87] On Rollock, see Bell, *Calvin and Scottish Theology*, 52-58.

[88] Calvin, *Inst.* II.10.2.

[89] Ibid., II.10.2.

[90] See ibid., IV.14.23.

emphasis upon the substantial continuity of the Old and New Testament sacraments, and the union with Christ they communicate, stands in some tension with his emphasis upon the necessity of communion with the life-giving humanity of Christ. Granted that the New Testament sacraments communicate the incarnate humanity of Christ in heaven to the believer on earth, how could the sacraments of the Old Testament communicate what did not yet exist? Calvin's opponents, particularly the high Lutherans, seized on this point, and it must be admitted that Calvin's responses were not entirely clear.[91]

In an effort to address this problem, later Reformed theologians turned to legal categories, a trend presaged by Calvin's successor, Theodore Beza. As Jill Raitt has shown, Beza distinguished between a presence *de iure* to Old Testament saints, and a presence *in actu* to New Testament believers. According to Beza, Old Testament believers became

> participators in the flesh of Christ, not in very actuality since it was not yet in existence, but according to the law only as they say, since they acquired the law in the flesh of Christ that was to be born. Now of course, since that flesh already exists, we receive the flesh itself in act, and therefore spiritually and through faith it is common to them and to us.[92]

It should be no surprise that the formulations of both Calvin and Beza did not persist. Instead, the idea of a legal union with Christ together with a virtual communion with the spiritual benefits of Christ common to both dispensations gradually won the day.

The terminology by which federal theology came to expression also played a role in shaping the motif of union with Christ. The emerging market economy, with its preoccupation with the legal and contractual, provided a ready store of images that were quickly put to use by federal theologians and preachers.[93] Quoting from a 1612 sermon by Puritan Thomas Newhouse, David Zaret writes,

> Puritan clerics cited written evidences in economic life in explaining the imputation of Christ's righteousness to the saints. They portrayed this as a contractual conveyance of right and title to property: "As the lands and goods of one man are made over unto another by deed of gift, sale, exchange or some like conveyance of law, both for title and use, even so the righteousness of Christ, by virtue of the free gift of God according to the tenure of the covenant of grace is truly and really conveyed unto us and made ours."[94]

In this context, the person of Christ came to be designated in two strikingly

---

[91] See, e.g., Calvin *Theological Treatises*, 281-290; *Comm.* 1 Cor. 10:4.
[92] Theodore Beza, *Apologia prima*, 302, quoted in Raitt, *Eucharistic Theology*, 39.
[93] This issue is explored, in the context of English Puritanism, by Zaret, *Heavenly Contract*, 163-198.
[94] Ibid., 177-78.

different ways corresponding to justification and sanctification. On the one hand, by the early to middle part of the seventeenth century, it was customary in the context of Reformed federal theology to speak of Christ as the "Surety" (*vadis*) of the Christian, a term rich in legal connotations.[95] On the other hand, Christ's spiritual relationship to the Christian was typically designated that of "Head" (*caput*). The result of this was that the application of the forensic and the transforming aspects of salvation were increasingly being discussed in very different terms. Francis Turretin (1623-87), the Genevan divine later to exert a strong influence upon the Princeton theologians in nineteenth-century America, writes:

> Just as Christ sustains a twofold relation to us of Surety and Head [*Vadis et Capitis*] (of surety, to take away the guilt of sin by a payment made for it; of head, to take away its power and corruption by the efficacy of the Spirit), so in a twofold way Christ imparts his blessings to us, by a forensic imputation, and a moral and internal infusion. The former flows from Christ as surety and is the foundation of our justification. The latter depends on him as head, and is the principle of sanctification. For on this account, God justifies us because the righteousness of our surety, Christ, is imputed to us. And on this account we are renewed because we derive the Spirit from our head, Christ, who renews us after the image of Christ and bestows upon us inherent righteousness.[96]

Given that the reception of justification and sanctification were being construed along increasingly different lines—involving two fundamentally different forms of relationship between Christ and the Christian (legal and spiritual)—it was probably inevitable that the notion of a legal union with Christ would evolve as a counterpart to the spiritual union concept inherited from the Reformers. As M. C. Bell suggests, tentative steps along this line apparently were first taken by Samuel Rutherford (1600-1661) in 1655. Discussing the grounds of forensic justification, Rutherford distinguishes between a natural or incarnational union, a legal union whereby Christ stands in a legal relationship with the Christian, and a federal union rooted in a pretemporal covenant of redemption between the Father and the Son:

> And the faith by which as by an instrument we are justified, presupposeth three unions, and maketh a fourth union. It presupposeth an union, (1) Naturall, (2) Legall, (3) Federall.
> 1. Naturall, that Christ and we are not only both mankind, for Christ and

---

[95] See *Oxford English Dictionary*, "Surety," 3173: "A person who undertakes some specific responsibility on behalf of another who remains primarily liable; one who makes himself liable for the default or miscarriage of another, or for the performance of some act on his part (e.g., payment of a debt, appearance in court for trial, etc.)."

[96] Francis Turretin, *Institutes of Elenctic Theology*, 3 vols., trans. George Musgrave Giger, ed. James T. Dennison (Phillipsburg, N.J.: Presbyterian and Reformed, 1992-97), II:647 (XVI.3.6). Similar language is found in Westminster Confession of Faith 26:1 and Larger Catechism Q. 71.

Pharaoh, Judas the Traitour and all the sons of perdition are one, *specie & natura*, true men, but one in brotherhood. He assuming the nature of man with a speciall eye to Abraham, Heb. 2.16. that is, to the elect and beleevers, for with them he is bone of their bone, and "is not ashamed to call them brethren," Heb. 2.11, 12. Ps. 22.22.

2. It presupposes a Legall union between Christ and them, that God made the debter and the Surety one in Law, and the summe one in so far as he laid our debts on Christ, Isa. 53.6. 2 Cor. 5:21.

3. It presupposes an union Federall, God making Christ our Surety, and he was willing to be our Surety, and to assume not only our nature in a personall union, but also our state, condition, and made our cause his cause, our sins his sins, not to defend them, nor to say Amen to them, as if we might commit them again, but to suffer the punishment due to them. And our faith makes a fourth union betwixt Christ and us, whether naturall, as between head and members, the branches and the Vine Tree, or mysticall, as that of the spouse and beloved wife, or artificiall, or mixed between the impe and the tree. Or 4. Legall, between the Surety and the Debter, the Advocate and the Client, or rather an union above all, is hard to determine, for these are but all comparisons, and this Christ prayes for, Joh. 17.23, "I in them, and thou in me, that they may be made perfect in one."[97]

Rutherford's suggestion here was quickly seized upon by other Scottish theologians, such that justification increasingly came to be described as involving a "legal" or "federal" union between Christ and the believer.[98] So much so that some years later (1720), Thomas Boston of Ettrick (1676-1732) would caution against a reduction of union to a mere legal relationship.[99]

---

[97] Samuel Rutherford, *The Covenant of Life Opened: Or A Treatise of the Covenant of Grace* (Edinburgh, 1655), 208-209. It is apparent that the "Legall" and "Federall" unions are closely related. On this development, see Bell, *Calvin and Scottish Theology*, 79, 89.

[98] With certain qualifications, M.C. Bell's argument at this point has merit: "There is in Rutherford's teaching, however, the beginning of a legal notion of this union which would, in the teachings of men such as [David] Dickson, [James] Durham, and [William] Guthrie, supercede that of a real, spiritual union." *Calvin and Scottish Theology*, 79. Bell's assertion (p. 85), however, that "Guthrie's conception of our union with Christ is little more than a legal relationship engendered by 'closing' with Christ through our act of faith" ill accords with what Guthrie actually wrote: "When a sinner closeth with Christ Jesus, there is presently an admirable union, a strange oneness between God and the man. As the husband and wife, head and body, root and branches, are not to be reckoned two but one; so Christ, or God in Christ, and the sinner closing with Him by faith, are one—'We are members of His body, of His flesh, and of His bones.' [Eph. 5:30.] He that is so 'joined unto the Lord is one spirit' [1 Cor. 6:17]; as the Father is in the Son, and Christ in the Father, so believers are one in the Father and the Son; they are one, as the Father and Son are one...O what a strange interweaving and indissoluable union here!" William Guthrie, *The Christian's Great Interest* (Edinburgh: Banner of Truth, 1969 [orig. 1658]), 140.

[99] Thomas Boston, *Human Nature in Its Fourfold State*, 255-256: "Though it is not a

This notion of a "legal" union between Christ and the believer is fundamentally extrinsic in character, and we may ask how this idea came to be articulated at this time (c. 1650-1660). This question is particularly important in that this concept of a "legal union" apparently arose in Scotland (with Rutherford) and is not found in Continental Reformed divines of the period (e.g., Francis Turretin). Though a precise genetic relationship is difficult to establish, circumstantial evidence points to the early and mid-seventeenth-century discussions of Original Sin in general, and the Placaean controversy over imputation in particular, as a factor in the development of this concept.

The doctrine of Original Sin underwent considerable development in Reformed circles between the death of Calvin and the mid-seventeenth century.[100] The Augustinian views of the Reformers were framed in opposition to the Nominalist *pactum* theory of Roman Catholics such as Ambrosius Catharinus. Augustine had explained the transmission of depravity and guilt from Adam to his posterity in terms of a shared disorder passed on by the human reproductive process. Adam's posterity is guilty and corrupted by the

---

mere legal union, yet is is a union sustained in law. Christ as the surety, and Christians as the debtors, are one in the eye of the law...When they believe on Him, they are united to Him in a spiritual marriage union; which takes effect so far, that what He did and suffered for them is reckoned in law, as if they had done and suffered it themselves."

Boston, *The Complete Works of the Late Rev. Thomas Boston*, ed. Samuel M'Millan, 12 vols. (London: W. Tegg & Co., 1853), I:546, goes on to write: "Some, to advance their legal scheme of doctrine, acknowledge no other union but a relative one betwixt Christ and believers, such as may be betwixt persons and things wholly separated."

The above statement might seem to confirm what we have termed the "replacement thesis," the argument that Calvin's view of spiritual union was replaced by a purely legal union. But this argument fails to account for the peculiar circumstances that obtained in late seventeenth- and early eighteenth-century Scotland, and in the Reformed world generally. David C. Lachman has shown that there was during this period a vigorous reaction against the antinomianism of the Commonwealth period in England and that there was a "majority in the Church of Scotland who represented in some degree a late seventeenth century tendency toward Legalism, Neonomianism and even Arminianism." See David C. Lachman, *The Marrow Controversy, 1718-1723: An Historical and Theological Analysis*, Rutherford Studies in Historical Theology (Edinburgh: Rutherford House, 1988), 491. To be sure, a significant group spoke of a purely legal union with Christ obtained upon the condition of faith and obedience, but this is rather inconsistent with the overall trajectory of Reformed thought. On the whole, it is more accurate to say that for British and American Reformed federal theology generally, union with Christ is bifurcated into federal (legal) and spiritual components. It would appear that the Torrances have read the legalizing tendency of this period back into earlier federal theology sources and figures.

[100]Helpful treatments of this development are found in Fisher, "Augustinian and Federal Theories"; Robert W. Landis, *The Doctrine of Original Sin as Received and Taught by the Churches of the Reformation* (Richmond: Whittet & Shepperson, 1884); John Murray, *The Imputation of Adam's Sin* (Grand Rapids: Eerdmans, 1959); Hutchinson, *Problem of Original Sin*, 8-11.

first sin because Adam's descendants were, seminally at least, present at the first transgression.[101] But Roman Catholic nominalists such as Catharinus denied that there is any such thing as a human "nature" common to all, or that sin can be passed on through natural generation. He argued instead that the state of moral disrepair in which all human beings find themselves is not in itself sinful since it is not freely chosen. Rather, Adam's posterity is liable to punishment for Adam's initial sin by virtue of a *pactum* between God and Adam in which Adam is deemed the legal representative of his offspring.[102]

The Pelagian implications of this nominalist theory were clear enough to Calvin and his contemporaries—there being no sinful "nature" in which to ground continuing depravity and a merely nominal guilt for another's sin. Calvin's doctrine of original sin therefore highlights the theme of inherited depravity.[103] But Calvin's view of original sin as inherited depravity was deemed inadequate by future generations of Reformed on both exegetical and theological grounds.[104] The mere transmission of depravity seemed an inadequate foundation on which to base human culpability for original sin. Some theory of responsibility appeared necessary if human beings were to be held legally accountable for their sinful condition, and, in one of the striking ironies of the history of Christian thought, Reformed theologians turned to a theory similar to the nominalist *pactum* against which Calvin had waged bitter battle. In short, these theologians posited a "covenant of works" in which Adam was designated the "federal head" of his posterity, thus acting as their legal representative. Because of this legal relationship between Adam and his posterity, the first sin of Adam is thereby imputed to his offspring and treated as their own.[105]

---

[101] On Augustine, see Hutchinson, *Problem of Original Sin*, 5-7; Fisher, "Augustinian and Federal Theories," 360-364.

[102] See Hutchinson, *Problem of Original Sin*, 7-8; Murray, *Imputation*, 12-14.

[103] See Calvin, *Comm.* on Rom. 5:12; *Inst.* II.1.5-11. See also Wendel, *Calvin*, 185-196; Niesel, *Theology of Calvin*, 80-88; Murray, *Imputation*, 17-18.

[104] Calvin's suggestion that *hēmarton* in Rom. 5:12 bears the sense of "to become corrupt" is questionable. See Turretin, *Institutes of Elenctic Theology*, I:618 (IX.16): "Now the word *hēmarton* cannot properly be drawn to a habit of sin or to habitual and inherent corruption, but properly denotes some actual sin and that, also, past (which can be not other than the sin of Adam itself)."

[105] Writing in 1626, Wollebius, *Compendium*, 69 (X.[I.2], V), evidences this new perspective: "Original sin is the innate evil of all mankind, engrafted into all who are naturally descended from Adam, on account of the guilt (*reatus*) of the first sin, by which freedom for good has been completely (*penitus*) lost and a tendency to do evil has arisen...Although the human soul is breathed into [the person] directly by God, yet from the first moment of being united to the body it is guilty of the first sin, which is imputed to the entire human race, and so it is corrupted by that sinfulness." Though clearly a "federal theologian," Wollebius' contemporary William Ames still viewed original sin primarily in Calvinian terms as inherited depravity: "a habitual deviation of the whole nature of man" and "the corruption of the whole man" (*Marrow*, 120).

It was in the context of this emerging federal theology consensus that the Placaean controversy over imputation and original sin occurred. Josué de la Place (Placaeus) was a colleague of Moises Amyraut at the French theological academy at Saumur, and is particularly known for his distinction between "immediate" and "mediate" imputation.[106] After his condemnation by the Reformed Synod at Charenton (1644-45) for allegedly teaching that original sin consists solely in hereditary corruption (to the exclusion of the imputation of the guilt of Adam's first sin), de la Place defended himself by distinguishing immediate and antecedent imputation from mediate and consequent imputation. Rather than denying imputation per se, de la Place contended that he only rejected an immediate imputation antecedent to depravity. Instead, he argued for an imputation of Adam's sin mediated through and resulting from inherited depravity.[107]

De la Place's proposal met with considerable opposition. Andrew Rivet (Rivetus) compiled a catalogue of quotations from earlier Reformed writers bearing on the matter, but the most substantial response came from the Swiss Reformed at Geneva, especially from Francis Turretin.[108] The Swiss objections

---

An important difference between this "federal theology" doctrine of original sin and the nominalist *pactum* theory should also be noted. While the nominalist *pactum* was merely a nominal arrangement rooted in the divine will, the federal theory attempted to combine nominalist and Augustinian concerns, an approach evident in The Westminster Larger Catechism (Q. 22): "The covenant being made with Adam as a publick person, not for himself only but for his posterity, all mankind descending from him by ordinary generation, sinned in him, and fell with him in that first transgression." On this, see Hutchinson, *Problem of Original Sin*, 9; Fisher, "Augustinian and Federal Theories," 379-384.

[106]Relatively little has been written on de la Place, though the distinction between "mediate" and "immediate" imputation has been of continuing importance for the tradition. For summary discussions of the Placaean controversy, see Charles Hodge, *Systematic Theology*, 3 vols. (New York: Charles Scribner's Sons, 1872-73), II:205-214; William G. T. Shedd, *A History of Christian Doctrine*, 2 vols., 14th ed. (New York: Charles Scribner's Sons, 1902), II:158-163; Fisher, "Augustinian and Federal Theories," 384-395; Warfield, "Imputation," 267-269; Murray, *Imputation*, 42-48; Armstrong, *Amyraut Heresy*, 104-105.

[107]De la Place's defense was eventually codified in his *De Imputatione Primi Peccati Adami Disputatio Bipertita* (1665). His argument involves a somewhat strained use of the term "imputation." The sin of Adam may be said to be "imputed" to his posterity only in that the depravity and sins of the latter are the remote result of the former, resulting in a unity of guilt before God. See Hutchinson, *Problem of Original Sin*, 10; Warfield, "Imputation," 267.

[108]A portion of Rivet's work was translated into English by Charles Hodge. See Charles Hodge, "Testimonies on the Doctrine of Imputation," *Princeton Review* 11 (1839): 553-579.

Turretin's *Institutio* devotes considerable attention to what were thought to be the errors emanating from Saumur. The *Formula Consensus Helvetica* (1675), written by J. H. Heidegger and Turretin, is largely intended to exclude views articulated by the

to the theory of mediate imputation were basically threefold. First, Turretin and his colleagues questioned whether mediate imputation was really imputation at all.[109] Second, they argued that the doctrine of original sin was imperiled by the theory. Mediate imputation reduced the doctrine to absurdity in that it would imply that Adam's posterity would be guilty of all Adam's sins, not just the first.[110] Moreover, the Swiss were convinced that the theory of mediate imputation undercut the second part of the doctrine (hereditary corruption) as well. Without some legal basis for the imposition of culpable depravity on Adam's offspring, they could hardly be held accountable for that depravity.[111] Third, and perhaps most important, Turretin believed that the hamartiological theory of mediate imputation threatened the soteriological imputation of Christ's righteousness to the Christian. The imputation of Adam's sin and the imputation of Christ's obedience are concepts cut from the same cloth in that both involve the ascription of the actions of one to another.[112]

By way of positive statement, the Swiss theologians reaffirmed the twofold relation involved in original sin (imputed guilt and hereditary depravity) and brought a new level of definition to the doctrine. In particular, the grounds of the imputation of Adam's sin were further explicated. Turretin holds that the immediate imputation of Adam's sin is rooted in a twofold relationship—natural and legal.

> For the bond between Adam and his posterity is twofold: (1) natural, as he is the father, and we are his children; (2) political and forensic, as he was the prince and representative head of the whole human race. Therefore the foundation of imputation is not only the natural connection which exists between us and Adam (since, in that case, all his sins might be imputed to us), but mainly the moral and federal (in virtue of which God entered into covenant with him as our head). Hence Adam stood in that sin not as a private person, but as a public and

---

Saumur theologians: against Louis Capellus the divine inspiration of the Hebrew vowel points is asserted (Arts. 2-3); against Amyraut's universal atonement theory a limited atonement is affirmed (Arts. 13-16); and against de la Place the theory of immediate imputation is affirmed (Arts. 11-12). An English translation of the *Formula* is found in A. A. Hodge, *Outlines of Theology*, rev. ed. (New York: Robert Carter, 1878), 656-663.

[109] See Turretin, *Institutes* (IX.9.6), I:615.

[110] See ibid., (IX.IX.11), I:616.

[111] See The Formula Consensus Helvetica (Arts. X, XII).

[112] Turretin, *Institutes* (IX.9.10), I:615-616, writes: "Imputation is either of something foreign to us or properly ours. Sometimes that is imputed to us which is personally ours...Sometimes that is imputed which is without us and not performed by ourselves. Thus the righteousness of Christ is said to be imputed to us, and our sins are imputed to him, although neither has he sin in himself, nor we righteousness. Here we speak of the latter kind of imputation, not of the former because we are treating of a sin committed by Adam, not by us." The phrase "without us" is particularly important here—we will argue below that Turretin's conception of immediate imputation is fundamentally that of an extrinsic relationship.

representative person—representing all his posterity in that action and whose demerit equally pertains to all.[113]

Several observations are in order at this point. The first relates to the passage quoted immediately above. Despite Turretin's vaunted reputation for precision, the relationship between the natural and the federal remains unexplained. Primary emphasis is placed on the federal bond ("the foundation of imputation is...mainly the moral and federal"). Given the overall structure of Turretin's argument, however, it seems that the natural and federal provide a "foundation" for imputation in rather different ways. The relationship of immediate imputation is a federal and legal one. The natural relationship, on the other hand, serves merely as a presupposition or precondition for the federal, ensuring that the federal relationship is fitting (e.g., it would not be appropriate to impute Adam's sin to an antelope).

A second observation has to do with the respective interests of the parties in the conflict. De la Place was concerned primarily to vindicate the justice of God by tying human culpability as closely as possible to personal sin and depravity. Turretin on the other hand wanted primarily to highlight the bond of union between Adam and his posterity so as to lay a foundation for the doctrine of total depravity and for soteriology. As a result, de la Place emphasized the quality or condition (depravity) shared by both Adam and his posterity, while Turretin paid careful attention to the forms of union involved. But the dichotomy posed by de la Place—either mediate imputation via a shared hereditary moral condition or an immediate imputation involving a fundamentally extrinsic legal relationship—served to set the parameters for future discussion.[114]

A third comment has to do with a subtheme underlying much of the discussion over imputation—the parallel between the imputation of Adam's sin to his posterity and the imputation of the righteousness of Christ to the Christian. While the Reformers, with their Pauline bent, inevitably had to reckon with the parallel between Adam and Christ drawn by Paul in Rom. 5:12-21, this parallel assumed particular importance for the federal theologians. Both Adam and Christ were viewed as federal heads of their respective communities, with their demerit or merit imputed to those in federal union with them.[115] In

---

[113] Turretin, *Institutes* (IX.9.11), I:616.

[114] On Placaean terms, for example, Calvin's view of the imputation of Christ's righteousness through participation in his incarnate humanity would inevitably be seen as an imputation mediated through participation in his sinless moral condition (i.e., as analytic justification).

[115] Commenting on Rom. 5:12ff., Turretin, *Institutes of Elenctic Theology*, I:617 (IX.9.15), writes: "It might seem strange and unusual for one to be justified by another's righteousness. Thus the apostle (by a comparison between Adam and Christ) proves the foundation of that mystery from its opposite—the condemnation which God willed to be derived upon all on account of the imputation of one sin. Therefore just as Adam was constituted by God the head and root of the human race (together with the guilt of his

contrast, those who in varying degrees were critical of the federal theology (such as de la Place) were inclined to minimize the extent of the parallel.[116]

The importance of this original sin/soteriology parallel is evident when we note the similarities between language used for union with Adam and union with Christ. It was becoming increasingly common to speak of a "natural" or incarnational union of Christ with all humanity, a union which serves largely as a presupposition for Christ's federal union with believers in much the same way that Adam's natural union with his posterity guarantees the fittingness of the imputation of Adam's sin.[117] But this natural union with Christ is still fundamentally extrinsic to the persons involved (a union of "species," as Rutherford terms it). Thus the structure and logic of federal theology pushed the conceptual framework of imputation in a more and more extrinsic direction.

The language of the Placaean debate (immediate vs. mediate imputation) and the Adam/Christ parallel so often involved in this debate had the effect of setting conceptual limits for future discussions and of forcing subsequent thinkers to frame imputation in primarily extrinsic categories. Rutherford was doubtless aware of these continental debates, and it is only reasonable to assume that the supralapsarian Rutherford took what seemed the logical step and spoke of justification in terms of a "legall union" between Christ and the believer.

The Influence of Pietism

The last significant factor to be discussed here is the influence of the concern for piety associated with English and American Puritanism.[118] It has been

---

sin), and from his sin death was spread through all; even so Christ, the second Adam, was made the head of all the elect, so that by his obedience justification might come upon all the elect."

[116]See Fisher, "Augustinian and Federal Theories," 390.

[117]See Rutherford, *Covenant of Life*, 208. The Westminster Larger Catechism (Q. 39) reads: "It was requisite that the Mediator should be man, that he might advance our nature, perform obedience to the law, suffer and make intercession for us in our nature, have a fellow-feeling of our infirmities; that we might receive the adoption of sons, and have the comfort and access with boldness unto the throne of grace." Along similar lines, Turretin, *Institutes* (XVI.3.5), II:647, writes concerning the "natural" union: "The former is the communion of nature by the Incarnation, by which Christ, having assumed our flesh, became our Brother and a true Goel, and could receive our sins upon himself and have the right to redeem us."

[118]On Puritan piety, see Geoffrey Fillingham Nuttall, *The Holy Spirit in Puritan Faith and Experience* (Oxford: Oxford University Press, 1946); Gordon Stevens Wakefield, *Puritan Devotion: Its Place in the Development of Christian Piety* (London: Epworth Press, 1957); F. Ernest Stoeffler, *The Rise of Evangelical Pietism* (Leiden: E.J. Brill, 1965), 24-108; Norman Pettit, *The Heart Prepared: Grace and Conversion in Puritan Spiritual Life*; Michael McGiffert, ed., *God's Plot: the Paradoxes of Puritan Piety, Being the Autobiography & Journal of Thomas Shepard* (Amherst: University of

customary for some to pit "pietism" against "orthodoxy," with pietism viewed as a reaction to the wooden precision of Protestant orthodoxy. Such a conclusion may be warranted if the later German pietism of Spener and Francke is in view, but a broader use of the term—embracing English Puritanism and Dutch precisianism—leads to different conclusions.[119] In fact, the leading lights of English Puritanism and the Dutch Second Reformation— William Perkins (1558-1602), Richard Sibbes (1577-1635), John Owen (1616-1683), Willem Teellinck (1575-1629), Gisbert Voetius (1588-1676), and Herman Witsius (1636-1708)—*were* orthodox divines. Despite differences of emphasis, pietist and non-pietist orthodox frequently worked together. Furthermore, the orthodoxy of Scottish Presbyterianism was thoroughly imbued with many of the concerns of their English Puritan neighbors to the south, so much so that Scottish divines such as Samuel Rutherford are often called "Puritans."[120]

Two general developments in Puritanism are of particular importance for our study. First, there was a new emphasis upon the contemplation of and communion with Christ, together with an appropriation of medieval "Jesus piety" models. Second, there was a corresponding deemphasis of the sacraments as means of union with Christ.

Devotional Communion with Christ

The distinctive Puritan emphasis upon devotional communion with Christ has been widely noted.[121] The prominent seventeenth-century Puritan preacher

---

Massachusetts Press, 1972); Charles E. Hambrick-Stowe, *The Practice of Piety: Puritan Devotional Disciplines in Seventeenth-Century New England* (Chapel Hill: University of North Carolina Press, 1982); Charles Lloyd Cohen, *God's Caress: The Psychology of Puritan Religious Experience*; Jerald C. Brauer, "Types of Puritan Piety," *Church History* 56 (1987): 39-58.

The relationship of Puritan piety and sacramental theology and practices is explored in E. Brooks Holifield, "The Renaissance of Sacramental Piety in Colonial New England," *The William and Mary Quarterly* 29 (1972): 33-48; *The Covenant Sealed: The Development of Puritan Sacramental Theology in Old and New England, 1570-1720* (New Haven: Yale University Press, 1974).

[119] On the Dutch Second Reformation movement generally, see Stoeffler, *Evangelical Pietism*, 109-162; and Joel R. Beeke, "The Dutch Second Reformation (Nadere Reformatie)," *Calvin Theological Journal* 28 (1993): 298-327. Connections between English Puritans and the Dutch Reformed are explored in Keith L. Sprunger, *The Learned Doctor Ames: Dutch Backgrounds of English and American Puritanism* (Chicago: University of Illinois Press, 1972); *Dutch Puritanism: A History of English and Scottish Churches of the Netherlands in the Sixteenth and Seventeenth Centuries* (Leiden: E.J. Brill, 1982).

[120] See Stoeffler, *Evangelical Pietism*, 22-23, 108.

[121] See Brauer, "Types of Puritan Piety," 47-50; Wakefield, *Puritan Devotion*, 94-108; Jonathan Jong-Chun Won, "Communion with Christ: An Exposition and

Richard Sibbes is representative of this tendency:

> What makes us, in the midst of all worldly discontentments, to think all dung and dross in comparison of Christ, but this sickness of love to Christ. If our love be in such a degree as it makes us sick of it, it makes us not to hear what we hear, not to see what we see, not to regard what is present. The soul is in a kind of ecstasy; it is carried so strongly, and taken up with things of heaven. It is deaded to other things, when our eyes are no more led with vanity than if we had none, and the flesh is so mortified as if we were dead men, by reason of the strength of our affections that run another way, to better things which are above.[122]

This Puritan concern for personal communion with Christ often came to expression in allegorical expositions of the Old Testament Song of Songs (i.e., Canticles or the Song of Solomon).[123] It is here that the Puritans tapped into the rich resources of medieval piety—trajectories that go back to Bernard of Clairvaux with his focus on devotion to the human nature of Christ.[124] Amidst trials and adversities, Puritan writers repeatedly directed their readers to the compassionate humanity of Christ. Thomas Goodwin (1600-1680) wrote:

> In Christ's human nature, though glorified, affections of pity and compassion are true and real, and not metaphorically attributed to him as they are unto God; and also more near and like unto ours here than those in the angels are; even affections proper to man's nature, and truly human...In all miseries and distresses you may be sure to know where to have a friend to help and pity you, even in heaven,

---

Comparison of the Doctrine of Union and Communion with Christ in Calvin and the English Puritans" (Ph.D. diss., Westminster Theological Seminary, 1989), 331-349. See also G.L. Prestige, *Fathers and Heretics* (London: SPCK, 1958), 180-207.

R. Tudor Jones, "Union with Christ: The Existential Nerve of Puritan Piety," *Tyndale Bulletin* 41 (1990): 186-208, shows that the themes of union and communion were of great importance to mainstream Puritanism, and that they also had considerable difficulty defining the nature of the *unio Christi*.

[122]Richard Sibbes, *The Complete Works of Richard Sibbes, D.D.*, ed. by Alexander B. Grosart, 7 vols. (Edinburgh: James Nichol, 1864), 2:125-126; quoted in Brauer, "Types of Puritan Piety," 50.

[123]Jerald Brauer, "Types of Puritan Piety," 48-49, notes: "What marks Puritan evangelical piety is the degree of fervor and intensity in speaking of the relations between Christ and the believer...Frequent allusions were made to Christ as the heavenly bridegroom who visits the soul of the believer. Evangelicals waxed eloquent in describing the relation between Christ and the church in terms of Canticles, one of their favorite biblical books." See also Won, "Communion with Christ," 116-131, 331-334.

[124]See Joseph B. Collins, *Christian Mysticism in the Elizabethan Age with Its Background in Mystical Methodology* (Baltimore: Johns Hopkins Press, 1940); Wakefield, *Puritan Devotion*, 94-99; Won, "Communion with Christ," 120-126. The interplay of Puritan and Catholic devotional practices is explored in Hambrick-Stowe, *The Practice of Piety*, 25-39.

Christ; one whose nature, office, interest, relation, all, do engage him to your succor.[125]

A result of this trend was that "communion with Christ" (a devotional matter) tended to displace "union with Christ" (a theological concept) for many of the later Puritans. Calvin had focused on union with Christ's incarnate humanity as the means whereby redemption is applied to the Christian, but the later Puritans viewed the humanity of Christ more as an object of contemplation and devotion.[126] This move was in part the result of pastoral concerns, but the Puritan pastors were also orthodox divines and Reformed theological developments worked against Calvin's formulations.

Puritans and the Sacraments

It is a commonplace of modern scholarship that Puritanism tended to depreciate the sacraments and sacramental efficacy.[127] But this eclipse of the sacramental was by no means total, and recent scholarship, especially that of E. B. Holifield, has underscored both the complexity and the diversity of Puritan opinion.[128] Here we can only touch on some of the more significant trends of

---

[125]Thomas Goodwin, *The Works of Thomas Goodwin, D.D.*, 12 vols. (Edinburgh: James Nichol, 1861), 4:140, 150; quoted in Won, "Communion with Christ," 250, 253.

[126]Jonathan Won, "Communion with Christ," 351, notes that "whereas Calvin placed more emphasis on union than on communion, the Puritans put more emphasis on communion than on union." When the theological significance of the humanity of Christ is discussed by the later Puritan writers, it is almost invariable viewed as a *conditio sine qua non* of redemption, rather than the means whereby redemption is applied. The mediatorial theme, so prominent in Calvin, is largely lost.

[127]See Nuttall, *Holy Spirit in Puritan Faith and Experience*, 90-101; Jens Glebe Møller, "Beginnings of Puritan Covenant Theology," *Journal of Ecclesiastical History* 14 (1963): 62-63; Holifield, *The Covenant Sealed*, ix, 73.

[128]A variety of reasons for this eclipse are suggested. In his influential study, G. F. Nuttall (*Holy Spirit in Puritan Faith and Experience*, 91-92) suggests that this was due primarily to the Puritan "movement toward immediacy" and their "violent reaction against everything savouring of papistry." John von Rohr (*Covenant of Grace*, 90) sees Puritan views of the sacraments as an example of the subordination of the institutional and sacerdotal to the personal and evangelical.

E. B. Holifield, *Covenant Sealed*, 2, argues that the eclipse of the sacraments among the Puritans was driven by philosophical convictions fundamental to Reformed theology generally—"a metaphysical contrast between spirit and flesh," and a belief that "the finite cannot contain the infinite" (expressed in the Latin dictum *finitum non capax infiniti*). In other words, Holifield detects a metaphysical dualism at the heart of the Reformed tradition, and he interprets both Reformed christology (with its insistence on the finitude of Christ's humanity) and Puritan sacramental views as the outworking of this dualism. Holifield here follows a vernerable line of Lutheran polemic against the Reformed.

Certain questions may be asked here, however. This argument is not supported by

the period.

Many early Puritans certainly intended to be Calvinistic in their view of the sacraments, and particularly in their view of the Supper.[129] But factors and influences were already at work that would push Puritan sacramental piety in a different direction. The Puritan stress on subjectivity led inexorably to a preoccupation with the faith of the recipient. While Calvin had emphasized the role of the Holy Spirit, Puritan writers often neglected to mention the work of the Holy Spirit in their discussions of the sacraments and instead stressed faith. As Holifield observes, the Westminster Confession "omitted specific mention of the Holy Spirit's activity in its paragraphs on the Lord's Supper."[130] More striking still is the description of the sacramental presence in the Catechism of John Owen (16116-1683). Responding to the question, "Do the elements remain bread and wine still, after the blessing of them?," Owen writes, "Yes; all the spiritual change is wrought by the faith of the believer, not the words of the giver; to them that believe, they are the body and blood of Christ."[131] Similarly, the Puritans framed sacramental efficacy in increasingly psychologistic terms, with extraordinary attention paid to the subjective state of the recipient. William Perkins asserted, for example, that as "the elements of bread and wine are present to...the receiver; at the verie same time the body and bloud of Christ are presented to the minde: thus and no otherwise is Christ truly present with the signes."[132]

Also evident is a move toward a "virtual" conception of the sacramental presence—a presence not of substance, but of the "virtue," or power and effects, of Christ's work. John Owen wrote:

> Faith is the grace that makes the soul to receive Christ, and whereby it doth actually receive him. To "as many as received him, to them gave he power to

---

Calvin's notion of divine grace communicated through spiritual union with the (finite) humanity of Christ, nor by with his concern for a true presence of that humanity in the Supper. That such a philosophical dualism is characteristic of Reformed theology generally may also be questioned. E. D. Willis, *Calvin's Catholic Christology*, 18, writes: "Here is one of the ironies continually emerging in the history of doctrines. Reformed Christology has been pilloried for refusing to recognize the capacity of the finite for the infinite. Here Reformed Christology asserts that this is but one fact; the other is the capacity of the infinite for the finite. In other words, can the infinite be related to the finite in a way not destructive to the finite?...Although none of the disputants put it this way, the logic of the Reformed position was that the majesty of the humanity of Christ consisted in the very fact that it remained finite and creaturely even when hypostatically joined to the infinite creator."

[129]See Holifield, *Covenant Sealed*, 57; Won, "Communion with Christ," 94.

[130]Holifield, *Covenant Sealed*, 131. See Westminster Confession of Faith, Chap. 29.

[131]John Owen, *The Works of John Owen*, ed. William H. Goold, 16 vols. (Philadelphia: The Leighton Publications, 1862-1871), I:492.

[132]William Perkins, *Reformed Catholike*, 590; quoted in Holifield, *Covenant Sealed*, 58.

become the sons of God, even to them that believe on his name"...it receives him by the gracious assent of the mind unto this truth the choice of him, cleaving and trusting unto him with the will, heart and affection for all the ends of his person and offices, as mediator between God and man: and in the sacramental mysterious proposal of him, his body and blood,—that is, in the efficacy of his death and sacrifice,—in this ordinance of worship, faith acts the whole soul in the reception of him unto all the especial ends for which he is exhibited unto us in this way and manner.[133]

It is also necessary here to distinguish between sacramental presence and sacramental efficacy. Many Puritans who stressed the efficacy of the sacraments also tended to minimize the real presence of Christ in them. Erastian controversialists such as William Prynne (1600-1669), in arguing for general admission to the sacraments, contended that the Lord's Supper should be viewed as a "converting ordinance"—the unregenerate should be admitted to the Supper in hopes that they might be converted.[134] But this emphasis led inexorably to a low view of the sacramental presence. As Holifield notes, "A vivid accent on the presence of Christ would have undermined their attempt to keep the Lord's Supper on exactly the same level as the Word and thus to open the sacrament to the unregenerate."[135]

While the idea of "converting ordinances" met with widespread opposition early on,[136] it eventually became common in Puritan New England as pastors agonized over the presence of large numbers of baptized but "unconverted" parishioners. What better way to foster conversions than to admit them to the Supper, argued the New England champion of this view, Solomon Stoddard (1643-1729). New England's Half-Way Covenant (permitting baptism of the children of the baptized but unconverted) in 1662, and the admission by Stoddard of baptized but unconverted persons to the Supper in 1677 (which then became widespread practice throughout New England) largely spelled the end of a high Calvinistic view of the presence of Christ in the Supper in Puritan New England.[137]

In summary then, we see that Puritan piety tended to push Reformed theology in particular directions. Calvin's view of union with the humanity of Christ as an instrument in the application of redemption largely disappears; instead, the humanity of Christ is viewed as the *conditio sine qua non* of redemption and as an object of devotion. Calvin's robust view of sacramental presence of Christ's humanity through the power of the Holy Spirit tend to be

---

[133]Owen, *Works*, VIII:562-3. Holifield, *Covenant Sealed*, 26, aptly notes, "Among later Reformed theologians, including English Puritans, some ministers were always tempted to describe the sacrament simply in terms of its efficacy."

[134]See Holifield, *Covenant Sealed*, 113-126.

[135]Holifield, *Covenant Sealed*, 126.

[136]See Wakefield, *Puritan Devotion*, 39.

[137]See Holifield, *Covenant Sealed*, 206-224; Edmund S. Morgan, *Visible Saints: the History of a Puritan Idea* (Ithaca: Cornell University Press, 1965), 113-152.

replaced by a "virtual presence" and by conceptions of psychologistic efficacy.

Conclusion: The Federal Orthodoxy Dilemma

This chapter began with the suggestion that the period of Reformed orthodoxy involved the confluence of Reformation, scholastic, and pietist influences. After Calvin's death, new issues, methods, terminology, and concepts evolved, and change was inevitable. At this point we may summarize the shifts which occurred during this period with respect to the theme of union with Christ. First of all, we must recall that for Calvin, there is a single, ineffable union of the believer with Christ through faith and the Holy Spirit. Through this union all the benefits of salvation—forensic as well as transforming—are communicated to the Christian. Calvin places particular emphasis on a "substantial" union with the incarnate humanity of Christ, through which salvation in its fullness is communicated.

During the orthodox period, however, Calvin's stress on a substantial union with the incarnate humanity of Christ increasingly drops out. While the humanity of Christ continued to be viewed as a *conditio sine qua non* of salvation and assumes new prominence as an object of devotion among Puritans during this period, it is deemphasized as a theological component. Reasons for this eclipse are several. In addition to the intrinsic conceptual difficulties involved in Calvin's emphasis on Christ's humanity, the increased use of Aristotelian categories, together with the logic of federal theology, with its tendency to accentuate the continuity of Old and New Testament dispensations, cut against Calvin's concerns here. In place of "substantial" union with Christ's incarnate humanity (inadequately explained by Calvin), theories of "virtual communion" come to the fore. Union with Christ comes to be seen as the reception of the forensic benefits of salvation and the experience of the transforming work of the Holy Spirit. Such "virtualism" began to become evident in the early seventeenth century, is apparent a bit later in Puritans such as Owen, and it subsequently becomes a touchstone of "orthodoxy" for nineteenth century federalists such as Charles Hodge and William Cunningham.

Also of crucial importance is the rise of the *ordo salutis* in Reformed circles in the early seventeenth century. Initially embraced to address assurance-related problems, the *ordo salutis* quickly became a bulwark against Rome. Forensic justification was firmly distinguished from sanctification as entirely different moments in a logical and temporal sequence, ostensibly to preserve the gratuity of forensic justification. Here the fundamental incompatibility of Calvin's view of union with Christ with the later *ordo salutis* should be noted. On Calvin's view, salvation is an organic unity communicated *in toto* through spiritual union with Christ. On the *ordo salutis* model, however, salvation is bestowed through a series of successive and discrete acts.

Related to the *ordo salutis* is the bifurcation of *unio Christi* undertaken by the federal theology. If the formal priority of union with Christ was to be maintained in an *ordo salutis* context, the theme needed to be recast. The logic and terminology of federal theology led to a bifurcation of union with Christ into the forensic benefits of salvation (i.e., an extrinsic, federal union issuing in justification) on the one hand, and the transforming benefits (i.e., a spiritual union issuing in sanctification) on the other. Initially, this bifurcation was implicit, as justifying and sanctifying unions with Christ were framed in increasingly disparate terms (a relationship of imputation with Christ as "Surety," and a relationship of infusion with Christ as "Head"). By the mid-seventeenth century, however, Samuel Rutherford and others began explicitly to distinguish various different unions with Christ—Legal, Mystical, etc. As the theme of *unio Christi* was thus accommodated to the *ordo salutis*, the principle of unity binding justification and sanctification together became purely formal, and the organic unity of salvation was obscured.

While this federal construction of the matter evidenced considerable longevity, problems inevitably emerged, many of which were related to the soteriological dualism inherent in the federal schema.[138] If there is both a federal union and a spiritual or mystical union, the question of the relationship between the two will inevitably be raised, hence the endless debates over various *ordo salutis* constructions in which the precise sequential order of the soteriological benefits was at issue. It is interesting to note that the British Reformed communities were torn by recurrent conflicts between Antinomians and Neonomians from the mid-seventeenth until the mid-eighteenth centuries, with antinomian parties emphasizing the priority and supremacy of justification at the expense of sanctification, and Neonomians reacting to antinomian excesses by emphasizing sanctification at the expense of forensic justification (note that this period was the heyday of the *ordo salutis*/federal theology model). Given the dualistic character of the federal paradigm, satisfying answers to this dilemma were difficult to find, and the Reformed federal tradition has tended to oscillate between the twin poles of legalism and antinomianism ever since.

The structural dualism inherent in federal theology spawned other dualisms as well. The legal relationship to Christ was abstracted from the personal relationship, with important implications for the doctrine of assurance. A dualism of the person and work of Christ is evident as well. Here the respective roles of the humanity of the incarnate Christ and the work of the Holy Spirit

---

[138]The term "dualistic" here denotes an approach viewing two realities as utterly distinct, making meaningful relationships impossible. The Reformed orthodox intent to safeguard the gratuity of justification by completely isolating it from sanctification issued in such a dualism.

On theological dualisms, see Colin E. Gunton, *Yesterday and Today: A Study of Continuities in Christology* (Grand Rapids: Eerdmans, 1983), 86. Gunton writes that "dualism...[need] not refer to a metaphysic in which two different kinds of reality are supposed, but one which conceives two realities as either opposites or contradictions of each other...Dualism denies such an interaction, either explicitly or by conceiving the two in such a way that it becomes impossible consistently to relate them."

were at issue. Calvin had closely related Christ's person and Christ's work—viewing Christ as clothed with his benefits and mediated by the Holy Spirit. For federal theology, however, the sanctifying work of the Holy Spirit *represents* rather than *mediates* Christ. In other words, the Holy Spirit functions as a surrogate for an absent Christ instead of mediating a personal presence, a perspective often reflected in federal views of the eucharist. Thus, the humanity of Christ often tended to become little more than a matter of historical importance, a necessary precondition for the atonement.

The eighteenth- and nineteenth-century period to which we now turn was a watershed period for the Reformed understanding of union with Christ. Federal theology still found articulate defenders in America, but the tide had turned against it. Critics of federal orthodoxy investigated a variety of other options—some attempted to return to Calvin while others explored new paths.

PART II

THE NEW ENGLAND TRAJECTORY: IMPUTATION ECLIPSED

CHAPTER 3

Jonathan Edwards on Salvation and Union with Christ

We turn now to the first of our American Reformed approaches to applied soteriology and the theme of union with Christ. Here we find, initially at least, considerable continuity with earlier Reformed thought, together with new directions that ultimately lead to a significant revision of the Reformed soteriological tradition. Of particular interest here is the progressive eclipse of imputation. In this portion of the book we will examine the thought of Jonathan Edwards, Samuel Hopkins, and Timothy Dwight.

The legacy of Jonathan Edwards has been subjected to a variety of appraisals. Though eulogized by his immediate New England successors, later in the nineteenth century Edwards' Calvinism was rejected as a tired vestige of New England's Puritan past.[1] The twentieth century has witnessed a revival of interest in Edwards, with assessments often bordering on the extravagant. Perry Miller, for example, finds Edwards "intellectually the most modern man of his age."[2] Sang Hyun Lee goes further, declaring Edwards to be "actually more radically 'modern' than Miller himself might have realized."[3] Such disparate appraisals alert one to the complexity of Edwards' thought and underscore the need for interpretive caution. We will examine Edwards' relation to the Reformed tradition, the philosophical and religious context within which he worked, and then turn to his views on union with Christ and related matters.

Edwards and the Reformed Tradition

Largely because of textbook presentations of his Enfield sermon "Sinners in the

---

[1]Helpful summaries of Edwards interpretation in America include Henry F. May, "Jonathan Edwards and America," in *Jonathan Edwards and the American Experience*, ed. by Nathan O. Hatch and Harry S. Stout (New York: Oxford, 1988), 19-33; William J. Scheick, "Introduction," in *Critical Essays on Jonathan Edwards*, ed. William J. Scheick (Boston: G.K. Hall, 1980), ix-xxv.

A variety of editions of Edwards' works are in circulation. Unless otherwise noted, quotations are from *The Works of President Edwards*, 4 vols. (New York: Robert Carter, 1868).

[2] Perry Miller, *Jonathan Edwards* (New York: William Sloane, 1949), 305.

[3]Lee, *Philosophical Theology of Jonathan Edwards*, 3.

Hands of an Angry God," and because of his masterwork *The Freedom of the Will*, a piece that confounded Arminian opponents for over a century, Edwards continues popularly to be viewed as an arch-Calvinist. Closer examination indicates, however, that his relationship to the tradition was complex. Edwards clearly had a deep appreciation for Calvin and for certain of the Reformed orthodox writers—especially Petrus van Mastricht and Francis Turretin.[4] On the other hand, Edwards was not afraid to depart from the received tradition when he deemed it necessary.

More recent scholarship has tended to find significant divergence at two important and related points—the federal theology and the doctrine of justification—both of which are significant for this present inquiry. Perry Miller, in large measure responsible for the twentieth-century revival of Edwards scholarship, argued that "the Federal Theology is conspicuous...by its utter absence."[5] More recently, Miller's view has been significantly qualified by those who discern considerable continuity with the federal tradition.[6] Edwards' conception of justification has also been a matter of dispute. In an influential article, Thomas A. Schafer argued that Edwards expands the concept of faith to include love and perseverance in a manner reminiscent of Tridentine Roman Catholicism, and that Edwards bypasses the doctrine of imputation in

---

[4] On Calvin, Edwards, *Freedom of the Will*, ed. Paul Ramsey (New Haven: Yale University Press, 1957), 131, writes: "I should not take it at all amiss, to be called a Calvinist, for distinction's sake: though I utterly disclaim a dependence on Calvin, or believing the doctrines which I hold, because he believed and taught them; and cannot justly be charged with believing in everything just as he taught." For Edwards' appreciation of van Mastricht and Turretin, see Stanley Williams, ed., "Six Letters of Jonathan Edwards to Joseph Bellamy," *New England Quarterly* 1 (1928): 229-230.

The most extensive study of Edwards' formative influences is William Sparkes Morris, *The Young Jonathan Edwards: A Reconstruction*, Chicago Studies in the History of American Religion, 14 (New York: Carlson Publishing, 1991). See also his "The Genius of Jonathan Edwards," in *Reinterpretation in American Church History*, ed. Jerald C. Brauer (Chicago: University of Chicago Press, 1968), 29-65.

[5] Miller, *Jonathan Edwards*, 30. As we have seen above, Miller viewed the federal theology as an Arminianizing attempt to bind the deity and to make room for human endeavor in salvation. But Edwards, Miller argues, emphasizes naked divine sovereignty in a manner markedly different in emphasis from federal theology.

P. Y. DeJong also views Edwards as departing from the federal theology of earlier Reformed thinkers. He contends that Edwards abandoned the organic connectionalism of federal theology for an individualistic, revivalist piety. See Peter Y. DeJong, *The Covenant Idea in New England Theology: 1620-1847* (Grand Rapids: Eerdmans, 1945), 136-152.

[6] See Bogue, *Jonathan Edwards and the Covenant of Grace*; Conrad Cherry, *The Theology of Jonathan Edwards: A Reappraisal* (Garden City, N.Y.: Anchor Books, 1966), 107-123; "The Puritan Notion of the Covenant in Jonathan Edwards' Doctrine of Faith," *Church History* 34 (1965): 328-341.

favor of the notion of "infused grace."[7] Against Schafer, Conrad Cherry and Samuel Logan argue that the substance of Edwards' doctrine of justification is largely consistent with classic Reformed orthodoxy.[8] As we examine this issue more closely below, we will discover that both sides are in part correct.

The Philosophical Context of Edwards' Thought

Jonathan Edwards was a contextual thinker, profoundly responsive to the needs and problems of his age. Indeed, he cannot profitably be understood apart from philosophical movements that arose in response to the Newtonian scientific revolution and the political and religious difficulties of seventeenth and eighteenth-century Europe. For example, if the material world was amenable to scientific description and explanation without recourse to immaterial or spiritual causes, the way was opened to full-fledged philosophical materialism—a move taken by Thomas Hobbes (1588-1679). But Hobbesian materialism was religiously unacceptable, and the French Protestant philosopher René Descartes (1596-1650) tried to preserve the interests of both science and religion by positing a dualism of spiritual mind and material body. Matter and spirit were seen as separate and antithetical substances, and their relationship became problematical.[9]

If Cartesian mind/body dualism presented ontological and epistemological difficulties, the search for certainty was exacerbated by the political and religious crises of seventeenth-century Europe. As traditional authorities (church, scripture, and tradition) were increasingly challenged, many followed Descartes in the quest for certainty by looking to innate ideas within the human mind. But the notion of innate ideas as a foundation for knowledge seemed increasingly questionable—it was criticized vigorously by John Locke (1632-1704)—and over against the prevailing dualism the most viable options seemed to be idealist illuminationism or materialist empiricism.

Of particular interest here are the thinkers Louis E. Loeb has termed the "theocentric metaphysicians" (e.g., Malebranche and George Berkeley [1685-1753]), primarily because of their influence on Jonathan Edwards.[10] While a

---

[7]Thomas A. Schafer, "Jonathan Edwards and Justification by Faith," *Church History* 20 (1951): 55-67. Morris, "Genius of Jonathan Edwards," 64, echoes Schafer at this point.

[8]See Cherry, *Theology of Jonathan Edwards*, 90-106; Samuel T. Logan, Jr., "The Doctrine of Justification in the Theology of Jonathan Edwards," *Westminster Theological Journal* 46 (1984): 26-52. See also Randall E. Otto, "Justification and Justice: An Edwardsean Proposal," *Evangelical Quarterly* 65 (1993): 131-145.

[9]See the helpful discussion by Wallace E. Anderson, "Editor's Introduction," in *Jonathan Edwards: Scientific and Philosophical Writings*, ed. Wallace E. Anderson, *The Works of Jonathan Edwards*, vol. 6 (New Haven: Yale University Press, 1980), 53-63.

[10]Here we follow Louis E. Loeb and Norman Fiering in diverging from the traditional textbook groupings of "Continental rationalism" (Descartes, Spinoza,

detailed examination of this trajectory is beyond the purview of this work, certain characteristics need to be noted, particularly its idealism and its theocentric view of causality and the God-world relationship. For these thinkers, as for Edwards, reality was conceived in primarily idealist terms. Epistemologically, all knowledge consists of ideas and there is no direct apprehension of material substance as such. Ontologically, existence itself is subordinated to knowledge and consciousness.[11] Strictly speaking, there is no material substance at all. George Berkeley's immaterialism is, of course, well known. Jonathan Edwards' somewhat similar denial of material substance is also of importance. Instead of separately subsisting material substance, Edwards concluded that the essence of the material is solidity, or resistance to division (rather than extension, as Descartes had supposed), and that this resistance is the result of immediate divine causation.[12]

According to Edwards, as also for Malebranche and Berkeley, the knowledge of ideas by finite minds results, not from sense perception, but from divine causation. W. E. Anderson writes:

> Edwards' phenomenalistic idealism, like that of Berkeley, assumes that there are many different created minds, each one conscious, capable of perception,

---

Leibniz) and "British Empiricism" (Locke, Berkeley, and Hume). Loeb has shown that Berkeley has more affinities with the Continental "rationalism" of Malebranche than with the "empiricism" of Locke and Hume. See Louis E. Loeb, *From Descartes to Hume: Continental Metaphysics and the Development of Modern Philosophy* (Ithaca: Cornel University Press, 1981). Loeb is followed by Norman Fiering, "The Rationalist Foundations of Jonathan Edwards's Metaphysics," in Jonathan Edwards and the American Experience, ed. Nathan O. Hatch and Harry S. Stout (New York: Oxford, 1988), 77, 95-96. See also Bruce Kuklick, *Churchmen and Philosophers: From Jonathan Edwards to John Dewey* (New Haven: Yale University Press, 1985), 15-22.

The roots of Edwards' thought have been much debated. G. P. Fisher viewed Edwards' metaphysics as Berkeleian. See his "The Philosophy of Jonathan Edwards," in *Discussions in History and Theology* (New York: Charles Scribner's Sons, 1880), 229-231. Perry Miller, *Jonathan Edwards*, 52, set the agenda for much mid-twentieth-century scholarship with his view that Edwards' reading of Locke was "the central and decisive event of his intellectual life." Norman Fiering (see above) more plausibly views Edwards in the tradition of Malebranche and Berkeley. A mediating proposal is found in George Rupp, "The 'Idealism' of Jonathan Edwards," *Harvard Theological Review* 62 (1969): 209-226.

[11] Jonathan Edwards, *Scientific and Philosophical Writings*, ed. Wallace e. Anderson, The Works of Jonathan Edwards, vol. 6 (New Haven: Yale University Press, 1980), 204, maintains that "nothing has any existence anywhere else but in consciousness. No, certainly nowhere else, but either in created or uncreated consciousness." See Fiering, "Rationalist Foundations," 82-83; Anderson, "Editor's Introduction," 75-80.

[12] See Edwards, *Scientific and Philosophical Writings*, 214-216, 351.

knowledge, and volition, and in each of which God excites an orderly train of ideas of sensation that comprise the bodies it perceives and affects.[13]

This clearly involves an extraordinarily theocentric view of causality, and of finite existence itself. The only truly subsistent "substance" is God; all finite reality is but the result of divine action.[14] Though not precisely and unequivocally identified, God and world are brought into the closest of relations in a way reminiscent of Neoplatonism.[15] Corollaries for Edwards of this divine omnicausality were the doctrine of continuous creation and an occasionalist view of causation. Strictly speaking, there is no secondary causation in the finite sphere—what we perceive as causes are merely the divinely constituted regular occasions for divine action.[16] Similarly, because the material world in itself is not substantial, it must be continuously created anew and upheld by divine action.[17]

---

[13]Anderson, "Editor's Introduction," 112. The close connection for Edwards of ontology and epistemology is evident in the following passage from his *Scientific and Philosophical Writings*, 344: "And indeed, the secret lies here: that which truly is the substance of all bodies is the infinitely exact and precise and perfectly stable idea in God's mind, together with his stable will that the same shall gradually be communicated to us, and to other minds, according to certain fixed and exact established methods and laws: or in somewhat different language, the infinitely exact and precise divine idea together with an answerable, perfectly exact, precise and stable will with respect to correspondent communications to created minds, and effects on their minds."

[14]Edwards, *Scientific and Philosophical Writings*, 215, writes: "The substance of bodies [is]...nothing but the Deity acting in that particular manner in those parts of space where he thinks fit. So that, speaking most strictly, there is no proper substance but God himself."

[15]Kuklick, *Churchmen and Philosophers*, 21, writes: "Edwards conceived God as an inexhaustible reality, an emanating light, communicating himself *ad extra* as the sun communicated its brilliance. The material world was thus not merely an idea in God's mind, but his eternal disposition, his will to display an idea...The world was not an act or state of the divine consciousness, but God operating, expressing himself in finite modes and forms according to a stable purpose and by an established constitution. This was Plotinus' idea mediated into the Christian tradition by Augustine and popular among the English Puritans." See also Anderson, "Editor's Introduction," 72-73; Fiering, "Rationalist Foundations," 83.

[16]Edwards writes: "In natural things means of effects in metaphysical strictness are not the proper causes of the effects, but only occasions. God produces all effects but yet he ties natural events to the operation of such means or causes them to be consequent on such means according to fixed, determinate, and unchangeable rules which are called the laws of nature." "Miscellanies," No. 629 (Thomas Schafer transcript), quoted in Fiering, "Rationalist Foundations," 81.

On the occasionalism of Malebranche and the modified occasionalism of Berkeley, see Loeb, *Descartes to Hume*, 194-248.

[17]See Anderson, "Editor's Introduction," 57; Fiering, "Rationalist Foundations," 78-81; Kuklick, *Churchmen and Philosophers*, 21.

In Edwards' day, the turn toward idealism enabled him to confront two philosophical threats to orthodoxy: the Cartesian dualism of mind and body, and the threat of materialism. But idealism was also useful in resolving religious and theological dualisms as well. The American awakenings of the eighteenth and nineteenth centuries posed other relational problems—divine sovereignty and human responsibility, the natural and the supernatural in conversion, and so forth. Bruce Kuklick writes:

> Edwards and the New England Theologians assumed a great divide between God and man, and between the realms of nature and grace. Both distinctions were reflected in the persistent exploration of human responsibility for sin and God's sovereignty over grace. God's omnipotence uneasily comported with man's accountability, especially when grace was so clearly supernatural. Bringing God and man and nature and grace into appropriate relations became central problems. The theologians again and again displayed an interest in idealist metaphysics that might overcome ostensible dualisms.[18]

The Religious Context of Edwards' Thought

Edwards' soteriological writings reflect concerns about two related and pressing issues of his time—the double threat of antinomianism and legalism on the one hand, and the problem of vindicating and shaping an emerging revivalist piety on the other. There is, in fact, general agreement that Edwards was concerned to walk a middle path between legalism and antinomianism, and that he was confronted by both positions.[19] Edwards himself says as much in a 1749 letter, remarking that it was necessary to "take heed and beware of the dangerous errors which many have run into; particularly the Arminian and Neonomian on the one hand, and the Antinomian and Enthusiastical on the other."[20] These tendencies, though present in New England before,[21] became

---

[18]Kuklick, *Churchmen and Philosophers*, 44.

[19]See, e.g., Joseph Haroutunian, *Piety Versus Moralism: The Passing of the New England Theology* (New York: Henry Holt and Company, 1932), 9-11; Schafer, "Edwards and Justification," 57; Conrad Cherry, *Theology*, 160-215; Logan, "Doctrine of Justification," 41. This theme is more fully developed in William Breitenbach, "Piety and Moralism: Edwards and the New Divinity," in *Jonathan Edwards and the American Experience*, ed. Nathan O. Hatch and Harry S. Stout (New York: Oxford University Press, 1988), 177-204.

[20]Quoted in Cherry, *Theology*, 161.

[21]The extent of the Arminian presence prior to the Great Awakening is a matter of some debate. Perry Miller, *Jonathan Edwards*, 107, for example, maintains that in 1734 "none in New England was an avowed follower of Arminius," although Miller also argues that the federal theology itself tended in an Arminian direction. More recently, Robert J. Wilson, III, *The Benevolent Deity; Ebenezer Gay and the Rise of Rational Religion in New England, 1697-1787*, (Philadelphia: University of Pennsylvania Press,

openly polarized in New England church life as a result of the religious cauldron of emerging revivalism we call the "First Great Awakening."

Arminian tendencies were evident in early eighteenth-century New England, and well before that in Britain. The "Age of Reason" had dawned, and traditionally optimistic Arminian views regarding human potential and action in the salvation process meshed well with the emerging rationalism of the period.[22] Arminian theological themes were increasingly popular among English dissenting divines, and books such as *A Discourse* (1710), by Daniel Whitby (1638-1726), which attacked the soteriology of the Synod of Dordt, and *The Scripture Doctrine of Original Sin Proposed to a Free and Candid Examination* (1738), by John Taylor (1694-1761), which focused criticism on the federal Calvinist hamartiological scheme, found an audience in New England. Thus it was that Jonathan Edwards, together with Calvinistic colleagues such as John White of Gloucester, sounded the alarm from the early 1730's.[23] Beginning with his 1734 Northampton sermons on "Justification by Faith Alone," Edwards embarked on the reasoned defense of Calvinistic orthodoxy that would occupy him for the remainder of his career. In particular, Edwards was deeply concerned to defend Reformed notions of the solidarity of human beings with Adam and with Christ against suggestions that Adam's sin had not determined the moral condition of his offspring, and that justification is

---

1984), 61-79, has found that Edwards' fears were not groundless.

[22]See Roland N. Stromberg, *Religious Liberalism in Eighteenth-Century England* (London: Oxford University Press, 1954), 110-122; Gerald R. Cragg, *The Church and the Age of Reason: 1648-1789* (Grand Rapids: Eerdmans, 1964), 37-80. The rise of liberal Puritanism in New England is chronicled in Conrad Wright, *The Beginnings of Unitarianism in America* (Boston: Starr King Press, 1955); James William Jones, *The Shattered Synthesis: New England Puritanism Before the Great Awakening* (New Haven: Yale University Press, 1973); and Wilson, *Benevolent Deity*. See also Francis Albert Christie, "The Beginnings of Arminianism in New England," *Papers of the American Society of Church History*, 2nd ser., 3 (1912): 153-172.

"Arminianism," named for the Dutch Reformed theologian Jacobus Arminius (1560-1609), was codified in the "Remonstrance" of students of Arminius in 1610. They denied total depravity, asserted that election was conditioned upon faith and obedience, proclaimed a universal Atonement (that Christ died for all rather than only for the elect), declared that divine grace was resistible by human beings, and that Christians could fall from grace. Against these Arminian tenets the Synod of Dordt (1618-19), called for the purpose of dealing with Arminianism, codified the so-called "Five Points of Calvinism": total depravity, unconditional election, limited Atonement, irresistible grace, and the perseverance of the saints. The Remonstrance and the Canons of the Synod of Dordt are found in Schaff, *Creeds of Christendom*, III:545-597. In speaking of New England "Arminianism," we recognize a marked affinity of concerns rather than a precise genetic relationship between the Remonstrants and liberal Puritanism.

[23]See John White, *New England's Lamentations* (Boston: T. Fleet, 1734); Jonathan Edwards, *Justification by Faith Alone*, in *The Works of President Edwards*, 4 vols. (New York: Robert Carter, 1868), IV:64-132. On these developments, see Miller, *Jonathan Edwards*, 101-126; Cherry, *Theology*, 186-215; Wilson, *Benevolent Deity*, 72-78.

to some degree predicated upon meritorious obedience to the divine law.

Antinomianism again was becoming a factor on the New England religious scene as the Awakening took hold in 1740. If the Arminian tendency in New England was to exalt the capacity of native human potential and to extol the importance of lawkeeping (as a preparation for salvation, as the means of salvation itself, and as evidence of one's state of grace), the Antinomian tendency was quite the opposite. The role of the divine in salvation was magnified. Grace was viewed in immediate terms (not as the infusion of gracious habits but as the direct action of the deity within the human soul). Obedience to the law was seen as of little importance since the hypocrite could be just as outwardly obedient as the saint.[24]

Not only did the Great Awakening bring these tendencies to light, but it acted as a catalyst in further polarizing them. Efforts by itinerant preachers to awaken staid congregations frequently involved attacks against allegedly "unconverted" ministers and against those who took comfort in their social respectability and outward morality. Such homiletical strategies were seen by many of the established clergy as personal attacks both upon themselves and upon the fabric of the social order itself.[25] More than a few of these pillars of the establishment—among them Charles Chauncy 1705-1787), Ebenezer Gay (1696-1787), and Jonathan Mayhew (1720-1766)—had Arminian tendencies and these predilections were reinforced by Awakening excesses.

Even more important for our study here is the way in which the Great Awakening sorely strained the traditional federal paradigm. As noted earlier, the soteriological dualism of the federal theology, with its *ordo salutis* and bifurcation of *unio Christi* into legal and spiritual unions, was unable meaningfully to relate the forensic and transformatory aspects of salvation. For this reason, the tradition tended to oscillate back and forth between the two poles of legalism and antinomianism. The Awakening, with its focus upon a "point in time" conversion experience, accentuated aspects of the federal tradition that already focused on the punctiliar moment of justification in the *ordo salutis*. Furthermore, by giving new prominence to the neonomian-antinomian tension, the Awakening highlighted a problem the traditional federal theology was incapable of solving. Confronted by this situation, Jonathan Edwards modified the Reformed federal tradition at the very points

---

[24]Studies of eighteenth-century New England Antinomianism include Williston Walker, "The Sandemanians of New England," *Annual Report of the American Historical Association for the Year 1901* I (1902): 133-162; Leigh Eric Schmidt, "'A Second and Glorious Reformation': The New Light Extremism of Andrew Croswell," *William and Mary Quarterly* 43 (1986): 214-244.

[25]Eighteenth-century declension from Calvinist orthodoxy was most pronounced among the more prosperous upper and upper-middle classes, in New England and elsewhere. The connection between social conservatism and eighteenth-century theological liberalism is explored in Daniel Walker Howe, "The Decline of Calvinism: An Approach to Its Study," *Comparative Studies in Society and History* 14 (1972): 306-327.

where it was weakest in dealing with the challenges presented by the Awakening. Equally important, these modifications established a trajectory for later New England thinkers.

Edwards on the Nature of Union with Christ

There is considerable continuity between Jonathan Edwards and his Reformed predecessors on the topic of union with Christ. Traditional Calvinian themes such as faith and the role of the Holy Spirit play key roles in Edwards' discussions. Consistent with the later federal bifurcation of union with Christ, Edwards distinguishes between a "vital" or spiritual union and a "relative" or legal union.[26] Edwards also speaks of a "natural" or incarnational union of Christ himself with human nature.[27] Furthermore, the theme of union with Christ continues to occupy a central place in his soteriological schema, functioning as an umbrella category for applied soteriology in general, just as it had for Calvin and federal orthodoxy.

> The Scripture is very plain and evident in this, that those that are in Christ are actually in a state of salvation, and are justified, sanctified, accepted of Christ, and shall be saved…But those that are not in Christ, and are not united to Him, can have no degree of communion with Him. For there is no communion without union. The members can have no communion with the head or participation of its life and health unless they are united to it.[28]

But such continuities should not lead us to overlook what is new in Edwards. One key to understanding Edwards' view of union with Christ is the way he approaches the topic from two directions or perspectives—the divine and the human: "There is a union with Christ, by the indwelling of the love of Christ, two ways. First, as 'tis from Christ, and is the very Spirit and life and fulness of Christ; and second, as it acts to Christ. For the very nature of it is love and union of heart to Him."[29] In the following sections we will explore Edwards' constructive approach to this theme. First we will look at the nature of union with Christ as it is described from both the human and the divine directions. Then we will examine the relationship between union with Christ and applied soteriology.

---

[26]See Edwards, *Justification by Faith*, *Works* IV:70; *Treatise on Grace and Other Posthumously Published Writings*, ed. by Paul Helm (London: James Clark, 1971), 73.

[27]Edwards, *Justification by Faith*, *Works* IV:95.

[28]Edwards, *Treatise on Grace*, 31.

[29]Ibid., 74. There is, of course, basic continuity here with Calvin's stress on union by faith and the Holy Spirit. Nevertheless, Edwards develops these ideas in unique ways.

The Human Perspective—Faith as Union with Christ

Edwards departs from previous Reformed thought by viewing faith, not as a means or "instrument" of union and the justification that flows from it, but as the act of union itself. Here Edwards is concerned to avoid any suggestion that faith is a meritorious work (as his Arminian opponents maintained). He writes, "God does not give those that believe, a union with or an interest in the Saviour, in reward for faith, but only because faith is the soul's active uniting with Christ, or is itself the very act of union, on their part."[30] Edwards further suggests that it is particularly "fitting" or "agreeable" for faith to be the act of union (from the human side) in light of the misery and helplessness of the sinner, the glorious invisibility of the Savior, and the wonderfully incomprehensible benefits received.[31]

Edwards' definition of this act of union, or faith, must be gathered from a variety of places. It is important to note that his definition is, by the standards of Reformed orthodoxy, rather broad. Against Arminian elements, whose view of faith tended toward mere rational assent (which was then assisted by moral behavior), and against antinomian interests, which exalted the initial act of faith and vigorously excluded works from the equation, Edwards' notion of faith includes elements traditionally subsumed under "sanctification." For example, faith is itself an expression of "true virtue": "Justifying faith is nothing else, but true virtue in its proper and genuine breathings adapted to the case, to the revelation made, the state we are in, the benefit to be received and the way and means of it, and our relation to these things.[32] Similarly, the essence of faith includes "hope" and "love."[33] Edwards goes so far as to define faith as both belief *and* obedience, as including the activity of the graced human disposition.

> As the whole soul in all its faculties is the proper subject and agent of faith, so undoubtedly there are two things in saving faith, viz., belief of the truth and an answerable disposition of heart. And therefore faith may be defined, a thorough believing of what the gospel reveals of a Saviour of sinners, as true and perfectly good, with the exercises of an answerable disposition towards him.[34]

---

[30]Edwards, *Justification by Faith, Works* IV:71. See *Observations Concerning Faith*, in *The Works of President Edwards*, 4 vols. (New York: Robert Carter, 1868), II:614-624. See also the helpful discussion in Cherry, *Theology*, 100-101.

[31]See Edwards, *Observations Concerning Faith, Works* II:614. See also pp. 616-18. Behind Edward's "fitness" argument is the notion of divine constitution.

[32]Ibid., 624. Edwards defines "true virtue" itself in terms of union with God, or "union of heart to Being simply considered." See his *A Dissertation on the Nature of True Virtue*, in *The Works of President Edwards*, 4 vols. (New York: Robert Carter, 1868), II:292; cf. p. 301.

[33]Edwards, *Observations Concerning Faith, Works*, II:612, 625.

[34]Ibid., 625. On p. 621, Edwards rejects a traditional scholastic definition of faith as consisting of three acts: assent, consent, and affiance. As Cherry, *Theology*, 17, notes, this construction implies a faculty psychology, with its discrete compartmentalization of

Clearly, this view of faith stands in some tension with earlier Reformed thinkers, who carefully sequestered faith and obedience, justification and sanctification.

The Divine Perspective—Union with God

Perhaps nowhere is the vaunted theocentricity of Jonathan Edwards more evident than at this point in his theology, as christology, soteriology, and Augustinian trinitarian doctrine are integrated in a striking manner. In his important *Treatise on Grace*, Edwards argues that union with Christ consists of partaking of the Holy Spirit: "All the blessedness of the redeemed consists in partaking of the fulness of Christ, their head and redeemer, which, I have observed, consists in partaking of the Spirit that is given Him not by measure."[35]

He also insists that this communion of the Holy Spirit involves the immediate agency of the third Person of the Trinity in the Christian.[36] At this point, Edwards knew he was arguing not only against the Arminians (whose desire to preserve human freedom led them to minimize direct divine agency), but also to some extent against the weight of the scholastic Reformed tradition with its carefully constructed dialectic of nature and grace.

A variety of metaphors and expressions are used to describe this immediate work of the Holy Spirit. Using the language of Reformed orthodoxy, Edwards refers to it as "physical" in order to emphasize the directness and permanence of the relationship.[37] This immediate divine grace is also depicted in terms of a Lockean "simple idea," a singular principle definable only in terms of itself which Edwards identifies as divine love: "That principle in the soul of the saints, which is the grand Christian virtue, and which is the soul and essence and summary comprehension of all grace, *is a principle of Divine love*."[38] This

---

reason, will, and emotion, which Edwards rejected.

Reformed orthodox divines show some diversity in their discussions of the aspects of faith. A more typical Reformed scholastic approach to the act of faith is to speak of *notitia* (knowledge), *assensus* (assent), and *fiducia* (trust). For discussions of various Reformed approaches to the "acts" of faith, see Turretin, *Institutio*, XV.8.1-XV.10.15; Heppe, *Reformed Dogmatics*, 530-534.

[35] Edwards, *Treatise on Grace*, 67-68. See also pp. 30-31, 62, 65; *Concerning Efficacious Grace*, in *The Works of President Edwards*, 4 vols. (New York: Robert Carter, 1868), II:595-96.

[36] Edwards, *Treatise on Grace*, 51-53. See also *Concerning Efficacious Grace*, *Works* II:567-569.

[37] See Edwards, *Concerning Efficacious Grace*, *Works* II:569. See the helpful discussion in Cherry, *Theology*, 36-37. This analysis of Edwards' terminology for divine grace is in part dependent on Ramsey, "Infused Virtues in Edwardsean and Calvinistic Context," 739-745.

[38] Edwards, *Treatise on Grace*, 40. On Edwards' use of the Lockean "simple idea," see Cherry, *Theology*, 18-19.

indwelling principle of divine love is nothing other than the personal presence of the Holy Spirit. Here Edwards introduces the Augustinian trinitarian schema in which the Holy Spirit proceeds from Father and Son as the bond of love between the first two Persons of the Trinity.

> The Scripture therefore leads us to this conclusion, though it be infinitely above us to conceive how it should be, that yet as the son of God is the personal word, idea, or wisdom of God, begotten by God, being an infinitely perfect, substantial image or idea of Himself...so the Holy Spirit does in some ineffable and inconceivable manner proceed, and is breathed forth both from the Father and the Son, by the Divine essence being wholly poured and flowing out in that infinitely intense, holy, and pure love and delight that continually and unchangeably breathes forth from the Father and the Son, primarily towards each other, and secondarily towards the creature, and so flowing forth in a different subsistence or person in a manner to us utterly inexplicable and inconceivable, and that this is that person that is poured forth into the hearts of angels and saints.
>
> Hence 'tis to be accounted for, that though we often read in Scripture of the Father loving the Son, and the Son loving the Father, yet we never once read either of the Father or the Son loving the Holy Spirit, and the Spirit loving either of them. It is because the Holy Spirit is the Divine love itself, the love of the Father and the Son.[39]

Edwards also uses the language of infused habits, albeit carefully, since he realized that such terminology connoted created rather than uncreated (immediate) grace. By using *habitus* language, Edwards emphasizes the permanence of the Spirit's presence in the soul of the Christian. All grace is immediate, but it is not for that reason intermittent or occasional. Rather, it becomes part of the structure of the saint's being. Note the way in which Edwards modifies the *habitus* terminology with the metaphor of illumination:

> We often, in our common language about things of this nature, speak of a principle of grace. I suppose there is no other principle of grace in the soul than the very Holy Ghost dwelling in the soul and acting there as a vital principle. To speak of a habit of grace as a natural disposition to act grace, as begotten in the soul by the first communication of Divine light, and as the natural and necessary consequence of the first light, it seems in some respects to carry a wrong idea with it. Indeed the first exercise of grace in the first light has a tendency to future acts, as from an abiding principle, by grace and by the covenant of God; but not by any natural force. The giving one gracious discovery or act of grace or a thousand, has no proper natural tendency to cause an abiding habit of grace for the future; nor

---

[39]Edwards, *Treatise on Grace*, 62-63. See also Edwards, "An Essay on the Trinity," in *Treatise on Grace and Other Posthumously Published Writings*, ed. Paul Helm (London: James Clarke, 1971), 99-131. For Augustine's view of the Holy Spirit as the bond of love between Father and Son, see *On the Trinity* (XV.17-19), in *Nicene and Post-Nicene Fathers*, 1st series, 14 vols., ed. Philip Schaff (New York: Christian Literature Co., 1886), III:215-220.

any otherwise than by Divine constitution and covenant. But all succeeding acts of grace must be as immediately, and, to all intents and purposes, as much from the immediate acting of the Spirit of God on the soul, as the first; and if God should take way His Spirit out of the soul, all habits and acts of grace would of themselves cease as immediately as light ceases in a room when a candle is carried out. And no man has a habit of grace dwelling in him any otherwise than as he has the Holy Spirit dwelling in him in his temple, and acting in union with his natural faculties, after the manner of a vital principle.[40]

A few preliminary observations may be made at this point. Given the extraordinary stress placed by Calvin on union with the incarnate humanity of Christ, and also the emphasis placed by Edwards' Puritan forbears on affectionate communion with Christ's humanity, it is interesting to note that in his presentation of the theme of union with Christ Edwards virtually ignores the humanity of Christ. This is doubtless because, for Edwards, the goal of salvation is an immediate union with the divine. While the humanity of Christ is relevant to the initial work of redemption (the active and passive obedience of Christ) and it has the role of mediating a revelation of the deity,[41] the Holy Spirit has to a great extent displaced the concrete theanthropic person of Christ in Edwards' presentation of applied soteriology.

This talk of immediate grace and divine indwelling raises a problem for Edwards, however. Does this not imply a mystical absorption into the divine? Edwards uses language that suggests deification and mysticism—more than once he cites 2 Peter 1:4, which in the Authorized Version speaks of human beings becoming "partakers of the divine nature."[42] Note also that here Edwards does not use the humanity of Christ as a hedge against mysticism as Calvin did. Furthermore, he frames the plausibility of immediate grace in terms of a chain-of-being schema reminiscent of Neoplatonism.

> And if it be reasonable to suppose it [an immediate work of the Holy Spirit] with respect to any part of the creation, it is especially so with respect to reasonable creatures, who are the highest part of the creation, next to God, and who are most immediately made for God, and have Him for their next head, and are created for the business wherein they are mostly concerned. And above all, in that wherein the highest excellency of this highest rank of beings consist, and that wherein he is most conformed to God, is nearest to Him, and has God for his most immediate object.

---

[40]Edwards, *Treatise on Grace*, 74-75. Also to be consulted is Edwards, *A Divine and Supernatural Light, Immediately Imparted to the Soul by the Spirit of God, Shown To Be Both a Rational and Scriptural Doctrine*, in *The Works of President Edwards*, 4 vols. (New York: Robert Carter, 1868), IV:438-450. On this indwelling principle of illumination, see Cherry, *Theology*, 27-31. See also Ramsey, "Infused Virtues in Edwardsean and Calvinistic Context."

[41]See, e.g., *The Excellency of Christ*, in *The Works of President Edwards*, 4 vols. (New York: Robert Carter, 1868), IV:179-201.

[42]See, e.g., *Concerning Efficacious Grace, Works* II:594; *Treatise on Grace*, 28.

> It seems to me most rational to suppose that as we ascend in the order of being we shall at last come immediately to God, the first cause. In whatever respect we ascend, we ascend in the order of time and succession.[43]

Despite these tendencies, Edwards himself vigorously rejects the mystical option (in the sense of "divinization"), arguing that Christians do not lose their personal distinctiveness through incorporation into the divine being.

> Not that the saints are made partakers of the essence of God, and so are "Godded" with God, and "Christed" with Christ, according to the abominable and blasphemous language and notions of some heretics; but, to use the Scripture phrase, they are made partakers of God's fullness (Eph. 3:17-19; John 1:16), that is, of God's spiritual beauty and happiness, according to the measure and capacity of a creature; for so it is evident the word "fullness" signifies in Scripture language.[44]

Edwards' presentation of the dynamic of union with Christ also seems to exclude the sort of all-encompassing "mystical" union that his language sometimes suggests, for he also argues that the union between Christ and the believer on this earth is both imperfect and incomplete.[45]

Edwards on Applied Soteriology

As early as 1734 Edwards was self-consciously framing his soteriological formulations over against the twin threats of neonomian Arminianism and antinomianism. In his sermon on "Justification by Faith Alone," Edwards begins by championing justification by faith alone and opposing Arminian contentions that God takes human effort and even imperfect obedience into account in the justification of the sinner. But he is equally concerned to answer the "objection, that is often made against this doctrine, viz., that it encourages

---

[43]Edwards, *Treatise on Grace*, 53; See also *Nature of True Virtue*, *Works* II:266. Lee, *Philosophical Theology*, 8, 172, cautions against simple identifications of Edwards as a Plotinian Neoplatonist at this point. Nevertheless, the degree of overlap between classical Neoplatonism and Edwards is striking.

[44]Jonathan Edwards, *Religious Affections*, ed. John E. Smith, *The Works of Jonathan Edwards*, vol. 2 (New Haven: Yale University Press, 1959), 203. See also his "Unpublished Letter on Assurance and Participation in the Divine Nature," in *Ethical Writings*, ed. Paul Ramsey, *The Works of Jonathan Edwards*, vol. 8 (New Haven: Yale University Press, 1989), 636-640.

Cherry, *Theology*, 30, argues with some plausibility that Edwards here makes use of the traditional Platonic notion of "participation," writing that "the gist of what Edwards intends to connote with the notion is that the Holy Spirit becomes the new principle for a new kind of exercise of the human faculties, without assuming an identity with human being as such."

[45]See Edwards, *Excellency of Christ*, *Works* IV:200.

licentiousness of life."⁴⁶ We shall see that in his effort to avoid both legalism and antinomianism Edwards proposes a christocentric applied soteriology which differs in important respects from the earlier federalism.

Justification by Faith

Edwards began his sermons on "Justification by Faith Alone" with a rejection of analytic justification; his scriptural text was Romans 4:5, which speaks of the justification of "the ungodly."⁴⁷ He then asserts, in classical Reformed orthodox fashion, that justification includes both forgiveness of sins and the positive imputation of the righteousness of Christ to the believer: "A person is said to be justified, when he is approved of God as free from the guilt of sin and its deserved punishment; and as having that righteousness belonging to him that entitles him to the reward of life."⁴⁸

---

⁴⁶Edwards, *Justification by Faith*, *Works* IV:128. This relatively early sermon, expanded for publication in 1738, is Edwards' most complete and important statement on this matter.

⁴⁷Ibid., 64.

⁴⁸Ibid., 66.

Brief mention of Edwards' view of the atonement is necessary at this juncture. His view is in large measure consistent with the Anselmian tradition as developed by federal orthodoxy. Sinners owe a infinite debt of guilt to God (*Works*, I:583; II:626) through their offence against God's moral governorship and against the divine majesty (I:590-591), and thus they incur the necessity of "condign punishment" (I:587). In payment of this infinite debt, Christ endured "infinite suffering," provided a "sacrifice of infinite value," and offered a sacrifice that was "fully and completely equivalent" (I:416, 606-607).

In both early and later works, Edwards defends the notion of imputation with some vigor. As with federal orthodoxy, there is a double imputation: of the sinner's guilt to Christ, and of Christ's obedience to the believer (I:594-596, 605-607; IV:93). Edwards also affirms a limited or definite atonement—Christ died with the specific intention of redeeming the elect (I:604-605).

Edwards does not limit himself to one "theory" of the atonement, however. Particularly striking is his use of the "Ransom" or "Christus Victor" theme reminiscent of the Eastern Fathers (IV:191): "The weapon with which Christ warred against the devil, and obtained a most complete victory and glorious triumph over him, was the cross…The devil had, as it were, swallowed up Christ, as the whale did Jonah; but it was deadly poison to him; he gave him a mortal wound in his own bowels; he was soon sick of his morsel, and forced to vomit him up again."

Secondary treatments of Edwards on the atonement include Haroutunian, *Piety vs. Moralism*, 157-160; Dorus Paul Rudisill, *The Doctrine of the Atonement in Jonathan Edwards and His Successors* (New York: Poseidon Books, 1971), 10-34. Edwards Amasa Park argues at length that the elder Edwards anticipates to some degree the "Governmental Atonement" theory of his New Divinity successors. See Park, "Introductory Essay," in *The Atonement: Discourses and Treatises* (Boston:

In his discussion of imputation, however, Edwards breaks new ground and departs in some important respects from federal orthodoxy. First, the role of faith in justification is significantly recast. Faith is not the "condition" of justification, nor is it the "instrument" whereby the human subject appropriates justification.[49] Rather, faith is the act of union itself from the human perspective. Second, Edwards departs from much of later federal orthodoxy by recasting the mode of imputation and moving decisively away from immediate imputation. While retaining the federal distinction between vital and legal unions, Edwards clearly assigns priority to the vital or spiritual relationship, contending that "the vital union between Christ and true Christians...is much more of a mystery than the relative union, and necessarily implies it."[50] Edwards goes on to observe: "What is real in the union between Christ and his people, is the foundation of what is legal; that is, it is something that is really in them, and between them, uniting them, that is the ground of the suitableness of their being accounted as one by the Judge."[51]

He is careful, however, to say that this "ground" of justification is in no sense a meritorious or analytic foundation. Here the concept of "fitness" via divine constitution is introduced. In the order of creation continually established by God, it is fitting that God justify those who join themselves by faith to Christ for salvation. This "fitness" is rooted in the divine being, and specifically in the divine love of order and beauty.[52] Edwards safeguards the gratuity of synthetic justification by distinguishing between "moral fitness" (the divine recognition of which would involve analytic justification) and a "natural fitness" rooted not in strict moral merit but in this divine love of order.

> A person has a moral fitness for a state, when his moral excellency commends him to it, or when his being put into such a good state is but a fit or suitable testimony of regard or love to the moral excellency, or value, or amiableness of any of his qualifications or acts. A person has a natural fitness for a state, when it appears meet and condecent that he should be in such a state or circumstances, only from the natural concord or agreeableness there is between such

---

Congregational Board of Publication, 1859), xii-xxxix.

[49] As we will see in the discussion of justification and sanctification, Edwards does not reject conditionality language in connection with justification. His point is that faith is not the "condition" of justification in any singular sense in that there are other "conditions" of justification as well, such as good works and perseverance.

"Instrumental" language is rejected by Edwards because of its lack of precision. Edwards finds it less than helpful to speak of one and the same act as the "instrument" of reception and also the reception itself. See *Justification by Faith*, *Works* IV:68.

[50] Ibid., 70.

[51] Ibid., 71.

[52] See ibid., 73. Schafer, "Edwards and Justification," 59, observes that this is an "aesthetic" argument. While there is some truth in this, we must also note that this aesthetic fitness arises out of divine will and wisdom itself, and is thus rooted in the divine being. See Edwards, *The Great Christian Doctrine of Original Sin Defended*, in *The Works of President Edwards*, 4 vols. (New York: Robert Carter, 1868), II:490.

qualifications and such circumstances; not because the qualifications are lovely or unlovely, but only because the qualifications and the circumstances are like one another, or do in their nature, suit and agree or unite one to another.[53]

Another intriguing and important aspect of Edwards' view of justification is his appropriation of the older Reformed theme of the resurrection justification of Christ.[54] He follows Olevian and van Mastricht in viewing the resurrection of Christ as a forensic justification which applies first of all to Christ himself and then, by participation, to the believer.

So Christ, our second surety (in whose justification all who believe in him, and whose surety he is, are virtually justified), was not justified till he had done the work the father had appointed him, and kept the Father's commandments through all trials; and then in his resurrection he was justified. When he that had been put to death in the flesh was quickened by the Spirit, 1 Pet. 3:18, then he that was manifest in the flesh was justified in the Spirit, 1 Tim. 3:16. But God, when he justified him in raising him from the dead, did not only release him from his humiliation for sin, and acquit him from any further suffering or abasement for it, but admitted him to that eternal and immortal life, and to the beginning of that exaltation that was the reward of what he had done. And indeed the justification of the believer is not other than his being admitted to communion in, or participation of the justification of this head and surety of all believers.[55]

Yet we may ask whether Edwards has successfully integrated this theme into his overall presentation of justification. The resurrection justification of Christ plays little role in Edwards' appeal to the "fitness" of justification by faith as determined by a divine "constitution," for the emphasis on divine constitution and sovereignty seems to render the resurrection justification of Christ somewhat superfluous, at least in terms of framing the mode of imputation. Furthermore, Edwards' conception of union focuses on the immediate reception of the Holy Spirit and not on union with the justified incarnate humanity of Christ. The connection between a forensic justification of Christ as the second Adam, the immediate presence of the Holy Spirit, and the forensic justification of the believer is by no means entirely apparent. We shall see below, however, that the resurrection justification of Christ is utilized in a new way. Edwards uses it in his effort against neonomianism and antinomianism, and here it serves to bind justification and sanctification together.

---

[53] Edwards, *Justification by Faith*, *Works* IV:72.

[54] The resurrection justification of Christ plays a role in two of Edwards' works: *Justification by Faith*, *Works* IV:66-67, 95-96, 106; and *Concerning the Perseverance of Saints*, in *The Works of President Edwards*, 4 vols. (New York: Robert Carter, 1868), III:513-514, 522. This aspect of Edwards' doctrine of justification is overlooked by a number of interpreters, including Perry Miller, Thomas A. Schafer, Conrad Cherry, and Samuel Logan. It is briefly noted by Otto, "Justification and Justice," 20, and Gaffin, *Resurrection and Redemption*, 123.

[55] Edwards, *Justification by Faith*, *Works* IV:66.

Imputation and Original Sin

Significantly, in both soteriology and hamartiology Edwards moves steadily in the direction of realistic conceptions of solidarity and away from the Reformed scholastic notion of immediate imputation. In this he represents a marked alternative to federal scholasticism. Edwards' reconceptualization of the doctrine of Original Sin has been extensively treated elsewhere, but several salient points require mention.[56]

In *The Great Christian Doctrine of Original Sin Defended* (1757), Edwards responded to a strategic attack by John Taylor on the weakest point in the federal doctrine of original sin—its conception of the solidarity between Adam and his posterity. Taylor in fact attacked both the realistic and the imputational poles of the federal doctrine of original sin, declaring the notions of inherited depravity and imputed guilt absurd and unjust. Here one finds an individualistic moralism in which human beings are held responsible for their own sins, not the sins of others. Responding to Taylor, Edwards first of all denies that original sin involves a quality that is infused into the soul, like a "taint" or "infection." He asserts that at creation God implanted within human beings two principles—inferior or "natural" (e.g., self-love) and superior or "supernatural" (the fruits of participation in divine love). With the Fall, the superior principles are withheld by God and cease to operate, leaving the inferior principles in control and introducing a tragic distortion into the operation of human faculties.[57] Inherited depravity, according to Edwards, is a matter of subtraction rather than addition.

Edwards' defense of imputed guilt is of particular importance. Responding to Taylor's argument that Adam and his posterity are distinct moral agents and that imputing the sin of one to the other is unjust and absurd, Edwards contends that Adam and his children are in fact one by virtue of a divine constitution, and that the sin of Adam is therefore imputed to his children. Edwards begins by employing the analogy of a tree where root and branches form an organic whole.[58] He goes on to argue that the communication of depravity and guilt is

---

[56]See, e.g., Frank Hugh Foster, *A Genetic History of the New England Theology* (Chicago: University of Chicago Press, 1907), 82-90; Miller, *Jonathan Edwards*, 265-282; H. Shelton Smith, *Changing Conceptions of Original Sin* (New York: Charles Scribner's Sons, 1955), 10-36; Murray, *Imputation of Adam's Sin*, 52-64; Clyde A. Holbrook, "Original Sin and the Enlightenment," in *The Heritage of Christian Thought: Essays in Honor of Robert Lowry Calhoun*, ed. Robert E. Cushman and Egil Grislis (New York: Harper & Row, 1965), 142-165; C. Samuel Storms, *Tragedy in Eden: Original Sin in the Theology of Jonathan Edwards* (Lanham, Md.: University Press of America, 1983); Randall E. Otto, "The Solidarity of Mankind in Jonathan Edwards' Doctrine of Original Sin," *Evangelical Quarterly* 62 (1990): 205-221.

[57]Edwards, *Original Sin*, *Works* II:476-481. Edwards of course realized that this resembled the Thomistic nature-grace view of original sin in which a *donum superadditum* was lost at the Fall. Despite his attempts distinguish his view from that of Thomas, the practical differences appear minimal. See also Miller, *Edwards*, 274-275.

[58]See Edwards, *Original Sin*, *Works* II:481.

grounded in a relationship of personal identity that is divinely constituted.

> From which it will follow, that both guilt, or exposedness to punishment, and also depravity of heart, came upon Adam's posterity just as they came upon him, as much as if he and they had all coexisted, like a tree with many branches...I think this will naturally follow on the supposition of there being a constituted *oneness* or *identity* of Adam and his posterity in this affair.[59]

But here the problems of justice and intelligibility must be addressed, and Edwards embarks on an extensive discussion of the nature of this constituted identity. He begins by suggesting that the notion of identity is a rather complex matter. For example, a hundred-year-old tree may not share a single atom with the sprout from which it grew, yet both sprout and tree share an identity according to the divinely constituted law of nature.[60] The personal identity of intelligent beings is more complicated still, Edwards concedes, for personal identity implies an identity of consciousness and a shared nature or substance. But even here, Edwards maintains that personal identity is only by divine constitution.[61] Behind this argument, of course, is Edwards' idealist ontology discussed above. Edwards, we will recall, was an omnicausalist for whom the only truly subsistent substance is God, and for whom all finite reality is the result of continuous creation *ex nihilo*.[62] Thus all continuity, personal and otherwise, stems from immediate divine agency and constitution.

> And there is no identity or oneness in the case, but what depends on the *arbitrary* constitution of the Creator; who by his wise sovereign establishment so unites these successive new effects, that he *treats them as one*, by communicating to them like properties, relations and circumstances; and so leads *us* to regard and treat them as *one*. When I call this an *arbitrary constitution*, I mean, it is a constitution which depends on nothing but the *divine will*; which divine will depends on nothing but the *divine wisdom*. In this sense, the whole *course of nature*, with all that belongs to it, all its laws and methods, and constancy and regularity, continuance and proceeding, is an *arbitrary constitution*...
>
> Thus it appears, if we consider matters strictly, there is no such thing as any identity or oneness in created objects, existing at different times but what depends on *God's sovereign constitution*.[63]

Having established the theoretical groundwork for the identity of Adam and

---

[59] Ibid., 481.

[60] Ibid., 486-87.

[61] Ibid., 487.

[62] Ibid., 489: "It will follow from what has been observed, that God's upholding created substance, or causing its existence in each successive moment, is altogether equivalent to an *immediate production out of nothing*, at each moment. Because its existence at this moment is not merely in part from God, but wholly from him, and not in any part or degree, from its *antecedent existence*."

[63] Ibid., 490.

his posterity, Edwards goes on to argue that the requisite identity of substance and consciousness does obtain between Adam and his posterity in that they share the "same depravity of disposition." Identity of consciousness is evident in that the posterity of Adam give a full and hearty consent to the first sin of Adam at the earliest possible moment in their own existence. Attendant to depravity of disposition there is "the first existence of an evil disposition of heart, amounting to a full consent to Adam's sin."[64]

Edwards then explains the imputation of Adam's sin. Just as in soteriological imputation, the real has priority over the legal. Edwards takes particular issue with the classical federal contention that depravity of heart is a consequence of imputed guilt. For him, imputation does not ground depravity, as classical federalism had asserted. Rather, the real union between Adam and his posterity has the priority. Here Edwards reasons from the constituted *identity* involved.

> The first being of an evil disposition in the heart of a child of Adam, whereby he is disposed to *approve* of the sin of his first father, as fully as he himself approved of it when he committed it, or so far as to imply a full and perfect *consent* of heart to it, I think, is not to be looked upon as a consequence of the imputation of that first sin...but rather *prior* to it in the order of nature. Indeed the derivation of the evil disposition to the hearts of Adam's posterity, or rather the *coexistence* of the evil disposition, implied in Adam's first rebellion, in the *root* and *branches*, is a consequence of the *union* that the wise author of the world has established between Adam and his posterity; but not properly a *consequence* of the *imputation* of his sin; nay, rather *antecedent* to it, as it was in Adam himself.[65]

In short, Edwards maintains that the sin of Adam is imputed to his posterity precisely because it is theirs: "And therefore the sin of the apostasy is not theirs, merely because God *imputes* it to them; but it is *truly* and *properly* theirs, and on that *ground*, God imputes it to them."[66]

Two general observations may be made at this point. First of all, the extent of Edwards' departure from classical federalism must be appreciated. The federal doctrine of immediate hamartiological imputation intended to explain how those who are personally distinct from Adam may nevertheless be charged with Adam's sin. Edwards, however, maintains that Adam's posterity is charged with the offense because it is theirs. Hamartiological imputation, for Edwards, consists of an analytic judgment grounded in a realistic, divinely constituted identity.[67]

---

[64]Ibid., 483. See also pp. 492-93.
[65]Ibid., 482.
[66]Ibid., 493.
[67]The precise nature of imputation here has been a matter of considerable dispute, doubtless because of the complexity of Edwards' proposal. Some suggest that Edwards taught mediate imputation consequent on inherited depravity. See William Cunningham, *The Reformers and the Theology of the Reformation* (Edinburgh: T. & T. Clark, 1866),

While Edwards sometimes uses the language of federal orthodoxy, he tends to recast it and turn it to his own use. Adam is the "federal head" and "surety" of the race; the divine constitution is termed a "covenant" with Adam, and so forth.[68] But when the matter was finally settled, Edwards found the classic federal view of solidarity inadequate. F. H. Foster writes:

> Yet he [Edwards] cannot accept the common view that men are charged with something which they have not done, any more than Taylor. Sin is imputed, he therefore says, but not in order to make it the sin of all men. It is imputed because it is the sin of all men, for they have committed it in Adam.[69]

Second, Edwards' proposal is also striking for the extraordinary weight it places on divine sovereignty. Despite the seemingly organic character of the tree illustration and other metaphors used by Edwards, there is nothing in the humanity of Adam or his posterity that in itself accounts for the transmission of depravity. Edwards nowhere develops a theory of "generic humanity," and he explicitly rejects the theory of an inherited "taint" in favor of pure privation Any solidarity is due to divine agency and constitution rooted in the divine wisdom. In actuality, Edwards' thought at this point is not organic at all. We will see that this emphasis on divine sovereignty is accentuated by Edwards' New Divinity successors, but diminishes in the New Haven theology of Timothy Dwight and Nathaniel William Taylor.

The Relation of Justification and Sanctification

In the work of Jonathan Edwards we find, despite his Reformed heritage, a much closer relationship of justification and sanctification than is typical of federal orthodoxy. Working as he was in a context dominated by conflict between antinomianism and legalism, Edwards struggled to formulate his soteriology in such a way that works of evangelical obedience and perseverance in faith stand in a *positive* relation to justification but without making obedience and perseverance the meritorious condition of that justification.

The difficulty of this task is compounded by the fact that Edwards imported certain fundamental aspects of the classical *ordo salutis* from his Reformed orthodox predecessors. Against the Arminians, he accepted the static and punctiliar conception of justification: "the sinner is actually and finally justified

---

384. Charles Hodge finds Edwards to be inconsistent, teaching immediate imputation at some points, mediate imputation at others, and realistic identity at still others. See Hodge, *Systematic Theology*, II:207-208. A few have even concluded that Edwards taught immediate imputation. See Murray, *Imputation of Adam's Sin*, 52-64.

[68]See, e.g., *Original Sin, Works* II:481, 485-486; *Perseverance of Saints, Works* III:512; *Justification by Faith, Works* IV:93.

[69]Foster, *Genetic History*, 87. See also Hodge, *Systematic Theology*, II:217-220; Smith, *Changing Conceptions of Original Sin*, 35; Otto, "Solidarity of Mankind," 211-215.

on the first act of faith."[70] But against antinomianism Edwards rejects the traditional Reformed orthodox view that perseverance and evangelical obedience are to be viewed simply as a *conditio sine qua non* of justification. Sanctification is not merely an inevitable concomitant of justification but rather stands in positive relation to it.

> Perseverance is acknowledged by Calvinian divines, to be necessary to salvation. Yet it seems to me, that the manner in which it is necessary has not been sufficiently set forth. It is owned to be necessary as a *sine qua non*: and also is expressed by this, that though it is not that by which we first come to have a title to eternal life, yet it is necessary in order to the actual possession of it, as the way to it; that it is as impossible we should come to it without perseverance, as it is impossible for a man to go to a city or town, without travelling throughout the road that leads to it. But we are really saved by perseverance; so that salvation has a dependence on perseverance, as that which influences in the affair.[71]

Edwards approaches this matter of positive "influence" and "dependence" in at least three discernibly different, though complementary, ways. First, he grounds the necessity of evangelical obedience and perseverance in divine constitution: "God has respect to the believer's continuance in faith, and he is justified by that, as though it already were, because by divine establishment it shall follow; and it being by divine constitution connected with that first faith, as much as if it were a property in it, it is then considered as such."[72] Again, this divine constitution is rooted in a fitness determined by the divine wisdom. Perseverance in faith is "one thing on which the fitness of acceptance to life depends."[73] Second, Edwards expands the scope of faith in a manner that would doubtless have surprised his Reformed predecessors. Faith, for Edwards, apparently can include not just the traditional assent and trust, but also repentance and even the works of evangelical obedience that flow from faith. Thus faith is defined as "a thorough believing of what the gospel reveals of a Saviour of sinners, as true and perfectly good, with the exercises of an answerable disposition towards him."[74] Repentance and turning from sin are "of the essence of justifying faith."[75] In a particularly striking passage, Edwards suggests that works of love are themselves acts of union with Christ.

---

[70] Edwards, *Justification by Faith*, *Works* IV:104.

[71] Edwards, *Perseverance of the Saints*, *Works* III:515. In *Justification by Faith*, *Works* IV:106, Edwards writes: "And that perseverance in faith is thus necessary to salvation, not merely as a *sine qua non*, or as a universal concomitant of it, but by reason of such an influence and dependence, seems manifest by many Scriptures."

[72] Edwards, *Justification by Faith*, *Works* IV:104.

[73] Ibid. See also *Perseverance of Saints*, *Works* III:515-517.

[74] Edwards, *Observations Concerning Faith*, *Works* II:625. In this same passage Edwards takes issue with the Reformed schoolbook tradition (here Thomas Goodwin) which rejects as "wicked" the Roman Catholic view that "love is the form and soul of faith." See also Cherry, *Theology*, 134-35; Schafer, "Edwards and Justification," 59-61.

[75] Edwards, *Justification by Faith*, *Works* IV:120-121.

The obedience of a Christian, so far as it is truly evangelical, and performed with the Spirit of the Son sent forth into the heart, has all relation to Christ, the Mediator, and is but an expression of the soul's believing union to Christ. All evangelical works of that faith that worketh by love; and every such act of obedience, wherein it is inward and the act of the soul, is only a new, effective act of reception of Christ, an adherence to the glorious Saviour.[76]

If this were all that Edwards had to say on the matter he might well be accused of an abstract fatalism on the one hand (for his appeal to divine constitution) and legalism (because of his expansion of faith). But a third approach to the matter is evident as the relationship between sanctification and justification is also grounded christologically and in the believer's union with Christ, a matter that requires careful examination. Edwards argues from the integrity of the person of Christ and of his offices, noting first of all that faith means accepting Christ not just as Priest but also as King: "Accepting Christ as a priest and king, cannot be separated. They not only cannot be separated, or be asunder in their subject, but they cannot be considered as separate things in their natures; for they are implied one in another."[77]

The inseparability of justification and sanctification is also rooted in the believer's participation in Christ as the second Adam, the one who is both justified and who persevered in faith and obedience. In developing this Edwards initially seems to present a circular argument. On the one hand, a person cannot be justified without perseverance, for it is a condition of justification: *"Perseverance* in faith is, in one sense, the condition of justification, that is, the promise of acceptance is made only to a persevering sort of faith, and the proper evidence of its being of that sort is actual perseverance."[78] On the other hand, Edwards also asserts in the same work that perseverance is contingent upon justification: "It is evident the saints shall persevere, because they are already justified."[79] The key to this, according to Edwards, is a christology in which vicarious perseverance and justification reside in a single person, namely Christ himself.

Adam would not have been justified till he had fulfilled and done his work...So, Christ having done our work for us, we are justified as soon as ever we believe in him, as being, through what he has accomplished and finished, now already actually entitled to the reward of life. And justification carries in it not only remission of sins, but also a being adjudged to life, or accepted as entitled by righteousness to the reward of life; as is evident, because believers are justified by communion with Christ in his justification, which he received when he was raised from the dead. But that justification of Christ which he was then the subject of, did most certainly imply both these things, viz., his being now judged free of that guilt which he had taken upon him, and also his having now fulfilled all

---

[76]Ibid., 106-7.
[77]Edwards, *Observations Concerning Faith, Works* II:629.
[78]Edwards, *Perseverance of Saints, Works* III:510.
[79]Ibid., 513.

righteousness, his having perfectly obeyed the Father, and done enough to entitle him to the reward of life as our head and surety; and therefore he then had eternal life given him as our head...Christ was then justified in the same sense that Adam would have been justified, if he had finished his course of perfect obedience; and therefore implies in it confirmation to a title to life, as tha[t] would have done; and thus, all those that are risen with Christ, and have him for their surety, and so are justified in his justification, are certainly in like manner confirmed.[80]

Edwards is careful, however, to avoid any suggestion that perseverance is a meritorious work undertaken in order to earn salvation. Again, a deep christocentrism is evident: the persevering soul must constantly look to Christ in faith, to the one who himself has persevered on the Christian's behalf and who is able to keep the Christian in the way of faith: "The believing soul is convinced of its own weakness and helplessness, its inability to resist its enemies, its insufficiency to keep itself, and so commits itself to Christ, that he would be its keeper."[81]

Edwards also had to deal with an obligatory question—the problem of reconciling Paul and James. It was to the second chapter of the Epistle of James that both the Roman Catholics and the Arminians of Edwards' day looked for particular comfort. Edwards adopts the common Reformed scholastic solution holding that Paul and James speak of different types of justification—Paul referring to forensic justification before God and James to a vindication of the Christian before human beings (termed by Edwards a "manifestative justification").

> To be justified, is to be approved and accepted: but a man may be said to be approved and accepted in two respects; the one is to be approved really, and the other to be approved and accepted declaratively. Justification is twofold; it is either the acceptance and approbation of the judge itself, or the manifestation of that approbation, by a sentence of judgment declared by the judge, either to our own consciences or to the world. If justification be understood in the former sense, for the approbation itself, that is only that by which we become fit to be approved: but if it be understood in the latter sense, for the manifestation of this approbation, it is by whatever is a proper evidence of that fitness...So in the sense in which the Apostle James seems to use the word *justify* for *manifestative justification*, a man is justified not only by faith but also by works; as a tree is manifested to be good, not only by immediately examining the tree, but also by the fruit.[82]

Edwards' adoption of this solution indicates the extent to which he continued to

---

[80]Ibid., 513-514; see also p. 522.

[81]Ibid., 514.

[82]Edwards, *Justification by Faith*, *Works* IV:125-26. Edwards may be dependent on Francis Turretin, *Institutio*, XVI.8.3. Elsewhere Edwards, *Observations Concerning Faith*, *Works* II:630-631, cites Puritan divine Thomas Manton (1620-1677). On this, see also Cherry, *Theology*, 138.

hold to the classical Reformed *ordo salutis*, with punctiliar justification occurring at the moment of an initial act of faith.

Summary—Edwards on Union with Christ

Edwards' relation to the federal theology tradition of Reformed orthodoxy is clearly complex. On the one hand, there is considerable continuity. He continues to utilize much of the language and terminology of the federal tradition, and he perpetuates the federal bifurcation of the *unio Christi* by speaking of "legal" and "vital" unions. Consistent with later federalism, union with Christ is defined largely in terms of faith and the work of the Holy Spirit, and the humanity of Christ is largely eclipsed as a theological factor. Finally, Edwards to a considerable degree accepts the *ordo salutis* framework by framing justification in static and punctiliar terms, though he then strives mightily to relate justification and ongoing renewal of life in some positive way.

The discontinuities are of even greater importance, particularly as we seek to understand the development of the New England theological trajectory. Divine grace is recast in terms of immediate, uncreated grace. The subtle balance of nature and grace involving the infusion of gracious habits, so characteristic of federal orthodoxy, is lost. Edwards also expands the scope of faith to include its "exercises," or the works that flow from faith, in ways that would doubtless have disquieted his Reformed predecessors.

The most significant shifts from federal orthodoxy involve imputation. In the context of original sin, the federal theory of hamartiological imputation is rejected in favor of a form of realistic identity rooted in divine constitution. On the soteriological side, Edwards departs from the federal consensus by according vital union priority over the legal union, thus giving sanctification explicit precedence in the *ordo salutis* over justification. Furthermore, as we survey Edwards' doctrine of justification we find a not altogether comfortable synthesis of the early and more dynamic Reformed biblical theology (concern for the humanity and resurrection justification of Christ, the continuous reception of Christ by faith) with the later static scholastic federalism (*ordo salutis*, punctiliar justification, etc.).

Despite the fact that much of Edwards' work was ostensibly directed against the neonomian Arminian threat, it appears that he was even more concerned to meet the Antinomianism of the revivalist left wing. This is doubtless due, not only to the fact that New Light Antinomianism was a considerable force in the post-Awakening situation, but also because Edwards and his fellow Calvinists with their federal theology legacy were persistently accused of antinomian tendencies by their Arminian opponents.[83] In order to obviate the practical

---

[83]Breitenbach, "Piety and Moralism," 186, observes that Edwards "realized that to defeat Arminianism, he had to devise a Calvinistic theology free from any taint of Antinomianism. Edwards's perception of the vulnerability of traditional New England

threat of legalism implicit in some of his contra-antinomian formulations, Edwards persistently accentuates the role of the divine—in every discussion of imputation and of "conditions" of justification he makes appeals to divine constitution rooted in a fitness determined by the divine wisdom, for this emphasis undercuts the notion of human merit before God.[84]

Other shifts can be cited as well. For example, the eclipse of the sacraments evident in later Puritanism is accelerated in Edwards and his successors, doubtless in part because of their revivalistic context, in part because of their opposition to the "converting-ordinance" sacramental theology of the Half-Way Covenant, and in part because of their extraordinary emphasis on divine sovereignty and immediate, uncreated grace, which tended to eclipse the sacramental means of grace.[85] The larger trend is clear, however. In a religious context dominated by conflict between neonomian and antinomian tendencies, the federal notions of legal solidarity and imputation were found wanting by Edwards. And this trend continues in the writings of his New England successors.

Calvinism to charges of Antinomianism pushed him in creative new directions during the 1750's." Breitenbach does not explore Edwards' revisioning of the doctrines of union with Christ and justification, and we would only observe here that Edwards' creativity at these points begins, not in the 1750's, but in the 1730's.

[84]Schafer, "Edwards and Justification," 59, notes that "Edwards was evidently not worried about making inherent states and qualities in the soul conditions of salvation so long as they were relieved of all meritorious connotations."

[85]For example, Edwards' view of the Lord's Supper is thoroughly Zwinglian. The elements symbolize an absent Christ; they do not mediate a real presence: "The sacramental elements in the Lord's Supper do represent Christ as a party in covenant, as truly as a *proxy* represents a prince to a foreign lady in her marriage; and our taking those elements is as truly a professing to accept Christ, as in the other case the lady's taking the proxy is her professing to accept the prince as her husband. Or the matter may more fitly be represented by this similitude: it is as if a prince should send an ambassador to a woman in a foreign land, proposing marriage, and by his ambassador should send her his *picture*, and should desire her to manifest her acceptance of his suit, not only by professing her acceptance in words to his ambassador, but in token of her sincerity openly to take or accept that picture, and so seal her profession, by thus representing the matter over again by a symbolical action." Jonathan Edwards, *An Humble Inquiry into the Rules of the Word of God, Concerning the Qualifications Requisite to a Complete Standing and Full Communion in the Visible Christian Church*, in *The Works of President Edwards*, 4 vols. (New York: Robert Carter and Brothers, 1868), I:146.

CHAPTER 4

Later New England Thought: Samuel Hopkins and Timothy Dwight

The death of Jonathan Edwards at Princeton in 1758 by no means put an end to the theological trajectory he initiated. New England pastors and educators such as Samuel Hopkins (1721-1803), Joseph Bellamy (1719-1790), Nathanael Emmons (1745-1840), John Smalley (1738-1808), Samuel Spring (1746-1819), Stephen West (1735-1818), and Jonathan Edwards, Jr. (1745-1801) carried on the theological interests of Edwards the elder, albeit with some significant shifts in emphasis. These New England successors of Edwards were referred to as "Consistent Calvinists," "Edwardseans," and "Hopkinsians," and their theology as a "New Divinity."

The New Divinity has been subjected to a variety of appraisals by nineteenth- and twentieth-century scholarship, and a major issue here has been the New Divinity's consistency, or lack thereof, with the thought of the elder Edwards. During the nineteenth century this was not a merely academic dispute, for, as Mark Noll has shown, both Congregationalists and New School Presbyterians on the one hand, and Old School Presbyterians on the other, contended for the mantle of the esteemed President Edwards.[1] Twentieth-century scholarship is also mixed. Frank Hugh Foster's *A Genetic History of the New England Theology* (1907) found considerable continuity between Edwards and his New Divinity successors, but the prevailing tendency during this period was to highlight the discontinuities between Edwards and his New Divinity successors. In 1932, Joseph Haroutunian argued that the New Divinity theologians replaced Edwards' theocentric piety with an anthropocentric moralism which paved the way for the incipient New England liberalism of Nathaniel William Taylor.[2] A bit later, Sidney Mead came to strikingly different conclusions. For him, the New Divinity represented the rationalization and desiccation of Edwards' thought. It was the "extraction by these unimaginative men of hard and solid metaphysical entities from Edwards'

---

[1] See Mark A. Noll, "Jonathan Edwards and Nineteenth-Century Theology," in *Jonathan Edwards and the American Experience*, ed. Nathan O. Hatch and Harry S. Stout (New York: Oxford University Press, 1988, 260-287. See also Joseph Conforti, "Antebellum Evangelicals and the Cultural Revival of Jonathan Edwards," *American Presbyterians* 64 (1986): 227-241.

[2] Haroutunian, *Piety Versus Moralism*.

writings...and pushing his implications without poetic insight to their logical, though bitter, limits."[3]

Since the mid-twentieth century, however, the increasing tendency has been to view the New Divinity thinkers more sympathetically as standing in at least partial continuity with Edwards. Joseph Conforti and William Breitenbach recognize that the New Divinity writers engaged in a vigorous theological and philosophical defense of absolute divine sovereignty, but that they also partook of the increasingly anthropocentrism, individualism, and moralism of the times in which they lived. Thus Conforti remarks that the "New Divinity was Janus-faced."[4] In their own ways, both Conforti and Breitenbach maintain that the New Divinity was concerned to do justice to both theocentric piety and moralism, an insight we have found useful here. Breitenbach also helpfully calls attention to the New Divinity polemics against the older Reformed federal theology.

Samuel Hopkins

Often referred to as the "codifier" of the Edwardsean New Divinity movement, Samuel Hopkins (1721-1803) was a student of the elder Edwards, his first biographer, and his literary executor. His theology, particularly as expressed in his *System of Doctrines* (1793), was exceedingly influential in New England, and "Hopkinsian" became a standard descriptive term for at least a portion of the Edwardsean school.[5]

---

[3]Sidney Earl Mead, *Nathaniel William Taylor, 1768-1858: A Connecticut Liberal* (Chicago: University of Chicago Press, 1942), 16.

[4]Joseph A. Conforti, *Samuel Hopkins and the New Divinity Movement* (Grand Rapids: Christian University Press, 1981), 118. See also his "Samuel Hopkins and the New Divinity: Theology, Ethics, and Social Reform in Eighteenth-Century New England," *William and Mary Quarterly* 34 (1977): 572-589; William K. Breitenbach, "The New Divinity and the Era of Moral Accountability" (Ph.D. diss., Yale University, 1978); "The Consistent Calvinism of the New Divinity Movement," *William and Mary Quarterly* 41 (1984):241-264; "Piety and Moralism."

Allen C. Guelzo also argues for a striking degree of continuity between the elder Edwards and his New Divinity successors. See his "Jonathan Edwards and the New Divinity: Change and Continuity in New England Calvinism, 1758-1858," in *Pressing Toward the Mark: Essays Commemorating Fifty Years of the Orthodox Presbyterian Church*, ed. Charles G. Dennison and Richard C. Gamble (Philadelphia: The Committee for the Historian of the Orthodox Presbyterian Church, 1986), 147-167. Most recently, Douglas A. Sweeney, *Nathaniel Taylor, New Haven Theology, and the Legacy of Jonathan Edwards* (New York: Oxford University Press, 2003), has convincingly argued for the continuity of an Edwardsean "theological culture" stretching from Jonathan Edwards to Nathaniel William Taylor.

[5]Unless otherwise noted, quotations from Samuel Hopkins are from his *The System of Doctrines, Contained in Divine Revelation, Explained and Defended*, second ed., 2 vols. (Boston: Lincoln and Edmands, 1811).

Hopkins' Contribution to New England Theology

Despite his obvious regard for his teacher, Hopkins was not content merely to recapitulate the theology of Jonathan Edwards. Three significant departures from the theology of Edwards demand our attention. First, in what turned out to be a highly significant move, Hopkins modified the definition of true virtue. Edwards had defined true virtue as "benevolence to Being in general."[6] And since Edwards' Neo-Platonic ontology implied that "God himself is in effect Being in general," he asserted that "true virtue must consist chiefly in love to God: the Being of Beings, infinitely the greatest and best of Beings."[7] Thus Edwards presents a highly theocentric view of ethics and virtue. He also closely associates ethics and aesthetics—virtue is defined in part by its beauty,[8] and like many other ethical theorists of his day he utilizes the concept of self-love, at least as a natural principle useful for the ordering of society.[9]

Hopkins, however, had a deep interest in the practical dimensions of piety, and Edwards' conception of virtue seemed to provide an insufficient basis for social ethics. He therefore defined sin as consisting in self-love, and he redefined virtue as "disinterested benevolence," as "love to God and our neighbors," and as "friendly affection to all intelligent beings."[10] This theory of

---

Biographical treatments of Hopkins include Stephen West, ed., *Sketches of the Life of the Late Rev. Samuel Hopkins, D.D., Pastor of the First Congregational Church in Newport, Written by Himself; Interspersed with Marginal Notes Extracted from His Private Diary* (Hartford, Conn.: Hudson and Goodwin, 1805); Edwards Amasa Park, *Memoir of the Life and Character of Samuel Hopkins, D.D.* (Boston: Doctrinal Tract and Book Society, 1854); Conforti, *Samuel Hopkins and the New Divinity Movement*.

[6]Edwards, *Nature of True Virtue, Works* II:262.

[7]Ibid., 301, 266.

[8]Ibid., 300: "That which is called *virtue*, is a certain kind of beautiful nature, form or quality that is observed in things." See also 262-63, 297.

[9]See ibid., 298-299. On this see Conforti, *Samuel Hopkins*, 113-116; Fiering, *Edwards's Moral Thought and Its British Context*, (Chapel Hill: University of North Carolina Press, 1981), 150-199; Stephen Garrard Post, *Christian Love and Self-Denial: An Historical and Normative Study of Jonathan Edwards, Samuel Hopkins, and American Theological Ethics* (Lanham, Md.: University Press of America, 1987).

[10]Samuel Hopkins, *An Inquiry into the Nature of True Holiness* (Newport: Solomon Southwick, 1773), 16; quoted in Conforti, *Samuel Hopkins*, 117. See also *System of Doctrines*, I:465-91. For a discussion of sin as consisting in self-love, see *System of Doctrines*, I:289-97.

The connection between "disinterested benevolence" and Hopkins' concern for social order and ethics is evident in *System of Doctrines* I:490, where he argues that the one so characterized "is devoted to the good of the public, and of the society to which he belongs, being ready to give up his private, personal interest, in any part or the whole of it, when the public interest demands it, and this is necessary for the good of the whole. This disinterested benevolence will lead every one to take his proper place, and to be industrious, active, prudent and faithful in his own business, and honest, upright, sincere and true in all his concerns and dealings with his fellow men."

virtue had implications both for Hopkins' anthropology and theology proper, and gave rise to one of the New Divinity distinctives—evidence of such disinterested benevolence on the part of human beings is the willingness of the truly regenerate to be damned for the glory of God.

> He who has a new heart, and universal disinterested benevolence, will be a friend to God, and must be pleased with his infinitely benevolent character, though he see not the least evidence, and has not a thought that God loves him, and designs to save him. And if he could know that God designed, for his own glory and the general good, to cast him into endless destruction; this would not make him cease to approve of his character; he would continue to be a friend of God, and to be pleased with his moral perfection.[11]

As the preceding quote indicates, Hopkins went on to maintain that the divine nature is also characterized by "disinterested benevolence."[12] In short, God is the benevolent moral governor of the universe, administering it for the ultimate good of human beings. Edwards' theocentric universe has given way to anthropocentrism, and as Conforti observes, at this point Hopkins "Arminianized Edwards's thought."[13] As we will see below, this understanding of the moral character of God would have a profound impact on Hopkins' doctrine of the atonement and applied soteriology.

Hopkins also accentuated the theme of divine sovereignty in ways that went significantly beyond his teacher Edwards. Seeking to safeguard both the sovereignty and the benevolent moral government of God, he adopted the supralapsarian position that God positively wills sin, rather than merely permits it, as the means of achieving the greatest good.[14] Further emphasizing divine sovereignty, Hopkins argued that regeneration is in no way conditioned upon the prior use of the means of grace—it is "a sovereign, undeserved, and unpromised favour" which is "wrought not gradually, but at once."[15] Against both the traditional Old Calvinists and the Arminians, who emphasized the use

---

Hopkins was a social reformer of some note. Even prior to the Revolution he preached against the slave trade. See Conforti, *Samuel Hopkins*, 125-158; David S. Lovejoy, "Samuel Hopkins: Religion, Slavery and the Revolution," *New England Quarterly* 40 (1967): 227-243; David E. Swift, "Samuel Hopkins: Calvinist Social Concern in Eighteenth-Century New England," *Journal of Presbyterian History* 47 (1969): 31-54.

[11]Hopkins, *System of Doctrines*, I:479. See also Foster, *Genetic History*, 154-158.

[12]Hopkins, *System of Doctrines*, I:308-309.

[13]Conforti, *Samuel Hopkins*, 117.

[14]See Samuel Hopkins, *Sin, thro' Divine Interposition, an Advantage to the Universe* (Boston: Daniel and John Kneeland, 1759). Edwards had followed the majority of Reformed theologians in viewing the divine decree regarding sin as one of permission. See Edwards, *Original Sin*, *Works* II:483.

[15]Hopkins, *System of Doctrines* I:452, 458. Regarding Hopkins' exaltation of divine sovereignty, see Stephen E. Berk, *Calvinism vs. Democracy: Timothy Dwight and the Origins of American Evangelical Orthodoxy* (Hamden, Ct.: Archon Books, 1974), 58.

of the means of grace (prayer, Bible reading, church attendance, etc.) as a preparation for conversion, Hopkins asserted that the awakened sinner who utilizes such means is more vile in the sight of God than the unawakened sinner.[16]

While Hopkins' view of the moral condition of the awakened sinner seemed perverse to the ecclesiastical sensibilities of his Old Calvinist contemporaries, it reveals some of his distinctive concerns. Wanting to safeguard divine sovereignty and further revivalist piety while avoiding both Arminian legalism and antinomianism, Hopkins utilizes Edwards' distinction between natural and moral inability to maintain both a form of human ability and total depravity. Adam's sin results in a total depravity of heart and will for his posterity. The problem is not that sinners *cannot* come, but that they *will not* come.[17] Hopkins therefore sought to remove any external impediments from the sinner's path to conversion, and preaching the use of means as a duty preliminary to conversion appeared to be such an impediment—it distracts sinners from their only duty, which is to repent and believe, and it fosters a false notion of inability which then serves as an excuse.[18] One also detects here, of course, a continuation of Edwards' conflict with the Old Calvinists over the Half-Way Covenant and the use of the means of grace. This continued reshaping of Calvinist soteriology along revivalist lines had the effect of further marginalizing the traditional means of grace, including the sacraments, from applied soteriology.

A third New Divinity contribution evident in the work of Samuel Hopkins is the governmental atonement theory, a matter regarded by several interpreters as the most distinctive contribution of the New England theology.[19] Here he follows his colleague Joseph Bellamy in advocating a view first propounded by the Dutch Arminian jurist Hugo Grotius (1583-1645) and later adopted by English Puritan divine Richard Baxter (1615-91).[20] The governmental theory maintains that God is to be viewed as a benevolent and loving moral governor

---

[16] Hopkins' views on this matter were first aired in his *An Inquiry Concerning the Promises of the Gospel* (Boston: W. M'Alpine and J. Fleeming, 1765); they are reiterated in *System of Doctrines* II:102-113.

The larger context of this controversy is treated in Conforti, *Samuel Hopkins*, 59-75; and William Breitenbach, "Unregenerate Doings: Selflessness and Selfishness in New Divinity Theology," *American Quarterly* 34 (1982): 479-502.

[17] Hopkins, *System of Doctrines*, I:260-289. In the interests of preserving moral accountability, Hopkins differs somewhat from Edwards by drawing a stronger distinction between moral powers (the will, which is depraved) and the natural powers (such as the intellect, which is not). See ibid., I:281. In this he moves in the direction of a faculty psychology. See Breitenbach, "Unregenerate Doings," 484.

[18] See Hopkins, *System of Doctrines* II:111.

[19] See, e.g., Park, "Introductory Essay," ix; Foster, *Genetic History*, 113-117.

[20] See Hugo Grotius, *A Defense of the Catholic Faith concerning the Satisfaction of Christ, against Faustus Socinus*, trans. Frank Hugh Foster (Andover, Mass.: W. F. Draper, 1889). Foster, *Genetic History*, 114, notes that both Grotius and Baxter were read in eighteenth-century New England.

rather than an offended, wrathful deity. God wishes to pardon sinners but cannot do so without a public display of punishment as a deterrent to wrongdoing. Thus, the death of Christ is not the satisfaction of a debt owed by sinners, but rather an exercise in deterrence designed to show God's disapproval of sin and to uphold the divine moral government of the universe.[21]

Several corollaries are implied by this general theory. First, a governmental atonement is in principle universal in scope. Reformed theology as codified at Dordt and Westminster had maintained that Christ died with the specific intention of saving the elect (many, of course, conceded that Christ's death was *sufficient* to atone for the sins the world, but was *efficient* only for the elect).[22] But this "limited" or "definite atonement" presupposes that Christ paid the penalty or debt owed by sinners, and no such limitation of scope applies if Christ's death is simply a demonstration that God disapproves of sin in general.[23]

Second, the notion of soteriological imputation has no real place in this scheme. Because Christ does not substitute in the strict sense for the sinner, there is no negative imputation of human sin to Christ, and no positive imputation of Christ's righteousness to the believer. Having satisfied the demands of general or public justice in Christ's death, God merely forgives the sinner.[24]

---

[21] It was common for the New Divinity thinkers to distinguish different types of justice. Jonathan Edwards, Jr. distinguishes "commutative justice" (having to do with commercial transactions), "distributive justice" (having to do with reward and punishment for personal moral conduct), and "general or public justice" (involving that which is agreeable to the good of the universe). For New Divinity thinkers, the Atonement involves general or public justice, and not commutative or distributive justice. See Jonathan Edwards, Jr., "Three Sermons on the Necessity of Atonement, and the Consistency between That and Free Grace in Forgiveness," in *The Atonement: Discourses and Treatises*, ed. Edwards A. Park (Boston: Congregational Board of Publication, 1859), 20-25.

[22] See Canons of Dordt, II:1-9, in Schaff, *Creeds of Christendom*, III:586-7; Westminster Confession of Faith, 8:5, 6, 8.

[23] For Hopkins' affirmation of a general atonement, see *System of Doctrines*, I:449; II:93.

[24] See ibid., II:73-79. Hopkins writes (II:73-74): "In the justification of the believer by the righteousness of Christ, it does not become his righteousness, so as that he is considered as having actually done and suffered, in his own person, what Christ did and suffered; for this is in no sense true, and cannot be made true...It would be needless to mention this particular, if some had not entertained this notion of the imputation of the righteousness of Christ, and represented it in this very absurd light." Hopkins redefines "imputation" as the way Christ's work "avails to procure all these benefits for them, in consequence of their union to him by faith" (I:429).

While Hopkins sometimes uses the terminology of the earlier Reformed theory (e.g., "propitiation" and "imputation"), close examination reveals significant differences. Christ's "propitiation" merely satisfies rectoral justice and does not satisfy the deity's wrath against sin. Similarly, the "imputation" of Christ's righteousness is simply favor

Third, there is a striking emphasis on the sufferings and atonement of Christ rather than on his lifelong obedience. The atonement, properly considered, consists only in the sufferings of Christ, and does not include his obedience: "The obedience of Christ, though most excellent and meritorious, is not an atonement for the sins of men, or really any part of it."[25] Furthermore, these sufferings do not constitute the exact penalty for sin which sinners would have suffered.[26] Thus, the death of Christ is not a *redemption* of sinners through the paying of a price. Rather, it clears the way for God to forgive sinners through an act of grace.

Within a brief period of time this governmental theory swept New England Calvinism, and it seems that the theory was attractive for a number of reasons. First of all, this theory enabled the New Divinity thinkers to balance divine sovereignty with the humanistic spirit of the age. While it presented God as a benevolent moral governor who administers the world in the interest of human beings, at the same time it safeguarded the freedom of God to save those whom God willed. Hopkins repeatedly emphasizes that the death of Christ places God under no obligation to save anyone.[27]

The governmental atonement theory also helped the New Divinity theologians to balance the universal and particularistic dimensions of soteriology. On the one hand, it served the interests of revivalism, by appearing more firmly to ground the free offer of the gospel to all. Hopkins writes:

"for the sake of Christ." Hopkins writes (II:77-78): "And this righteousness avails to their complete justification; their sins are pardoned for the sake of Christ, who is the propitiation for their sins." Hopkins' New Divinity successors were more forthright in their rejection of the terminology, as well as the substance, of Reformed federal orthodoxy. See the essays in Edwards Amasa Park, *The Atonement: Discourses and Treatises* (Boston: Congregational Board of Publications, 1859).

[25] Hopkins, *System of Doctrines*, I:427. Hopkins thus avoids the traditional terminology speaking of Christ's "active" and "passive" obedience," for it implied the notion of the imputation of that obedience to the Christian.

[26] Ibid., 408: "The Mediator did not suffer precisely the same kind of pain, in all respects, which the sinner suffers when the curse is executed on him: He did not suffer that particular kind of pain which is the necessary attendant, or natural consequence of being a sinner, and which none but the sinner himself can suffer."

Hopkins, nevertheless, approaches the traditional Reformed doctrine by maintaining that Christ suffered "as much and as great evil, as the law denounces against transgression" (I:408). His New Divinity successors were more forthright and consistent in saying that Christ in fact did not suffer the penalty the law demanded, but that the suffering were sufficient to uphold the moral government of God. See, e.g., Jonathan Edwards, Jr., "Three Sermons on the Necessity of the Atonement," 34-35; Edward D. Griffin, "An Humble Attempt to Reconcile the Differences of Christians Respecting the Extent of the Atonement," in *The Atonement: Discourses and Treatises*, ed. Edwards A. Park (Boston: Congregational Board of Publication, 1859), 239-40.

[27] See, e.g., Hopkins, *System of Doctrine*, I:421, 458. See also, Park, "Introductory Essay," xlviii-xlix.

> The Redeemer has made an atonement sufficient to expiate for the sins of the whole world; and, in this sense, has tasted death for every man, has take away the sin of the world, has given himself a ransom for all, and is the propitiation for the sins of the whole world...Therefore, the gospel is ordered to be preached to the whole world, to all nations, to every human creature.[28]

On the other hand, a governmental atonement also enabled them to undercut arguments for universal salvation prevalent in late eighteenth-century New England. A type of federal Calvinist universalism was advocated at this time by James Relly (1722?-1788), John Murray (1741-1815), and Joseph Huntington (1735-1794), who argued from the parallel between Adam and Christ; just as all fell in Adam, so all will be saved in Christ.[29] In all of this, traditional federal notions of union with Christ and imputation played a key role. Christ has taken a "universal human nature," and by virtue of this the sins of all humanity are imputed to Christ, and his active and passive obedience are in turn imputed to all humanity.[30]

Hopkins' response to Relly is significant, for, as we shall see, the universalist controversy was of considerable importance in shaping the New Divinity view of union with Christ. He stresses the *discontinuities* of the Adam-Christ parallel; while Adam is united to the entire race by "nature" and by "divine constitution," the union of Christ with believers is different.

> The last Adam, the Redeemer of men, has no such particular relation and union to all the human race, either by nature, or divine constitution, as the first Adam had...But there is no provision or security in any divine constitution, or the covenant of redemption between the Father and the Mediator, that all shall believe on him and unite themselves to him.[31]

---

[28] Hopkins, *System of Doctrines*, I:449. See also II:93, 157.

[29] See James Relly, *Union: or, A Treatise on the Consanguinity and Affinity between Christ and His Church* (Boston: White and Adams, 1779); John Murray, *Universalism Vindicated: Being the Substance of Some Observations on the Revelation of the Unbounded Love of God* (Charlestown, Mass.: J. Lamson, 1798); Joseph Huntington, *Calvinism Improved: or, the Gospel Illustrated as a System of Real Grace, Issuing in the Salvation of All Men* (New London: Samuel Green, 1796).

On Relly and the Universalist controversy, see Foster, *Genetic History*, 190-210; Wright, *Beginnings of Unitarianism*, 189-199; Russell E. Miller, *The Larger Hope: The First Century of the Universalist Church in America, 1770-1870* (Boston: Unitarian Universalist Assoc., 1979), 3-33; Conforti, *Samuel Hopkins*, 164-66; Sweeney, *Nathaniel Taylor*, 104-105.

[30] See the helpful discussion and quotes in Foster, *Genetic History*, 190-192.

[31] Hopkins, *System of Doctrines*, II:58. Hopkins' view of original sin evidences both continuity and discontinuity with that of Edwards. Gone is any imputation of Adam's sin to his posterity, and with it Edwards' speculative theory of identity. At the same time, even more emphasis is placed on notions of divine constitution and consent: "But all that is asserted, as what the scripture teaches on this head is, that by a divine

Instead, believers are united with Christ by a faith union consisting in "mutual voluntary consent" and "cordial approbation of Christ."[32] Thus, the Universalist controversy influenced the New Divinity by rendering obnoxious both the notions of soteriological imputation and realistic solidarity with the humanity of Christ. The governmental atonement theory obviated the need for either.

The governmental theory also enabled the New Divinity to counter an apparent tendency within federal theology toward antinomianism. If Christ paid the debt of sin owed by the believer, and the righteousness of Christ is imputed, it was argued, then the believer is freed from any obligation to obey the law of God. In response, Hopkins repeatedly asserts that despite the death of Christ, the Christian remains just as guilty as ever in the sight of God and just as deserving of eternal punishment. The death of Christ merely makes divine forgiveness possible; it carries no entitlement to salvation.

> It has been shown, that the sinner who is interested in the atonement of Christ, and is delivered from the curse of the law, is left as ill deserving as he ever was, in his own person; and this his ill desert, never will, or can be removed...And the least thought to the contrary would be infinitely criminal, and a most ungrateful and horrid abuse of the atonement and righteousness of Christ.[33]

Hopkins' vehemence here underscores his deep concern about the antinomian threat he saw as implicit in the federal theology. He resoundingly declares that the Christian is in no sense released from the obligation to obey the law, and he countenances no doctrine of atonement or justification that appears in any way antinomian.[34]

Finally, the governmental theory enabled the New Divinity thinkers to frame their soteriology in terms consistent with theories regarding moral agency and responsibility emerging out of the Scottish Enlightenment. For these thinkers, such as the Common-Sense philosopher Thomas Reid, moral responsibility

---

constitution, there is a certain connection between the first sin of Adam, and the sinfulness of his posterity; so that as he sinned and fell under condemnation, they in consequence of this became sinful and condemned" (I:268).

As for any parallel between Adam and Christ, Hopkins declares that such is to be found not in imputation, as federal theology had maintained, but in consent (II:57): "It has been thought by some, that if the sin of Adam be not imputed to his posterity... there is no parallel...But...this objection is groundless. As the posterity of Adam become guilty, and fall under condemnation, by consenting to his sin, and a union of heart to him, as a transgressor; that is, by sinning themselves: so the righteousness of the Mediator comes upon men...by their uniting themselves to him in a cordial approbation of his righteousness, and his holy character. It is true there is a necessary difference in many respects, but in this there is a parallel." See also ibid., I:283.

[32]Ibid., I:448; II:60.
[33]Ibid., I:445-6. See also I:405, 421; II:73-75.
[34]See ibid., II:84.

requires both personal identity and free will, and notions of "serial identity" implied by federal conceptions of solidarity were viewed as absurd.[35] By the late eighteenth century, it was axiomatic to most (except the beleaguered defenders of federal theology) that merit and guilt inhered in individual "moral character" and that moral merit and demerit are therefore not transferable to another.[36] But the governmental model required no transfer of demerit from the believer to Christ or merit from Christ to the believer.

Hopkins on Applied Soteriology and Union with Christ

In typical Reformed dogmatic fashion, Hopkins includes a discussion of union with Christ in the opening section of his chapter on "the application of redemption."[37] Thus the theme, as in earlier Reformed theology, continues to denote the application of redemption in its totality. Also, as we might expect from the previous material, Hopkins' view of union with Christ and applied soteriology displays both continuity and discontinuity with the elder Edwards. The discontinuities are sometimes evident more in what is not said than in what is explicitly affirmed. Bearing in mind the hazards of an argument from silence, Hopkins' silence at certain points is nevertheless deafening.

In describing union with Christ, Hopkins closely follows Edwards in approaching the issue from two perspectives—the divine agency of the Holy Spirit and the human response of faith.

---

[35]Thomas Reid had written: "If one set of ideas makes a covenant, another breaks it, and a third is punished for it, there is reason to think that justice is no natural virtue in this system." Quoted in S. A. Grave, *The Scottish Philosophy of Common Sense* (Oxford: Clarendon Press, 1960), 202. See also pp. 190-223.

[36]In his doctrine of original sin, Edwards had sought to meet both requirements with his theory of personal identity and with his distinction between natural and moral inability. The New Divinity thinkers found his theory of personal identity implausible, and therefore they declared that merit and demerit are nontransferable functions of individual moral character. See Hopkins, *System of Doctrines*, I:421-2: "His [the sinner's] ill desert is according to his whole moral character, according to what he is, and has done, as a moral agent...Had Adam persevered in obedience, to the end of the time of his trial, by his vicarious obedience, all his children would have been admitted to the enjoyment of the favour of God, and eternal life; but this vicarious obedience of their substitute would not have rendered them in the least degree more deserving of such favour, than if there had been no such obedience. For Adam's obedience was not their personal obedience, and never could be; and therefore could not be considered as such. So the sufferings of Christ, not being the sufferings of the sinner, but of a substitute, cannot render the sinner less ill deserving in himself, or personally considered, more than the vicarious obedience of a substitute can render those for whom he obeys more worthy of reward."

[37]Ibid., I:447-451.

> This union of the believer to Christ may be considered as consisting in two things, viz. 1. In Christ's uniting himself to him by his Spirit, by which he takes possession of him, is formed in him, and dwells in him...2. In the believer's uniting himself to Christ, by actually cleaving to him, trusting in him, and loving him; all which is implied in saving faith, or *believing* on Christ.[38]

But omissions and differences in emphasis are immediately evident as well. Having dispensed with imputation, Hopkins does not utilize, as Edwards had, the crucial federal distinction between legal and vital unions. Furthermore, while Edwards had strongly emphasized the immediate work of the Holy Spirit, Hopkins focuses on faith and largely takes the immediate work of the Holy Spirit in regeneration for granted.

Hopkins' description of faith extensively utilizes Edwards' notions of consent and agreement.[39] It is, in fact, a mutual and reciprocal union of consent on the part of both Christ and the Christian: "This union, by divine constitution and appointment, is to take place and consist in a mutual voluntary consent; the Redeemer offering himself to them, and they consenting and complying with his proposal and offer, and accepting of him, and trusting in him as their Redeemer."[40] But in the increasing absence of Edwards' idealist metaphysic, the notion of "consent" in Hopkins begins to assume a somewhat extrinsic and moralistic cast.

> Saving faith is the proper, active union of the soul to Jesus Christ, as he is revealed in the gospel. But such union with Christ consists in the actual agreement of the heart with Christ, and suiting and adapting itself to him and redemption by him...When the soul actively conforms in its views and exercises to such a revelation and testimony as this, and acquiesces in the truths and objects revealed, as certain realities, excellent and divine, it does actively unite itself to Jesus Christ; and in this active union to him consists.[41]

In fact, Hopkins often describes this union of consent and agreement as a "moral union," a term that for Hopkins denotes a voluntary, mutual sharing of purpose and moral concern.[42]

---

[38] Ibid., I:450.

[39] Edwards uses the notion "consent" in connection with original sin and his discussion of true virtue, but it is not extensively utilized in his treatment of union with Christ. See Edwards, *Original Sin*, *Works* II:482, 493; *Nature of True Virtue*, *Works* II:262, 270-71, 301. Note that Edwards' theory of virtue, and its attendant notion of union as "consent," is rooted in his Neo-Platonic ontology. See especially *Nature of True Virtue*, *Works* II:301: "Virtue...consists in the cordial consent or union of Being to Being in general."

[40] Hopkins, *System of Doctrines*, I:448.

[41] Ibid., II:40-41.

[42] Hopkins, ibid., II:56, writes: "But he will as certainly perish in his sins, as if there had been no such Redeemer, unless a moral union take place between him and the

Hopkins summarizes his most extensive discussion of union with Christ by describing it as "a moral and spiritual union."[43] That is, it involves the immediate work of the Holy Spirit together with a human response consisting in a voluntary sharing of purpose and moral concern. Thus, union with Christ is defined almost exclusively in terms of the individual's experience of sanctification. The first major result of this is that Hopkins' applied soteriology has a moralistic, and even legalistic, tenor. This is evident, first of all, in the way the scope of faith is expanded even beyond the broad parameters set by Edwards. As with Edwards, love is of "the essence of saving faith" and "true repentance is included in saving faith."[44] In fact, Hopkins is impatient with attempts to distinguish faith and works, or to suggest that works are merely the inevitable result of faith: "Saving faith does not *produce* obedience, or the latter flow from the former, as the effect from the cause; but faith itself is evangelical obedience, and cannot be distinguished from it."[45] Note also that faith is repeatedly depicted as a "condition" of salvation and as a duty commanded by God.[46]

We see from this that Hopkins' view of the *ordo salutis* closely parallels that of Edwards, though with some differences. Regeneration is an instantaneous work of divine grace acting immediately in the heart, and this grace removes moral inability and gives rise to the act of faith on the part of the human being. With this initial act of faith, the sinner enters into a "justified state," but Hopkins insists that perseverance is necessary for continued justification and

---

Saviour, by his hearty approbation of his character, of his design, and of what he has done and suffered for the salvation of men; and he, cordially unite himself to him in the character he sustains, as the Redeemer of sinners...It is not proper...that he should have any interest in the atonement and righteousness of Christ, so as to be pardoned and received to favour, out of respect to that, while with his whole heart he opposes and rejects him, and is disposed not to come to him that he might have life; because by this there is a moral discord between him and the Redeemer, and opposition to him, and refusal to be in any union or relation to him." See also I:451.

[43] Ibid., I:451.

[44] Ibid., II:16, 19.

[45] Ibid., II:28. On p. 48 Hopkins writes, "From the view we have had of saving faith, we may learn why pardon of sin and salvation are in the Bible promised to the least degree of true holiness and christian obedience...The reason is, not because evangelical holiness in the least degree of it, is only *a sign of faith*, as something distinct from it; but because it is saving faith itself, and that in the exercise of which the soul does unite itself to Christ."

This conflation of faith and works is evident as well in Hopkins' reconciliation of Paul and James. While the elder Edwards had argued that Paul and James had different kinds of justification in mind, Hopkins suggests nothing of the sort. Instead, he maintains that Paul and James speak of different kinds of works, and that the "works" Paul opposes to faith are "obedience to the law as a covenant of works, in order to obtain the righteousness of the law, to be thereby recommended to the favour of God." Ibid., II:43; see also II:31, 47-48.

[46] Ibid., II:19, 45, 73, 88.

union with Christ.[47] Having dispensed with imputation entirely, and defined justification as forgiveness of sins and reception to divine favor, Hopkins is in somewhat better position than the elder Edwards to insist on the real necessity of perseverance in faith, albeit at the cost of again introducing a measure of legalism. Once again, the contra-antinomian motive is paramount. Hopkins stresses that sins are "not so blotted out, or covered, as not to be any more seen or remembered." They are merely forgiven for Christ's sake, and if union with Christ were to cease, "all his past sins would be remembered against him, and he fall into condemnation."[48]

The legalistic danger in Hopkins' approach is particularly evident in his view of Christian assurance, a point where he diverges to some degree from his teacher. To be sure, Edwards had viewed sanctification as the primary evidence of regeneration, but he cautioned against undue introspection and he directed the anxious to the objective promises and love of God as revealed in the gospel.[49] For Hopkins, however, assurance derives exclusively from the "practical syllogism"; that is, in the detection of the fruits of sanctification through an introspective process.

> Assurance of salvation, therefore, consists in a person's consciousness of the acts of his own heart, that he does believe in Christ; and knowing from intuition or reflection, that he has attained to those things which imply saving faith, and do accompany salvation, being infallibly connected with it, by the promise of God, in the covenant of grace...There is no other way of obtaining this assurance, but by having such high degree of christian holiness, in actual exercise; and accompanied with such spiritual discerning, as that it is seen and known by the person who has it, to be real gospel holiness, or true, saving faith.[50]

Not surprisingly, Hopkins seems to view firm assurance of salvation as more the exception than the rule among Christians: "The assurance of salvation is not common to all christians; may [sic] never attain to it, and few, or none of those who do, have it constantly, without interruption."[51] Hopkins' theory of virtue complicates the matter as well. He views the very concern for one's salvation as evidence of self-love, and thus the anxious believer is placed in a bind—even to ask the question of assurance is evidence that one is not regenerate.[52] In

---

[47]Ibid., II:71-72.

[48]Ibid., II:73-74.

[49]See Edwards, *A Treatise Concerning Religious Affections*, in *The Works of President Edwards*, 4 vols. (New York: Robert Carter, 1868), III:56-57, 64. See also the helpful treatment of Edwards' view of assurance in Cherry, *Theology*, 143-158.

[50]Hopkins, *System of Doctrines*, II:126, 128. See also p. 137. Again responding to the antinomian threat, Hopkins also declares that assurance does not come from any "immediate, suggestion, revelation, or testimony" by the Holy Spirit to the believer (II:130).

[51]Ibid., II:130.

[52]Ibid., II:141: "There are some, who earnestly desire and long for assurance that they shall be saved, and feel that if they could obtain this, they should be happy...These

light of this, Hopkins' own lack of pastoral success is understandable.

A second major characteristic of Hopkins' soteriology, in addition to its moralistic bent, is its striking individualism. We have already seen how federal notions of solidarity, both hamartiological and soteriological, have been systematically excluded by Hopkins. As for original sin, neither shared guilt nor an inherited depravity remain. All rides on a divine constitution that Adam's posterity will behave in substantially the same sinful way he did. On the soteriological plane, we see a similar breaking of traditional theological ties—the federal union of Christ and believer, the double imputation of sin to Christ and Christ's righteousness and obedience to the Christian. But on Hopkins' New Divinity model, there is no imputation to or from Christ; there is no mention of participation in the resurrection justification of Christ. Also, one detects little of the "affectionate communion" between the believer and the incarnate humanity of Christ that characterized much earlier Puritan thought. All rides on a somewhat abstract divine constitution, a divine intention to forgive those individuals who fulfill the conditions of repentance and belief.

This soteriological individualism and legalism is, not unexpectedly, reflected in Hopkins' ecclesiology. His fundamental view of the church is that of a "voluntary society," the aggregate of individuals who choose to repent and believe, and who thus become "friends" of Christ.

> It is reasonable and important, that the friends of the Redeemer should be his professed friends...Accordingly, Christ has enjoined upon his friends and disciples, to confess him before men, and to form themselves into a public society, or particular societies...The church of Christ is a free, voluntary society, in opposition to any force or compulsion used to oblige the members of it to join and come into it, contrary to their consent and free choice. All are invited to be members of it, and none are to be rejected, who appear willing to come and to conform to the rules which Christ has given.[53]

In keeping with this, considerable stress is placed on the individual right of private judgment in matters of religion: "Every member of the church has a right to judge for himself what are the laws of Christ, and what is his duty, being accountable to none but Christ for his judgment and conduct; and none have a right or authority to dictate to him, or control him in these matters."[54]

As we might expect, in view of Hopkins' notion of immediate grace in regeneration, his presentation of the traditional means of grace tends toward

---

are not seeking the assurance which the christian desires...it follows, that the true believer prizes holiness more than assurance, and is more concerned to obtain the former, than the latter...Indeed, the true christian, in the exercise of holy affection, or disinterested benevolence to God and man, is seeking more important objects and events, than his own salvation."

[53] Ibid., II:225. One of Hopkins' favorite soteriological metaphors is that of "friendship" to Christ. See II:224-5, 228, 251, 259, 262-3, 343.

[54] Ibid., II:226.

Zwingli rather than Calvin. We find, for example, little trace of the traditional Reformed emphasis upon the bond of Word and Spirit, for "the word of truth does not make the evil, hard, selfish heart, good; but where it finds such an heart, it produces no saving good, but leaves it as bad as it finds it."[55] In his treatment of baptism and the Lord's Supper, Hopkins overwhelmingly prefers the term "ordinance" to "sacrament."[56]

Hopkins' treatment of the Lord's Supper is surprisingly brief.[57] While "Christ is exhibited as an all-sufficient Saviour, and the promise of salvation is expressed and sealed to all his friends," the emphasis falls on the Supper as the believer's outward expression of an inward moral union with God and with other Christians: "And the church by coming together, and celebrating this holy supper, not only profess their love to Christ, and union of heart to him; but that peculiar love and union to each other, which takes place between the true disciples of Christ, and is essential to their character."[58]

Hopkins' section on baptism is much more extensive and more intriguing. He virtually ignores the issue of baptismal efficacy; again, the conceptual framework is essentially Zwinglian. In the case of adults, baptism is essentially an expression of "friendship" to Christ, and is to be administered only to the "really holy."

> The proper subjects of baptism, if adult, are those who by profession, and in appearance, are believers in Christ, and true friends to him...They must therefore be really holy, in order to put on this visibility and profession of it, with propriety and truth, which they do in baptism...Therefore none are to be admitted to this ordinance, but those who in the view of the church appear to be true friends of Christ, or believers in him, and really holy, and are justly considered by them as such, who can judge only by outward appearance, and cannot certainly know what is in the heart.[59]

Having closely connected baptism with "real holiness," Hopkins then must justify the baptism of infants, whose moral character is not yet apparent.[60] Here Hopkins advances the surprising theory that the infant children of believers are

---

[55] Ibid., II:14.

[56] See, e.g., ibid., II:257-347.

[57] It covers less than six pages. In contrast, baptism is treated in over eighty pages.

[58] Hopkins, *System of Doctrines*, II:343.

[59] Ibid., II:262-3. There are relatively few references to union with Christ in Hopkins' discussion of baptism. Those that are present usually occur in quotations from earlier Reformed writers. See II:336-7.

[60] Some seventy-nine pages of Hopkins' *System* are devoted to infant baptism, an indication of the Baptist threat to Congregational churches in late eighteenth-century New England. On the rise of Baptist churches in New England during this period, see Clarence C. Goen, *Revivalism and Separatism in New England, 1740-1800: Strict Congregationalists and Separate Baptists in the Great Awakening* (New Haven: Yale University Press, 1962); William G. McLaughlin, *Isaac Backus and the American Pietistic Tradition* (Boston: Little, Brown and Co., 1967).

to be baptized because holy parents tend to transmit good moral character to their children: "the piety and obedience of them, who love God, and keep his commandments, is in mercy visited upon their children, transmitting a good moral character to them."[61] Sensing a conflict with his earlier statements regarding means and the immediacy of divine grace, Hopkins argues that while regeneration is an immediate work of God, by divine constitution God has purposed to convey grace to the children of faithful parents.

> It is true, that holiness is wrought in the heart, by the power and energy of the holy Spirit, and cannot be communicated to children by any means or endeavours used by parents; but is wholly effected by divine influences. In this view and sense, parents do not convey grace to their children: this is wholly out of their power: It is the work of God. But it does not follow from this, that God has not so constituted the covenant of grace, that holiness shall be communicated by him to the children, in consequence of the faithful, commanded endeavors of their parents, so that, in this sense, and by virtue of such a constitution, they do, by their faithful endeavors, convey saving blessings to their children.[62]

As the preceding quotation indicates, Hopkins highlights the importance of Christian nurture and education in the home, even affirming that children whose Christian parents faithfully discharge their covenant responsibilities will be saved according to divine promise and constitution.[63] Here, of course, one senses a marked conflict with Hopkins' earlier emphasis on divine sovereignty and the unconditionality of regeneration. But he was apparently willing to put aside concerns for theocentric piety and divine sovereignty when moral responsibility was being evaded.

> This is a maxim often mentioned by parents, when the faithful education of their children is brought into view, and urged, that parents cannot give grace to their children, however faithful they are in their education. This is not true, in the sense now mentioned, if the covenant of grace contains a promise that their children shall be holy, if they will use all proper and commanded endeavors to this end, by which there is a constituted connection between such means, and the end...There is reason to fear, and even to believe, that the above maxim is too often mentioned by parents, in order to exculpate and excuse themselves from fault, when their children grow up ungoverned, ignorant and vicious. In this view it is desirable it should be laid aside.[64]

---

[61] Hopkins, *System of Doctrines*, II:268.

[62] Ibid., II:334-5.

[63] Ibid., II:292-319.

[64] Ibid., II:335. Thus the baptismal covenant is conditional upon the faithfulness of parents in fulfilling their responsibilities of spiritual nurture. Much of Hopkins' extensive treatment of infant baptism deals with these parental duties. Hopkins also addresses the objection that this baptismal promise constitutes a "legal scheme" of salvation by works, in this case, the works of the parents. He responds that no merit is

Summary

As we survey Hopkins' contribution to the New England soteriological trajectory, we see that a good deal of Edwards' legacy is present, but in new and modified forms. Themes of divine constitution, benevolence, and union as consent are readily apparent. Likewise, we also find the bi-directional view of union with Christ, and the expansion of faith to include nonmeritorious works. And like Edwards, Hopkins is more concerned to counter antinomianism than legalism. But many of these themes are developed, or given significantly new twists. Of crucial importance is the redefinition of virtue as *disinterested* benevolence, and its application both to human beings and especially to God. For Hopkins, God is the benevolent moral governor of the universe, who rules with the best interests of God's subjects in view. Edwards' theocentric universe has become anthropocentric, and nowhere is this shift more evident than in Hopkins' governmental atonement theory. Here the death of Christ does not propitiate divine wrath or pay a debt owed by sinners; rather, it is a public demonstration designed to deter sin by exhibiting God's disapproval of it. The stage is then set for a significant recasting of the theme of union with Christ. With the governmental theory, there is no need for soteriological imputation of any sort. Furthermore, the solidarity between Christ and the sinner is notably lessened. Justification is no longer "in Christ" but somehow on the basis of what Christ has done.

With soteriological imputation gone, the older federal bifurcation of union into federal or legal and vital or spiritual no longer obtains. Instead, Edwards' bi-directional conception of vital union and his concept of union as consent are developed and combined with Edwards' expansion of faith in such a way as to increase markedly the role and importance of faith. Faith, for Hopkins, constitutes a "moral union," a voluntary sharing of purpose and moral concern. In view of this concept of "moral union" and the way "faith" has been expanded to include all the "exercises" of the regenerate soul, it becomes apparent that Hopkins defines union with Christ almost entirely in terms of *sanctification*. Earlier notions of a mystical union are gone. What remains is an extrinsic, moralistic, voluntary union that fit well the increasingly individualistic and moralistic tenor of the times.

The theme of union with Christ is also less prominent in Hopkins than in his Reformed predecessors, including Edwards. Historically, the appeal of the *unio Christi* for Reformed thinkers had been its umbrella function linking justification and sanctification. But for Hopkins with his moralistic and contra-antinomian concerns, justification had been recast as little more than an appendage of sanctification, and the need for an overarching theme such as

---

involved, and that hence there is no "legal scheme" (II:330-31).

Doubtless reflecting his own pastoral experience, Hopkins pessimistically observes that while "Paedobaptists believe infant baptism to be a divine institution...most of them, if not all, refuse to comply with, and practise the most important and essential duties implied in the institution, which they solemnly profess and engage to do" (II:340).

union with Christ was lessened. We will see that this trend continues in Hopkins' New England successor Timothy Dwight.

A final observation is necessary. Hopkins and the New Divinity were known, of course, for their vigorous defense of divine sovereignty and moral inability. But as notions of a universal, governmental atonement came to the fore, divine sovereignty and particularity were no longer fully integrated with soteriology (as they had been in the earlier federal theology). In fact, a governmental atonement stood in considerable tension with the theory of moral inability—the death of Christ is not a deterrent if human beings are morally unable anyway. Thus, it is not surprising that the New England successors of Hopkins began to modify the tradition with regard to divine sovereignty and human inability.[65]

The Rational Evangelicalism of Timothy Dwight

An outstanding New England representative of the generation following Hopkins is Timothy Dwight (1752-1817), the distinguished Connecticut pastor, educator, poet, and president of Yale College from 1795 until his death in 1817.[66] A stout defender of New England Federalism and the Congregationalist establishment, Dwight exercised considerable influence in both the ecclesiastical and political spheres. Dwight's theological influence was also considerable. His dogmatics, *Theology: Explained and Defended*, took the form of 173 doctrinal sermons initially presented to students at Yale. First published in 1818, it went through numerous editions.[67] Later New England theologian Nathanael William Taylor studied under Dwight at Yale, and acknowledged his

---

[65]Sweeney, *Nathaniel Taylor*, 98-104, helpfully explores the theological and cultural factors in the early national period pulling the New Divinity to expand the role and place of human ability.

[66]General biographical treatments of Dwight include "Memoir of the Life of President Dwight," in Timothy Dwight, *Theology; Explained and Defended in a Series of Sermons*, 11th ed., 4 vols. (New Haven: T. Dwight & Sons, 1843), I:3-61; and Charles E. Cuningham, *Timothy Dwight, 1752-1817* (New York: Macmillan, 1942).

[67]Citations from Dwight's *Theology* are taken from Timothy Dwight, *Theology; Explained and Defended, in a Series of Sermons*, 11th ed., 4 vols. (New Haven: T. Dwight & Sons, 1843).

Dwight's theology is examined in Wayne C. Tyner, "The Theology of Timothy Dwight in Historical Perspective," (Ph.D. diss., University of North Carolina at Chapel Hill, 1971); Berk, *Calvinism vs. Democracy*; John R. Fitzmier, "The Godly Federalism of Timothy Dwight, 1752-1817: Society, Doctrine, and Religion in the Life of New England's 'Moral Legislator,'" (Ph.D. diss., Princeton University, 1986), which includes nuanced discussions of biographical matters; *New England's Moral Legislator: Timothy Dwight, 1752-1817* (Bloomington, IN: Indiana University Press, 1998; and Annabelle S. Wenzke, *Timothy Dwight (1752-1817)* (Lewiston, N.Y.: Edwin Mellen Press, 1989). See also Foster, *Genetic History*, 361-66.

considerable theological debt to the college president.[68]

Dwight's Relation to Earlier New England Thought

The nature and antecedents of Dwight's theology have been a matter of some dispute. On the one hand, he was clearly indebted to the theological trajectory initiated by Jonathan Edwards. A grandson of Jonathan Edwards the elder, he studied theology under his uncle, Edwards the younger, who preached his ordination sermon.[69] On the other hand, his relationship to the New Divinity of Hopkins, Emmons, and Edwards the younger is more ambiguous, for he evidences both continuity and discontinuity with New Divinity thought.[70]

The lines of continuity, first of all, are substantial. With the New Divinity thinkers (and in a manner consistent with larger trends of religious thought), the benevolent character of God as moral governor of the universe is viewed as the foremost of the divine moral attributes.[71] In keeping with this view of divine benevolence, and consistent with earlier New Divinity thought, the death of Christ is viewed in terms of a governmental atonement, and soteriological imputation is denied.[72] Also as in Hopkins, divine and human virtue is defined primarily in terms of disinterested benevolence: "God...is infinitely benevolent,

---

[68]See Mead, *Nathanael William Taylor*, 25-33.

[69]Jonathan Edwards, Jr., *The Faithful Ministration of the Truth, the Proper and Immediate End of Preaching the Gospel. A Sermon Delivered November 5, 1783, at the Ordination of the Reverend Timothy Dwight, to the Pastoral Office over the Church in Greenfield* (New Haven: Thomas and Samuel Green, 1783).

[70]Foster, *Genetic History*, 361-2, does not view Dwight as a New Divinity thinker. Regarding Dwight's *Theology*, he writes: "But in a peculiar degree it represented no special school in the New England divinity, and did not lie in the line, proceeding through Hopkins and Emmons...It stands largely by itself." Stephen Berk, *Calvinism vs. Democracy*, 49-73, views Dwight as a representative of "Evangelical New Divinity" along with Joseph Bellamy. John R. Fitzmier, "Godly Federalism," 111-158, is critical of Berk, and contends that Dwight is not a New Divinity representative. Sweeney, *Nathaniel Taylor*, places Dwight firmly in the New Divinity trajectory.

Much of the difficulty here stems from, first of all, the lack of a fully satisfactory functional definition of "New Divinity," and secondly, from the fact that Dwight was clearly an eclectic thinker. The complexities involved here are apparent in Fitzmier's cross-bench conclusion that Dwight is an "Edwardsean," who "did not adopt the New Divinity system in its entirety. But those elements of the system that he did adopt became the...intellectual means by which Edwardseanism was effectively dissolved." "Godly Federalism," 233.

While this larger question cannot be adjudicated here, suffice it to say that at critical soteriological points of importance to this study, Dwight stands in considerable continuity with Hopkins' New Divinity, and in fact, represents the further development of themes evident in Hopkins.

[71]Dwight, *Theology*, I:166-191.

[72]Ibid., II:194-229.

and wholly disinterested. Christ has also been proved to sustain the same character. That *the same mind was in* the Apostles, *which was also in Christ*, cannot be disputed, that it is possessed by every good man, and is that which constitutes the excellence of his character."[73]

Dwight's conception of original sin also closely parallels that of Hopkins. He repeatedly insists that guilt is not transferable, and thus the imputation of Adam's sin is denied.[74] In treating the connection between the sin of Adam and the sinfulness of his posterity, Dwight also appeals to the notion of divine "constitution," and like Hopkins he eschews metaphysical speculation regarding an "identity" of Adam and his offspring.[75] Like his Edwardsean and New Divinity predecessors, Dwight also distinguishes between natural or "physical" inability and moral inability, affirming the latter but not the former.[76]

Like his predecessors, Dwight clearly favors the "gathered church" concept, and he opposes the Half-Way Covenant practices of the Old Calvinists: "The Church of Christ ought to consist of Christians only."[77] Dwight also reflects the New Divinity heritage in the consistently moralistic tenor of his presentation. He is much concerned to answer the antinomian threat, and like Hopkins he particularly endeavors to counter suggestions that the Reformed doctrine of justification undercuts the Christian's legal obligations of obedience.[78] Furthermore, Dwight continues the New Divinity emphasis on the practical syllogism as the primary source of assurance.[79]

Points of discontinuity are present as well. There is, compared with the New Divinity thought of Hopkins, a deemphasis of divine sovereignty and a correspondingly increased stress on human agency. Dwight clearly departs from the supralapsarianism of Hopkins—there is no positive divine decree willing the existence of sin; God merely permits its existence.[80] Dwight's discussion of divine decrees places more emphasis on divine foreknowledge than on decrees *per se*, and he expends considerable effort defending the compatibility of human freedom and divine foreknowledge.[81] Similarly, human

---

[73]Ibid., II:474. Dwight is careful, however, to exclude certain New Divinity extrapolations from this principle such as the willingness to be damned for the glory of God. He affirms that natural affection is "no part of selfishness" (II:472). He also distinguishes between "disinterestedness" and "uninterestedness," arguing that in "aiming at our own happiness there is no necessary selfishness" (II:492-3).

[74]Ibid., I:478-9. See also II:219, 306.

[75]Ibid., I:479-80. Cf. Hopkins, *System*, I:268.

[76]Dwight, *Theology*, II:401.

[77]Ibid., IV:207. For his rejection of Half-Way Covenant sacramental practices, see IV:341-44.

[78]Ibid., II:358-69.

[79]See ibid., II:426; III:27-52.

[80]Ibid., I:255-6.

[81]Ibid., I:244-47, 256-59.

free agency is treated as an indubitable datum of human experience.[82] And despite his strong affirmation of the need for spiritual regeneration to overcome moral inability, Dwight argues that grace is resistible, although it is "never resisted."[83] Here Dwight's lack of philosophical consistency is apparent; his formulations are driven more by pastoral and pedagogical considerations.[84]

In keeping with his emphasis upon human agency, Dwight gives considerably more prominence to the means of grace than did Hopkins. Particular attention is given to the "ordinary means"—the preaching of the gospel, Bible reading, prayer, "correspondence with religious men," religious meditation, and the religious education of children—all of which are intended to impress sacred truths upon "the human Understanding, or Affections."[85] He is also careful to reject the New Divinity suggestion that awakened sinners who use the means of grace are more vile than sinners who do not.[86]

A final difference between Dwight and many of the New Divinity thinkers is evident in his theological method. There are, for example, more appeals to human experience. Though perhaps not a Scottish Common Sense philosopher in the strict sense, Dwight frequently appeals to human "common sense."[87] There is also a disinclination to press matters to what might seem to be their logical conclusion; we have already seen how the rough edges of the New Divinity, arising from its speculative tendency, are removed by Dwight.[88]

---

[82]Ibid., I:256: "men are intuitively conscious of their own free agency, being irresistibly sensible, that they act spontaneously, and without any coercion, or constraint."

[83]Ibid., II:400.

[84]Wenzke, *Timothy Dwight*, 105, remarks that "Timothy Dwight was not a philosopher...although Dwight's theology lacked philosophical consistency, it made good sense."

[85]Dwight, *Theology*, IV:49-50. The contrast with Hopkins here, though real, is not absolute, for Hopkins also placed extraordinary emphasis upon the religious education of children.

Dwight's conception of the efficacy of the means of grace is rather naturalistic; there is little mention of the agency of the Holy Spirit or of the bond of Word and Spirit: "I consider none of these as Means of Grace, in any other sense, than as they display, and impress upon the mind, the Truth of God." Ibid., IV:50.

[86]Ibid., II:448; IV:60-74.

[87]See ibid., I:255; IV:260.

[88]George Park Fisher, "Channing as a Philosopher and Theologian," in *Discussions in History and Theology* (New York: Charles Scribner's Sons, 1880), 259, speaks of "the moderation of Dwight in his theological statements" and "his strenuous opposition to Hopkinsian extravagances."

Dwight's theological method and approach to human reason has been the subject of disparate appraisals. Fitzmier, "Godly Federalism," 157, suggests that an essential difference between Dwight and the New Divinity is that Dwight "believed that human reason had bounds, that the endless application of logic to the things of God ended in futility, and that an appreciation of the divine mystery ought to characterize the Christian's heart and mind." In contrast, Wenzke, *Timothy Dwight*, 105-110, views

In summary, while Dwight manifests both continuity and discontinuity with his New Divinity predecessors, with respect to crucial soteriological elements (governmental atonement, eclipse of imputation, etc.) he stands squarely in the trajectory that leads from Edwards through Hopkins and the New Divinity. This conclusion is confirmed as we turn to his treatment of the theme of union with Christ.

Dwight on Applied Soteriology and Union with Christ

In Dwight's presentation of soteriology we find both considerable continuity with New Divinity formulations and also the accentuation of certain trends already evident in the New Divinity thought of Samuel Hopkins. The focus here will be primarily on those elements where further development is evident.

We find in Dwight, first of all, a more rationalistic and moralistic conception of faith. Faith for Dwight is primarily belief and trust in a set of abstract propositions rather than the union with Christ of Edwards and Hopkins. The "object of faith" is not so much Christ himself, but "the Gospel…for by this Gospel only do we become acquainted with the character, mission, doctrines, precepts, or even the existence of a Savior." Similarly, saving faith is "faith in the atonement preeminently," and "in the moral character of God."[89] Faith is also construed as a "duty" and a virtuous, moral act undertaken voluntarily and subject to reward: "Faith, and its opposite, disbelief, are, in all moral cases, voluntary exercises of the mind; are proper objects of commands and prohibitions; and proper foundation of praise and blame, reward and punishment."[90]

Faith is further viewed as issuing in a "moral union" with God—note the shift in focus from union with Christ to union with God. This union is characterized by a confluence of minds, a voluntary sharing of moral concerns.

> By faith we intend Confidence in the moral character of God and the Redeemer. This confidence is plainly the beginning, and the continuance, of union and attachment to our Creator; while, on the other hand, distrust is a complete separation of the soul from the Author of its being. It is plainly impossible for

---

Dwight's *Theology* as an example of "supernatural rationalism" characterized by the synthesis of "reason, revelation, and experience." Part of the disagreement here is due to different uses of the term "reason." To be sure, Dwight has little patience for the speculative flights of the New Divinity—this is due largely to the fact that almost nothing of Edwards' idealism remains in Dwight. On the other hand, Dwight is more open than the New Divinity thinkers to the use of practical reason, evidential argument, and common sense—a rationalism of a different sort.

[89] Dwight, *Theology*, II:124, 224, 333. The overwhelming centrality of the atonement in Dwight's presentation of the work of Christ is striking. The incarnation and resurrection are presented largely as precondition and addendum to the atonement.

[90] Ibid., II:313.

him, who distrusts God, to have any moral union to him, or any devotion to his pleasure.[91]

Dwight never ceases to highlight the moral implications of faith and right belief. To have faith is to share in the "mind of Christ," that is, to be characterized by "disinterested benevolence."[92] Furthermore, right belief is vindicated by the individual and social morality it engenders—Dwight repeatedly suggests that Unitarian and Socinian beliefs demonstrate a negative "moral tendency," while the Calvinistic system of belief encourages obedience.[93]

Dwight's moralistic bent is further evident in the *ordo salutis* implicit in his system. As with Edwards and Hopkins, sanctification precedes justification. At regeneration, a "relish for Spiritual objects" is imparted and the Holy Spirit is infused.[94] Only then, upon the exercise of faith, is the person justified. Interestingly, Dwight views the time of justification as a matter of "little importance."[95]

The most dramatic development, however, is the almost complete eclipse of the theme of union with Christ itself in Dwight's *Theology*. As noted earlier, the theme is somewhat deemphasized in Hopkins, but the nearly total absence of the theme here is nevertheless remarkable, given its historic prominence in Reformed soteriology. Union with Christ no longer functions as an umbrella concept unifying the legal and transformatory elements of salvation, and it is entirely absent from Dwight's discussions of justification, sanctification, and baptism—*loci* where the theme historically played an important theological role. A survey of Dwight's *Theology* reveals only three substantive references to the theme of union with Christ—most of which occur in the context of moral exhortation.[96] Thus we may conclude that the theme of union with Christ is not a theological factor in the theology of Timothy Dwight, and that occasional references to a "moral union" with God have largely replaced union with Christ. A review of subsequent New England thinkers, such as Nathaniel William Taylor, shows that the theme continues in eclipse.[97]

---

[91] Ibid., II:335. See also II:542; III:6; IV:32-37.

[92] Ibid., II:474.

[93] Ibid., II:369, 414.

[94] Ibid., II:418, 549.

[95] Ibid., II:338-344. Like Hopkins, Dwight finds Jonathan Edwards' reconciliation of Paul and James unconvincing. He stresses that James writes in opposition to antinomianism and that he merely highlights the inseparability of faith and obedience. See ibid., II:348-57.

[96] The first brief reference (Ibid., II:224) occurs in the context of an exhortation against doubt. The second is found in a discussion of the necessity of faith and repentance for obedience (IV:32-34). The last occurs in a section treating the voluntary, moral union of Christians with one another (IV:364).

[97] See, e.g., Nathaniel W. Taylor, *Essays, Lectures, Etc. Upon Select Topics in Revealed Theology* (New York: Clark, Austin & Smith, 1859), 310-372; esp. pp. 321,

The larger New England trend here involves the progressive effacing of federal notions of imputation and legal union, followed by the eclipse of the theme of union with Christ itself. The Christian's relationship with Christ is thus revised along moralistic and extrinsic lines. Several interrelated factors appear to account for this development. The first has to do with Hopkins' and Dwight's notion of a "moral union." Because the central focus here is the voluntary sharing of moral concern, it can only denote an extrinsic relationship, and it describes at best only a part of the soteriological complex. In short, "moral union" now becomes merely a synonym for sanctification. A second major influence is the New Divinity governmental atonement theory. Because this theory involves no "legal union" between Christ and the believer, and no imputation of merit and demerit, justification is no longer "in Christ," but rather is "on the basis of" what Christ has done in his atoning death. The relationship to Christ here is clearly more remote than that envisioned by Calvin or the federal theologians. It is not surprising, therefore, that Dwight persistently modifies scriptural occurrences of the phrase "in Christ" to read "through Christ."[98] Finally, the eclipse of union with Christ itself is doubtless due in large measure to the fact that its earlier function of unifying imputed and actual righteousness was less necessary in the absence of imputation itself.

Conclusions and Observations

Our survey of New England developments has covered only a little over eighty years—from Jonathan Edwards' sermons on justification by faith in 1734 to the death of his grandson Timothy Dwight in 1817. But this brief period was one of enormous change for New England Calvinism. In particular, Reformed soteriology was revisioned on a grand scale as the venerable federal theology edifice was subjected to searching critique, found wanting, and replaced.

Several general aspects of this critique deserve mention. First of all, Edwards and his successors were primarily concerned with the antinomian threat they saw as implicit in the federal theology. Repeatedly this anxiety causes them to move in directions that earlier generations of Reformed thinkers would have viewed as legalistic. Second, Edwards and his successors found this threat of antinomianism in the federal theology's notion of legal solidarity, a "legal union" with Christ, and particularly in the fact that the relationship between this legal union (justification) and spiritual union (sanctification) was unclear. As we have seen, Reformed federal theology never entirely succeeded in establishing a meaningful relationship between justification and sanctification, and the New England theology addressed this precise problem by subordinating justification to sanctification and rejecting the notion of

---

367-8, where union with Christ is mentioned only in connection with the rejected notion of soteriological imputation.

[98]See, e.g., Dwight, *Theology*, II:67-68, 412.

imputation altogether.[99] Finally, once these modifications were made, the theme of union with Christ itself began to recede—an eclipse evident in Hopkins and nearly complete in Dwight.

The theological legacy of this trajectory may only be briefly touched on here. The historical connection between the New England theology described here and the Evangelical theology of mid-nineteenth century trinitarian Congregationalism and New School Presbyterianism is undeniable.[100] A clear though somewhat convoluted line can and must be drawn from Edwards the elder through Hopkins and Dwight to Lyman Beecher, the Congregationalist and sometime New-School Presbyterian, and Nathaniel William Taylor of Yale. Thus these New England thinkers provided an important formative influence on what has been called the "Evangelical United Front," with its phalanx of missionary and Bible societies, temperance organizations, Sunday schools, and the like.[101]

The religious legacy of the New England theology is susceptible of varying interpretations. Particularly as it was further shaped by the moderate revivalism of Asahel Nettleton and the more radical revivalism of Charles Grandison Finney and Nathaniel William Taylor, the trajectory had considerable popular appeal. But popularity and religious adequacy not always the same thing, and there is considerable evidence that the later New England theology was not meeting the religious needs of many people.[102] The difficulties here revolved to a large degree around the problem of assurance. As we have seen, the New England theology increasingly emphasized the practical syllogism. People were urged to look within themselves for evidence of sanctification and regeneration, and the standard of proof was heightened by moralistic legalism. Furthermore, the itinerant revivalists of the period saw it as their job to destroy the (presumably false) assurance of their audiences, rather than nurture it. The New England theology, however, provided little in the way of religious resources for anxious Christians. Having minimized the objective solidarity of the Christian with Christ, and having robbed the sacraments of objective efficacy, the anxious were relegated to their own subjectivity. It is little wonder, then, that a reaction emphasizing the spiritual objectivity of union with Christ and the sacraments would be spawned, and it is to this response that we now turn.

---

[99]Perhaps the most sustained and concerted New England polemic against the federal Reformed soteriology and notions of legal union is found in Griffin, "Humble Attempt to Reconcile the Differences of Christians Reflecting the Extent of the Atonement," 210-248.

[100]A point emphasized by Berk, *Calvinism vs. Democracy*, 194-205; and Wenzke, *Timothy Dwight*, 1-8. On the New England Theology roots of New School Presbyterianism, see George M. Marsden, *The Evangelical Mind and the New School Presbyterian Experience* (New Haven: Yale University Press, 1970), 31-58.

[101]See, e.g., Charles I. Foster, *An Errand of Mercy: The Evangelical United Front, 1790-1837* (Chapel Hill: University of North Carolina Press, 1960).

[102]See Haroutunian, *Piety vs. Moralism*, 174-76.

PART III

THE MERCERSBURG SOTERIOLOGY

CHAPTER 5

John W. Nevin and Organic Union with Christ

A distinctively new approach to soteriology is evident in the work of John Williamson Nevin of the German Reformed Seminary at Mercersburg, Pennsylvania. Drawing on the Reformation thought of John Calvin and Philip Melanchthon, and on the German mediating theology of Schleiermacher's successors, Nevin's formulations stood in self-conscious contrast to the federal theology of Calvinist orthodoxy and to the moralistic Calvinism of the New England tradition.

Biography

The scion of a Pennsylvania Scots-Irish family, John Williamson Nevin (1803-1886) was raised in the bosom of the older Presbyterian tradition.[1] Moving to the rhythm of the sacramental communion seasons, its catechetical training was informed by the federal theology of the Westminster Standards. Young Nevin was prepared in Latin and Greek for further education by his gentleman-farmer father, and in 1817 he journeyed to Schenectady, New York, to attend Union College.

At Union College, a cooperative venture of New England Congregationalist and Presbyterian interests, Nevin was introduced to the New England theology of Edwards and his successors, with its revivalist, moralist, and reformist

---

[1] Two helpful general treatments of Nevin and the Mercersburg movement are Luther J. Binkley, *The Mercersburg Theology* (Lancaster, Pa.: Franklin and Marshall College, 1953); and James Hastings Nichols, *Romanticism and American Theology: Nevin and Schaff at Mercersburg* (Chicago: University of Chicago Press, 1961). On Nevin in particular, see Theodore Appel, *The Life and Work of John Williamson Nevin* (Philadelphia: Reformed Church Publication House, 1889); D. G. Hart, *John Williamson Nevin: High Church Calvinist* (Phillipsburg, NJ: Presbyterian & Reformed, 2005). Of considerable importance is Nevin's autobiographical *My Own Life: The Earlier Years* (Lancaster, Pa.: Historical Society of the Evangelical and Reformed Church, 1964). This work was initially published in serial form in the *Reformed Church Messenger* (March 2-June 22, 1870). It covers the period from 1803 until the call to Mercersburg in 1840. Written long after the events it describes, it presents Nevin's own theological interpretation of his religious journey.

impulse.[2] Here the young Nevin first experienced the phenomenon of New England revivalism under the ministry of the Connecticut revivalist Asahel Nettleton (1783-1844), a protégé of Timothy Dwight. At the age of seventeen Nevin had a conversion experience, but the subjective piety encouraged at Union coupled with his own tendency toward introspection led to an extended episode of "dyspepsia," or nervous exhaustion. The nearly constant critique of "Puritanism" during Nevin's later career must be seen in light of these early experiences.

Following his graduation with honors from Union College in 1821, and after a period of physical recuperation, Nevin enrolled at Princeton Seminary. Here he excelled at the study of Hebrew, and was called in 1826 to substitute for his teacher Charles Hodge in the Department of Oriental and Biblical Literature while Hodge studied in Europe for two years. While at Princeton he wrote his widely circulated and reprinted *Biblical Antiquities*.[3] Despite his academic success, however, the religious struggles of his Union College days had not completely disappeared. Many years later, Nevin spoke of the tension at Princeton between the churchly piety of Reformed orthodoxy and the more individualistic, moralistic, and subjective piety of the American awakenings.

> There were in fact two different theories or schemes of piety at work in my mind, which refused to coalesce. One was the New England Puritanic theory, as it had taken possession particularly of the revival system, which was now assuming to be the only true sense of the Gospel all over the country; the other was the old proper Presbyterian theory of the seventeenth century...There was, for me, a difference between the two systems, which I could feel without being able to explain...Our teaching was not steadily and consistently in one direction.[4]

Nevin was subsequently to react against these two systems of piety, and to present a cogent alternative to both.

Upon Hodge's return from Europe, Nevin was called to occupy the chair of Biblical Literature at the newly established Western Theological Seminary in Allegheny, Pennsylvania. While there, the indefatigable Nevin taught courses, supplied a variety of pulpits, and edited a reformist magazine, *The Friend*. Even more important for his subsequent career, he began to become more familiar with German scholarship, particularly the writings of the church historian J. A. G. Neander (1789-1850). Nevin's seminary courses in church history had

---

[2]Nevin, *My Own Life*, 7-11.

Jonathan Edwards the Younger was president of Union College from 1799 until his death in 1801. While there he was instrumental in establishing the Plan of Union of 1801, an alliance of Presbyterian and Connecticut Congregationalist churches.

[3]John W. Nevin, *A Summary of Biblical Antiquities; for the Use of Sunday School Teachers and for the Benefit of Families*, 2 vols. (Utica: Western Sunday School Union, 1828).

[4]Nevin, *My Own Life*, 22-23.

utilized the German rationalist Mosheim for facts and the English evangelical Milner for piety, but neither text made history come alive for the young student.[5] It was Neander, Nevin remarked later, who roused him from his historiographical "dogmatic slumbers."[6]

> He caused church history to become for me like the creations of poetry and romance. How much I owe to him in the way of excitement, impulse, suggestion, knowledge, both literary and religious, reaching onward into all my later life, is more than I can pretend to explain, for it is in truth more than I have power to understand.[7]

Nevin's call in 1840 to teach at the German Reformed Seminary at Mercersburg signaled a new chapter in his career. Here his initial colleague was F. A. Rauch (1806-1841), a German classicist who introduced the Hegelianism of his teacher Karl Daub to America.[8] Rauch bequeathed to Nevin a set of categories—the organic nature of human life, a unified psychology of the human being, the foundational nature of self-consciousness for the human organism—that Nevin was to find extraordinarily useful in coming years.[9] Upon Rauch's death in 1841 Nevin was left to carry on the educational program of both the college and the theological seminary until the arrival of the young Philip Schaff from Germany in 1844, whom Nevin found a learned and congenial colleague.

Almost immediately upon his reception by the German Reformed Church, Nevin noticed the inroads of Charles Finney's "New Measures" revivalism among the churches.[10] Sensing a threat to the theology and order of the church, Nevin penned *The Anxious Bench* in 1843, followed by an expanded second edition of the same work in 1844.[11] This second edition is significant, not only

---

[5]Ibid., 40-41. See Johann Lorenz Mosheim, *Ecclesiastical History, Ancient and Modern, From the Birth of Christ to the Beginning of the Present Century*, 6 vols., trans. by Archibald Maclaine (Charlestown, Mass.: Samuel Etheridge, 1810-11); Joseph Milner, *History of the Church of Christ*, 2nd ed., 5 vols. (Boston: St. Armstrong and Crocker & Brewster, 1822).

[6]Nevin, *My Own Life*, 143.

[7]Ibid., 139.

[8]See Frederick A. Rauch, *Psychology: Or, A View of the Human Soul: Including Anthropology, Adapted for the Use of Colleges*, second ed. (New York: M. W. Dodd, 1841). This second edition includes a "Preliminary Notice" by Nevin. On Rauch, see Howard J. B. Ziegler, *Frederick Augustus Rauch: American Hegelian* (Lancaster, Pa.: Franklin and Marshall College, 1953).

[9]See Nichols, *Romanticism*, 48.

[10]See Don Yoder, "The Bench vs. the Catechism: Revivalism and Pennsylvania's Lutheran and Reformed Churches," *Pennsylvania Folklife* 10 (Fall 1959): 14-23.

[11]John W. Nevin, *The Anxious Bench*, 2nd ed. (Chambersburg, Pa.: Publication Office of the German Reformed Church, 1844). The text is reprinted in *Catholic and Reformed: Selected Theological Writings of John Williamson Nevin*, ed. Charles

as a sophisticated deconstruction of the psychology of revivalism, but also as the first systematic statement of what came to be known as the "Mercersburg Theology." Here the crucial themes of organic union with Christ, the generic humanity of Christ and Adam, the mediation of the church, and the priority of the general over the individual all come to expression for the first time. Nevin wrote:

> The sinner is saved then by an inward living union with Christ as real as the bond by which he has been joined in the first instance to Adam. This union is reached and maintained through the medium of the Church by the Power of the Holy Ghost. It constitutes a new life, the ground of which is not the particular subject of it at all, but in Christ, the organic root of the church. The particular subject lives, not properly speaking in the acts of his own will separately considered, but in the power of a vast generic life that lies wholly beyond his will, and has now begun to manifest itself through him as the law and type of his will itself as well as of his whole being.[12]

These themes were then further developed later that year in Nevin's sermon, entitled "Catholic Unity," given to the Joint Convention of the Reformed Dutch and German Reformed Churches on August 8, 1844.[13]

In 1846 Nevin published his best-known theological work, *The Mystical Presence*.[14] Here a searching indictment was leveled against his Reformed contemporaries in Presbyterianism and New England Congregationalism. Both traditions, Nevin maintained, had departed markedly from the sacramental theology of Calvin and the Reformed confessions. But *The Mystical Presence* was much more than an historical study of sacramental doctrine—it was a treatise on applied soteriology as a whole, with union with Christ as the central theme. The work provoked spirited reaction from a variety of quarters, including Charles Hodge of Princeton, whose lengthy but less-than-charitable review of the book elicited an even more detailed response from Nevin.[15]

Yrigoyen, Jr. and George H. Bricker (Pittsburgh: Pickwick Press, 1978), 9-126. Citations from *The Anxious Bench* are taken from this more accessible edition.

[12]Nevin, *Anxious Bench*, 107-8.

[13]This sermon is reprinted in James Hastings Nichols, ed., *The Mercersburg Theology* (New York: Oxford University Press, 1966), 33-55.

[14]John W. Nevin, *The Mystical Presence: A Vindication of the Reformed or Calvinistic Doctrine of the Holy Eucharist* (Philadelphia: J. B. Lippincott, 1846).

[15]See Hodge, "Doctrine of the Reformed Church." Nevin's response to the Hodge review was published in the summer of 1848 in *The Weekly Messenger* of the German Reformed Church. A more extensive response is found in Nevin's "Doctrine of the Reformed Church on the Lord's Supper," *Mercersburg Review* 2 (1850): 421-548. Much of this latter work is reprinted in John W. Nevin, *The Mystical Presence and Other Writings on the Eucharist*, ed. Bard Thompson and George H. Bricker., Lancaster Series on the Mercersburg Theology 4 (Boston: United Church Press, 1966), 267-401.

Despite their earlier ties, the relationship between Nevin and Hodge was strained

In January of 1849, Nevin and Schaff launched *The Mercersburg Review* with the intention of gaining a greater audience for their views. Nevin contributed many of the articles for the initial issues, and some are significant for this study. The *Review* was needed because of the opposition the Mercersburg theologians were incurring both within the German Reformed Church and without, and because the denominational organ (*The Weekly Messenger*) eventually declined to publish the volume of articles generated by both sides.[16]

During and after 1849, Nevin was taken up with what he often termed "the church question." Ever more critical of the sectarian tendency in American Protestantism, and engaged in detailed historical study of the early church, Nevin wrote extensively on the Apostles' Creed, the Oxford Movement, and on the "catholic" nature of the church. By 1851, Nevin was seriously considering the claims of Rome, and he entered a lengthy period of ecclesial uncertainty, which contemporaries termed "Nevin's Dizziness."[17] His resignation from the seminary was submitted in 1851 and accepted by the German Reformed Synod in 1852.

Nevin's retirement from the seminary at Mercersburg signaled the end of the creative period of the Mercersburg Theology. Philip Schaff remained until 1865, and he subsequently continued his distinguished career at Union Theological Seminary in New York. By 1854, Nevin had decided to remain within the Protestant fold. He resumed his involvement in German Reformed affairs, served on a controversial liturgical commission of the church, and as President of Marshall College in Lancaster from 1866 until his retirement in 1876.

Considerable attention has been paid here to Nevin's life for two reasons. First, Nevin's theology arose out of deep personal engagement with the issues addressed. As we will see, his educational and religious experiences in the contexts of New England Puritanism and Old School Presbyterianism left indelible marks, and his subsequent theological journey can only be understood in light of these experiences.[18] Second, it is necessary for the purposes of this

---

after this point. See George H. Shriver, "Passages in Friendship: John W. Nevin to Charles Hodge, 1872," *Journal of Presbyterian History* 58 (1980): 116-122.

[16] On the controversies of this period, see Nichols, *Romanticism in American Theology*, 140-191; Binkley, *Mercersburg Theology*, 110-120; D. Bard Thompson, "The Mercersburg Divines," (Unpublished paper read before the Avon Literary Club, May 4, 1962).

[17] For sensitive historical treatments of this period in Nevin's life, see Nichols, *Romanticism*, 192-235; Hart, *John Williamson Nevin*, 139-168.

[18] Nevin's chief foil in the writings of his Mercersburg period was "Puritanism," a term sometimes referring specifically to the New England tradition of Edwards and his successors, and sometimes more generally to both the New England and federal theology traditions. In his "Puritanism and the Creed," *Mercersburg Review* 1 (1849): 602, Nevin wrote: "The hardest Puritan we have to do with always, is the one we carry,

study to delimit the field of examination to a portion of Nevin's years at Mercersburg, and the justification for this must be made in light of the interrelationship of Nevin's life and thought. This chapter focuses on the period between Nevin's initial statements of the distinctive Mercersburg Theology in 1844 and his departure from Mercersburg in 1852. Prior to this period, he had not publicly broken with the federal theology of Princeton; after this period his relationship to the Reformed tradition is less clear. During his Mercersburg period, however, Nevin articulated a distinctive and yet self-consciously Reformed soteriological position.[19]

The Mercersburg Theology

While the Mercersburg Theology of Nevin and Schaff has been the subject of numerous treatments and appraisals, attention has focused primarily on three major areas—the Mercersburg sacramental theology, the liturgical dimension of the Mercersburg movement, and the ecumenical and ecclesial implications of the movement.[20] In these, the relationship between union with Christ and

---

by birth and education, in our own bosom."

[19] A word is in order regarding sources. Because they were written for a larger audience and with more care, special attention here is given to Nevin's monographs and to his essays in the *Mercersburg Review*. Prior to establishing the *Review* in 1849, he also contributed to *The Weekly Messenger* of the German Reformed Church. These latter articles, though important for a reconstruction of debates within the German Reformed church during this period, are often more occasional in nature and they are inaccessible to most scholars as well.

Special attention is also given to Nevin's 1851 lectures in theology to students at Mercersburg. Nevin's 1851 lectures were collated by William H. Erb from three separate (though very similar) sets of student notes, and published as William H. Erb, ed., *Dr. Nevin's Theology: Based on Manuscript Class-Room Lectures* (Reading, Pa.: I. M. Beaver, 1913).

[20] The body of literature on the Mercersburg movement is large and increasing. The best general discussion of Nevin's theology and the Mercersburg movement remains James Hastings Nichols' *Romanticism in American Theology*. On the Mercersburg Theology generally, see George Warren Richards, "The Mercersburg Theology, Historically Considered," *Papers of the American Society of Church History*, second series, vol. 3 (1912): 119-149; "The Mercersburg Theology: Its Purpose and Principles," *Church History* 20 (1951): 42-55.

Dissertations on Nevin's theology include Kenneth Moses Plummer, "The Theology of John Williamson Nevin in the Mercersburg Period, 1840-1852" (Ph.D. diss., University of Chicago, 1958); William L. Carlough, "A Historical Comparison of the Theology of John Williamson Nevin and Contemporary Protestant Sacramentalism" (Ph.D. diss., New York University, 1961).

Important studies of Nevin's sacramental theology are Brian A. Gerrish, *Tradition and the Modern World: Reformed Theology in the Nineteenth Century* (Chicago: University of Chicago Press, 1978), 49-70; E. Brooks Holifield, "Mercersburg,

applied soteriology, while certainly recognized, has not been exhaustively treated, particularly the relation between union with Christ, imputation, and justification. In this chapter, we will see that Nevin rejects both the federal and New England approaches. Instead he attempts to return to Calvin while recasting the thought of the Reformer in ways that compromise, to some extent, Calvin's basic intentions.

German Influences on the Mercersburg Theology

The period between the death of Edwards and the beginning of the nineteenth century saw the introduction to America of the empirical philosophy known as Scottish Common Sense Realism.[21] Suffice it at this point to note that the Common Sense philosophy was characterized by a reflexive dualism and predilection for making distinctions (between mind and matter, subject and object, body and soul, flesh and spirit, finite and infinite, the natural and the supernatural, cognitive faith and religious experience, and so forth). Along with this came a focus on truth as static and particular, and a preoccupation with the inductive, or "Baconian," method in both the natural sciences and in theology. By the middle of the nineteenth century in America, however, the limitations of Scottish Common Sense Realism were becoming evident, and the attention of many thinkers turned increasingly to a variety of theological and idealist philosophical currents of thought coming out of Germany.[22] Several distinct influences must be identified here—an idealist ontology together with its implied epistemology, organic views of history, and christocentric approaches

---

Princeton, and the South: The Sacramental Controversy in the Nineteenth Century," *Journal of Presbyterian History* 54 (1976): 238-257. Nevin's ecclesiology is addressed in Walter H. Conser, *Church and Confession: Conservative Theologians in Germany, England, and America, 1815-1866* (Macon, Ga.: Mercer University Press, 1984), 273-297; W. Clark Gilpin, "The Doctrine of the Church in the Thought of Alexander Campbell and John Nevin," *Mid-Stream* 19 (1980): 417-427; John B. Payne, "Schaff and Nevin, Colleagues at Mercersburg: The Church Question," *Church History* 61 (1992): 169-190; Charles Yrigoyen, "Mercersburg's Quarrel with Methodism," *Methodist History* 22 (1983): 3-19; John F. Wolverton, "John Williamson Nevin and the Episcopalians: The Debate on the 'Church Question,' 1851-1874," *Historical Magazine of the Protestant Episcopal Church* 49 (1980): 361-387. For an analysis of liturgical developments, see Jack Martin Maxwell, *Worship and Reformed Theology: The Liturgical Lessons of Mercersburg* (Pittsburgh: Pickwick Press, 1976).

Nevin's doctrine of sanctification is treated in Glenn A. Hewitt, *Regeneration and Morality: A Study of Charles Finney, Charles Hodge, John W. Nevin, and Horace Bushnell* (Brooklyn, N.Y.: Carlson Publishing, 1991), 89-123.

[21] The nature and theological influence of Scottish Common Sense philosophy will be treated more extensively in the next chapter.

[22] This shift has been ably chronicled by Kuklick, *Churchmen and Philosophers*, 117-229.

to theology—together with the "Mediating Theologians" who propagated and popularized these ideas.

IDEALIST ONTOLOGY AND EPISTEMOLOGY

The nineteenth-century idealist ontology and epistemology took shape in response to the epochal work of Immanuel Kant (1724-1804).[23] Awakened from his "dogmatic slumber" by David Hume, Kant sought to deal with the skepticism of Hume by positing a distinction between noumena and phenomena. Human beings can know the phenomenal, the thing as it appears, but can never penetrate to know the noumenal, the thing in itself, through metaphysical inquiry. But where metaphysics fail, practical (i.e., moral) reason comes to the fore, as Kant argues that theologically significant matters such as the reality of God, human freedom, and immortality are to be viewed as postulates of practical reason. In addition, Kant called attention to the mind's extensive contribution to what is subjectively known. Even time and space, he argued, are *a priori* intuitions imposed by the mind.

Kant's proposals caused a crisis of theological method. The subject-object distinction common both to Scottish Common Sense Realism and to the rationalist-supernaturalism of earlier German thinkers was undercut. In view of the limits of reason and the mind's substantial epistemological contribution, it was increasingly difficult to view theological truth as a set of static, objective propositions to which the mind gave assent. And if this is the case, how is the theological enterprise to be funded, and to what do theological statements refer?

Such concerns prompted methodological developments in two broad directions. First, since the mind was no longer viewed as a primarily passive receptor of external "objects" of knowledge, there was a new emphasis in theology on subjectivity and experience as a source of truth. Friedrich D. E. Schleiermacher (1768-1834), for example, sought to move beyond the Kantian noumenal-phenomenal and metaphysical-moral dualisms by finding a level antecedent to cognition and morality—feeling (*Gefühl*)—where God is immediately present to pretheoretical human consciousness.[24] Another response to Kant was the metaphysical idealism of Schelling and Hegel. Kant's stark dualisms were intolerable to these thinkers, and they embarked on a quest

---

[23]Helpful treatments of Kant's significance for theology include Emil L. Fackenheim, "Immanuel Kant," in *Nineteenth Century Religious Thought in the West*, ed. by Ninian Smart, *et al*, 3 vols. (New York: Cambridge University Press, 1985), 17-40; Hans W. Frei, "Niebuhr's Theological Background," in *Faith and Ethics: The Theology of H. Richard Niebuhr*, ed. Paul Ramsey (New York: Harper & Brothers, 1957), 9-64, esp. 16-21, 32-40.

[24]See Friedrich Schleiermacher, *The Christian Faith*, ed. by H. R. Mackintosh and J. S. Stewart (Edinburgh: T. & T. Clark, 1928), 5-26. See also Brian Gerrish, "Friedrich Schleiermacher," in *Nineteenth Century Religious Thought in the West*, 3 vols., ed. Ninian Smart *et al* (New York: Cambridge University Press, 1985), I:123-156.

for the inner unity of all reality, an inner unity framed in terms of an idealist ontology which posited an absolute, creative mind as the source and ground of all finite particularity.[25] Finite reason, argued Hegel, is but Absolute reason coming to self-consciousness. All world process—nature, history, and finite thought—is seen as the dialectical unfolding of the Absolute.

This idealist ontology effaces many traditional epistemological distinctions. Subject and object, *a priori* and *a posteriori*, and so forth are transcended, as is the absoluteness of metaphysical distinctions such as the finite and the infinite, matter and spirit, natural and supernatural. Furthermore, the religious and theological implications of this integrative idealist ontology are highly significant. If world process is the unfolding of the Absolute, the God-world relationship is framed in terms very different from the older orthodoxy—the relationship is no longer one of absolute difference but dialectical identity *and* difference.[26] Recast in idealist terms, the christological question no longer revolves around a paradoxical union of two antithetical "natures" but rather focuses on the explicit realization of the (already implicit) idea of divine-human unity.[27]

ORGANIC VIEWS OF HISTORY

The rise of metaphysical idealism spawned a new interest in history. If world process is the unfolding of the Absolute, then history is invested with ultimate significance. Again the German philosophers Schelling and Hegel play a crucial role, although predecessors such as Herder and Lessing had already begun to view history in terms of progress and development.[28] As G. A. Benrath has noted, this view of history as the organic unfolding of the divine life involves the "sacralization" of history.[29] The identification of divine becoming and historical process is such that history *is* ultimate reality. In light of this, the intense interest that the nineteenth century as a whole displayed in historical studies, and theology in particular with the discipline of church history, becomes understandable.

Organic, developmental views of history, however, stood in stark tension

---

[25]See Frederick C. Coppleston, *Fichte to Nietzsche, A History of Philosophy*, vol. 6 (London: Burns and Oates, 1965), 1-31.

[26]For helpful overviews of Hegel's theological significance, see Karl Barth, *Protestant Theology in the Nineteenth Century* (Valley Forge: Judson Press, 1973), 384-421; Emil Fackenheim, *The Religious Dimension of Hegel's Thought* (Bloomington: Indiana University Press, 1967); Peter C. Hodgson, "Georg Wilhelm Friedrich Hegel," in *Nineteenth Century Religious Thought in the West*, 3 vols., ed. Ninian Smart and others (New York: Cambridge University Press, 1985), I:81-119.

[27]See Hodgson, "Hegel," 102-105.

[28]See Paul Collins Hayner, *Reason and Existence: Schelling's Philosophy of History* (Leiden: E. J. Brill, 1967), 17-21.

[29]Gustav Adolf Benrath, "Evangelische und katholische Kirchenhistorie im Zeichen der Aufklärung und der Romantik," *Zeitschrift für Kirchengeschichte* 82 (1971): 209.

with the static historiography characteristic of earlier Protestant thought and of the Scottish Common Sense thinkers. As this organic perspective was introduced to America in the 1840's, particularly by Philip Schaff of Mercersburg, one immediate result was to open the vexed question of continuity and discontinuity—between pre-Reformation Catholicism and Reformation thought, and between Reformation and nineteenth-century theology. Common Sense historians, with their focus on static doctrinal truth, could dismiss as "heretical" whole epochs of church history. But if the history of the church is viewed as an ongoing organic unfolding, then the question of continuity between the Roman Catholic and Protestant traditions becomes much more pressing. Yet another result of the organic, developmental historical perspective was the realization that there could be no simple repristination of past formulations. Continuity with the past would of necessity take the form of a *critical* continuity which took account of both old formulations and the new situation.

CHRISTOCENTRIC APPROACHES TO THEOLOGY

Yet another aspect of German influence is the rise in the early nineteenth century of what may be termed "christocentric" approaches to theology, in which christology becomes the central organizing principle.[30] In contrast to much of the earlier Enlightenment theology, in which Jesus was viewed as little more than a moral example and teacher of rational religion, German theology beginning with Schleiermacher entered a new period in which the figure of Jesus assumed central importance. Schleiermacher's well-known definition of the Christian religion illustrates this trend: "Christianity is a monotheistic faith, belonging to the teleological type of religion, and is essentially distinguished from other such faiths by the fact that in it everything is related to the redemption accomplished by Jesus of Nazareth."[31]

Schleiermacher used a number of themes to illuminate the uniqueness of Jesus. His method, in short, was to reason from the religious consciousness of the Christian community to the historical ground of that consciousness. Central to Schleiermacher's argument is the claim that in Jesus the archetypal ideal (*Urbild*) of humanity has been fully realized in history. The content of this "ideality," or *Urbildlichkeit*, consists in the "constant potency of his God-consciousness" and his "unclouded blessedness" (i.e., sinlessness).[32]

---

[30] For two appraisals of this shift, see Eugene TeSelle, *Christ in Context: Divine Purpose and Human Possibility* (Philadelphia: Fortress Press, 1975); Richard A. Muller, "Emanuel V. Gerhart on the "Christ Idea" as Fundamental Principle," *Westminster Theological Journal* 48 (1986): 97-117.

[31] Schleiermacher, *Christian Faith*, 52.

[32] On Schleiermacher's view of Jesus as the archetypal ideal, see Richard R. Niebuhr, *Schleiermacher on Christ and Religion* (New York: Charles Scribner's Sons, 1964), 219.

Throughout, Schleiermacher seeks to avoid natural/supernatural dualism that had dogged the earlier rationalistic supernaturalism, and to present a theology consistent with immanent, historical existence. In place of the traditional two-natures doctrine, which he views as intolerably dualistic,[33] Schleiermacher asserts that the "Redeemer...is like all men in virtue of the identity of human nature, but distinguished from them all by the constant potency of His God-consciousness, which was a veritable existence of God in Him."[34]

With the introduction of this new level of God-consciousness, Schleiermacher argues that Jesus embodies the culmination of creation. In Jesus the creation of humanity reaches its conclusion, and Christ is thus termed the "Second Adam."[35] Clearly, the coming of Christ involves not simply the restitution of a previously lost state, but the positive elevation of human nature. It is also apparent that in Schleiermacher we find a kind of christology "from below," in which Christ's humanity is the starting point for reflection. In the final analysis, the "deity" of Christ consists in a function (God-consciousness) of his archetypal humanity.

The importance of this archetypal humanity becomes apparent when Schleiermacher's view of the application of redemption is examined. Schleiermacher's Reformed heritage becomes apparent as the application is described as a *unio Christi* involving the assumption of the believer "into the power of His God-consciousness" and "into the fellowship of His unclouded blessedness."[36] Schleiermacher insists that this assumption is "mystical," by which he means that it is a corporate phenomenon taking place in the life of the church and occurring in human consciousness through the preaching of the word and through the effect of the sacramental symbols.[37]

Schleiermacher's influence on the methodology and content of subsequent nineteenth-century German theology was pervasive. In particular, his christocentrism became common currency on the continent. Several aspects of Schleiermacher's christocentricity are directly relevant to this study. First, it helped to overcome the creation/redemption dualism of Protestant orthodoxy, implicit in which was a natural/supernatural dualism as well. Schleiermacher solves this relational difficulty by viewing Christ as the Second Adam and

---

[33] Schleiermacher, *Christian Faith*, 389-413.

[34] Ibid., 385. The God-consciousness of Jesus differs in degree, rather than kind, from the God-consciousness of other human beings. See p. 476.

[35] See ibid., 367, 389.

[36] Ibid., 425, 431. On this, H. R. Mackintosh, *The Doctrine of the Person of Christ* (New York: Charles Scribner's Sons, 1912), 254, writes: "A light is cast on Schleiermacher's deeply Christian conception of the Saviour by his mystical view of His redeeming work...Its cardinal idea is that of vital union with Christ. It is by taking us up into the energies of His God-consciousness and the fellowship of His perfect blessedness that He reconciles and saves."

[37] Schleiermacher, *Christian Faith*, 428-429, 611-655. See also the discussion in TeSelle, *Christ in Context*, 79-82.

redemption as the completion of creation, thus in essence subordinating redemption to creation and the supernatural to the natural.[38]

Another result was the ascription of a new dogmatic significance to union with the humanity of Christ. As we have already seen, Reformed federal theology tended to view the humanity of Christ as little more than a *conditio sine qua non* of salvation. For Schleiermacher, however, the emphasis is on participation in the archetypal humanity of Christ as the means whereby all the benefits of salvation are received and find their unity.[39] Although they reached their respective conclusions by very different routes, there is nevertheless a striking parallel between Calvin's notion of union with the incarnate humanity of Christ and Schleiermacher's idea of assumption into the God-consciousness of Jesus' archetypal humanity.[40]

THE MEDIATING THEOLOGIANS

Particularly important for our purposes were the theologians who sought to mediate between Schleiermacher and Hegel on the one hand and orthodoxy on the other.[41] These "mediating theologians"—especially J. A. G. Neander

---

[38] This subordination is not quite complete, however. The introduction of the archetypal principle into history involves at least a relative miracle (*Christian Faith*, 381). Thus, an act of God is necessary to instantiate the principle within the historical continuum. Schleiermacher, 430, writes that "the beginning of the Kingdom of God is a supernatural thing, which, however, becomes natural as soon as it emerges into manifestation."

[39] See ibid., 478.

[40] Schleiermacher's method of doing christology "from below" means that the humanity of Christ must carry considerably more theological freight than is necessary with Calvin's two-natures christology. The result of this, as several generations of Schleiermacher interpreters have noted, is a certain docetic tinge. For example, Schleiermacher's Christ is not only sinless but also immune to temptation (*Christian Faith*, 415). Furthermore, the emphasis on the "constant potency of his God-consciousness" ill accords with the Christ's cry of dereliction on the Cross. This point is forcefully made by Gunton, *Yesterday and Today*, 98-100. See also Mackintosh, *Person of Christ*, 255; TeSelle, *Christ in Context*, 82-83.

Schleiermacher's relationship to the Reformed tradition is explored in Wilhelm Niesel, "Schleiermachers Verhältnis zur reformierten Tradition," *Zwischen den Zeiten* 8 (1930): 511-525; Walter L. Moore, "Schleiermacher as a Calvinist: A Comparison of Calvin and Schleiermacher on Providence and Predestination," *Scottish Journal of Theology* 24 (1971): 167-183; B. A. Gerrish, *Tradition and the Modern World*, 13-48; "Theology Within the Limits of Piety Alone: Schleiermacher and Calvin's Notion of God," in *The Old Protestantism and the New: Essays on the Reformation Heritage* (Edinburgh: T. & T. Clark, 1982): 196-207.

[41] On the German mediating theology, see Otto Pfleiderer, *The Development of Theology in Germany Since Kant: and Its Progress in Great Britain Since 1825*, trans. by J. Frederick Smith (New York: Macmillan, 1893), 131-153; Ragnar Holte, *Die Vermittlungstheologie. Ihre theologischen Grundbriffe, kritisch untersucht* (Uppsala:

(1789-1850), I. A. Dorner (1809-1884), Richard Rothe (1799-1867), and Carl Ullmann (1796-1865)—modified the views of Schleiermacher and Hegel in a number of important ways, generally in the direction of orthodoxy.[42] With regard to the doctrine of God, both the "pantheism" of Hegel and the Sabellianism of Schleiermacher were treated with suspicion as the mediating theologians moved toward supernaturalistic conceptions of the God-world relationship, and toward more personal conceptions of the divine modes of being.[43]

The mediating theologians also granted, with Hegel and against Schleiermacher, the possibility of objective theological knowledge. Schleiermacher's attempt to view the object of all theological reflection as analysis of Christian self-consciousness seemed too subjective for many. While commending Schleiermacher for progressing beyond the intellectualism of the older orthodoxy and the moralism of Kant, the mediating theologians sought to integrate intellect, will, and feeling in a new epistemological synthesis which gave a larger place to objective supernatural revelation.[44]

Almquist & Wiksell, 1965); Claude Welch, *Protestant Thought in the Nineteenth Century*, 2 vols. (New Haven: Yale University Press, 1972, 1985), I:269-291.

[42]It was typical for these thinkers to view Schleiermacher in particular, not as the founder of a new epoch in theology, but as a bridge between rationalism and orthodoxy. Philip Schaff, *Germany: Its Universities, Theology, and Religion* (Philadelphia: Lindsay and Blakiston, 1857), 320, writes: "Schleiermacher first built a bridge over the abyss that divides the dismal swamp of skepticism from the sunny hills of faith, and kindled again the flame of religion and of the Christian consciousness." See also p. 154; Welch, *Protestant Thought*, I:269-273.

Ullmann's "Das Wesen des Christentums," *Studien und Kritiken* (1845) was loosely translated by John W. Nevin as "Preliminary Essay," in *The Mystical Presence: A Vindication of the Reformed or Calvinistic Doctrine of the Holy Eucharist* (Philadelphia: J. B. Lippincott, 1846), 13-47. This piece provides a brief presentation of the mediating theology's christocentric concerns.

[43]On the mediating theologians rejection of Sabellianism, see I. A. Dorner, *System of Christian Doctrine* [excerpts], in *God and Incarnation in Mid-Nineteenth Century German Theology*, ed. and trans. by Claude Welch (New York: Oxford University Press, 1965), 184-189, 209-215.

The mediating theologians' suspicion of impersonal pantheism is evident in Ullmann, "Preliminary Essay," 28: "The main contradiction lies between the pantheistic speculation, which resolves the idea in question into a general fact belonging to the phenomenology of spirit, and the proper Christian view, by which all is made to rest on the acknowledgment of a personal God and a positive revelation, as something historically real and individual. The difference is complete." See also I. A. Dorner, "On the Proper Version of the Dogmatic Concept of the Immutability of God," in *God and Incarnation in Mid-Nineteenth Century German Theology*, ed. and trans. by Claude Welch (New York: Oxford University Press, 1965), 119.

[44]Ullmann, "Preliminary Essay," 27, wrote: "Schleiermacher, in full conformity with the prevailingly subjective character of his theological views, and his conception of

Schleiermacher and Hegel were also criticized for an inadequate view of sin. Schleiermacher, for example, is chided for his neglect of the real estrangement between God and human beings due to sin, and for his corresponding slighting of an objective atonement.[45] In addition, the idealist tradition of Hegel was roundly criticized, particularly by Julius Müller, for making sin and estrangement a necessary moment in the dialectic (i.e., a metaphysical necessity) rather than a contingent and fundamentally moral disaster.[46]

Finally, the mediating theologians made significant moves back toward the traditional two-natures doctrine in christology, though they expressed it in somewhat more dynamic terms. Agreeing with the Hegelian tradition that the highest form of religion involves the union of the divine and the human, they nevertheless insisted (against Strauss and the Hegelian left wing) that a real, historical union of God with a complete humanity took place in the person of Jesus Christ. Like Schleiermacher, they started with the archetypal humanity of Christ as the "Second Adam" and, utilizing a "christology from below," they deduced the presence of the divine from the character of Jesus' humanity.[47] Considerable attention was also directed to the relationship between the divine and human in Christ. Unlike earlier orthodoxy, which often presented the "two natures" of Christ as static and ontologically antithetical realities, the mediating theologians stressed the compatibility and dynamic interaction of the divine and human in Christ.[48] We will see that the so-called "Mercersburg Theology," articulated by John Williamson Nevin and his colleague Philip Schaff, recast a good deal of this German mediating theology in a form that addressed the

---

religion as a form of feeling, has here also confined himself exclusively to what is matter of inward experience, and Christian salvation as carried forward in the life of the subject. But it is an inadequate view of religion to place it in feeling, to the exclusion of knowledge and action. A full, sound piety embodies the understanding and will also as original elements in its constitution."

[45] See Ullmann, "Preliminary Essay," 26-27.

[46] See Julius Müller, *The Christian Doctrine of Sin*, 2 vols., trans. William Urwick (Edinburgh: T. & T. Clark, 1868). See also Ullmann, "Preliminary Essay," 32; Barth, *Protestant Theology*, 592-93.

[47] The popularity of notions of Jesus' "archetypal humanity" is noted by I. A. Dorner, *A System of Christian Doctrine*, 4 vols, trans. Alfred Cave and J. S. Banks (Edinburgh: T. & T. Clark, 1882), III:254-255 (reprinted in Welch, *God and Incarnation*, 183-184, 239-247).

The apologetical use of the archetypal humanity is evident in Carl Ullmann, *Die Sundlosigkeit Jesu: eine apologetische Betrachtung*, 7 Aufl. (Gotha: Friedrich Andreas Perthes, 1863); *The Sinlessness of Christ: An Evidence for Christianity*, trans. by Sophia Taylor (Edinburgh: T. & T. Clark, 1882); and Philip Schaff, *The Moral Character of Christ, or the Perfection of Christ's Humanity a Proof of His Divinity* (Chambersburg, Pa.: M. Kieffer, 1861).

[48] Note especially Dorner's idea of a "developing incarnation" in Welch, *God and Incarnation*, 247-256. See also Ullmann, *Sinlessness of Jesus*, 180-206.

peculiarities of the American situation.[49]

Nevin's Theological Method

Though his 1851 theological lectures are preserved in good form, Nevin never wrote a complete dogmatics. The order of presentation in the lectures is conventional, beginning with prolegomena and revelation, and moving on to the attributes of God, anthropology, christology, soteriology, and ecclesiology.[50] The distinctiveness of his theology is more a matter of content than form. As his invitation to teach at Princeton indicates, Nevin was well versed in the biblical languages. His references to Scripture are extensive, and he was conservative on matters of biblical higher criticism.[51] Nevin also

---

[49]Although Nevin's dependence upon the German mediating theologians was recognized early on, there has nevertheless been recent scholarly disagreement regarding the relative influence of a variety of strains of German theology. K. M. Plummer, "Theology of John Williamson Nevin, 383-390, while noting the variety of influences and the difficulty of characterizing this complex thinker, finally describes Nevin's theology as "Lutheranizing." J. H. Nichols, *The Mercersburg Theology*, 16, also emphasizes the Lutheran roots, and suggests that the "Mercersburg Theology, then, may be triangulated from high-church Lutheranism and Anglo-Catholicism." B. A. Gerrish, *Tradition and the Modern World*, 49-70, presents Nevin in a more Reformed light, and emphasizes the influence of Schleiermacher. Finally, J. B. Payne, "Schaff and Nevin," 175, returns to the influence of the mediating theologians, viewing Nevin as most strongly influenced by the theologians of the Prussian Union church.

As we will see, this study of the Mercersburg soteriology repeatedly reveals the powerful influence of Schleiermacher and his "mediating" successors. Applying their insights to the American Reformed situation, Nevin himself sought to mediate between New England moralism and the doctrinal emphasis of Princeton. Christianity, Nevin argued together with Schleiermacher, is neither a knowing nor a doing, but a life. Nevin also follows Schleiermacher in his christocentrism—Nevin's "second Adam" christology with Christ as the goal of creation is scarcely imaginable without the impetus of Schleiermacher. This influence is also evident in Nevin's interrelation of self-consciousness, faith, and union with Christ, and also in his non-dualist approach to the relationship of the natural and the supernatural. Finally, Schleiermacher's famous conception of religious dependence is reflected in Nevin's characterization of the religious consciousness as dependence: "The first utterance of religious consciousness is that the whole world is directly dependent upon God." Erb, *Nevin's Theology*, 153.

For a sympathetic examination of Schleiermacher's influence on Nevin and the Mercersburg Theology, see William M. Reily, "Schleiermacher and the Theology of the Mercersburg Review," *Mercersburg Review* 18 (1871): 165-182. See also John W. Nevin, "Our Relations to Germany," *Mercersburg Review* 14 (1867): 627-633.

[50]The order of treatment is probably due to Nevin's use of a theological textbook by the Scottish Seceder theologian John Dick (1764-1833). First published in America in 1835, Dick's *Lectures on Theology* attained wide usage during the mid-nineteenth century. The volume is strongly oriented toward the federal theology tradition.

[51]Though aware of the critical currents coming out of Germany, Nevin affirmed the

ascribed remarkable weight to the tradition of the church, viewing it as foundational both for the interpretation of scripture and for the theological enterprise. In particular, the Apostles' Creed was regarded as the interpretive crux, and the Protestant rule of faith (*sola scriptura*) is significantly qualified in favor of tradition.[52]

Nevin insists that Christianity is primarily life rather than doctrine or ethics. It is participation in the life of Christ, but this life is not to the exclusion of dogma, for it is the nature of the Christian religion to involve the human being in its totality, including the intellect.

> Christianity is indeed primarily life, not doctrine; but it is such a life as requires to take full possession, in the end, of our whole human being. This includes knowledge as well as action; and why then should not the contents of the new creation lay claim to our understanding full as much as our Will?...It is just *because* Christianity is a new life, that it must work like leaven into our whole existence, generating a theology or theoretic religion in its own form, as well as a religion of mere feeling and practice.[53]

Furthermore, because theology springs from this new life, Nevin adopts the Augustinian and Anselmian stance of *credo ut intelligam* and *fides quaerens intellectum*. Theology is to be done from inside the circle of faith.[54]

Throughout his writings from this period, the influence of German idealism, and particularly the organic idealism of Schelling is readily apparent.[55] It is

---

traditional authorship ascriptions for all the biblical books. See Erb, *Nevin's Theology*, 20-24.

[52] See especially John W. Nevin, "The Apostles' Creed," *Mercersburg Review* I (1849):105-127, 201-221, 313-347; "Puritanism and the Creed"; Erb, *Nevin's Theology*, 55-58.

[53] John W. Nevin, Review of *God in Christ*, by Horace Bushnell, *Mercersburg Review* 1 (1849): 312.

[54] See Nevin, "Apostles' Creed," 207, 211, 345; *My Own Life*, 69; Erb, *Nevin's Theology*, 294. Thus Nevin breaks decisively with the empiricist Scottish Common Sense tradition he had been taught at Princeton.

[55] Nevin's organic idealism is evident in this quote from 1846: "We take *Idea* here in its true sense, by which it expresses the very inmost substance of that which exists, as distinguished from its simply phenomenal character in time and space. As such it is not opposed to what is actual, but constitutes rather its truth and soul. All life is Ideal, that is, exists truly in the form of possibility, before it can become actual; and it is only in the presence and power of this potential life, this invisible, mysterious living nature which lies behind and beyond all outward manifestations, that these last can ever be said to carry with them any reality whatever...But it is the most real of all realities that God has established in this world." John W. Nevin, "The Church," in *The Mercersburg Theology*, ed. James Hastings Nichols (New York: Oxford University Press, 1966), 58.

The philosophical influences on Nevin and the Mercersburg are treated in Kuklick, *Churchmen and Philosophers*, 171-183; Linden Jay DeBie, "German Idealism in

especially evident in Nevin's nearly constant polemic against what he terms the "outward" or "extrinsic," the "mechanical," and the "abstract," and in his turn toward the "inward," the "organic," and the "concrete." We see here a vigorous methodological tendency toward unity and integration rather than disjunction, toward the *a priori* and ideal over against the *a posteriori* and empirical, and toward the general over the particular. Here the study of history seems to have been the catalyst for Nevin. Regarding his stance prior to his idealist period Nevin later wrote:

> I had not yet awaked at all to the apprehension of what history necessarily is for the life of humanity and the moral world in every view. It was, for me, still a system only of dead outward facts. I had no sense of its constitutional relation everywhere to the inmost significance of these facts themselves. I saw in it no science, much less a philosophy. Its necessary *a priori* principles and postulates, as connected with the general scheme of the world, had not begun to dawn upon my mind.[56]

Similarly, in his apologetics and theology generally Nevin departs from the dualistic "rationalistic supernaturalism" so prevalent during his day by bringing nature and supernature into organic relationship: "Miracles are not external to the whole course of nature, nor do they violate the established laws; but they are comprehended in the original law of nature. They belong to the process of this world...A new order of things is then introduced, but in a natural way."[57] Likewise, Nevin's approach to ethics involves an organic synthesis of liberty and authority. These must be united if the idea of true moral freedom is to be realized.[58]

Nevin's ecclesiology exhibits the same integrative tendency. He decries the proliferation of sects, and their tendency "to drive all religion into a system of outward notions and abstractions...They hold not so much in the actual apprehension of divine realities by faith, as in the mere notion of them by the imagination."[59] In keeping with their focus on the external, Nevin observes that the sects show great concern for "law" and *de jure divino* conceptions of the

---

Protestant Orthodoxy: The Mercersburg Movement, 1840-1860," (Ph.D. diss., McGill University, 1987); William DiPuccio, "Nevin's Idealistic Philosophy," in *Reformed Confessionalism in Nineteenth-Century America*, ed. Sam Hamstra and Arie J. Griffioen (Lanham, MD: Scarecrow Press, 1995), 43-67.

[56]Nevin, *My Own Life*, 40.

[57]Erb, *Nevin's Theology*, 30. See also Nevin, *My Own Life*, 106-116.

[58]See John W. Nevin, *Human Freedom and A Plea for Philosophy: Two Essays* (Mercersburg, Pa.: P. A. Rice, 1850).

[59]John W. Nevin, "The Sect System," in *Catholic and Reformed: Selected Theological Writings of John Williamson Nevin* (Pittsburgh: Pickwick Press, 1978), 150. This article originally appeared in the *Mercersburg Review* 1 (1849): 482-507; 521-539.

church, while ignoring its inward life and spirit.[60]

As this tendency toward integration is worked out, Nevin reveals himself to be an intuitive and thematic thinker rather than a systematic one. In this, too, he reflects the German idealist heritage. There are, to be sure, loose ends and ambiguities in Nevin's thought, but these emerge because of Nevin's unswerving commitment to certain basic themes. This general integrative bent is perhaps most evident in Nevin's soteriology, and particularly in his view of union with Christ.

The Nature of Union with Christ

With regard to the centrality of union with Christ, Nevin stands squarely in the Reformed tradition, and here he rests explicitly on the legacy of Calvin. Nevin's greatest theological work, *The Mystical Presence* (1846), while ostensibly a defense of Calvin's eucharistic doctrine, in a deeper sense is a theological treatise on the *unio Christi*. Nevin wrote: "The *Question of the Eucharist*...may be regarded as in some sense central to the whole Christian system. For Christianity is grounded in the living union of the believer with the person of Christ; and this great fact is emphatically concentrated in the mystery of the Lord's Supper."[61]

In *The Mystical Presence* and other works from this period, Nevin distances his own view from the two prevailing American Protestant theories. First, union with Christ is not to be construed as merely the voluntary sharing of moral purpose and concern. It is more than the "moral union" of Samuel Hopkins and his New England successors. There is nothing distinctively Christian about such a union, and it reduces religion to a flat moralism.

> In this view, the relation is more again than a simply *moral* union. Such a union we have, where two or more persons are bound together by inward agreement, sympathy, and correspondence. Every common friendship is of this sort. It is the relation of the disciple to the master, whom he loves and reveres. It is the relation of the devout Jew to Moses, his venerated lawgiver and prophet. It holds also undoubtedly between the believer and Christ...But Christianity includes more than such a moral union, separately considered. This union itself is only the result here of a relation more inward and deep.[62]

Nevin just as strongly opposes the compound view of union found in federal orthodoxy, that is with the notion of an extrinsic "legal" union (involving immediate imputation) and a "spiritual union" consisting of the efficacy of the Holy Spirit as the representative of an absent Christ.

---

[60]Ibid., 151. See also "The Anglican Crisis," *Mercersburg Review* 3 (1851): 374-77.
[61]Nevin, *Mystical Presence*, 51.
[62]Ibid., 55-56. See also idem, "The New Creation in Christ," *Mercersburg Review* 2 (1850): 1-11.

> The relation of believers to Christ, then, is more again than that of a simply *legal* union. His is indeed the representative of his people, and what he has done and suffered on their behalf is counted to their benefit, as though it had been done by themselves. They have an interest in his merits, a title to all the advantages secured by his life and death. But this external imputation rests at last on an inward, real unity of life, without which it could have no reason or force...Of course, once more, the communion in question is not simply with Christ in his *divine nature* separately taken, or with the *Holy Ghost* as the representative of his presence in the world. It does not hold in the influences of the Spirit merely, enlightening the soul and moving it to holy affections and purposes.[63]

Nevin also insightfully suggests that this extrinsic federal approach to justification and legal union constitutes an unstable synthesis, tilting toward a theoretical antinomianism but with the potential to fall into a practical legalism at the same time.

> It is well to note how generally the sect system adheres to the article of *justification by faith*, and how prone it is to run this side of Christianity out to a false extreme, either in the way of dead antinomianism or wild fanaticism...They...turn justification by faith into a complete abstraction, and so nullify the law in one form, only to come too generally under the yoke of it in another.[64]

Nevin's positive presentation of union with Christ blends elements of Calvin, Reformed orthodoxy, Schleiermacher, and the German mediating theologians into a new and striking synthesis. With Calvin, whom Nevin regarded as "the great theologian of his age,"[65] Nevin stresses that the believer is united with the "substance" of Christ, and particularly with Christ's incarnate humanity.[66] Furthermore, this union involves faith and the work of the Holy

---

[63] Nevin, *Mystical Presence*, 57. See also Erb, *Nevin's Theology*, 291. Nevin regarded bicovenantal federalism as having been "formulated by the celebrated Witsius." See Erb, *Nevin's Theology*, 202. Nevin frequently uses the terminology of federalism, but almost always redefines it.

On the surface, Nevin appears to misinterpret the federal view of the Holy Spirit's activity, viewing it as "mediate," as nothing more than "moral suasion," and as "appeals addressed to the understanding and will." See *Mystical Presence*, 187-88. The federal tradition had generally insisted that the action of the Holy Spirit is "physical" rather than merely "moral," and Charles Hodge's treatment of this matter seems to respond directly to Nevin's misapprehension. See Hodge, *Systematic Theology*, II:684-87. On the deeper level, however, the Scottish Common Sense apologetic of Princeton Seminary was expressly directed toward the intellect. Here one perceives a tension between the Princeton soteriology and the Princeton apologetic. See Cornelius Van Til, *The Defense of the Faith*, 3rd ed. (Philadelphia: Presbyterian & Reformed, 1967), 79-90.

[64] Nevin, "Sect System," 160-61.

[65] Nevin, *Mystical Presence*, 67.

[66] See Nevin, "Catholic Unity," in *The Mercersburg Theology*, ed. James Hastings

Spirit.[67] Also as in Calvin, the humanity of Christ serves as a hedge against mysticism in that the Christian's union with the divine is mediated through the humanity of Christ, "the indispensable medium of our participation in his person as divine."[68]

But the overwhelming importance of Christ's humanity becomes evident in Nevin's treatment of the Incarnation. It is, for Nevin, the central event of all history, the ontological ground of all created reality, and the epistemological key to all truth: "The Incarnation is the deepest and most comprehensive fact, in the economy of the world. Jesus Christ authenticates himself, and all truth and reality besides; or rather all truth and reality are such, only by the relation in which they stand to him, as their great centre and last ground."[69] In the Incarnation, humanity is united with the eternal Logos so as to introduce a new principle of existence into the world, the epochal significance of which is highlighted by Nevin's frequent use of the Pauline (and Schleiermacherian) christological term "second Adam."

In discussions of the rationale for the Incarnation, Nevin is emphatic that the Incarnation is much more than a *conditio sine qua non* of the Atonement. There is, in fact, a certain logical as well as temporal priority here: "The true order is, the mystery of the Incarnation first, and then the atonement, as growing forth from this."[70] The logic of his position implies, and Nevin at times suggests, that the Incarnation would have occurred even apart from sin.[71] The heart of

---

Nichols (New York: Oxford University Press, 1966, 38-39; *Mystical Presence*, 54-62; Erb, *Nevin's Theology*, 291-92.

[67]Nevin declares: "The mystical union is accomplished by the Holy Spirit on the one side and faith on the other, not including nor acting independently of each other, but as counterparts. Both the activity of the Spirit and the exercise of faith are necessary for the mystical union." Erb, *Nevin's Theology*, 291.

[68]Nevin, *Mystical Presence*, 171.

[69]Nevin, "Apostles' Creed," 315. See also *Mystical Presence*, 199-201; Erb, *Nevin's Theology*, 127-28.

Nevin's treatment of the Incarnation is traditional, and he affirms the "two-natures doctrine" of Chalcedonian orthodoxy. See *Mystical Presence*, 210; Erb, *Nevin's Theology*, 239-247. His emphasis, however, falls more on the unity of the person of Christ than on the distinction and integrity of the two natures. That is to say, Nevin's christology is Alexandrian rather than Antiochene.

[70]Nevin, "Apostles' Creed," 343. See also *Mystical Presence*, 165; Erb, *Nevin's Theology*, 221.

[71]See Nevin, *Mystical Presence*, 165-66. Nevin paid closer attention to this matter in 1850-51, when he reviewed (without definitive comment) two important German works on the subject—one by T. A. Liebner (who rejected the hamartiological rationale for the Incarnation) and one by Julius Müller (who affirmed it, and argued against the views of Liebner and Dorner). See "Liebner's Christology," *Mercersburg Review* 3 (1851): 55-73; and "Cur Deus Homo," *Mercersburg Review* 3 (1851): 220-238.

Following the lead of the mediating theologians, Nevin elsewhere suggests that "the Messianic idea" of the God-Man "has its necessity in the constitution of humanity." Erb,

Nevin's soteriology, however, is evident in the positive reason adduced for the Incarnation. The Logos has been united with fallen human nature, has sanctified it, and thus has raised humanity to a new level of existence Nevin terms the "New Creation." As the bearer of this new principle of existence, Christ is the "second Adam," the root and source of a new humanity made up of those in mystical union with him.

> The Word accordingly became flesh, that is assumed humanity into union with itself...The object of the incarnation was to couple the human nature in real union with the Logos, as a permanent source of life. It resulted from the presence of sin only, (itself no part of this nature in its original constitution,) that the union thus formed called the Saviour to suffer. As the bearer of a fallen humanity he must descend with it to the lowest depths of sorrow and pain, in order that he might triumph with it again in the power of his own imperishable life. In all this, he acted for himself and yet for the race he represented at the same time. For it was no external relation simply, that he sustained to this last. He was himself the race. Humanity dwelt in his person as the second Adam, under a higher form than ever it carried in the first.[72]

Nevin insists that the old and new creations do not stand in opposition to one another. Rather, in view here is a process of sublation, as the old is taken up into the new and elevated by the introduction of a new divine principle. This new creation "must of necessity take up into itself the entire compass and power of the old creation; not destroying its constituent elements and laws, but fulfilling their inmost sense rather and raising them to their highest power."[73]

How, then, is the humanity of Christ to serve as the medium for the communication of the New Creation? Here Nevin introduces a crucial distinction between individual and generic humanity, between "the simple man and the universal man."[74] Both the first and second Adams serve as generic heads of their respective communities. The first Adam has to do with humanity as originally created, the second with humanity as recreated and elevated through union with the Logos.

Nevin's Theology, 236.

[72] Nevin, *Mystical Presence*, 165-66. Here one detects elements of Irenaeus's theory of recapitulation, which Nevin frequently echoes. See "Noel on Baptism," *Mercersburg Review* 2 (1850): 248, 250; Erb, *Nevin's Theology*, 267.

Nevin's insistence that Christ assumed a "fallen" human nature represents a departure from previous Reformed thought. While affirming the impeccability of Christ, Nevin nevertheless stresses Christ's solidarity with humanity: "In taking our nature upon him, he was made in all respects like as we are, only without sin...The humanity which he assumed was fallen, subject to infirmity, and liable to death." *Mystical Presence*, 223.

[73] Nevin, "Noel on Baptism," 250. See also "New Creation in Christ," 8; *Mystical Presence*, 167.

[74] Nevin, *Mystical Presence*, 173. See also pp. 165-174; "Catholic Unity," 40-41; *Anxious Bench*, 107-111.

> Adam was not simply *a* man, like others since born, but he was *the* man, who comprehended in himself all that has since appeared in other men. Humanity as a whole resided in his person. He was strictly and truly the world. Through all ages, man is organically one and the same. And parallel with this precisely is the constitution of the Church. The second Adam corresponds in all respects with the first. He is not a man merely, an individual belonging to the race, but he is *the* man, emphatically the *Son of Man*, comprising in his person the new creation, or humanity recovered and redeemed as a whole.[75]

Nevin further explains this generic identity as consisting in an organic law, a single principle of existence that determines the identity and character of those in relationship with the head. With regard to the first Adam, Nevin argues that there is an organic law of personal identity antecedent to any dualistic division into body and soul.[76] Likewise, with the second Adam a new and higher principle or law, pertaining to the human being as a whole, is introduced into the sphere of human existence. Though supernatural, and therefore not explainable solely in terms of the old creation, it nevertheless becomes integral and congruent with human existence. It is, in short, *organically* human.

> Christ's life as a *whole* is borne over into the person of the believer as a like *whole*. The communication is central, and central only; from the last ground of Christ's life to the last ground of ours; by the action of a single, invisible, self-identical, spiritual law. The power of Christ's life lodged in the soul begins to work there immediately as the principle of the new creation. In doing so, it works organically according to the law which it includes in its own constitution. That is, it works as a *human* life; and as such becomes a law of regeneration in the body as truly as in the soul.[77]

This distinction between individual and generic humanity, Nevin believes, enables one to affirm a real union without effacing personal distinctions. Thus, regarding Adam Nevin remarks that "the individual is not blended with his posterity in any such way, as to lose his own personality or swallow up theirs. His identity with his posterity is generic; but not the less real or close on this account."[78] Similarly, with respect to the second Adam, Nevin argues,

---

[75]Nevin, "Catholic Unity," 40. Nevin goes on to argue that the parallel is not complete in that Christ sustains a more profound relation to the new creation than Adam does to the old. See *Mystical Presence*, 173.

On Nevin's rejection of both the body-soul dualism and the disjunctive faculty psychology, see Hewitt, *Regeneration and Morality*, 100, 107-8; and Plummer, "Theology of John Williamson Nevin," 172-74.

[76]See Nevin, *Mystical Presence*, 165.
[77]Ibid., 172.
[78]Ibid., 165.

> We not only spring from Christ, so far as our new life is concerned, but stand in him perpetually also as our ever living and ever present root...And yet there is no mixture, or flowing of one into the other, as individually viewed...Just as little does it imply any like dissipation of Christ's personality into the general consciousness of the Church, when we affirm that it forms the ground, out of which and in the power of which only, the whole life of the Church continually subsists.[79]

The corporate character and comprehensiveness of Nevin's vision of humanity is evident throughout, and he frequently condemns the prevailing nominalism that reckoned humanity to be no more than a vast "sand-heap," the mere aggregate of individuals.[80] The organic principle in question underlies all of human life and existence, encompassing the race as a whole and all aspects of individual existence. It was necessary for Christ to sanctify all stages of fallen human life from infancy to adulthood, from birth to death.[81] Similarly, Christ's person, as the ground of the new creation, encompasses the race as a whole (numerically considered) in that it constitutes the goal for all humanity, and the new creation in Christ is diachronically comprehensive in that it has reference to all of human history.[82]

Nevin is quick to draw out the ecclesiological implications of this corporate christological vision. The church is a unity, the body of Christ. Thus, it is a continuation of the Incarnation, the mode of Christ's presence on earth.[83] Because the general principle or law always precedes the individual manifestation, Nevin insists that ecclesial reality is antecedent to the experience of the individual Christian.

> Due regard is had to the idea of the Church as something more than a bare abstraction, the conception of an aggregate of parts mechanically brought together. It is apprehended rather as an organic life springing perpetually from the same ground, and identical with itself at every point. In this view the Church is

---

[79] Ibid., 173.

[80] See, e.g., Nevin, "New Creation," 7; *Mystical Presence*, 164.

[81] Here an echo of Irenaeus is apparent. See "Noel on Baptism," 248-250; Erb, *Nevin's Theology*, 267.

[82] See Nevin, "Catholicism," *Mercersburg Review* 3 (1851): 5, 23; "Noel on Baptism," 248.
In explaining the comprehensive character of the Incarnation, Nevin rejects both Calvinist particularism (with its "limited" or "definite" atonement) and also universalism. Both are "abstract" in that they view humanity individualistically—either as a group of individuals singled out from the whole, or as the aggregate totality of the race. See "Catholicism," 18-19; "Noel on Baptism," 247-48.

[83] Nevin, "The Church," 66, writes: "In a deep sense, then, Christ himself is made perfect in the Church, as the head in our natural organization requires the body in order to its completion. There can be no Church without Christ, but we may reverse the proposition also and say, no Church, no Christ."

,truly the *mother* of all her children. They do not impart life to her, but she imparts life to them. Here again the general is left to go before the particular, and to condition all its manifestations. The Church is in no sense the product of individual Christianity...but individual Christianity is the product, always and entirely, of the Church as existing previously and only revealing its life in this way.[84]

In speaking of the relationship between the New Creation in Christ and the church as it exists empirically, Nevin distinguishes between the "ideal" and the "actual church." The ideal church is "the power of a new supernatural creation, which has been introduced into the actual history of the world by the Incarnation of Jesus Christ."[85] But this ideal church cannot simply remain ideal, for "it includes in itself the necessity of a visible externalization in the world."[86] The actual church, however, falls short of fully realizing the ideal, and this accounts for the ecclesial defects evident throughout church history.[87]

Yet how is this organic law carried over from the person of Christ to the church and to the individual Christian? A variety of metaphors and expressions are utilized, including infusion and participation.[88] Here Nevin's teaching on faith and the Holy Spirit is crucial. He stresses, first of all, that faith is essentially receptive; it is an organ of reception analogous to the sense of sight.

> It is the organ by which we perceive and apprehend the spiritual and eternal; the telescope, through which our vision is carried far over the confines of time and sense, into the regions of glory that lie illimitable beyond; the very eye itself rather, that enables us to "look at things unseen," and causes their presence to surround us as a part of our own life.[89]

Furthermore, this organ stands in the closest relation to its object; in a sense it is constituted by its object: "They are different sides only of the same fact, each being what it is wholly by the correspondence in which it stands with the other."[90]

This receptive faith is closely connected with consciousness, for human personality "is constituted by self-consciousness."[91] Nevin views faith as a

---

[84]Nevin, *Anxious Bench*, 110-111. See also "Catholic Unity," 40-41.

[85]Nevin, "The Church," 57. Note that Nevin's idealism led him to shift away from the traditional Reformed scholastic distinction between the "visible" and "invisible" church.

[86]Ibid., 60.

[87]Ibid., 62.

[88]See Nevin, "New Creation," 2-5; *Mystical Presence*, 55, 176.

[89]Nevin, "Apostles' Creed," 208.

[90]Ibid., 207.

[91]Nevin, *Mystical Presence*, 169. Here the influence of Nevin's first colleague at Mercersburg, F. A. Rauch, is apparent. See Rauch, *Psychology*, 175-180. Nevin goes on to develop a teleology of religions framed in terms of the development of individual

form of self-consciousness, and union with Christ and salvation itself as the impartation of a higher form of self-consciousness, the gradual formation of a perfect personality in the Christian. Schleiermacher's statement that "Living faith in Christ...is nothing but the self-consciousness of our union with Christ" is quoted with approval.[92] Again echoing Schleiermacher, Nevin writes in an important passage,

> But the *Christian* consciousness carries in its very nature, such a reference to the person of Jesus Christ. It consists in the active sense of this relation, as the true and proper life of its subject. The man does not connect with Christ the self-consciousness that he has under a different form, in the way of outward reference merely; but this reference is comprehended in his self-consciousness itself, so far as he has become spiritually renewed. Christ is felt to be the centre of his life; or rather this feeling may be said to be itself his life, the form in which he exists as a self-conscious person. It is with reason, therefore, that Schleiermacher speaks of the communication which Christ makes of himself to believers, as moulding the *person*; since he imparts, in fact, a new higher consciousness, that forms the basis of a life that was not previously at hand, the true centre of our personality under its most perfect form. In this case the person of Christ is the ground and fountain of all proper Christian personality in the Church. It is only as he is consciously in communication with Christ as his life centre, (which can only be through an actual self-communication—*Wesenmittheilung*—of Christ's life to him for this purpose,) that the believer can be regarded as a *Christian*, or new man in Christ Jesus.[93]

Nevin also explains the role of the Holy Spirit in effecting this conscious union with Christ. Particularly important is the close relationship between the Holy Spirit and the incarnate humanity of Christ. We have already noted Nevin's contention that the Spirit is not a proxy for an absent Christ, but rather that the Spirit mediates the presence of Christ to the believer. The Spirit is the "sphere" of the mystical union, the mode of Christ's presence with the Christian.

> Here then we see the nature of the mystical union, as it holds between Christ and his people. It falls not, in any sense, within the sphere of nature as such, and we cannot say of it in this view that it is physical. But just as little are we at liberty to

---

consciousness (animal consciousness, world consciousness, and sense of absolute dependence). Nevin correlates this somewhat loosely with the rise from nature religion, to polytheism, to Judaism, and finally to Christianity as the absolute religion. See Erb, *Nevin's Theology*, 13-16, 38, 58-64, 185. Here the influence of Schleiermacher as well is apparent. See Plummer, "Theology of John Williamson Nevin," 201.

Nevin's view of the Trinity is also framed in terms of a dialectic of self-consciousness reminiscent of right-wing Hegelianism: "God becomes self-conscious in His Son, who is derived eternally from the Father." Erb, *Nevin's Theology*, 104.

[92] Nevin, *Mystical Presence*, 176.
[93] Ibid., 169. See also pp. 176, 221; *Anxious Bench*, 109.

conceive of it as merely moral. Its sphere is that of the Spirit. In this sphere, however, it is in the highest measure real; far more real, indeed, than it could possibly be under any other conceivable form.[94]

Nevin brings together his emphasis on union with the incarnate humanity of Christ and his stress upon the work of the Holy Spirit in a remarkable integration of trinitarian theology, theological anthropology, christology, and pneumatology. This work of the Spirit is conditioned, first of all, by the Incarnation, resurrection, and ascension; that is, since these events, the Spirit's work is profoundly different than it was before: "John goes so far as to say there was no Holy Spirit...till Jesus was glorified (John vii.39). This does not mean of course that he did not exist; but it limits the proper effusion of the Spirit, as known under the New Testament, to the Christian dispensation as such."[95]

Nevin goes on to argue that the fallen (albeit sinless) humanity of Christ has been elevated by virtue of its union with the Logos into the realm of Spirit, and thus has been made accessible to the believer: "His whole humanity has been taken up into the sphere of the Spirit, and appears transfigured into the same life. And why then should it not extend itself...over into the persons of his people?[96] The crucial event in this elevation of humanity is the final triumph over death in the resurrection of Christ, for it constitutes the point of transition from the realm of the "flesh" to the realm of the "spirit."[97] For Nevin, then, the humanity of Christ has been decisively transformed by being imbued with the power of the Holy Spirit. Christ's post-resurrection mode of human existence—body and soul—is thoroughly bound up with the Holy Spirit.[98]

Two areas of ambiguity are evident in Nevin's teaching at this point, however. He equivocates, first of all, on the question whether this elevation of fallen humanity is due to its incarnational union with the Logos or to the work of the Holy Spirit. Both concepts are even used in the same context.

> Humanity itself in this way, as joined with the everlasting Word, is made to triumph over the law of infirmity and mortality, to which it was previously subject in its own nature, and takes henceforth the character of *spirit*, in distinction from

---

[94] Nevin, *Mystical Presence*, 229.

[95] Ibid., 222. See also Erb, *Nevin's Theology*, 138.

[96] Nevin, *Mystical Presence*, 176.

[97] Ibid., 223-24; Erb, *Nevin's Theology*, 349. See also Nevin, "Jesus and the Resurrection," *Mercersburg Review* 13 (1861): 169-190.

[98] Nevin, *Mystical Presence*, 223-24, writes: "The victory however must be understood to extend to the whole man, external as well as internal, transforming the very flesh itself into spirit. It is the full triumph of Christ's higher life over the limitations with which it had been called to struggle in its union with our fallen humanity; by which this humanity itself is raised into the sphere of the same life, and completely transfused with its power, in the everlasting glorification of the Son of Man."

mere flesh...With the final triumph of the Spirit in the glorified humanity of Christ, this higher order of life began to reveal itself with power on the day of Pentecost.[99]

Another point of ambiguity has to do with the identity of the Spirit, which Nevin often describes in impersonal and transpersonal terms—as the "higher nature" of Christ, as a "sphere" of power, and so forth. This impression of ambiguity is heightened by the way in which Nevin alternates the use of personal and impersonal pronouns. Nevin writes:

> It [the Spirit] denotes then his higher nature, in the power of which his whole person was, by this triumph, raised into a new undying state, and clothed with the attributes and prerogatives of a divine existence. In Rom. viii. 11, the resurrection of Christ is inseparably joined with the third person of the ever blessed and glorious Trinity, as one and the same life. Whether as the Spirit of the Father, or as the Spirit of Christ himself, his agency, proceeding as it does from both, constitutes the form, in which the new creation in Christ Jesus is carried forward, first in his own person and subsequently with the Church. The resurrection state of the Saviour then, especially as made complete at his ascension, is itself *spirit* (*pneuma*), in the way of distinction from the *flesh* (*sarx*) or common mortal state in which he had appeared before.[100]

A partial answer to both of these problems lies in Nevin's integrative theological method, for everywhere he tends toward integration rather than disjunction, and in how this was applied to the Trinity. Nevin was quite aware that speaking of the Spirit as the "higher nature of Christ" had a Sabellian ring, and he sought to distance himself from this charge. Nevertheless, he affirms the closest of intra-trinitarian and redemptive-historical relations between the Christ and the Spirit.

---

[99]Ibid., 222. See also pp. 165-66; "New Creation," 9.

Bruce L. McCormack has shown that the Reformed tradition generally has denied that the Logos assumed a "fallen" humanity. Furthermore, it has generally maintained that the sanctification of Christ's human nature is through the agency of the Holy Spirit and not through the hypostatic union of humanity with the Logos. See his *For Us and Our Salvation: Incarnation and Atonement in the Reformed Tradition*, Studies in Reformed Theology and History I:2 (1993), 17-22. In an interesting parallel to Nevin's teaching at this point, Edward Irving was deposed from the ministry of the Church of Scotland for teaching that Christ assumed a fallen human nature. Irving's views were published in his *The Orthodox and Catholic Doctrine of Our Lord's Human Nature* (London: Baldwin and Cradock, 1830). On the influence of Irving at this point, see F. F. Bruce, "The Humanity of Jesus Christ," in *A Mind for What Matters: Collected Essays of F. F. Bruce* (Grand Rapids: Eerdmans, 1990), 248-258. More recently, this idea has been forcefully advocated by Scottish theologian T. F. Torrance. See chap. 8 below.

[100]Nevin, *Mystical Presence*, 223. On this point, Charles Hodge, "Doctrine of the Reformed Church," 276-77, criticized Nevin's "unintelligible" language and his "affinity for Sabellianism."

The persons of the adorable Trinity are indeed distinct. But we must beware of sundering them into abstract subsistences, none without the other. They subsist in the way of the most perfect mutual inbeing and intercommunion. The Spirit of Christ is not his representative or surrogate simply, as some would seem to think; but Christ himself under a certain mode of subsistence.[101]

Union with Christ and Applied Soteriology

According to Nevin, union with Christ is foundational for all salvation. It is through union with Christ that all soteriological benefits are applied to the believer.[102] Extraordinary emphasis is also placed on the unity of salvation found in Christ. In particular, Nevin rejects the standard federal explanation of salvation—with its bifurcation of the forensic and transformatory—as abstract and lacking mystery. It is but a series of disjointed divine acts abstracted from the life of Christ. Such a salvation is not really *in Christ*.

A very common view appears to be, that the whole salvation of the gospel is accomplished, in a more or less outward and mechanical way, by supernatural might and power, rather than by the Spirit of the Lord as the revelation of a new historical life in the person of the believer himself. So we have an outward imputation of righteousness to begin with; a process of sanctification carried forward by the help of proper spiritual machinery brought to bear on the soul, including perhaps, as its basis, the notion of an abrupt creation *de novo*, by the fiat of the Holy Ghost; and finally, to crown all, a sudden unprepared refabrication of the body, as an entirely new product of Almighty power at the moment, to be superadded to the life of the spirit already complete in its state of glory. But the Scriptures sanction no such hypothesis in the case…It is a new creation *in Christ Jesus*, not by him in the way of mere outward power.[103]

Sanctification in Christ

Nevin's view of sanctification does not depart markedly from the position of Reformed orthodoxy, and thus may be treated briefly. Sanctification is rooted in union with Christ, and is viewed as a lifelong process that is not completed in this life.[104] It is furthered by the means of grace, particularly the word and sacraments.[105] Also as in many of the earlier Reformed scholastics, the

---

[101] Ibid., 225. Because of this link between christology and pneumatology, Nevin was a firm defender of the *filioque*. See Erb, *Nevin's Theology*, 133-38.

[102] See Nevin, "New Creation"; Erb, *Nevin's Theology*, 311.

[103] Nevin, *Mystical Presence*, 228.

[104] See Nevin, "Noel on Baptism," 252; Erb, *Nevin's Theology*, 314. For an extensive treatment of Nevin on sanctification, see Hewitt, *Regeneration and Morality*, 89-123.

[105] See Erb, *Nevin's Theology*, 314-15.

principle and process of sanctification is framed in terms of infused grace: "The new life lodges itself, as an efflux from Christ, in the inmost core of our personality. Here it becomes the principle or seed of our sanctification; which is simply the gradual transfusion of the same exalted spiritual quality or potence through our whole persons."[106] Also in good Reformed fashion, a certain priority is assigned to justification. Nevin repeatedly declares that the objective change in status before God (justification) is the germ and ground of the subjective change experienced in sanctification.[107] Clearly no antinomian, Nevin also insists on the necessity of sanctification: "The full salvation of man turns ultimately on his full sanctification."[108]

Justification in Christ

Nevin's doctrine of justification is less conventional, and thus requires considerably more attention and discussion. His views must be reconstructed from a variety of sources—polemical articles and book reviews, monographs, and theological lectures. An additional complication is the fact that the Mercersburg position on justification became a bone of contention. Nevin's writings on the subject were often forged in the heat of controversy, and they sometimes generate more heat than light. Also, while Nevin's Mercersburg writings evidence considerable thematic continuity, some uncertainties and points of ambiguity remain. In the final analysis, however, it is apparent that Nevin realized that he was proposing a view of justification in marked variance with the prevailing theories of American Reformed Protestantism.

Nevin subjected the federal and New England theories of justification to searching criticism. Frequently noting the tendency to make justification by faith the touchstone of orthodoxy, Nevin suggests that the doctrine of justification was overemphasized and that other doctrines such as sanctification had been neglected.[109] As a result, the spectre of antinomianism posed a real threat. But Nevin's most fundamental objections have to do with what he viewed as the "abstract" and extrinsic character of the prevailing doctrines: "The tendency...is to over-emphasize the external side of the transaction and to ignore the internal or organic relation."[110] Thus, in his discussions of justification Nevin repeatedly stresses the priority of the real, the inward, the organic, and the personal over the extrinsic and merely legal.

In a number of ways Nevin echoes traditional Reformed themes in his treatment of justification. Justification is an objective work of God, in contrast

---

[106] Nevin, *Mystical Presence*, 168.
[107] See Erb, *Nevin's Theology*, 222, 295-310.
[108] Nevin, "Catholicism," 9.
[109] Nevin, "Sect System," 160-61; "Apostles Creed," 345; "Catholicism," 7.
[110] Erb, *Nevin's Theology*, 203.

to sanctification which involves a process of change within the Christian.[111] Furthermore, the importance of faith is consistently stressed.[112] Nevin also argues that justification is not merely negative, in that sins are remitted, but also positive in the sense that the righteousness of Christ is imputed to the Christian.[113] But Nevin's view of justification and the forensic dimension of salvation also diverges from much earlier Reformed thought in important ways, especially with regard to the concept of imputation, his view of the atonement, and in his understanding of the *ordo salutis*. With respect to each of these matters, Nevin's statements, while not exhaustive, are sufficient to establish his position with some precision.

Nevin shows considerable independence in his views on imputation, both hamartiological and soteriological. Here the parallel between the first and second Adams plays a decisive role, for the mode of imputation is precisely the same with respect to both.[114] With regard to hamartiological imputation, Nevin argues for what is in fact a type of mediate imputation: the "punishment of sin is reached only through the mediation of personal sin."[115] The federal doctrine of an extrinsic, immediate imputation is rejected as an abstract fiction. Because all human beings share in Adam's sinful generic humanity, they are accounted guilty.

> The fall of Adam was the fall of the race. Not simply because he represented the race, but because the race was itself comprehended in his person...But the human race is not a sand-heap. It is the power of a single life. It is bound together, not outwardly, but inwardly. Men have been one before they have been many; and as many, they are still one. We have a perfect right then to say that Adam's sin is imputed to all his posterity. Only let us not think of a mere outward transfer in the case. Against such imputation the objection commonly made to the doctrine has force. It would be to substitute a fiction for a fact. No imputation of that sort is taught in the Bible. But the imputation of Adam's sin to his posterity involves no

---

[111]Nevin (Ibid., 313) writes: "The distinction between justification and sanctification is that the former is an act of God, and the latter is a work springing from God also, but involving the idea of a process in the subject. Justification is objective; sanctification is subjective...Justification is the commencement of sanctification and underlies its whole process...These two also differ with respect to what they remove. Both have a relation to sin, but in a different respect. Justification changes the state of man; sanctification induces a new inward habit as far as it prevails."

[112]See ibid., 298, 305-6.

[113]Nevin, ibid., 296-97, writes: "If justification was only a freeing from guilt, we would have an abstract view; but if we hold that the sinner also becomes united to Christ and thereby made righteous, since thus the righteousness of Christ is imputed to the sinner, then we have the proper view." In this context Nevin also rejects the Arminian theory that justification may be earned by imperfect but sincere obedience to the law of Christ.

[114]See Nevin, *Mystical Presence*, 164, 166, 190-91.

[115]Erb, *Nevin's Theology*, 218.

fiction. It is counted to them simply because it is theirs in fact. They are born into Adam's nature, and for this reason only, as forming with him the same general life, they are born also into his guilt.[116]

A presupposition behind Nevin's rejection of immediate imputation is that merit and demerit inhere in persons, and cannot be abstracted from personality: "For righteousness, like guilt, is an attribute which supposes a subject in which it inheres, and from which it cannot be abstracted without ceasing to exist altogether."[117] Echoing Calvin's insistence that union with Christ's humanity is necessary for reception of justification, Nevin repeatedly declares that the merits of Christ inhere only in the mediatorial life of Christ: "The imagination that the *merits* of Christ's life may be sundered from his life itself, and conveyed over to his people under this abstract form, on the ground of a merely outward legal constitution, is unscriptural and contrary to all reason at the same time."[118] Yet like Calvin, Nevin has considerable difficulty explaining how the realistic and the forensic categories fit together. And in pressing the point, Nevin more than once lapses into the language of mediate forensic imputation.

The moral relations of Adam, and his moral character too, are made over to us at the same time. Our participation in the actual unrighteousness of his life, forms the ground of our participation in his guilt and liability to punishment. And in no other way, we affirm, can the idea of imputation be satisfactorily sustained in the case of the second Adam. The scriptures make the two cases, in this respect, fully parallel.[119]

In the same context Nevin also adopts a proleptic analytic conception of justification. Justification may be ascribed proleptically to the believer because the life of Christ communicated in the mystical union includes potentially all that belongs to Christ.

In the very act of our justification, by which the righteousness of Christ is accounted to be ours, it becomes ours in fact by our actual insertion into Christ himself. He is joined to us mystically by the power of the Holy Ghost, and becomes in this way the principle of a new creation within us, which from the very start includes in itself potentially, all that belongs to it already in his own person.[120]

In this connection, Nevin also insists that the justification of the Christian is not Calvin's synthetic "justification of the ungodly," but rather the analytic

---

[116]Nevin, *Mystical Presence*, 164. See also Erb, *Nevin's Theology*, 204, 218.

[117]Nevin, *Mystical Presence*, 191. Note that Nevin shared this notion with the New England trajectory described earlier.

[118]Ibid., 191. See also pp. 57, 197, 240.

[119]Ibid., 190-91. See also p. 166.

[120]Ibid., 191-92.

justification of the at least partly (and potentially completely) righteous.

> The judgment of God must ever be according to truth. He cannot reckon to anyone an attribute or quality, which does not belong to him in fact. He cannot declare him to be in a relation or state, which is not actually his own, but the position merely of another...The law in this view would be itself a fiction only, and not the expression of a fact. But no such fiction, whether under the name of law or without it, can lie at the ground of a judgment entertained or pronounced by God.[121]

We see, then, that the forensic is consistently subordinated to the realistic, to the point that an important Reformation insight (the synthetic justification of the ungodly) is jeopardized. Further evidence of this tendency is the manner in which Nevin virtually equates justification and imputation with the mystical union.[122] Central to Nevin's argument is the frequent contention that justification is "not a mere forensic act" and that it "implies a certain investiture of positive righteousness." He goes on explicitly to identify soteriological imputation as "the infusion of the sinner with the life of Christ and the favor of God."[123] Earlier we noted that faith and union with Christ are construed in terms of an elevated self-consciousness, and it is therefore no surprise that justification itself is also viewed in these terms.

> Justification takes hold of the subject in a living way. It never completes itself as a divine act until it has entered the consciousness of the subject. Justification stands under an objective form and completes itself in the consciousness of the subject more or less clearly, and so carries with it the power of a new life.[124]

This form of self-consciousness is not simply the subjective awareness of an objective forensic justification, but is part and parcel of the act of justification itself. Nevin notes that the "sense of justification in the sinner's mind is itself personal righteousness," and he adds that the "sinner cannot be pardoned unless

---

[121]Ibid., 189. Nevin saw no contradiction between Paul and James, though he argues that Paul's view of faith is more expansive. In Erb, *Nevin's Theology*, 306, Nevin writes: "There is no great difficulty in reconciling them, if we keep in view what Paul means by faith. He always takes it as a life, necessarily including other affections and graces, such as love and hope, as well as corresponding outward acts. A faith including nothing would not come up to Paul's conception. The corresponding outward acts simply unfold completely the proper sense of faith itself."

[122]Nevin makes the surprising suggestion, Erb, *Nevin's Theology*, 295, that "justification stands related to the mystical union as form and contents." Traditional Reformed theology would have reversed the order in that it viewed the mystical union as an umbrella category under which are subsumed a variety of benefits.

[123]Ibid., 296.

[124]Ibid., 307. See also p. 311, where justification is described as "a new state of consciousness induced by union with Christ."

he has the sense of forgiveness."[125]

Nevin's doctrine of the atonement also departs in important ways from the prevailing Reformed theories. The governmental theory characteristic of New England Calvinism is rejected because it renders the death of Christ an empty show and takes away all force from the event.[126] Similarly, the hypothetical universalism of the Amyraldian theory prevalent among some New School Presbyterians is condemned for making the Atonement "a vague and indefinite affair."[127] But Nevin's deepest strictures are reserved for the traditional Reformed federal theory of a limited atonement, as representing abstract and extrinsic thinking at its worst.[128] Here Nevin reasons from the Incarnation to an atonement of universal significance. As the "second Adam," Christ's death must have reference to the race as a whole.[129] Yet, in affirming the universal significance of the Atonement, Nevin nevertheless rejects an explicit soteriological universalism.[130]

Implied in this rejection of a limited atonement is a corresponding rejection of Calvin's particularistic doctrine of the decrees of election and reprobation. Here Nevin shows a deep concern for the integrity of historical process and for the economy of salvation. Central to Nevin's theology, and indeed to his piety, was the conviction that the means of grace are effectual. He was convinced that Calvin's "abstract" doctrine of the decrees rendered the Incarnation, the atonement, and the sacraments a charade.[131] Equally important was Nevin's deep concern for safeguarding human freedom, and he argues that even divine knowledge is conditioned by human freedom: "Human liberty requires that there should be actions which are independent even of foreknowledge in an unerring wisdom. There must be actions which are beyond all calculations."[132]

Nevin goes on to revision the divine decrees along idealist lines. Instead of divine decrees wholly separate from history, Nevin argues that the decrees

---

[125]Ibid., 307-8. See also p. 299. Here again the influence of Schleiermacher is apparent. See Schleiermacher, *Christian Faith*, 498-99.

[126]See Erb, *Nevin's Theology*, 94, 258-60.

[127]Ibid., 151. The New England revisionist theory of Horace Bushnell is also rejected. Nevin, "Review of *God in Christ*," 312, remarks that Bushnell "seems to us to turn it [the atonement] into a pure fiction."

[128]See Nevin, "Noel on Baptism," 247-48; Erb, *Nevin's Theology*, 142, 156-57.

[129]See Nevin, *Mystical Presence*, 166.

[130]See Erb, *Nevin's Theology*, 142-43; 261-63. The work of Christ is potentially universal, but it becomes "particular in its actualization" (p. 261).

[131]See John W. Nevin, "Hodge on the Ephesians," *Mercersburg Review* 9 (1857): 61-2.

[132]Erb, *Nevin's Theology*, 147. In seeking to reconcile divine omniscience and human freedom, Nevin embraces the Jesuit notion of *scientia media*, holding that in addition to the "knowledge of simple intelligence" and the "knowledge of vision," God also possesses a "middle knowledge" of futuribles, i.e., what a person *would* do under any circumstances. See pp. 82, 138-40, 144, 193.

relate to the world as "ideal" and "actual."

> The only true view is to regard the decrees as the ideal side of what became actual in the creation of the world…All misconceptions of God's decrees arise from a false view of the relation of time to eternity. We must firmly hold to this conception, that the decree of God is the idea of the world as it becomes actual in the course of creation, and thus underlying, supporting and accompanying the creation. In this manner God's decree becomes substantially the same with creation and providence, and providence the manifestation of the decree.[133]

Clearly this involves a closer God-world relationship than much of the Reformed tradition was willing to affirm,[134] and by 1848 Nevin had publicly and decisively broken with high Calvinism's doctrine of the decrees. Thereafter, he pits Calvin's sacramental theology against Calvin's predestinarianism, and he trumpets the distinctive identity of the German Reformed tradition as Calvinian on the sacraments and Melanchthonian on the decrees.[135]

Nevin's positive presentation of the atonement includes a variety of themes, not all of which cohere comfortably. He approaches traditional Reformed doctrine in his insistence, against the New England trajectory, that the death of Christ propitiates divine wrath and satisfies the demands of divine justice. By virtue of his hypostatic union with the Godhead, the sufferings of Christ are of infinite value.[136] On balance, however, more stress is placed in Nevin's published writings upon what Gustav Aulén more recently termed the "classic" or *Christus Victor* theme of the atonement, in which Christ's death and resurrection constitute the triumph of humanity over the forces of sin and death. Once again, the forensic is subordinated to the realistic.

> The passion of the Son of God was the world's spiritual crisis, in which the principle of health came to its last struggle with the principle of disease, and burst forth from the very bosom of the grace itself in the form of immortality. This was

---

[133]Ibid., 192-3.

[134]See also ibid., 141; *Human Freedom*, 11-12. Here Nevin approaches the panentheism of the Hegelian tradition. As a hedge against the threat of "pantheism," Nevin regularly appealed to the "personality" of God: "Is not God the last ground of all personality? But does this imply any pantheistic dissipation of his nature, into the general consciousness of the intelligent universe?" (*Mystical Presence*, 173). See also Erb, *Nevin's Theology*, 85, 90, 132-33, 141, 165.

[135]See Nevin, "Doctrine of the Reformed Church," 372-3. See also Nichols, *Romanticism*, 99-100.

[136]See Erb, *Nevin's Theology*, 124-5, 258-60. Plummer, "Theology of John Williamson Nevin," 195, denies that this element is present in Nevin. Here he was hampered by his failure to consult the theological lectures collated by Erb.

the atonement, Christ's victory over sin and hell. As such it forms the only medium of salvation to men.[137]

Nevin's distance from federal orthodoxy is also evident in his comments on matters relating to the *ordo salutis*. He was clearly uncomfortable with the punctiliar dimensions of both revivalism and federal orthodoxy. In *The Anxious Bench*, Nevin presents a searching critique of the revivalist "system of the anxious bench." Here "all is made to hang methodistically on sudden and violent experiences belonging to the individual separately taken, and holding little or no connection with his relations to the Church previously."[138] In its place Nevin recommends the "system of the catechism," where a relatively uneventful process of Christian nurture is the norm. In this system, Nevin argues, it is "altogether natural that children growing up in the bosom of the Church under the faithful application of the means of grace should be quickened into spiritual life in a comparatively quiet way."[139]

In contrast to federal orthodoxy, with its concern for the precise time of regeneration and justification, Nevin's approach is considerably more dynamic. Both these elements of the *ordo* may involve a lengthy process in the individual Christian.

> Hence, what can be more uncertain and precarious than to fix the point of what is called the regeneration of believers; for it rests upon a series of preceding exercises in the form of conversion, springing from the operations of God's grace, with respect throughout to what is finally reached. The act of justification must be taken in the same view. It is not exactly correct to make this instantaneous or sudden. It is a single act on the part of God, but a certain period of time may be required to complete the act, so far as the subject is concerned.[140]

In short, Nevin thinks in terms of an ongoing economy of faith, moving to the rhythm of the sacraments and the means of grace, rather than an *ordo salutis* in the technical sense.

Union with Christ and the Sacraments

Nevin's sacramental theology, particularly his view of the Lord's Supper, has

---

[137]Nevin, *Mystical Presence*, 166. See also "Jesus and the Resurrection." For a history and commendation of this theme, see Gustav Aulén, *Christus Victor*, trans. A. G. Hebert (New York: Macmillan, 1969). See also Plummer, "Theology of John Williamson Nevin," 195.

[138]Nevin, *Anxious Bench*, 112. Cf. Schleiermacher, *Christian Faith*, 487.

[139]Nevin, *Anxious Bench*, 111. In his later writings, Nevin often refers to this as "educational religion." See *My Own Life*, 2; "Noel on Baptism," 252, 264; Erb, *Nevin's Theology*, 382.

[140]Erb, *Nevin's Theology*, 304. See also pp. 299-300, 303.

been treated extensively elsewhere, but some comments must be made here. As is apparent above, the objective efficacy of the sacraments was a foundational principle for Nevin, and he maintains that "there can be no full, sound and healthy religion without appreciating the sacramental side of Christianity."[141] He decries the non-sacramental direction of much contemporary Protestantism, emblematic of which was the terminological shift from "sacrament" to "ordinance."[142] In his definition of a sacrament, Nevin echoes the classic Reformed language. The sacrament consists of an outward sign and an inward grace, with the two united by a sacramental or mystical union.

> A sacrament in the true church sense is not a mere outward rite, made obligatory by divine appointment. It carries in itself a peculiar constitution of its own. It consists, according to the old definition, of two parts, one outward and the other inward, a visible terrene sign and an invisible celestial grace; not related simply as corresponding facts, brought together by human thought; but the one actually bound to the other in the way of most real mystical or sacramental union, causing the last to be objectively at hand in one and the same transaction with the first.[143]

The sacraments and the sacramental principle are accorded extraordinary importance by Nevin: "Baptism and the Lord's Supper are the central institutions of Christianity."[144] In Nevin's view the sacraments are not merely vehicles of salvation; the prelapsarian situation in the Garden of Eden was sacramental as well.[145] Furthermore, Nevin's conception of reality in general is profoundly sacramental: "The whole constitution of the world is sacramental, as being not simply the sign of, but the actual form and presence of invisible things."[146]

---

[141] Ibid., 404. See also Nevin, "Apostles' Creed," 334; "Noel on Baptism," 243; "Anglican Crisis," 372.

[142] Nevin, "Sect System," 147-48.

[143] Nevin, "Noel on Baptism," 243-44. See also Erb, *Nevin's Theology*, 360.

[144] Erb, *Nevin's Theology*, 372.

[145] Nevin identifies the tree of the knowledge of good and evil and the tree of life as sacraments. See ibid., 214-15.

[146] Ibid., 373. With the focus of his piety on Incarnation and sacrament, Nevin manifests something of what David W. Tracy has termed the "Catholic analogical imagination." Tracy, "The Catholic Analogical Imagination," *Proceedings of the Catholic Theological Society of America* (1977), 235-36, writes: "Rather when we imagine, especially when we imagine the reality inspired and nourished by God's gift of faith and revelation, we redescribe the creative possibilities of all reality...We literally reimagine reality as a new series of ordered possibilities; we then choose some central clue for the whole of reality—for Catholics that central clue to the whole—to the relationship between God and humanity, the individual and society—is found in what T. S. Eliot called the half-guessed, the gift—half-understood—incarnation as *the* secret of both God and humankind and the relationship of both church and cosmos as finally sacramental."

Nevin's emphasis on the sacraments leads to a marked deemphasis of the written and preached Word as a means of grace. We must note, however, that all of this flows from the incarnational focus of his theology in general. The written Word, first of all, is clearly subordinate to the incarnate Word of God,[147] and by extension the written Word is also subordinate to the sacraments, which mediate union with the Word incarnate: "the sacraments as means for the application of redemption have certain priority over the Word, which has power to reach us only as we stand in proper relation to God by the sacraments."[148] In view of this incarnational focus, Nevin also distinguishes between the sacraments of the Old Testament period and those of the New; those of the old are "relative," while those of the new are "absolute."[149]

While Nevin devoted considerably more attention to the Eucharist, he was not silent on baptism. In particular, Nevin insists on the thoroughly objective character of baptism as a means of grace, though he then struggles to reconcile this with other aspects of his soteriology.[150] But this concern for objective efficacy created friction at two closely related points—the necessity of faith and the central importance of union with Christ as the mediator of salvation. Here the problem is simple: given the Reformed insistence on faith for regeneration, union with Christ, and justification, what is the efficacy of infant baptism? This problem was especially pressing for Nevin, because in Schleiermacherian fashion he viewed faith (a state of self-consciousness) as constitutive for both *unio* and justification. This dilemma is particularly evident in Nevin's 1851 theological lectures, and Nevin suggests that in the case of infants, there may be a justification prior even to faith and union with Christ.

> The object of Christianity is the salvation of the individual, and this can be accomplished only by a union with Christ...The mystical union must be regarded as originating in the divine mind, but not as something abstract; so, also, the justification of infants who die. They cannot realize the mystical union. Yet, if we

---

[147]Nevin, "Apostles Creed," 212-13, writes: "For Christianity...is in a deep sense identical with the life of Christ itself. It is not the words he spoke, nor the works he wrought, as something sundered from his own person, but the living fountain of all these as introduced into the world in the mystery from which his person springs. He is the word itself made flesh; grace and truth enshrined in living *shekinah*; the life of God disclosed, to the fullest possible extent of revelation, in the very bosom of man's life." See also Erb, *Nevin's Theology*, 43, 56, 282-85.

[148]Erb, *Nevin's Theology*, 285. Along these lines, Nevin also subordinates the written Word to the tradition of the church, insofar as the tradition of the church is the product of the church's consciousness of union with the incarnate Christ. See Nevin, "Apostles' Creed," 338-340.

[149]Nevin, *Mystical Presence*, 250-51.

[150]Two of Nevin's Mercersburg-era essays, "Noel on Baptism" and "The Anglican Crisis," are particularly important here, as are the theological lectures collated by Erb.

grant that children are saved, then there is an objective justification before the infant can embrace it. This is of force to prove the validity of infant baptism.[151]

In explaining this justification of infants through baptism, Nevin comes remarkably close to the Roman Catholic doctrine of baptism. In short, baptism removes the curse of original sin: "The sins of the baptized are so forgiven that they are no longer involved in the curse of original sin, so far as their present condition is concerned...If they die, they are saved, if they have not fallen after baptism.[152] Apparently Nevin's intense concern for the objective efficacy of the sacraments was such that he was willing to sacrifice both the necessity of faith and the centrality of union with Christ.

As we have seen, the Lord's Supper was a central concern for Nevin, and all the more so because of the close relation between the eucharist and union with Christ: "Any theory of the eucharist will be found to accord closely with the view that is taken, at the same time, of the nature of the union generally between Christ and his people."[153] As we might expect, Nevin opposes the eucharistic doctrines of both New England Calvinism and federal theology—the first because it evacuates the sacrament of all objective efficacy, and the second because it is "abstract."[154]

Much of Nevin's doctrine of the eucharist may be inferred from his view of union with Christ discussed above, but some account must be made at this juncture of the development evident in his understanding of Calvin and of the "real presence." In *The Mystical Presence*, Nevin took issue with Calvin at three points, each connected with what Nevin believed to be a "false psychology." First of all, Nevin criticized Calvin for a preoccupation with the flesh of Christ as material and local instead of understanding the "flesh" or

---

[151]Erb, *Nevin's Theology*, 293-94.

[152]Ibid., 390. See also p. 263. For the remarkably similar Roman Catholic doctrine, see "The Canons and Decrees of the Council of Trent," Fifth Session, 1-5, in Schaff, *Creeds of Christendom*, II:83-88. Nevin does not, however, echo the Roman Catholic emphasis on the vicarious faith of the parents.

[153]Nevin, *Mystical Presence*, 54. Consistent with this emphasis, Nevin followed Schleiermacher in his suggestion that for Calvin there was a special communion with Christ in the Supper, a communion different in kind from that to be had through the ministry of the Word. See *Mystical Presence*, 118, 182; "Doctrine of the Reformed Church," 344, 358. As Gerrish, *Tradition and the Modern World*, 62, notes, "The truth seems to be, not that Nevin exaggerated the role of the sacraments in Calvin's theology, but that he underestimated the significance Calvin attributed to the preached Word."

[154]For example, New Englanders Jonathan Edwards and Timothy Dwight are criticized for reducing the Supper to an evocative event on the order of "a common Fourth of July celebration...a mere occasion by which the religious affections are excited and supported in the breast of the worshiper." Nevin, *Mystical Presence*, 119, 122. Federal theologians such as Charles Hodge, Nevin argued, allow for an objective efficacy, but reduce it to the work of the Holy Spirit and limit the scope of this work by the doctrine of predestination. See "Doctrine of the Reformed Church," 289-90.

humanity of Christ as "organic law." Second, Nevin suggests that Calvin had an inadequate apprehension of the unity of Christ's person. Finally, Calvin failed to make a distinction between the individual and the generic life of Christ.[155] Shortly after the publication of *The Mystical Presence*, Nevin received a copy of the second volume of August Ebrard's eucharistic history, and the influence of Ebrard is apparent in Nevin's subsequent reply to Charles Hodge.[156] Ebrard's interpretation of Calvin not only vindicated the Reformer but it enabled Nevin to frame his own doctrine with greater precision.

Following Ebrard, Nevin presents a dynamic interpretation of Calvin's view of Christ's presence in the Supper, and so also of the believer's union with the humanity of Christ. Thus, the presence of Christ's humanity is not at all to be viewed as *material* substance, but as activity and power. Here Nevin's earlier language of "organic law" is somewhat recast. Nevin writes:

> Christ's flesh and blood are at hand, not in the bread and wine as such, but in the transaction; not materially or by mechanical contact in space, but *dynamically*, in the way of living substance and power; not for the outward man primarily and separately, as Luther contended, but for the *soul* (by no means to be confounded here with mere understanding or mind), as the central life of the whole person, so as to flow out from this to the *body* also as the true pabulum of immortality.[157]

Nevin goes on to note that the presence of Christ's body and blood, that is, his humanity, certainly must not be abstracted from his presence as a person with the believer.

> It is a most low view of the body, in any case, to make it consist of a given quantum of matter in space; its fundamental character is found only in the psychic force that comes to its revelation in this form. So Calvin saw and felt, and in such view it is that he rejects the crass notion of Luther—not to sunder the body of Christ from the mystery of the Holy Eucharist, but only to make the more sure of its presence in its true vital energy and virtue.[158]

Nevin develops this dynamic understanding in a number of ways. First,

---

[155] Nevin, *Mystical Presence*, 156-60.

[156] See August Ebrard, *Das Dogma vom heiligen Abendmahl und seine Geschichte*, 2 vols. (Frankfurt am Main: Zimmer, 1845-46). On this see Nichols, *Romanticism*, 100-101.

[157] Nevin, "Doctrine of the Reformed Church," 316. See also pp. 317-19, 346-50. On p. 347, Nevin quotes the following passage from Ebrard: "What sort of substance does Calvin mean? The substance of Christ's body and blood" or the substance of his person generally: Undoubtedly the latter. And is the term substance, it is impatiently asked, any better in such case than puppet play, contrived to deceive the unwary? Is the substance of Christ's *person*, with which we are fed, anything more at last, in Calvin's mind, than Christ's *spiritual power*?"

[158] Ibid., 317.

spatial concerns are transcended. The humanity of Christ has surmounted the limitations of the material and has entered the realm of the spiritual.

> In the glorification, the dualism between animating spirit and matter needing animation is brought to an end; the glorified body is through and through the *manifestation of spirit, life clear of space* although through and through *life*; it has the power to *take volume* at its own pleasure (John 20:19; Luke 24:16); but still in such a way that it shall rule the matter so assumed, and not be ruled by it as an outward limitation.[159]

Consistent with this, Nevin goes on to argue that heaven is not to be thought of as a *place* in any local sense of the term, and the *sursum corda*, upon which Calvin had placed such emphasis, is viewed in strictly metaphorical terms.[160] Temporal constraints are likewise transcended to some degree by this dynamic approach. Calvin, of course, had taught that the substance of the sacraments was the same in both the Old and New Testament dispensations, and the federalist Charles Hodge regarded this principle as decisive against Nevin's view of union with the humanity of Christ.[161] Viewed in terms of efficacy and vital power rather than material substance, Nevin argues, it is quite reasonable that the Old Testament saints would receive the saving virtue the flows from Christ's humanity.[162]

---

[159] Ibid., 348.

[160] Ibid., 351-52; Erb, *Nevin's Theology*, 272. See also Nichols, *Romanticism*, 101-103. Despite the arguments of Ebrard, it is apparent that Nevin's thoroughgoing relational conception here goes beyond Calvin, for whom the spatial and local character of heaven was preserved. See *Inst*. IV.17.12, 26-27.

In his theological lectures, Nevin appears to favor a Lutheran view of the ubiquity of Christ's humanity: "Among the Lutherans were two views concerning the ubiquity of Christ's human nature. One party maintained that Christ's divinity made His humanity ubiquitous; the other party implied the possibility of Christ's human nature being present where it was His will to be present. The latter may be admitted without the supposition of any attributes in Christ's humanity being essentially divine. There is no reason (and without asserting the deification of Christ's flesh) why it is not possible to assert the presence of Christ's glorified body in the way of power wherever He is co-extensive with His mediatorial presence. Christ could make Himself present or invisible after His resurrection. Whatever difficulty there may be in supposing Christ's humanity as present at different places at the same time, it is no more difficult and unsatisfactory than to suppose it fixed to one place or to give dimensions." Erb, *Nevin's Theology*, 246.

[161] See Hodge, "Doctrine of the Reformed Church," 252. Nevin responds in "Doctrine of the Reformed Church," 352-54. See also Calvin, *Inst*. IV.14.23.

[162] Nevin, "Doctrine of the Reformed Church," 353, writes: "But who may not see that it comes to nothing, so far as the objection is concerned, whether Calvin understood the "efficacy of Christ's body" in the sense of his proper human life, or in some lower sense, so long as his *body* in any way is taken to be its seat and source? It must in any view be still dependent, according to the objection, on the fact of the incarnation, and so

Interpretive Questions and Observations

A number of interpretive questions emerge from our examination of Nevin's soteriology. The first has to do with his relationship to the Reformed tradition. As we have seen above, by 1846 Nevin had rejected predestinarian Calvinism. But what about his relationship to the federal theology in which he was trained at Princeton Seminary? To be sure, the federal doctrine of imputation and legal union is rejected as abstract. Similarly, the venerable covenantal argument for infant baptism is conspicuous by its total absence.

But some aspects of the federal tradition do remain. Nevin retains the scholastic distinction between the covenant of grace and a pretemporal covenant of redemption, and he continues to maintain that faith is the condition of the covenant of grace.[163] In other cases, federal language is used but redefined or placed in a new context which significantly alters the meaning. For example, a "federal" union or relationship is occasionally mentioned but is always redefined and reoriented in a realistic direction.[164] Similarly, in federal fashion Christ is termed a "surety," but the nature of the relationship is clearly recast.[165] Nevin also speaks of a "covenant of works," but in the end it is apparent that "covenant" is nothing more than a metaphor for the realistic relationship between Adam and his posterity.[166] In the final analysis, rather little substance of the federal tradition remains.

Nevin's relationship to Calvin is more ambiguous. *The Mystical Presence* was ostensibly a defense of Calvin's eucharistic doctrine. At very least, Nevin retrieved and made a case for Calvin's notion of soteriological and sacramental union with the incarnate humanity of Christ.[167] Furthermore, in contrast to the dualism of the federal tradition, his stress on the unity of salvation in Christ echoes Calvin's concerns at key points. But in crucial areas, Nevin departs from Calvin and the tradition generally. The ministry of the Word is eclipsed to some degree by the sacraments. Furthermore, Nevin's subordination of the forensic to the realistic jeopardizes the Reformation concern for the synthetic justification of the ungodly. Finally, one may at least ask whether Nevin was

---

out of reach for the Old Testament saints."

[163] Erb, *Nevin's Theology*, 222, 228.

[164] See Nevin, *Mystical Presence*, 189, 211-12.

[165] See Erb, *Nevin's Theology*, 221-22.

[166] See ibid., 202-208. On pp. 207-8 Nevin writes: "As a reality is attached to the idea of guilt, so must a reality be attached to the idea of merit. It lies in the inmost nature of things that obedience to the law should be rewarded, and should issue into life. The contrary opinion is a result of adhering too strictly to the idea of a covenant. To say that man would have no claim except by the virtue of this covenant transaction implies a false view. The word, covenant, is used here as an accommodation, and expresses what was necessary in the actual nature of things."

[167] In this, Nevin received some support from outside the German Reformed Church, notably John B. Adger of Columbia Seminary. See Holifield, "Mercersburg, Princeton, and the South."

too quick to conclude that the sacramental and predestinarian strains in Calvin's thought were mutually exclusive. Certainly there is ample precedent in the Western Christian tradition—here one thinks of Augustine, Lombard, Aquinas, and Luther, to name a few—for their combination.

One final observation has to do with the criticisms persistently leveled against Nevin and the Mercersburg movement. As noted earlier, Nevin was the subject of intense criticism, both within and without the German Reformed church. A common denominator in many of these attacks was a concern that Nevin was slighting justification and the forensic side of soteriology. The Princeton federalist, Charles Hodge, criticized Nevin's *Mystical Presence* on many points, but first and foremost Hodge was concerned to defend the doctrines of immediate imputation and forensic justification. Responding to Nevin's views on imputation, Hodge waved the bloody shirt of the Reformation martyrs:

> Here we reach the very lifeblood of the Reformation. Is justification a declaring just, or a making just, inherently? This was the real battle-ground on which the blood of so many martyrs was spilt. Are we justified for something done for us, or something wrought in us, actually our own?...We consider Dr. Nevin's theory as impugning here, the vital doctrine of Protestantism.[168]

Concern at this point was not limited to proponents of the federal theology. While generally sympathetic to Nevin, and convinced that "he honestly holds the old forensic aspect of redemption in connexion...with his peculiar theanthropic doctrine," New York Calvinist Tayler Lewis (1802-1877) expressed some dismay at the eclipse of the forensic in the Mercersburg Theology and argued for the priority of the atonement over the Incarnation.[169] Within the German Reformed Church itself opposition in some quarters was fierce. In a blistering tract, Jacob Helfenstein contended, "With the *legal* aspect of the atonement or of Justification, the Mercersburg system seems to have but little connexion."[170] Criticism on this point even came from Germany as the venerable mediating theologian I. A. Dorner, whose own influence on Nevin was substantial, expressed reservations about Nevin's soteriological program. According to Dorner, Nevin had subordinated imputation to impartation; his theory "says little of justification, but rather merges this in sanctification."[171]

---

[168]Hodge, "Doctrine of the Reformed Church," 271-72.

[169]See Tayler Lewis, "The Mercersburg School," *Literary World*, 114, 115 (April 7, 14, 1849): 332. Nevin responded to Lewis in "The Apostles' Creed," 342-43. See the discussion in Nichols, *Romanticism in American Theology*, 97.

[170]Jacob Helfenstein, *A Perverted Gospel; or, The Romanizing Tendency of the Mercersburg Theology* (Philadelphia: William S. Young, 1853), 13.

[171]I. A. Dorner, *The Liturgical Conflict in the Reformed Church of North America, with Special Reference to Fundamental Evangelical Doctrines* (Philadelphia: Loag, 1868). This work was written after Dorner's name was drawn into the controversy

Dorner went on to suggest that Nevin's view that "we first obtain justification by *participating in the human nature of Christ*, is a manufactured theory which cannot support itself by the Holy Scriptures."[172]

Summary and Conclusions

In many respects, the soteriology of John Nevin represents a return to Calvin, whose concerns for sacramental efficacy, for the unity of salvation in Christ, and for the importance of union with the incarnate humanity of Christ find a powerful voice here. Here too, a number of the critical soteriological innovations of federal Calvinism are rejected—the notion of an extrinsic legal or federal union with Christ, the dualistic bifurcation of union into legal and spiritual, and the federal understanding of a sequential *ordo salutis*.

This return to Calvin was driven by a keen awareness of the weaknesses inherent in the federal and New England approaches. For the acute religious sensibilities of Nevin, the nineteenth-century New England Calvinist combination of mechanistic revivalism and moralism was both shallow and barren. Similarly, the dualism of the federal paradigm offered little promise of an integrated and satisfying Christian experience.

Despite its depth at certain points, Nevin's creative recasting of the sacramental Calvin in the language of nineteenth-century German organicism and idealism was not an unmitigated success from the standpoint of Reformational thought. While sharing Calvin's intuition that the forensic dimension of salvation is tied to union with the humanity of Christ, Nevin also failed (as did Calvin) to establish sufficiently the connection between Christ's person and the forensic benefits accruing from Christ's work. Instead, Nevin recasts soteriological imputation as mediate, that is, as grounded in the believer's participation in a new and renovated moral state. Here a critical Reformation insight—the synthetic justification of the sinner—is subverted. Nevertheless, Nevin's trenchant criticisms of federal orthodoxy helped to provoke further soteriological reflection and development on the part of federal thinkers, and it is to this further process of development that we now turn.

---

surrounding the revised liturgy of the German Reformed Church in America. For accounts of this liturgical controversy, see Nichols, *Romanticism in American Theology*, 281-307; Maxwell, *Worship and Reformed Theology*, 323-370.

[172]Dorner, *Liturgical Conflict*, 38. On p. 52 he goes on to argue that Mercersburg neglects the Christ *pro nobis* in favor of the Christ *in nobis*. Nevin was clearly stung by these criticisms. He responded to Dorner in "Answer to Professor Dorner," *Mercersburg Review* 15 (1868): 532-646.

PART IV

THE PRINCETON DEFENSE OF IMPUTATION

CHAPTER 6

The Federal Theology of Charles Hodge

The establishment of Princeton Seminary in 1811 was to be of extraordinary significance for Reformed theology in America during the nineteenth century. Here a succession of capable theologians—Archibald Alexander (1772-1851), Charles Hodge (1797-1878), Archibald Alexander Hodge (1823-1886), and Benjamin Breckinridge Warfield (1851-1921)—occupied the chair of theology, and each was a defender of the federal theology that had reached maturity in seventeenth-century. Until the publication of Charles Hodge's own *Systematic Theology* in 1871-3, the text of choice was Francis Turretin's *Institutio Theologicae Elencticae*, first published in 1679-85.

In an earlier chapter, we noted that the federal soteriology was characterized by increasingly strict adherence to an *ordo salutis* framework, the bifurcation of union with Christ into an extrinsic and legal union on the one hand and a vital or spiritual union on the other, and the virtual eclipse of the humanity of Christ as a material element in the application of salvation. The difficulties inherent in this approach invited opposition from a variety of quarters, and in mid-nineteenth-century America a battle raged for the soul of American Calvinism between the revisionist Calvinism of the New England successors of Edwards, the idealist Reformed perspective of Mercersburg, and the defenders of federal theology at Princeton. Here it is critical to note that the Princeton defense of the federal soteriology, an effort largely undertaken by Charles Hodge, was no mere recapitulation. Despite his repeated contention that "a new idea never emerged in this Seminary,"[1] Hodge radicalized certain elements of federalism, particularly the emphasis on the extrinsic. In this he unwittingly paved the way for the further decline of the tradition.

---

[1] Quoted in A. A. Hodge, *The Life of Charles Hodge* (New York: Charles Scribner's Sons, 1880), 521. Hodge and other Princetonians persistently claimed that there was no distinctive "Princeton theology," and that what was taught was simply "Calvinism." See Mark A. Noll, "Introduction," in *The Princeton Theology, 1812-1921* (Grand Rapids: Baker, 1983), 38-40. On this period of Princeton Seminary, see William K. Selden, *Princeton Theological Seminary: A Narrative History, 1812-1992* (Princeton, N.J.: Princeton University Press, 1992), 6-79; and David B. Calhoun, *Princeton Seminary (1812-1862): Faith and Learning* (Carlisle, Pa.: Banner of Truth, 1995).

Biography

The last of five children born to Hugh and Mary Blanchard Hodge (only two of whom survived childhood), Hodge was raised by his widowed mother who instructed him in the Westminster Shorter Catechism.[2] As a child, he attended the Second Presbyterian Church of Philadelphia, then pastored by Ashbel Green, who was later to teach Hodge at Princeton Seminary. After graduating from the College of New Jersey at Princeton in 1815, he entered Princeton Seminary, graduating in 1819.[3] In 1820 he became Assistant Instructor in the Original Languages of Scripture at the Seminary, thus beginning an association with Princeton Seminary as a teacher that would continue until his death. In 1822 he was named Professor of Oriental and Biblical Literature, a post he occupied until 1840 when he replaced his teacher Archibald Alexander in the chair of Exegetical and Didactic Theology.

Sensing the need for further education, Hodge spent two years (1826-28) in Europe, studying in Paris, Halle, and Berlin, with further stops at Göttingen, Bonn, and England. While at Halle, he became a friend of the pietist F. A. G. Tholuck (1799-1877). At Berlin he heard Schleiermacher preach, and he became acquainted with many luminaries of the Prussian religious scene.[4]

As important as his teaching career was, Hodge's literary efforts were both voluminous and significant. In 1825 he began the *Biblical Repertory*, which was soon renamed *The Biblical Repertory and Theological Review* in 1829, and then dubbed *The Biblical Repertory and Princeton Review* in 1837. This journal, which was edited by Hodge until 1872, served as the major organ of the Princeton theology, and Hodge contributed many articles and reviews to it.[5]

---

[2]For biographical treatments of Hodge, see A. A. Hodge, *Life of Charles Hodge*; C. A. Salmond, *Princetoniana: Charles and A. A. Hodge, with Class and Table Talk of Hodge the Younger* (New York: Scribner & Welford, n.d.), 11-52; John Oliver Nelson, "Charles Hodge: Nestor of Orthodoxy," in *The Lives of Eighteen from Princeton*, ed. Willard Thorp (Princeton, N.J.: Princeton University Press, 1946), 192-211.

General treatments of Hodge's theology include Ralph J. Danhof, *Charles Hodge as a Dogmatician* (Goes, the Netherlands: Oosterbaan & le Cointre, 1929); David F. Wells, "Charles Hodge," in *Reformed Theology in America: A History of Its Modern Development*, ed. David F. Wells (Grand Rapids: Eerdmans, 1985), 36-59.

[3]Entries from Hodge's personal journal during the period between his graduation from seminary and his call to teach are published in Charles D. Cashdollar, "The Pursuit of Piety: Charles Hodge's Diary, 1819-1820," *Journal of Presbyterian History* 55 (1977): 267-283.

[4]On Hodge's understanding of European theology, see B. A. Gerrish, "Charles Hodge and the Europeans," in *Charles Hodge Revisited: A Critical Appraisal of His Life and Work*, ed. John W. Stewart and James H. Moorhead (Grand Rapids: Eerdmans, 2002), 129-158.

[5]On the history of this journal and Hodge's involvement with it, see Mark A. Noll, "The Princeton Review," *Westminster Theological Journal* 50 (1988): 283-304.

Because the articles in *The Biblical Repertory and Princeton Review* (hereafter cited

In addition to his many articles, Hodge published commentaries on four Pauline epistles—Romans (1835), Ephesians (1856), 1 Corinthians (1857), and 2 Corinthians (1859). A variety of other historical and theological works followed, culminating in his three-volume *Systematic Theology* (1871-73).[6] Because of the abbreviated character of many discussions in the *Systematic Theology*, a fuller understanding of his theology must utilize other sources as well.

Hodge was also involved in ecclesiastical affairs, and his theology arose out of a deep concern for the life of the church. Serving as a delegate to the Old School General Assembly in 1842, 1846, and 1847, Hodge was elected moderator of the Assembly in 1846. Furthermore, his annual synopsis of the Assembly was a fixture of the July issue of the BRPR from 1835 onward. Hodge also served on a variety of church boards, including Foreign Missions (1846-1870), Domestic Missions (1840-1870), and Education (1861-1870), and as a trustee of Princeton College and of the Presbyterian Historical Society.[7]

The Method and Context of Hodge's Theology

The method and content of Charles Hodge's theology must be understood in light of the institutional and ecclesiological context within which he worked. As a leading professor at the flagship seminary of the Presbyterian Church, Hodge viewed himself not only as a spokesman for the Presbyterian church as a whole, but as a guardian of American Calvinism. As such, Hodge had an apologetic concern for all of doctrine; he frequently would write against a particular view of theological anthropology or original sin because of its potential impact on other doctrines.

Scottish Common Sense Realism

The philosophy of Scottish Common Sense Realism took shape in response to

---

as BRPR) are unsigned during this period, the use of an index is essential. See the history of Hodge's involvement in the journal and a list of his articles in *Biblical Repertory and Princeton Review: Index Volume from 1825 to 1868* (Philadelphia: Peter Walker, 1871), 200-211. A more accurate index covering the years 1829-1868 is found in Earl William Kennedy, "Authors of Articles in *The Biblical Repertory and Princeton Review*," (Typescript, Speer Library, Princeton Theological Seminary, 1963).

[6]Charles Hodge, *Systematic Theology*, 3 vols. (New York: Charles Scribner's Sons, 1871-72). See also *The Constitutional History of the Presbyterian Church in the United States of America*, 2 vols. (Philadelphia: William S. Martien, 1839-40); *The Way of Life* (Philadelphia: American Sunday School Union, 1841); *What Is Darwinism?* (New York: Scribners, Armstrong, and Co., 1874). Hodge's notes from his Sunday afternoon devotional meetings with students were published as *Conference Papers* (New York: Charles Scribner's Sons, 1879).

[7]See A. A. Hodge, *Life of Charles Hodge*, 343, 384-87.

the skeptical empiricism of David Hume (1711-1776), who had argued that all ideas consist of discrete impressions or perceptions, and that these sensory data are not in themselves verifiable.[8] What we perceive as "cause and effect," Hume argued, is simply the succession of isolated perceptions. The skeptical and irreligious implications of this radical empiricism were apparent—metaphysical claims, arguments for cause and effect, probability, and so forth were ruled out of court. Even the concept of mind is undercut—what we conventionally call "mind" is nothing but a series of isolated perceptions. Hume was countered by Thomas Reid (1710-1796), who concluded that the root of Hume's skepticism lay in Locke's representational epistemology (with its notion of "ideas") mediated to his successors Berkeley and Hume. Interpreting Locke as teaching that the mind is only immediately aware of its own ideas (implying that the connection between ideas and things is uncertain), Reid concluded that this representationalism led inexorably to skepticism regarding our knowledge of the world as it is. His response was to challenge the notion of "ideas" itself. The knower apprehends reality directly and unmediated rather than through ideas. An "idea" is not a mental entity or object to be known, but a mental "act." Reid wrote that he took "the idea of an object and the perception of an object to be the same thing," and he argued that there are but three elements in the process of knowing—"the mind that perceives, the operation of the mind, which is called perception, and the object perceived."[9]

The way beyond Hume's skepticism was, according to Reid, illuminated by the "common sense" possessed by all. There are certain things foolish or dangerous to deny—the existence of material objects, the existence of the knowing self, and so forth.[10] This "common sense," furthermore, could be sustained theoretically through the rigorous, inductive study of the human mind and its operations. The beliefs of common sense arise, Reid thought, from the constitution of the human mind itself. The perception of an object is not reducible to sensory impression, but also involves the application of axiomatic

---

[8]On Scottish Common Sense Realism in general, see James McCosh, *The Scottish Philosophy* (New York: Robert Carter, 1874); S. A. Grave, *The Scottish Philosophy of Common Sense* (Oxford: Clarendon Press, 1960).

On the influence of Scottish Realism on American thought and theology, see Sydney E. Ahlstrom, "The Scottish Philosophy and American Theology," *Church History* 24 (1955): 257-272; Henry May, *The Enlightenment in America* (New York: Oxford University Press, 1976); Theodore Dwight Bozeman, *Protestants in an Age of Science: The Baconian Ideal and Antebellum Religious Thought* (Chapel Hill, N.C.: University of North Carolina Press, 1977); E. Brooks Holifield, *The Gentlemen Theologians: American Theology in Southern Culture, 1795-1860* (Durham, N.C.: Duke University Press, 1978), 110-126; Mark A. Noll, "Common Sense Traditions and American Evangelical Thought," *American Quarterly* 37 (1985): 216-238.

[9]Thomas Reid, quoted in Grave, *Scottish Philosophy*, 20, 22. See also Holifield, *Gentlemen Theologians*, 114-115.

[10]See Grave, *Scottish Philosophy*, 57-60, 82-93.

principles constitutive of the mind's operation.

Although recent scholarship has been less kind to the Scottish Realists, Reid's ideas met with extraordinary acceptance in the late eighteenth and early nineteenth century period. Scottish Realism appeared to have conquered Hume's skepticism, secured the self and the reliability of its knowledge, and laid a firm methodological foundation for scientific endeavor and, many thought, for theology.[11] Dugald Stewart (1753-1828), Reid's great friend and popularizer, disseminated Reid's views, which found an eager audience in both Europe and America. Scottish Realism was introduced to America by John Witherspoon (1723-1794), who came from Scotland to be president of the College of New Jersey at Princeton in 1768. Taking a dim view of the idealism prevalent at the college upon his arrival, he moved quickly to dismiss the Edwardsean tutors, Jonathan Edwards the younger among them.[12] Witherspoon's nineteenth-century successors continued the Reid-Stewart tradition at Princeton College, and from there Scottish Realism was disseminated by its graduates throughout American Protestantism.

Certain characteristics of Scottish Common Sense Realism crucial for this study require mention. The first is its reflexive dualism. Reid and his successors fully accepted the venerable Cartesian distinction of mind and matter, resisting both the idealist subordination of matter to mind, and the materialist reduction of mind to matter.[13] But this foundational mind/matter dualism implied or was accompanied by a number of other dualisms as well—subject and object, body and soul, flesh and spirit, finite and infinite, natural and supernatural, creator and creation, cognitive faith and religious experience.[14]

Related to this is the Scottish Common Sense approach to truth itself. Here

---

[11] See Ahlstrom, "Scottish Philosophy," 267-268.

[12] See Henry May, *Enlightenment in America*, 62-63; Kuklick, *Churchmen and Philosophers*, 66-72; Bozeman, *Age of Science*, 22.

[13] See Grave, *Scottish Philosophy*, 131-135; Bozeman, *Age of Science*, 53-55.

[14] See Woodbridge Riley, *American Thought: From Puritanism to Pragmatism and Beyond* (New York: Henry Holt, 1915), 123; Lefferts A. Loetscher, *Facing the Enlightenment and Pietism: Archibald Alexander and the Founding of Princeton Seminary* (Westport, Conn. Greenwood Press, 1983), 33; Kuklick, *Churchmen and Philosophers*, 78. Ahlstrom, "Scottish Philosophy," 267-268, writes regarding the appeal of the Common Sense philosophy: "The Scottish Philosophy was an apologetical philosophy, *par excellence*. And the secret of its success, I think, lay in its dualism, epistemological, ontological, and cosmological. Its other advantages were auxiliary. Reid's theory affirmed a clean subject-object distinction. The world which men perceived was in no sense constituted by consciousness. On the mind-matter problem dualism facilitated an all-out attack on both materialism and idealism, as well as the pantheism that either type of monistic analysis could lead to. Furthermore, by a firm separation of the Creator and His creation, the Scottish thinkers preserved the orthodox notion of God's transcendence, and made revelation necessary...The Scottish philosophy, in short, was a winning combination."

the emphasis falls overwhelmingly on static particularity. Writing in *The Biblical Repertory and Princeton Review*, James Clement Moffatt argued:

> To know a truth or fact precisely, is not only to apprehend it intelligently, but also to perceive just what it amounts to in itself, and how all its elements stand related to each other, and what its boundaries are, so that you can pick it up out of the mass of other knowledge, and hold it before you as a complete, distinct, and practicable entity.[15]

This concern for the particular is reflected in the striking preoccupation of Scottish Common Sense thinkers with induction. As T. D. Bozeman has shown, rather than deducing truth from general first principles, Reid and his followers stressed the observation of discrete phenomena and generalizations therefrom. The name of Francis Bacon (1561-1626) became the watchword of methodological orthodoxy in a vast array of disciplines—from geology to theology.[16]

This bent toward particularity in turn shaped a disjunctive theological method based on Common Sense principles and particularly on Baconian induction. For Old School Presbyterians in particular, methodological continuity between the physical sciences and theology were asserted, and theology was viewed as a science dealing inductively with the data of Scripture. Charles Hodge provides the classic statement here. After distinguishing three approaches to theological method—the speculative, the mystical, and the favored inductive method—Hodge goes on to declare that all theological "facts" are to be found in scripture and that the task of the theologian is the orderly, inductive collection and systematization of these facts.

> If natural science be concerned with the facts and laws of nature, theology is concerned with the facts and the principles of the Bible. If the object of the one be to arrange and systematize the facts of the external world, and to ascertain the laws by which they are determined; the object of the other is to systematize the facts of the Bible, and ascertain the principles or general truths which those facts involve.[17]

The Scottish Realist optimism regarding the innate powers of "common sense" also affected the form and language of theological controversy in the early and mid-nineteenth century. We will recall the prominent role of the category of "mystery" in Calvin's sacramental discussions, and appeals to

---

[15]James Clement Moffatt, "Popular Education," *The Biblical Repertory and Princeton Review* 29 (1857), 615. Citing this statement by Moffatt, Bozeman, *Age of Science*, 57, speaks of a "radically nominalist vision" of reality on the part of American Common Sense thinkers.

[16]See Bozeman, *Age of Science*, 23-30, 44-70.

[17]Hodge, *Systematic Theology*, I:18. See also pp. 3-17.

divine mystery are by no means absent in later orthodoxy.[18] But what had been "mystery" to earlier generations of Reformed theologians often becomes unacceptably "irrational" to nineteenth-century American Presbyterians. This is a matter of considerable importance for, as we shall see, Calvin's view of union with Christ is derided as "irrational," "impossible," or worse.

Charles Hodge was in many ways a child of the Scottish Enlightenment.[19] Here we find frequent appeals to "common sense," to "intuitive principles," and to the "consciousness of every man."[20] The reflexive dualism so characteristic of Common Sense thinkers is present as well—distinctions between body and soul, subject and object, the natural and the supernatural, and doctrine and experience are frequently emphasized. And with these dualisms came an increased distinction between imputation and impartation in both hamartiology and soteriology. Indeed, the soteriological paradigm of federal theology found defenders almost entirely among the devotees of Scottish Common Sense. Finally, Hodge's methodological orientation toward the particular and the individual at the expense of the general lends a nominalistic caste to his theology.[21]

Religious Experience

Counterbalancing the empiricist rationalism of the Common Sense philosophy one also finds a deep strain of theocentric piety and concern for religious experience at work in Hodge's theology. Hodge was quite willing to limit the role of reason where it seemed to conflict with his theology, and he was not afraid to appeal to religious experience where he deemed it helpful. As we will see below, when responding to attacks by New England Calvinists (who shared his Common Sense presuppositions) on the doctrine of imputation, Hodge stressed the limits of reason and the necessity of faith in an inscrutable God. But when responding to John Nevin of Mercersburg (whose idealist metaphysic

---

[18] See Calvin, *Inst.* IV.14.5; IV.17.5, 33, 36.

[19] The influence of the Scottish philosophy on Hodge is treated in James L. McAllister, Jr., "The Nature of Religious Knowledge in the Theology of Charles Hodge" (Ph.D. diss., Duke University, 1957), 58-122; John C. Vander Stelt, *Philosophy and Scripture: A Study in Old Princeton and Westminster Theology* (Marlton, N.J.: Mack Publishing Co., 1978), 120-147.

[20] See, e.g., Charles Hodge, "The Nature of Man," BRPR 37 (1865): 111, 126.

[21] This was, in fact, a persistent charge leveled against Hodge by his contemporaries. See, e.g., Philip Schaff, "Additions" in J. P. Lange and F. R. Fay, *The Epistle of Paul to the Romans*, trans. J. F. Hurst (New York: Charles Scribner, 1869), 193; Landis, *Doctrine of Original Sin*, 67, 336, 345, 385, 403-4.

While Hodge occasionally distanced himself from nominalist formulations, the charge has considerable basis in his own way of thinking. See especially Charles Hodge, "The First and Second Adam," BRPR 32 (1860): 335-376; "Nature of Man," 111-132.

he did not share) Hodge sounded a more rationalistic note.[22]

An interesting dimension of Hodge's piety was his ambivalent attitude toward revivalism. Though he had a "conversion experience" while a college student at Princeton, it seems that Hodge shared none of Nevin's introspective tendencies. W. A. Hoffecker, in his study of Hodge's piety and devotional writings, speaks of his "lack of emotional excesses."[23] Always critical of the emotional extravagances that often accompanied revivals, Hodge's writings became increasingly caustic as the "New Measures" revivalist practices of Charles Finney were more and more identified with New England revisionist Calvinism and with Arminianism.[24] Like Nevin in *The Anxious Bench*, Hodge advocated a system of Christian nurture rooted in the ongoing life of the church.[25]

The Reformed Tradition

Hodge's theology was also conditioned by an emphasis on the received tradition of federal Calvinism. He had read widely and deeply in the Reformed tradition, and he often quotes promiscuously from the first generation of Reformers up through the period of high orthodoxy in the seventeenth century, with scattered quotations from eighteenth-century luminaries such as Jonathan Edwards. In this he manifests a certain lack of historiographical sophistication.[26] But Hodge was not utterly devoid of historical consciousness, and he was aware of differences between Calvin and the later federalists. In debates over the Reformed doctrine of the Lord's Supper and Original Sin, Hodge was quite willing to concede the fact of diversity, which he explained in terms of a teleology of Reformed doctrinal development, a process that culminated in the high federalism of the middle and late seventeenth century. Briefly put, Hodge contended that a range of views were present among the early Reformers, but gradually the inner logic of the central tradition (thought by Hodge to consist in the doctrines of the authority of Scripture and justification by faith) exerted itself and the "uncongenial foreign elements" were eliminated.[27] In this, Hodge's preference for seventeenth-century

---

[22] When it suited his purposes, Hodge could be critical of a naive reliance on "common sense." See, e.g., Charles Hodge, "Is the Church of Rome a Part of the Visible Church," BRPR 18 (1846): 321.

[23] W. Andrew Hoffecker, *Piety and the Princeton Theologians* (Phillipsburg, N.J.: Presbyterian and Reformed, 1981), 54. Ambivalence toward the phenomenon of American revivalism was characteristic of Princeton Seminary from its inception. See Loetscher, *Facing the Enlightenment and Pietism*, 161-175.

[24] See Hoffecker, *Piety*, 71-79, for a fine treatment of Hodge's critique of revivalism.

[25] See, e.g., Charles Hodge, "Bushnell on Christian Nurture," *BRPR* 19 (1847): 502-539. See also Hoffecker, *Piety*, 76-79.

[26] On this point, see Noll, "Introduction," 28.

[27] See Hodge, "Doctrine of the Reformed Church," 251; "First and Second Adam,"

scholasticism is apparent—the federalism of Francis Turretin and the Westminster Standards is the norm by which earlier formulations are judged.[28]

> We accordingly find in the history of Protestant theology much more of inconsistency and confusion during the sixteenth than during the seventeenth century. It was not until after one principle had been allowed to modify another, that the scheme of doctrine came to adjust itself into the consistent and moderate form in which it is presented in the writings of Turretin and Gerhard.[29]

Hodge, however, was not a slavish disciple of the seventeenth-century theologians, nor could he be. Federal theology faced new and severe challenges during the nineteenth century, both from American culture generally and from within the Reformed tradition itself. The increasingly individualistic, optimistic, and democratic character of American culture rendered Calvinistic notions of corporate solidarity in sin, and by extension, in salvation, increasingly implausible to many, and Hodge bitterly opposed the New England attempt to revise the Reformed tradition along these more modern lines. Likewise, he opposed the Mercersburg proposals regarding solidarity in sin and salvation, proposals that were directed against both Princeton federalism and New England individualism. Thus, the thought of Charles Hodge represents an important chapter in the later history of federal theology.

The Problem of Solidarity—The Defense of Imputation

The questions of hamartiological and soteriological solidarity came to a focus for Hodge in the defense of the doctrine of forensic imputation. Early in his literary career, Hodge expressed himself strongly on this point, and in this he followed the lead of his teacher Archibald Alexander. In January 1830 Alexander had written:

> Now we confess ourselves to be of the number of those who believe, whatever reproach it may bring upon us from a certain quarter, that if the doctrine of imputation be given up, the whole doctrine of original sin must be abandoned.

338-39.

[28]Hodge found the seventeenth-century scholastics preferable in particular to the theology of nineteenth-century Germany: "After all the alleged improvements in theological research, we never feel so much disposed to take down one of the old Latin dogmatic writers of the seventeenth century, as immediately on closing a fresh work from Germany. These antiquated writers have a thousand faults, it may be; they are stiff, they are prolix, they are technical, they are intolerant and austere, they are scholastic in their distinctions, but they have one great merit—they always let us know what they mean. Their atmosphere, if wintry and biting, is clear." Charles Hodge, "Neander's History," *BRPR* 16 (1844): 182.

[29]Hodge, "First and Second Adam," 338. See also "Doctrine of the Reformed Church," 253.

And if this doctrine be relinquished, then the whole doctrine of redemption must fall; and what may then be left of christianity, they may contend for that will; but for ourselves, we shall be of opinion, that what remains will not be worth a serious struggle.[30]

Hodge signaled his agreement, adding that "the denial of the doctrine of imputation not only renders that of original sin untenable; but involves, either the rejection or serious modification of those of atonement and justification."[31] For Princeton, hamartiological and soteriogical imputation stood and fell together.

Original Sin and the Solidarity with Adam

Although Charles Hodge's doctrines of original sin and hamartiological imputation have received attention elsewhere, his distinctive view of solidarity with Adam must be touched on here.[32] His distinct approach to the topic was framed in conscious opposition to the rejection of federal theology that increasingly characterized the New England trajectory. With some warrant, Hodge discerned a natural progression from the denial of imputation to the denial of innate depravity and moral inability.[33] Hodge's formulations must also be understood as a response to problems within the federal theology itself. Before this, federal theologians had framed original sin in terms of an unstable dialectic of inherited corruption and of imputed guilt grounded in a

---

[30]Archibald Alexander, "The Early History of Pelagianism," *BRPR* 2 (1830): 92-93; quoted in Charles Hodge, "Inquiries Respecting the Doctrine of Imputation," *BRPR* 2 (1830): 431.

[31]Hodge, "Inquiries Respecting the Doctrine of Imputation," 472.

[32]Helpful treatments include Earl William Kennedy, "A Historical Analysis of Charles Hodge's Doctrines of Sin and Particular Grace," (Th.D. diss., Princeton Theological Seminary, 1968); Hutchinson, *Problem of Original Sin*, 28-35. See also Fisher, "Augustinian and Federal Theories Compared."

[33]See, e.g., Hodge, "Inquiries Respecting the Doctrine of Imputation"; "The New Divinity Tried," BRPR 4 (1832): 278-304. In his "Beecher's Great Conflict," *BRPR* 26 (1854):104, Hodge quotes New Englander Edward Beecher on this progression. Beecher had written: "They deny the imputation of Adam's sin to his posterity—that is, they deny that God regards as their act that which was not their act, and that on this ground he inflicts on them the inconceivably severe penalty alleged by the Old-school divines. They also deny the existence in man of a nature in the strict sense sinful, and deserving of punishment, anterior to knowledge and voluntary action, and teach that all sin and holiness consist in voluntary action. As a natural result, they also deny the doctrine of the absolute and entire inability of the sinner to do the duties required of him by God. The inability asserted in the Scriptures they hold to be, according to the just laws of interpretation, merely a fixed unwillingness to comply with the will of God, which is not inconsistent with a real and proper ability to obey, but derives its character of inexcusable guilt from the existence of such ability."

representative federal relationship, each buttressing what was lacking in the other. When the justice of inherited corruption was questioned, federal theologians appealed to the representative relation. Likewise, when the justice of the federal relationship was challenged, the innate hereditary sinfulness was cited. The difficulties here were increasingly obvious.[34] If federalism was to be defended, it would have to be recast. Such was the challenge facing this defender of Reformed orthodoxy.

Hodge operated in a context where both imputation and inherited depravity were questioned. If the imputation of Adam's sin was to be maintained, Hodge could do this either by making the representative aspect stand on its own as a purely extrinsic relation, or he could move in the direction of realistic participation and ground imputation in the participation of Adam's posterity in his actual sin. Hodge's choice here was determined by both philosophical and theological considerations. As a Scottish Common Sense thinker, the empiricist Hodge had little regard for the philosophical idealism that often accompanied the realist-participationist option. As we will see below, Hodge had nothing but scorn for idealist theories of "generic identity" and traducianist views of the origin of the soul. Equally important was the parallel Hodge perceived between the double imputation of Christ's righteousness to the Christian and the Christian's guilt to Christ on the one hand, and the imputation of Adam's sin to his posterity. If the first is an extrinsic, legal relationship, the second must be as well by virtue of the typological relationship between Christ and Adam as presented by St. Paul in the fifth chapter of Romans. Hodge writes, "As we have been condemned for a sin which is not our own, so are we justified for a righteousness which is not our own.[35] Thus it was that Hodge undertook to make the representative relationship, the federal union, stand on its own. And for this reason, federal theology here assumes an even more extrinsic mode.

Hodge initially seems to echo the earlier formula by affirming a two-fold relationship to Adam: "The ground of the imputation of Adam's sin to his posterity, is the union between them, which is two-fold, a natural union, as between a father and his children, and the union of representation, which is the main idea here insisted upon."[36] It is apparent, however, that the federal or legal relationship is by far the more important, for "over and beyond this natural relation...there was a special divine constitution by which he was appointed the head and representative of his whole race."[37] The natural union is, for Hodge, a sort of *conditio sine qua non* which assures the fitness of the

---

[34]This problem was noted by New England thinkers. See George Park Fisher, "Original Sin: The State of the Question," *The New Englander* 18 (1860): 698-700.

[35]Hodge, "Inquiries Respecting the Doctrine of Imputation," 468. See also "First and Second Adam," 339-41; *Systematic Theology*, II:195, 212-13, 225.

[36]Hodge, "Inquiries Respecting the Doctrine of Imputation," 436. See also *Systematic Theology*, II:196-97.

[37]Hodge, *Systematic Theology*, II:197.

transaction, but the representative relationship is determinative. Commenting on the natural relation and its omission from the Westminster Larger Catechism, Hodge wrote: "It is neglected because of its secondary importance, representation being the main ground of imputation; so that when representation ceases, imputation ceases, although the natural bond continues."[38]

Hodge goes on to insist on the extrinsic and purely representative character of both relationships. Against realists, he argues that there is no personal or numerical identity involved, for representation and identity are not the same thing at all: "A union of representation is not a union of identity. If Adam and his race were one and the same, he was not their representative, for a thing cannot represent itself."[39] Against New Englanders who assumed that merit and guilt inhered only in actual moral character, Hodge maintains that imputation involves no "transfer of moral character" as would render one actually righteous or unrighteous.[40] Thus, for Hodge, imputation involves neither meaningful personal identity nor mutual participation in a moral condition. It is an entirely extrinsic and legal matter.

Hodge goes on to define this legal and extrinsic relationship of imputation as the imputation of guilt. By "guilt," he means neither actual moral pollution nor demerit, but merely the legal obligation to satisfy the demand of justice. By implication, the evils consequent upon this imputation—moral corruption and death—are understood as penal.

> To impute sin, in Scriptural and theological language, is to impute the guilt of sin. And by guilt is meant not criminality or moral ill-desert, or demerit, much less moral pollution, but the judicial obligation to satisfy justice. Hence the evil consequent on the imputation is not an arbitrary infliction; not merely a misfortune or calamity; not a chastisement in the proper sense of that word, but a punishment, i.e., an evil inflicted in execution of the penalty of law and for the satisfaction of justice.[41]

Here certain distinctions critical to Hodge's argument are utilized. In the quotation immediately above, three elements are distinguished—actual moral

---

[38] Charles Hodge, "The Doctrine of Imputation," in *Princeton Theological Essays*, ed. Patrick Fairbairn (Edinburgh: T. & T. Clark, 1856), 162. See also "First and Second Adam," 340. On this priority of the forensic, see Hutchinson, *Problem of Original Sin*, 29-30.

[39] Hodge, "Inquiries Respecting the Doctrine of Imputation," 437.

[40] Ibid., 436-37, 442. See also the discussion in Hutchinson, *Problem of Original Sin*, 29-30. It was suggested by New England critics that the imputation of believer's sin to Christ would compromise his sinlessness. See, e.g., John Smalley, "Justification Through Christ, An Act of Free Grace," in Edwards A. Park, ed., *The Atonement: Discourses and Treatises* (Boston: Congregational Board of Publication, 1859), 57.

[41] Hodge, *Systematic Theology*, II:194.

pollution, demerit, and judicial obligation to satisfy justice. Agreeing with New England that merit and demerit are tied to actual moral character, Hodge drew a marked distinction between demerit and the obligation to satisfy justice, that is, the classic scholastic distinction between *reatus culpae* and *reatus poenae*.[42] Imputation, according to Hodge, has only to do with the latter. As we will see below, this same framework is carried over into soteriology, with unfortunate results. The utility of this distinction for Hodge was substantial, however. It enabled him to evade the New England jibe that shared guilt in Adam's transgression implied the absurdity that Adam's posterity should feel remorse for that sin. Furthermore, Hodge hereby avoided any suggestion that the imputation of the believer's sin to Christ involved Christ in moral turpitude.[43]

Another intriguing element of Hodge's doctrine of original sin is evident in his doctrine of universal infant salvation. Hodge staunchly maintained that all children dying in infancy are among the elect and thus are saved from eternal damnation. He held that such children are saved by grace, but he also argued that the imputation of Adam's guilt, or liability to punishment, in itself is not a sufficient ground for eternal condemnation. Rather, this imputation is the ground of inherited corruption, the outworking of which in turn merits eternal judgment.

> All who die in infancy are doubtless saved, but they are saved by grace. It is nevertheless important that the real views of the Reformed Churches, on the doctrine of immediate imputation, should be clearly understood. Those churches do not teach that the first sin of Adam is the single and immediate ground of the condemnation of his posterity to eternal death, but that is the ground of their forfeiture of the divine favour from which flows the loss of original righteousness and corruption of our whole nature, which in their turn become the proximate ground of exposure to final perdition, from which, however, as almost all Protestants believe, all are saved who have no other sins to answer for.[44]

---

[42]This distinction arose out of the medieval Roman Catholic penitential system, which held that the satisfaction of Christ atoned for the guilt of sin, but that a guilt or liability to temporal punishment remained to be dealt with by penitential disciplines. This is reflected in "Canons and Decrees of the Council of Trent," Session 14, chap. 8; in Schaff, *Creeds of Christendom*, II:155-58. On the history of this distinction, see also Richard A. Muller, *Dictionary of Latin and Greek Theological Terms* (Grand Rapids: Baker, 1985), 258.

Reformation and Reformed orthodox thinkers generally rejected the relevance of the distinction, contending that the satisfaction offered by Christ is sufficient for both the expiation of guilt and the satisfaction of divine justice. See, e.g., Calvin, *Inst.* III.4.30; and Turretin, *Institutes*, (XIV.12.13), II:441, who dismissed the distinction as absurd.

[43]That these two concerns were on Hodge's mind is apparent in "Inquiries Respecting the Doctrine of Imputation," 436-37.

[44]Hodge, *Systematic Theology*, II:211-12. See also I:26; III:605; "First and Second Adam," 342.

One senses here an inconsistency borne of both sentimentalism and the desire to defend Calvinist orthodoxy in an increasingly hostile environment. If the imputed guilt of Adam is not a sufficient ground of eternal punishment, then it is by no means clear that those dying in infancy need to be "saved by grace" in the first place.

Hodge was also concerned to defend the doctrine of inherited depravity and inability. As noted above, he viewed moral corruption as a penal infliction or punishment grounded in the imputation of an obligation to satisfy justice to Adam's posterity.[45] But Hodge was also aware of the problems associated with a naive realism, and he insists that this inherited corruption is not an inherited taint or change in the essence of the soul, for this would make the creator God the author of sin. Rather, the "corrupt nature" inherited from Adam is the result of a judicial abandonment, the withdrawal of divine favor and sustaining grace.[46]

Hodge's reformulation of the Reformed doctrine of hamartiological imputation along consistently extrinsic and forensic lines met with considerable opposition within the American Reformed community. On the one hand, Hodge persistently had to defend his formulations over against New England Calvinism, which, he thought, made too little of solidarity with Adam by its denial of imputation and apparent minimizing of inherent corruption. On the other hand, he also argued against various forms of realism, which made, Hodge thought, too much of it with notions of participation in a "generic humanity" and the like.

Hodge's defense of imputation against New England involved him in a vigorous dispute with Moses Stuart of Andover over the exegesis of Romans 5:12-21.[47] Even more interesting is the opposition incurred by Hodge from

---

D. F. Wells has found that the issue of infant salvation was a major element in the Unitarian polemic against orthodox Calvinism. See Wells, "Charles Hodge," 43, 58 note 27. Prior to the late eighteenth century the majority of Reformed theologians expressed confidence that children of the believers dying in infancy were saved, but were cautiously agnostic with respect to the children of unbelievers. Later, however, came a decided shift toward the conviction that all dying in infancy are elect, a tendency reflected in Hodge as well. See Benjamin Breckinridge Warfield, *Two Studies in the History of Doctrine* (New York: Christian Literature Co., 1897), 195-220.

[45]See Hodge, "Inquiries Respecting the Doctrine of Imputation," 456. 471; *Systematic Theology*, II:206.

[46]See Hodge, "First and Second Adam," 362; *Systematic Theology*, II:253.

[47]On the Hodge-Stuart debate, see Stephen J. Stein, "Stuart and Hodge on Romans 5:12-21: An Exegetical Controversy about Original Sin," *Journal of Presbyterian History* 47 (1969): 340-358. Many of the responses to Hodge from various quarters are listed in Earl William Kennedy, "Writings about Charles Hodge and His Works, Principally as Found in Periodicals Contained in the Speer Library, Princeton Theological Seminary, for the Years 1830-1880 (Typescript, Speer Library, Princeton Theological Seminary, 1963).

Presbyterian contemporaries. There were, first of all, realists such as Samuel J. Baird (1817-1893), and the New School Presbyterian William G. T. Shedd (1820-1894), who opposed Hodge's notion of a purely legal relationship, and argued that the sin of Adam is imputed to his posterity because they were present "in the loins of Adam" as to their human nature.[48] This involved two crucial ideas with which Hodge took exception: a traducianist view of the origin of the human soul, and a distinction between individual and generic human identity. Against traducianism, Hodge provides the standard scholastic arguments—that the sinful acts of all ancestors would be imputed as well, that the impeccability of Christ is threatened because he possesses a human nature, and that it implies a holy nature can be transmitted by natural generation as well as a sinful one. He adds that the realist approach is grounded in a "philosophy" (i.e., forms of idealism) alien to the Bible.[49] Against notions of generic human identity (formulations holding that moral attributes and responsibility may be credited to a corporate human nature antecedent to individual human existence), Hodge argues in Common Sense and nominalist fashion that the distinction between generic and individual identity is "absurd," and that substantial identity therefore cannot be separated from the numerical identity of individual persons.[50]

But perhaps the most trenchant criticisms of Hodge came from the pen of Robert W. Landis (1809-1883), an Old School theologian who taught for a time at the Presbyterian seminary in Danville, Kentucky. In a series of articles, he accused Hodge of advocating a "strictly gratuitous" imputation of sin to humanity.[51] With considerable cogency, Landis argued, first of all, that

---

Among Hodge's more important responses to New England hamartiological thought are the following: New England denials of imputation are addressed in "Inquiries Respecting the Doctrine of Imputation"; Charles Finney's views on inherent corruption are examined in "The New Divinity Tried,"; Edward Beecher's advocacy of the pre-existence of the soul is treated in "Beecher's Great Conflict."

[48]Samuel J. Baird, *The First Adam and the Second: The Elohim Revealed in the Creation and Redemption of Man* (Philadelphia: Lindsay & Blakiston, 1860); William G. T. Shedd, *Dogmatic Theology*, 3 vols. (New York: Charles Scribner's Sons, 1891), II:6-94; 168-257. See the discussion in Hutchinson, *Problem of Original Sin*, 36-59.

[49]See Hodge, "First and Second Adam," 363-66; *Systematic Theology*, II:223-26.

[50]See Charles Hodge, "Nature of Man." Here Hodge attacks both the more traditional traducianism of Shedd and the German idealism of Mercersburg.

[51]See Robert W. Landis, "Imputation, Part I," *The Danville Quarterly Review* I (1861): 390-427; "Imputation, Part II, Antecedent Imputation and Supralapsarianism," *The Danville Quarterly Review* I (1861): 553-613; "Imputation, Part III, Imputation and Original Sin," *The Danville Quarterly Review* II (1862): 58-111, 248-282, 514-578; "Unthinkable Propositions and Original Sin," *Southern Presbyterian Review* 26 (April 1875): 298-315; "The Gratuitous Imputation of Sin," *Southern Presbyterian Review* 27 (1876): 318-353. Much of the material contained in these articles was republished in Landis, *Doctrine of Original Sin*.

Hodge's theory is vitiated by philosophical nominalism and by a rationalistic reliance on "common sense."[52] In this emphasis upon the dictates of human reason, Landis argued, Hodge is no different than the Socinians of the Reformation period or the German rationalists Hodge himself impugned. Landis also insisted that Hodge's "gratuitous imputation" had no real precedent in the Reformed tradition, and he demonstrates with copious citations that Reformed thinkers had, with almost complete uniformity, assumed some sort of real participation in the sin and/or sinfulness of Adam as a ground of corporate guilt.[53] Not content to present Hodge as merely an innovator, Landis also suggests that where meaningful antecedents of Hodge's theory do exist, they are to be found in the works of Roman Catholic nominalists such as Catharinus and Pighius, and in Socinian and Arminian thinkers.[54] Third, Landis gets to the heart of the matter by questioning the justice of Hodge's arrangement: "the question simply is, whether sin may be gratuitously imputed or charged upon the guiltless."[55] With other critics of Hodge, Landis demanded that imputation be grounded in more than a merely legal and extrinsic relationship. Finally, Landis went on to argue that Hodge's theory of original sin, assuming as it does a strict parallel between the imputation of Adam's sin and the imputation of Christ's righteousness, has decidedly unfortunate consequences for soteriology. Landis and others correctly discerned that Hodge's doctrine of original sin stood in service to his soteriology, and it is to this that we now turn.

Soteriology and Solidarity with Christ

Hodge echoes much of the earlier tradition in his affirmation of the importance and centrality of union with Christ. Through union with Christ by faith, the Christian receives the benefits of salvation, including justification, participation in Christ's life, peace with God, assurance of salvation, and sanctification.[56]

For a helpful and more extended treatment of Landis's critique of Hodge, see Hutchinson, *Problem of Original Sin*, 64-71.

[52]See Landis, *Doctrine of Original Sin*, 13, 60, 67, 178-79, 196, 333.

[53]Ibid., 11, 41-43, 158.

[54]Ibid., 31, 218-227, 276-77, 279, 344-45, 392-98, 403. Catharinus stressed a forensic imputation while minimizing inherited moral corruption as a factor. The Socinians and Arminians, while avoiding the notion of an imputation of guilt, nevertheless viewed the condition of Adam's posterity as a "calamity" that is not grounded in any real participation in the guilt of Adam. In this the similarities to Hodge lie.

[55]Ibid., 27. See also pp. 190, 407-467.

[56]Hodge, *Systematic Theology*, III:104-110. In "Beman on the Atonement," *BRPR* 17 (1845): 115, Hodge wrote: "Again, can any reader of the Bible, can any Christian at least, doubt that union with Christ, was to the apostles one of the most important and dearest of all the doctrines of the gospel; a doctrine that lay at the root of all the other doctrines of redemption, the foundation of their hopes, the source of their spiritual life."

This union involves, first of all, a "federal union" rooted in the pretemporal covenant of redemption between the first and second Persons of the Trinity. However, this union must be actualized in the lives of believers: "But it was also...included in the stipulations of that covenant, that his people, so far as adults are concerned, should not receive the saving benefits of that covenant until they were united to Him by a voluntary act of faith."[57]

In describing the character of this temporal union, Hodge emphasizes the importance of subjective faith and the objective work of the Holy Spirit. From one perspective, the *unio Christi* may be defined in terms of faith: "To be in Christ, and to believe in Christ, are, therefore, in the Scriptures convertible forms of expression. They mean substantially the same thing...the same effects are attributed to faith as are attributed to union with Christ."[58] From the other perspective, union with Christ involves a "participation in the life of Christ," here construed in terms of the efficacy of the Holy Spirit.

> As the principle of animal life is located in the head, through the complicated yet ordered system of nerves extending to every member, diffuses life and energy through the whole body; so the Holy Spirit, given without measure to Christ the head of the Church, which is his body, diffuses life and strength to every member. Hence, according to Scripture, Christ's dwelling in us is explained as the Spirit's dwelling in us. The indwelling of the Spirit is the indwelling of Christ.[59]

In this connection, Hodge argues against those in the New England tradition who were inclined to make too little of the union by reducing it to shared sentiment. He insists that the union is not "merely moral, arising from the agreement and sympathy."[60] Furthermore, he laments the tendency, so evident

---

[57]Hodge, *Systematic Theology*, III:104. See also "Beman on the Atonement," 134.

Hodge's doctrine of union with Christ emphasizes the pretemporal "covenant of redemption" between the first and second Persons of the Trinity to a greater extent than some earlier Reformed divines. He does this in part to mitigate an element of potential legalism implicit in his soteriology—particularly his view that faith is a "condition" of the covenant of grace—and in part to safeguard the gratuity of justification in the context of an *ordo salutis* where regeneration precedes faith and justification. We will see below that this pretemporal covenant plays an even more important role in the soteriology of Hodge's successors.

[58]Hodge, *Systematic Theology*, III:104. See also, "Doctrine of the Reformed Church," 247.

Hodge viewed faith in traditional Reformed terms as involving knowledge, assent, and trust. See *Systematic Theology*, III:42-53. Though not a meritorious act, the exercise of faith is viewed as a condition of the covenant of grace. See *Systematic Theology*, III:105.

[59]Hodge, *Systematic Theology*, III:105-6. In II:396, Hodge speaks of a three-fold union with Christ (federal, vital, and conscious). His basic structure is two-fold, however.

[60]Hodge, "Doctrine of the Reformed Church," 228. See also *Systematic Theology*,

in New England Calvinism with its governmental theory of the atonement, for the theme of union with Christ to be effaced.

> But according to the theory that Christ's death is a mere symbolical method of instruction, an expression of a great truth, that it merely opens the way for mercy, what can union with Christ mean? In what sense are we in him? How are we his members? How is it that we die, that we live, that we are to rise from the dead in virtue of that union? What is meant by living by faith of which he is the object? The fact is this theory changes the whole nature of the gospel; every thing is altered; the nature of faith, the nature of justification, the mode of access to God, our relation to Christ, the inward exercises of communion with him, so that the Christian feels disposed to say with Mary, They have taken away my Lord, and I know not where they have laid him.[61]

But if Hodge was concerned to oppose those who made too little of union with Christ, he was equally anxious to resist those who, he believed, made too much of it—particularly those who affirmed a union with the humanity of Christ. Much of this polemic is found in the context of Hodge's arguments against the sacramental theology of Mercersburg's John W. Nevin. In his review of Nevin's *The Mystical Presence*, Hodge concedes Nevin's point that Calvin had affirmed such a union, but argues that Zwingli is the true father of the Reformed sacramental doctrine and view of union with Christ at this point.[62] He goes on to argue that the mystical union of the believer with Christ involves no real union with Christ's incarnate humanity, but rather the reception of the Spirit.

> The same apostle [St. Paul] tells us that believers are one body and members of one another, not in virtue of their common human nature, nor because they all partake of the humanity of Christ, but because they all have one Spirit. Such as we understand it is the doctrine of the Reformed church and of the Bible as to the mystical union.[63]

But Hodge does affirm a certain connection with the humanity of Christ as to its "virtue and efficacy." This efficacy of the incarnate humanity, or body and blood of Christ, is then defined as "their virtue as a body broken and of blood as shed, that is, their sacrificial, atoning efficacy."[64] Note that here the "presence" of Christ's humanity is framed primarily in terms of its legal significance for justification. Thus we see already that, in typical federal

---

III:106.

[61] Hodge, "Beman on the Atonement," 115. See also *Systematic Theology*, III:127. Other treatments of the atonement by Hodge include "Bushnell on Vicarious Sacrifice," BRPR 38 (1866): 161-194; *Systematic Theology*, II:480-591.

[62] Hodge, "Doctrine of the Reformed Church," 230-36, 251.

[63] Ibid., 256. See also p. 258.

[64] Ibid., 229, 249.

theology fashion, Hodge has incorporated an implicit bifurcation into his doctrine of union with Christ—the reception of the work of the Spirit on the one hand, and a legal relation on the other.[65]

Hodge's opposition to notions of realistic union with the humanity of Christ is rooted in a number of considerations, and these require attention because they reveal a good deal about Hodge's theological method and concerns. First of all, there are philosophical objections rooted in Hodge's commitment to Scottish Common Sense Realism. He regarded the notion of participation in a "generic humanity," either of Adam or Christ, as absurd. If a generic humanity is real, he contended, it must be a "substance," but substantial and numerical identity cannot be separated: "If...the generic life of man means anything more than the same kind of life, it must mean that that which lives in all men is identically the same numerical substance."[66] In nominalistic fashion, Hodge consistently regards the general and generic as merely linguistic phenomena which do "not convey any definite idea beyond the facts themselves."[67]

Hodge's Scottish Common Sense Realism is also evident in his consistent contention, against Nevin, that Christ's humanity is not physically and locally present to the believer.[68] The denial of a "local presence" is indeed a distinctive of Reformed theology, but while Calvin and Nevin sought to understand how Christ's humanity might be present in a non-local and spiritual mode, Hodge concluded that no realistic presence existed, only a presence of "efficacy and virtue." Here his Scottish Common Sense metaphysic largely determined his conclusion. For Hodge, body and blood are material substances, and to speak of something material as actually present in a non-material and non-local mode is sheer nonsense.

Another set of objections to realistic union with the humanity of Christ is rooted in Hodge's dualistic anthropology, and by extension in his christology. The notion of a generic humanity entailed, as Hodge realized, an implicitly monistic anthropology—a principle of generic identity which then gives rise to both the material and spiritual dimensions of the human being.[69] Against this, Hodge argued for what he termed "realistic dualism," and he contended for this, first of all, on Common Sense grounds: "It may be said, therefore, despite of materialists and idealists, that it is intuitively certain that matter and mind are two distinct substances. And such has been the faith of the great body of

---

[65]This bifurcation is noted in Kennedy, "Historical Analysis," 331-32, though the implications of it are not explored.

[66]Hodge, "Nature of Man," 125. See also pp. 134-35.

[67]Ibid., 124. See also Charles Hodge, "What is Christianity," *BRPR* 32 (1860): 136-37.

[68]See Hodge, "Doctrine of the Reformed Church," 244-46, 255.

[69]See, e.g., Nevin, "Doctrine of the Reformed Church," 318; *Mystical Presence*, 171-72; Shedd, *Dogmatic Theology*, II:22-23.

mankind."[70]

But Hodge was also convinced that many of the central doctrines of the faith depend on this anthropological dualism, and he therefore regarded this as no minor matter.

> It is evident that these views of the nature of man which seem to be everywhere assumed in the Bible, must determine in large measure the view taken of our relation to Adam, of the nature of original sin, of the constitution of Christ's person, and of other important doctrines of the Scriptures. If Christ took upon himself our nature, we cannot agree as to what he assumed, unless we are agreed as to what human nature is.[71]

Believing that the conceptual categories of anthropology, christology, theology, and soteriology were closely intertwined, Hodge detected, first of all, a set of analogies between anthropology on the one hand, and theology and christology on the other. Arguing particularly against Nevin at this point, Hodge contended that if the soul and body are seen as a single life, with the soul externalizing itself in the body, then by analogy the relation of God to the world will be seen in similar terms. From a faulty anthropology comes a faulty theology, in this case an implicit pantheism.[72] Thus Hodge argued that "the anthropology of this system...destroys the essential difference between the creator and his creatures, between God and man."[73]

The christological implications of this anthropology are equally harmful, according to Hodge. A monist anthropology implies a monist christology as well: "As in man there is no dualism between soul and body, so in Christ there is no dualism between his divine and human nature. They are *one* life."[74] Thus Hodge accused Nevin, Schleiermacher, Ullmann, Dorner, and the like of Eutychianism and of denying the traditional two-natures doctrine of

---

[70]Charles Hodge, "Nature of Man," 112; see also p. 126. On pp. 115-16, Hodge further explains this anthropological dualism: "The doctrine...asserts the existence of two distinct *res*, entities, or substances; the one extended, tangible, and divisible, the object of the senses; the other, unextended, and indivisible, the thinking, feeling, willing subject in man. This doctrine stands opposed, 1st, to materialism and idealism, which, although antagonistic systems in other respects, agree in denying any dualism of substance. The one makes the mind a function of the body, while according to the other the body is a form of the mind."

[71]Hodge, "What Is Christianity?," 124.

[72]See Hodge, *Systematic Theology*, III:20-21.

[73]Ibid., III:21. On Hodge's relationship with John Nevin, see Shriver, "Passages in Friendship." Shriver notes that Nevin took umbrage at Hodge's charges of Hegelian pantheism and denying the divinity of Christ. See also Hodge's response to Nevin's complaint in *Systematic Theology*, III:655.

[74]Hodge, "What Is Christianity," 146. See also "Doctrine of the Reformed Church," 264-65.

Chalcedon.[75]

Hodge also took exception to Nevin's view that the Logos assumed a "fallen human nature" (i.e., the generic humanity derived from Adam), that this fallen human nature is then gradually sanctified through its contact with the Logos, and that the Christian is then sanctified and justified through union with this deified human nature and its merits. Hodge argued that the impeccability of Christ is destroyed if a fallen human nature was assumed.[76]

Perhaps most importantly, Hodge also thought that the notion of union with the humanity of Christ involved a vital threat to soteriology, and particularly to the doctrine of forensic justification. Hodge consistently opposed Nevin's view that the saving merits of Christ inhere in his person, such that union with Christ's person is necessary to receive the forensic benefits of Christ's work.[77] For Hodge, who insisted that justification is synthetic and *extra nos*, the "justification of the ungodly," this alternative could be nothing but a "subjective justification." And we noted in the previous chapter, Hodge had some reason for concern at this point.

This was clearly a matter of existential importance for Hodge; his whole system of piety was at stake. Peace with God, he declared, is dependent on the imputation of a righteousness that is *extra nos*, that is more sure and secure than the shifting sands of the inner life of the psyche.

> This system, therefore, sends the sinner naked and shivering into the presence of God, with nothing to rely upon but the modicum of theanthropic life that flickers in his own bosom. He has not righteousness but what is inherent. All he has of righteousness, holiness, joy, or glory, is in himself, in that life which is as much his as the life he derived from Adam, the heights and depths of which are sounded by his own consciousness. If he feels himself to be wretched, and miserable, and poor, and blind, and naked, he is so, and there is no help for him. All his treasures are within himself.[78]

This, Hodge adds, "is not a doctrine on which the soul can live."[79]

Finally, Hodge repeatedly objected to what he saw as the depersonalization implicit in the notion of generic humanity. Nevin had defined generic identity in terms of an "organic law," and Hodge failed to see how such a notion could involve a personal presence.

---

[75]Hodge, "Doctrine of the Reformed Church," 265; "What Is Christianity," 138-140.

[76]See Hodge, "What Is Christianity," 147-49; "Doctrine of the Reformed Church," 261, 270.

[77]See Hodge, "What Is Christianity," 151-54; "Doctrine of the Reformed Church," 270-71.

[78]Hodge, "What Is Christianity," 159. See also "Doctrine of the Reformed Church," 271-72; *Systematic Theology*, III:209-212.

[79]Hodge, "What Is Christianity," 161.

Then what becomes of a personally present Christ? All Christ does for us is to implant a new law in our nature, which by its natural, historical development works out our salvation...It is not for other men to say how a theory lies in the minds of its advocates, or to sit in judgment on their religious experience; but they have the right to protest against any theory which, in their apprehension of it, takes away their personal Saviour and gives them nothing but a new invisible law in their members; which substitutes for the Incarnate Son of God "the organic law of Christ's human life."[80]

Thus we see that Hodge's view of union with Christ is largely consistent with the federal theology of his predecessors. There is a federal union rooted in the eternal covenant of redemption, and the legal benefits promised by this covenant and merited by the work of Christ are imputed through faith to the believer in an extrinsic relationship. Any source or locus of legal merit, such as the humanity of Christ, remains utterly outside the Christian. There is also a vital or spiritual union, in which the believer receives the Holy Spirit as a representative of Christ, a Christ who is most certainly absent with respect to his incarnate humanity.

Applied Soteriology—The *Ordo Salutis*

The critical role of the *ordo salutis* in federal theology has already been noted, and it continues to have an important function in Hodge's soteriology. A temporal as well as logical order in the application of redemption is evident in Hodge. This order begins with regeneration or the initial quickening that gives rise to faith. Faith then is the instrument of a legal union with Christ in justification. After justification the Holy Spirit is imparted to the believer, resulting in a vital or spiritual union with Christ in sanctification. Hodge writes:

As soon, however, as it exercises faith, it receives the imputation of the righteousness of Christ, God's justice is thereby satisfied, and the Spirit comes and takes up his dwelling in the believer as the source of all holy living. There can therefore be no holiness until there is reconciliation with God, and no reconciliation with God except through the righteousness imputed to us and received by faith alone. Then follow the indwelling of the Spirit, progressive sanctification, and all the fruits of holy living.[81]

Regeneration is defined in traditional federal terms. Solely an act of divine grace, it is neither a change in the substance of the human soul (as some New England theologians accused the federalists of teaching) nor is it merely a change in the exercises of the soul (as some successors of Edwards

---

[80]Hodge, *Systematic Theology*, III:660. See also "Doctrine of the Reformed Church," 276; "What Is Christianity," 161.

[81]See *Systematic Theology*, III:172; see also pp. 104-105.

maintained). Furthermore, it is not a mere external moral suasion. Rather, it is "physical," the immediate impartation by the Holy Spirit of a new *habitus* or principle to the soul, or as Hodge put it, "those immanent dispositions, principles, tastes or habits which underlie all conscious exercises, and determine the character of a man and of all his acts."[82]

Hodge is also careful to resist any conflation of regeneration with subsequent elements of the *ordo salutis*, i.e., with either justification or sanctification. Against Ebrard and Nevin, Hodge argues that their view of regeneration substitutes union with the theanthropic Christ for the efficacy of the Holy Spirit, and that they are "confounding the work of the Holy Spirit in regeneration, with the judicial, objective act of justification."[83] In short, regeneration is a work of prevenient grace which is completely antecedent to union with Christ.

Similarly, against New England theologians who equated regeneration with sanctification (and thus placed sanctification prior to justification in the *ordo*), regeneration is not to be conflated with sanctification.[84] But here Hodge was faced with a problem, for if regeneration involves the infusion of gracious habits, then it looks rather like sanctification. Furthermore, if regeneration involves an actual change for the better in a person, does not that imply that sanctification in some sense precedes justification, and also imply that justification is not the gratuitous exoneration of the "ungodly"? Hodge replied with two arguments. First, he diffidently suggested that this might be viewed as a question of logical rather than temporal succession.

> It may be said that this scheme involves an inconsistency. There can be no holiness until there is reconciliation, and no reconciliation (so far as adults are concerned) until there is faith. But faith is a fruit of the Spirit, and an act of the renewed soul. Then there is and must be, after all, holy action before there is reconciliation. It might be enough to say in answer to this objection, that logical order and chronological succession are different things; or that the order of nature and order of time are not to be confounded.[85]

But this solution was not entirely satisfactory to Hodge, probably because it

---

[82] See ibid., III:35. Hodge's extensive reply to New England and New School Presbyterians is found in his "Regeneration, and the Manner of Its Occurrence," *BRPR* 2 (1830): 250-297. Here the notion of the infusion of gracious habits is defended at great length (pp. 267-274), and the idea of "physical" regeneration is explained (pp. 261-65).

[83] Hodge, *Systematic Theology*, III:24.

[84] Ibid., III:7-8. Hodge's treatment of sanctification is conventional. It is attributed to the work of the Holy Spirit (III:215-16). It is distinguished from regeneration in that regeneration occurs in an instant while sanctification is a process that takes place over a lifetime. Furthermore, this process is described in terms of mortification and vivification (III:221).

[85] Ibid., III:172-73.

does not remove the difficulty at hand, and it also tends to undermine the notion of an *ordo salutis*, which for Hodge has an obviously temporal dimension, and so Hodge attempted to address the gratuity problem by grounding regeneration itself in the intercession of Christ, a solution that he realized was not without difficulties.

> The intercession of Christ secures for those given to Him by the Father the renewing of the Holy Ghost. The first act of the renewed heart is faith; as the first act of a restored eye is to see. Whether this satisfies the understanding or not, it remains clear as the doctrine of the Bible that good works are the fruits and consequences of reconciliation with God, through faith in our Lord Jesus Christ.[86]

Hodge's inflexible commitment to a strict *ordo salutis* framework clearly involved him in considerable perplexities. For example, the distinction between regeneration and sanctification was rather artificial.[87] He also faced considerable opposition from theologians within the Presbyterian camp who disagreed with his *ordo*, particularly from those who argued that a real spiritual union with Christ must ground the relation of imputation in justification.[88] The increasing abstractness of the federal soteriology was unappealing to many.

In his reply to the stock New England charges of antinomianism against federal theology, Hodge appealed in traditional Reformed fashion to the unity of salvation in Christ. With some hyperbole, Hodge declared:

> Antinomianism has never had any hold in the churches of the Reformation. There is no logical connection between the neglect of moral duties, and the system which teaches that Christ is a Saviour as well from the power as from the penalty of sin; that faith is the act by which the soul receives and rests on Him for sanctification as well as for justification; and that such is the nature of the union with Christ by faith and indwelling of the Spirit, that no one is, or can be partaker of the benefit of his death, who is not also partaker of the power of his life.[89]

Having bifurcated *unio Christi* into two very different unions—legal and spiritual—Hodge could not appeal to the integrity of the Christian's experience

---

[86] Ibid., III:173.

[87] See Hewitt, *Regeneration and Morality*, 58. This problem was recognized by his son, A. A. Hodge, who does not attempt to distinguish regeneration and sanctification as markedly as does Charles Hodge, and who then modifies the *ordo salutis* to account for this.

[88] The following statement by Shedd, *Dogmatic Theology*, II:534, is typical: "Upon this spiritual and mystical union, rests the federal and legal union between Christ and his people. Because they are spiritually, vitally, eternally, and mystically one with him, his merit is imputable to them, and their demerit is imputable to him." See also Baird, *First Adam and the Second*, 429-30, 435, 448, 494-95; John B. Adger, "Calvin's Doctrine of the Lord's Supper," *The Southern Presbyterian Review* 35 (1885): 787.

[89] Hodge, *Systematic Theology*, III:241. See also III:141.

of redemption in Christ as the bond of unity. The unity of justification and sanctification is not to be found in the efficacy of faith or in the experiential union with Christ, but in theology proper, in the pretemporal covenant of redemption between the Father and the Son.[90]

Applied Soteriology—Justification

Hodge's soteriological innovations are to be found particularly in his treatment of imputation and justification. We must recall that Hodge had not been afraid even to criticize the esteemed Calvin, whose sacramental theology and realistic doctrine of union with Christ Hodge believed subverted the material principle of the Reformation, justification by faith.[91] Ironically, however, this very doctrine that Hodge was so keen to protect underwent a significant change in his hands, a change that was to have an important influence on subsequent conservative Reformed theology.

Hodge is careful to define justification as an extrinsic "forensic act" which changes the status of a person with reference to divine justice, but which does not effect an inward change of moral condition. Justification, therefore, is completely distinct from sanctification. In opposition to the Roman Catholic conflation of justification and sanctification, Hodge noted that "the two gifts, although inseparable, are distinct, and that justification, instead of being an efficient act changing the inward character of the sinner, is a declarative act, announcing and determining his relation to the law and justice of God."[92] Throughout his career, one of Hodge's great fears was anything that hinted of "subjective justification," that is, making justification contingent on an immanent moral condition or change.[93]

Hodge also insists against New England that justification is not mere pardon, or forgiveness of sins. Here Hodge was keenly concerned to defend the attribute of divine justice.[94] Because God is not a mere moral governor, but is also a judge, justification is not an executive remitting punishment, but rather is a judicial act: "To justify is to declare not guilty; or worthy of punishment; or that justice does not demand punishment; or that the person concerned cannot be justly condemned."[95] A fundamental assumption here is that both

---

[90] See ibid., III:226-27; "Beman on the Atonement," 134.

[91] See Hodge, "Doctrine of the Reformed Church," 253.

[92] Hodge, *Systematic Theology*, III:119.

[93] See Hodge, "First and Second Adam," 339, 341, 374-75; "Doctrine of the Reformed Church," 272; *Systematic Theology*, II:201, 213; III:118, 125, 129-32, 209-210.

[94] This is defended largely on "common sense" grounds. See *Systematic Theology*, III:123: "But the human soul knows intuitively...there is such an attribute as justice. It knows that the demands thereof are inexorable because they are righteous." See also "Beman on the Atonement," 87-88.

[95] Hodge, *Systematic Theology*, III:121.

justification and condemnation as forensic acts involve the satisfaction of divine justice.[96] Hodge also maintained that mere pardon would not satisfy the conscience of the sinner: "But pardon does not produce peace...There can be no satisfaction to the mind until there is satisfaction of justice."[97] Finally, mere pardon would not, Hodge argued, give positive title to eternal life. Here earlier Reformed statements about the imputation of the merits of Christ are echoed.[98] We will see below, however, that Hodge's modification of the tradition creates difficulties at precisely this point, and also at the point where Hodge thought his position to be strongest—the existential problem of the sinner's conscience before God.

In keeping with his *ordo salutis* approach, Hodge also treats justification in punctiliar terms as occurring at a point in time. Justification precedes sanctification in time as well as in logical priority: "the gift of righteousness precedes that of sanctification. We are justified in order that we may be sanctified."[99] Hodge further described justification as a "transient act," in contrast to sanctification which is a "progressive work."[100] But the heart and distinctiveness of Hodge's doctrine is found in his treatment of the imputation of righteousness. As in the context of the doctrine of original sin noted earlier, Hodge distinguishes between moral and forensic senses of the term *righteous*. Soteriological imputation, like hamartiological imputation, has to do solely with the latter.

> The word *dikaios*, "righteous," or "just," has two distinct senses, as stated above. It has a moral and also a legal, forensic, or judicial sense. It sometimes expresses moral character, sometimes simply a relation to law and justice. In one sense to pronounce a man just, is to declare that he is morally good. In another sense, it is to declare that the claims of justice against him are satisfied, and that he is entitled to the reward promised to the righteous. When God justifies the ungodly, he does not declare that he is godly, but that his sins are expiated, and that he has a title founded in justice to eternal life.[101]

A number of important results flow from Hodge's preoccupation with the forensic. Because of the focus on the forensic obligation to satisfy justice, Hodge emphasizes the so-called "passive obedience" of Christ over the "active obedience." Traditional Reformed orthodoxy had distinguished between the

---

[96] See ibid., III:125.

[97] Ibid., III:128. See also p. 163.

[98] Hodge, ibid., III:129, writes: "Pardon is purely negative. It simply removes a penalty. It confers no title to benefits not previously enjoyed. Eternal life, however, is suspended on the positive condition of perfect obedience. The merit of Christ is entitled to the reward. And the believer, being partaker of that merit, shares in that title."

[99] Ibid., III:157.

[100] Ibid., III:213.

[101] Ibid., III:141-42.

passive obedience (Christ's passion and death on the cross) and his active obedience (his sinless life); both were viewed as necessary for full justification. While Hodge speaks of both, the weight lies decidedly with the former.[102]

Hodge's forensic focus also necessitates a redefinition of soteriological "merit." Though he sometimes spoke of the "merits" of Christ, he also maintained that both hamartiological and soteriological imputation have nothing to do with personal merit or demerit as such, but only with a relation to the judicial activity of God. Implicit here is Hodge's distinction between "demerit" (*reatus culpae*) and "guilt" (*reatus poenae*; i.e., liability to punishment).[103] While the notion of guilt as liability to punishment is at least coherent (if perhaps reductionistic), Hodge had difficulty framing the notion of positive merit in purely legal terms, hence the decided preference for the notion of "passive obedience" noted above. When Hodge does speak of the active obedience, this is cast in terms of Christ's fulfillment of the terms of the "covenant of works."[104]

Hodge's forensic focus also involves a psychological reductionism in that the problem of conscience is reduced to the merely legal or forensic. The problem of conscience is seen as purely one of legal liability: "What satisfies the justice of God, satisfies the conscience of the sinner...He does not lose his sense of personal demerit, but the conscience ceases to demand satisfaction."[105] In contrast to Turretin, who strongly asserted that the work of Christ addresses both *reatus culpae* and *reatus poenae*, Hodge effectively conceded that in justification only the "liability to punishment" is expiated; the "demerit" remains.

> There is a great deal of difference, as often remarked, between demerit and guilt. The latter is the liability in justice to the penalty of the law. The former is personal ill-desert. A criminal who has suffered the legal punishment of his crime, is not

---

[102]See ibid., III:143; see also pp. 150, 161. This perhaps accounts for John Nevin's frequent insistence on the importance of Christ's active obedience. See Erb, *Nevin's Theology*, 226-27, 311.

[103]See Hodge, *Systematic Theology*, III:178.
Having denied any realistic union with the incarnate humanity of Christ, Hodge also argues that the righteousness of Christ is primarily to be thought of as divine rather than human. In *Systematic Theology* III:143, Hodge writes: "The righteousness of Christ on the ground of which the believer is justified is the righteousness of God. It is so designated in Scripture not only because it was provided and is accepted by Him; it is not only the righteousness which avails before God, but it is the righteousness of a divine person; of God manifest in the flesh." Such a divine righteousness is "infinitely meritorious" because it is an "adequate satisfaction" for the sins of the world. See ibid., III:156, 176. Hodge clearly had considerable difficulty defining the positive role of Christ's humanity.

[104]See Hodge, "Beman on the Atonement," 135; *Systematic Theology*, III:164-65.

[105]Hodge, *Systematic Theology*, III:128.

longer justly exposed to punishment for that offence. He however thinks of himself no better than he did before...And so it is with the believer; he knows that, because of what Christ has done for him, he cannot be justly condemned, but he feels and admits that in himself he is as hell-deserving as he was from the beginning.[106]

Hodge did conceive that this view presents certain religious and pastoral difficulties.[107] His suggestion at this point is for the believer to avoid undue introspection, and to find comfort in an extrinsic piety.

> Many sincere believers are too introspective. They look too exclusively within, so that their hope in graduated by the degree of evidence of regeneration which they find in their own experience. This, except in rare cases, can never lead to the assurance of hope. We may examine our hearts with all the microscopic care prescribed by President Edwards in his work on "The Religious Affections," and never be satisfied that we have eliminated every ground of misgiving and doubt. The grounds of assurance are not so much within, as without us.[108]

One can imagine, of course, how someone of tender and precarious conscience such as Nevin would have found such a doctrine barren. Furthermore, when this was combined with Hodge's predestinarianism, the pastoral consequences were likely to be unhappy.[109]

In Hodge we find a fundamentally different form of piety than is evident in Nevin, or in Calvin for that matter. Calvin's argued that "as long as Christ remains outside of us...all that he has suffered and done for the salvation of the human race remains useless and of no value to us," and this assertion was firmly rooted in a piety that placed a premium on the ongoing life of faith.[110] But Hodge, whose soteriology at this point is largely determined by the federal bifurcation of *unio* and by the *ordo salutis* framework, effectively reverses Calvin's principle here—it is only as Christ remains outside that what he has suffered for the race can avail for salvation. Replying to Mercersburg criticisms of his extrinsic doctrine, Hodge wrote:

---

[106] Ibid., III:178.

[107] See, e.g., ibid., III:178.

[108] Ibid., III:107.

[109] Mark A. Noll, "Charles Hodge as an Expositor of the Spiritual Life," in *Charles Hodge Revisited: A Critical Appraisal of His Life and Work*, ed. John W. Stewart and James H. Moorhead (Grand Rapids: Eerdmans, 2002), 181-216, contends that Hodge failed to provide a coherent account of the dynamic of the Christian life. Noll attributes this to a failure to integrate the objective ground of Christian faith and subjective experience. Our treatment of Hodge in this chapter suggests that the problems go still deeper. With his resolutely punctiliar and extrinsic piety, Hodge was ill-equipped to account for the importance of the ongoing life of faith.

[110] Calvin, *Inst.* III.1.1.

What is urged as an objection to the doctrine is true. It does concern what is outward and objective; what is done for the sinner rather than what is done within him. But then it is to be considered, first, that this is what the sinner needs. He requires not only that his nature should be renewed and that a new principle or divine life should be communicated to him; but also that his guilt should be removed, his sins expiated, and justice satisfied, as the preliminary condition of his enjoying this new life, and being restored to the favour of God...It is only by ignoring this objective work of Christ, or by merging justification into inward renovation, that this objection has force or even plausibility.[111]

Ecclesiology and the Sacraments

While Hodge's three-volume *Systematic Theology* contains no extensive section on ecclesiology, he was not silent on the subject. He wrote an extensive *Constitutional History* of American Presbyterianism as a defense of the Old School's 1837 exclusion of the New School, and he generated a number of important articles dealing with the church, particularly between 1845 and 1860.[112] These polemical pieces are directed primarily against the "ritualism" of the Oxford Movement in Anglicanism and a resurgent Roman Catholicism, and also against some of Hodge's Old School Presbyterian critics, many of whom found his ecclesiology distressingly "low." Little is said in these works expressly in opposition to the ecclesiology of Mercersburg.[113]

---

[111]Hodge, *Systematic Theology*, III:179. Hodge frequently gives expression to this "extrinsic piety." See, e.g., "What Is Christianity," 161; *Systematic Theology* II:213; III:107, 160, 194-95.

[112]Among his more important articles are "The General Assembly," *BRPR* 17 (1845): 444-471; "Is the Church of Rome a Part of the Visible Church," *BRPR* 18 (1846): 320-344; "Theories of the Church," *BRPR* 18 (1846): 137-158; "The Idea of the Church," *BRPR* 25 (1853): 249-290, 339-389; "Visibility of the Church," *BRPR* 25 (1853): 670-685; "Bishop McIlvaine on the Church," *BRPR* 27 (1855): 350-59; "The Church—Its Perpetuity," *BRPR* 28 (1856); "The Church Membership of Infants," *BRPR* 30 (1858): 347-389; "Presbyterianism," *BRPR* 32 (1860): 546-67. A portion of Hodge's ecclesiological writings were collected and published as Charles Hodge, *The Church and Its Polity*, ed. William Durant (London: Thomas Nelson, 1879).

For an extensive and helpful treatment of Hodge's ecclesiology, see John Jey Deifell, Jr., "The Ecclesiology of Charles Hodge," (Ph.D. diss., University of Edinburgh, 1969).

[113]Reasons for this may include Hodge's sense that the Mercersburg ecclesiology was too esoteric to appeal to many, the fact that Nevin's dalliance with Roman Catholicism had discredited it in the eyes of many American Protestants, and the fact that the Mercersburg ecclesiology had met with spirited opposition within the German Reformed Church itself. The Mercersburg ecclesiology is mentioned, however, in works having to do more expressly with soteriology. See, e.g., "What Is Christianity," 120. Hodge took particular exception to Nevin's notion of the church as a continuation of the theanthropic life of Christ, and thus of the Incarnation. See "Doctrine of the Reformed

Hodge's ecclesiology is largely shaped by the theological method and, even more importantly, by his soteriology discussed above. With regard to the latter, Hodge himself frequently noted the connection, arguing that "there is a necessary connection between a certain scheme of doctrine and a certain theory of the Church," and that the "nature of the Church is then determined by the nature of the gospel."[114] Here we will recall the implicit nominalism and disjunctive dualism of Hodge's method, which inclined him toward the individual at the expense of the general and corporate, as well as Hodge's firm commitment to an *ordo salutis* and his bifurcation of union with Christ into legal and vital unions, the goal of which was decisively to separate justification and sanctification. Both factors drove him inexorably toward an individualistic ecclesiology and sacramental theology.[115]

Hodge distinguishes three major "theories" of the church: the Rationalistic (which denies the essentially supernaturalistic character of the church), the Ritualistic (in which the church mediates saving grace to the individual), and the Evangelical (which views the church as the body of those who by the act of faith and the work of the Holy Spirit are united with Christ).[116] In his description of the "Evangelical" theory, Hodge repeatedly refers to union with Christ as the foundation of the church.[117] This union with Christ, however, is entirely an individual matter between the believer and God: "The life of the believer is not a corporate life, conditioned on union with any outward organization, called the Church, for whosoever...looks to Him as his God and Saviour, shall be saved, whether in a dungeon or alone in a desert."[118] This individualistic focus is also evident in Hodge's insistence that the church is constituted by the effectual call by God of individuals: "It is not organization, but evocation, the actual calling out and separating from others, that makes the

---

Church," 263-64.

[114]Hodge, "Idea of the Church," 253, 347. See also "Theories of the Church," 138, 157-58.

[115]Hodge's ecclesiological individualism is a major focus of Deifell, "Ecclesiology of Charles Hodge." Deifell attributes this primarily to Hodge's "metaphysical Calvinism" (i.e., his predestinarianism) and to his failure sufficiently to ground soteriology in christology. Deifell's work is to be faulted on two counts. First, he fails to take adequate account of Hodge's theological method and its impact on his ecclesiology. Second, excessive weight is placed on Hodge's predestinarianism. This argument fails to explain how southern Presbyterians such as J. H. Thornwell and John Adger, who were every bit Hodge's equal with respect to "metaphysical Calvinism," had different ecclesiologies.

[116]See Hodge, "Theories of the Church," 138-42; "Idea of the Church," 340-43. In his *Systematic Theology*, III:543-46, Hodge presents a somewhat different typology of ecclesiological theories, distinguishing the Roman Catholic, Puritan, and Common Protestant.

[117]See Hodge, "Theories of the Church," 140-41.

[118]Hodge, *Systematic Theology* II:397. See also "Idea of the Church," 345.

Church."[119] Thus, in the final analysis, the true church for Hodge is simply the "aggregate" of individuals that have believed on Christ.[120]

Hodge perceived a discrepancy, however, between the church as the "body of Christ" and the church as it manifested itself in external organization, and to account for this inconsistency he introduced a programmatic distinction between what he variously called the "invisible" and the "visible" church, the "true" and the "nominal" church, the "true" church and the "outward" church. The former consists of those truly united with Christ by faith and the Holy Spirit, the latter of those who have made profession of faith.[121] Despite occasional protestations to the contrary, however, Hodge viewed the "true" or "invisible church" as the real entity, with the "visible church" being little more than a contingent matter of convenience: "True believers constitute the true Church; professed believers constitute the outward Church. These two things are not to be confounded. The external body is not, as such, the body of Christ."[122]

This, of course, led to a marked de-emphasis of the visible church (in comparison with many previous Reformed thinkers) that is evident in a number of ways. According to Hodge, one illustration of the relationship between the visible and invisible church is the anthropological analogy of soul and body.[123] Just as the soul can live without the body, so the invisible church may exist without the external structure of the visible church, and Hodge repeatedly asserts both that the visible church may completely cease to exist as to organized structure, and that an individual may be a member of the invisible church but not a member of any organized group. The true church may continue to exist in the form of isolated individuals without any external structure. Indeed, "there have been periods when the whole external organization lapsed into idolatry or heresy."[124]

---

[119] Hodge, "Idea of the Church," 255.

[120] See Hodge, ibid., 350; "Visibility of the Church," 675. Note the contrast with John W. Nevin, who castigated those who view the church as a mere "sand-heap" or aggregate of individuals.

[121] Hodge, "Theories of the Church," 142: "In like manner there is a real and a nominal, a visible and an invisible church, a body consisting of those who are truly united to Christ, and a body consisting of all who profess such union."
In his *Systematic Theology*, III:548, Hodge somewhat expands the requirements for membership in the visible church, requiring "competent knowledge, and a credible profession of faith and obedience."

[122] Hodge, "Visibility of the Church," 680. One is less certain what Hodge means when he proceeds to state: "Neither are they to be separated as two churches; the one true and the other false, the one real and the other nominal." He appears to have separated them in just these terms.

[123] See ibid., 673, 675.

[124] Ibid., 677. See also "The Church—Its Perpetuity," 696, 708. Thus, Hodge was not troubled by the question of historical continuity that was so pressing for Nevin. Nor was

As union with the Church depends solely on union with Christ its head, by faith, and not on union with the external societies; and as union with these societies, though a duty, is not in all cases essential, of course there may be members of the Church who are not members of these societies, as there are members of these societies who are not members of the church.[125]

Not surprisingly, Hodge also refused to apply the traditional creedal "marks" or characteristics of the church to the visible church in any meaningful way.[126] Even the "visible church" is effectively redefined as having nothing at all to do with external structure. Rather, the visible church is necessarily "visible" only insofar as individual believers exist in embodied form and may be seen as different from the world.[127] Interestingly, however, Hodge believed he could affirm Cyprian's ecclesiological dictum, *non salus extra ecclesiam*, albeit in a qualified way: "When it is said, in our Confession of Faith, that out of this visible church, there is no ordinary possibility of salvation, it is only saying that there is no salvation without the knowledge and profession of the gospel."[128]

As suggested earlier, reasons for this individualistic ecclesiology are not difficult to find. The dualism of a visible and invisible church coheres well with Hodge's disjunctive theological methodology. Just as Hodge had difficulty viewing the human organism as an organic unity of body and soul, so also he had problems conceiving of the church in its spiritual and outward aspects as a unity. Hodge's doctrine of salvation also plays a role here. Controlled as it was by a strict *ordo salutis* in which union with Christ was bifurcated into a justification component and a sanctification component, Hodge's soteriology was designed to explain how *the individual* is saved without any admixture of human merit. Having begun with the individual Christian, Hodge then found it difficult to include a more corporate dimension. Even more importantly, despite Hodge's frequent references to union with Christ in ecclesiological contexts, one is struck by the almost total absence of christology, and particularly the humanity of Christ, as a material factor in his ecclesiology. For example, the Incarnation makes no real difference to Hodge's doctrine of the church.[129]

---

he particularly concerned about the dangers of ecclesiastical schism. See "The Church—Its Perpetuity," 714-15; "Theories of the Church," 154.

[125]Hodge, "Bishop McIlvaine on the Church," 353. See also "Idea of the Church," 250; "Theories of the Church," 145; The Church—Its Perpetuity," 703, 711.

[126]See Hodge, "Idea of the Church," 278.

[127]See Hodge, "Visibility of the Church," 671.

[128]Hodge, "Theories of the Church," 147. See also "General Assembly," 463. Here one recalls Hodges's frequent jibes against "High-churchism," "Churchianity," and all that is "churchy." See, e.g., "Idea of the Church," 341; "Theories of the Church," 150; "Doctrine of the Reformed Church," 273. See also, Deifell, "Ecclesiology of Charles Hodge," 123.

[129]This is evident in Hodge's insistence that the essence of the church is identical in both the Old and New Testament dispensations. See *Systematic Theology*, III:549: "The

Because there is no real union with Christ's humanity, there is no ontological basis for a common corporate identity, only an occasional divine activity common to all individual Christians. Thus J. J. Deifell aptly writes, "It is Hodge's inadequate understanding of the humanity of Christ which led to this view of the Church's disconnected spirituality, individualism, rationalism and sectarianism."[130]

Hodge's view of the sacraments is closely connected and consistent with his ecclesiology and soteriology. In his *Systematic Theology*, he articulates three major principles of his sacramental theology. First, the sacraments are "real means of grace...appointed by Christ for conveying the benefits of his redemption to his people."[131] Second, the sacraments have "no inherent efficacy." And third, Hodge affirms the necessity of faith (in the case of adults) for sacramental efficacy.[132] Elsewhere, Hodge provides two additional principles: the sacraments do not convey a special grace available nowhere else, and the grace conveyed in the sacraments is identical in both the Old and New Testament dispensations.[133] These principles are, in turn, conditioned by other theological commitments—in this case a thoroughgoing spiritual occasionalism and commitment to an *ordo salutis* framework.

Hodge repeatedly insists that whatever efficacy the sacraments may have is due to the work of the Holy Spirit, who works as the divine will decrees: "The Spirit, it is to be ever remembered, is a personal agent who works when and how He will."[134] In baptism and the Lord's Supper, as well as in the ministry of the Word, the Spirit works as the Spirit pleases, and there is no assurance that one will in fact encounter divine grace in the so-called "means of grace": "The Spirit does not always cooperate with the truth as heard, to make it a means of

---

Church under the New Dispensation is identical with that under the Old." See also p. 559.

[130] Deifell, "Ecclesiology of Charles Hodge," 393. See also pp. 6, 21, 27-28, 38, 143. There are aspects in Hodge which suggest a more corporate understanding of the church. For example, he decried the revivalist tendencies so evident during his time. Furthermore, he lamented the decline in family religion (what Nevin termed "the system of the catechism") and practices of Christian nurture. See *Systematic Theology*, III:572; and especially his "Bushnell on Christian Nurture." In the context of his soteriology, however, these emphases appear somewhat vestigial, and are to be accounted for in part, at least, by Hodge's well-known social conservatism and his antipathy to the social disorder and democratization produced by revivalism. On this, see Glenn A. Hewitt, *Regeneration and Morality*, 83. Hodge's social conservatism is detailed by David Neil Murchie, "Morality and Social Ethics in the Thought of Charles Hodge," (Ph.D. diss., Drew University, 1980), who speaks of Hodge's "Hamiltonian Federalism" (p. 2). See also pp. 132-192.

[131] Hodge, *Systematic Theology*, III:499.
[132] See ibid., III:500, 579.
[133] Ibid., III:581-82.
[134] Ibid., III:500.

grace; neither does He always attend the administration of baptism, with his sanctifying and saving power."[135]

The influence of the *ordo salutis* framework is also quite evident in Hodge's view of the sacraments. Here we will recall that the order of application for Hodge is regeneration, exercise of faith, justification, and sanctification. In order to safeguard Evangelical doctrine from any taint of ritualism, Hodge insists that the sacraments do not convey divine grace in its inception, but rather serve to strengthen union with Christ by faith.

> That union with the visible church, and participation of the sacraments, are not the indispensable conditions of our union with Christ, neither are they the means of communicating, in the first instance, his benefits and grace, but rather the appointed means by which our union with Christ is acknowledged, and from time to time strengthened.[136]

Thus Hodge insists that the sacraments do not communicate either regeneration or justification, but rather they may be used by the Spirit as a means of furthering the believer's sanctification as they help to strengthen faith.[137] In this way, union with Christ in the sacraments is almost completely abstracted from justification and from the problem of conscience in the believer's relationship with God.

Hodge's doctrine of baptism reflects these emphases. His favored definition is taken verbatim from the Westminster Shorter Catechism, but his explanation of the doctrine reveals certain other themes as well.[138] In large part because of his occasionalism, Hodge adopted the Roman Catholic distinction between sacramental "efficacy" and "validity." While a person's baptism may never be accompanied by the work of the Holy Spirit, it is nevertheless "valid" if it is undertaken using the proper form (with water in the name of the Trinity) and

---

[135]Ibid., III:588. See also pp. 470-79, 505-7, 582, 622. Hodge's occasionalism is noted in Gerrish, *Tradition and the Modern World*, 62, who argues that Hodge operated "from the standpoint of a radical occasionalism, according to which there is no antecedent guarantee, not even a divine pledge, that the reality will be united with the sign, but only the expectation that, at least sometimes, the Spirit may choose to act upon the elect concurrently with the administration of the sacrament."

The occasionalism of Hodge's doctrine of word and sacrament stands in remarkable contrast with Calvin, for whom word and Spirit are not to be separated, and for whom the sacraments are never bare signs. See *Inst.* IV.8.13; IV.14.7.

[136]Hodge, "Idea of the Church," 343.

[137]Regarding baptism, Hodge, *Systematic Theology*, III:588, writes: "the Spirit makes the truth signified in baptism the means of sanctification." With respect to the Lord's Supper, Hodge specifically notes that "the effect intended is not regeneration, nor justification." Hodge, *Conference Papers*, 331. See Deifell, "Ecclesiology of Charles Hodge," 188.

[138]See Westminster Shorter Catechism, Q. 94; Hodge, *Systematic Theology*, III:526; "General Assembly," 445.

with the proper intention (to perform a Christian baptism).[139]

When the efficacy of baptism was discussed, Hodge was keen to eliminate any suggestion of baptismal regeneration in order to protect the gratuity of justification and the integrity of the *ordo salutis*. In adults, the efficacy of baptism presupposes faith, and thus Hodge tended to present baptism primarily as a "confession" or "profession of faith" already enjoyed.[140] The situation is not radically different with infant baptism. Here again, faith logically precedes baptism, even though the sacrament, or "ordinance" (the term Hodge seemed to prefer), temporally precedes the act of faith.[141]

In describing the efficacy of baptism, Hodge attributes it on the one hand to the act of faith (which instrumentally appropriates Christ and his benefits), while also suggesting that the Holy Spirit sometimes uses the sacrament as a means of sanctification. Just as the Spirit on occasion will use the Word to elicit or evoke faith, so also with baptism.

> Unless the recipient of this sacrament be insincere, baptism is an act of faith, it is an act in which and by which he receives and appropriates the offered benefits of the redemption of Christ. And, therefore, to baptism may be properly attributed all that in the Scriptures is attributed to faith. Baptism washes away sin (Acts xxii. 16); it unites to Christ and makes us the sons of God (Gal. iii. 26, 27); we are therein buried with Christ (Rom. vi. 3); it is (according to one interpretation of Titus iii. 5) the washing of regeneration. But all this is said on the assumption that it is what it purports to be, an act of faith...it is plain that baptism is as truly a means of grace as the Word. It conveys truth to the mind; it confirms the promise of God; and it is the means in the hands of the Spirit of conveying to believers the benefits of redemption.[142]

By earlier Reformed standards generally, and particularly in comparison with Calvin, this is a rather low view of sacramental efficacy. The question arises, then, as to the necessity and desirability of baptism. With respect to the necessity of baptism, Hodge appeals to its preceptive status as divine command.[143] While there is no absolute necessity for baptism, in the normal order of events it is appropriate for a believer to confess his or her faith in baptism and to join the visible church. Only in this limited sense may baptism

---

[139] See Hodge, "General Assembly," 445-449; *Systematic Theology*, III:523-25. Hodge first presented this distinction in the context of his defense of Roman Catholic baptism against an overwhelming decision by the 1845 Old School General Assembly declaring "Romish" baptisms to be invalid. Hodge went on to argue that the Roman Catholic church, while defective, is part of the visible church. See "Is the Church of Rome a Part of the Visible Church?"

[140] See Hodge, *Systematic Theology*, III:601. See also pp. 585, 589-90.

[141] See ibid., III:590. Hodge's views on infant baptism are developed in "The Church Membership of Infants."

[142] Hodge, *Systematic Theology*, III:589-90. See also p. 588.

[143] See ibid., III:586, 590, 612.

be regarded as necessary.[144] But while not absolutely necessary, baptism is nevertheless desirable. It is "not to be neglected," because it "may be made effectual."[145] Noting that membership in the visible church is a "great advantage," Hodge lamented the decline of infant baptism among Presbyterians and Congregationalists.[146]

Hodge's view of the Lord's Supper is also consistent with his general approach to soteriology, and particularly with his conception of union with Christ. As we have seen above, it was in the context of the Lord's Supper that Hodge, like many other Reformed theologians, clarified what he meant by the *unio Christi*. In his treatments of the matter, which cover an almost thirty-year period, one sees both remarkable continuity of concern and some development at certain points.

Despite his occasionalism, Hodge sometimes spoke of the Supper in extravagant terms.

> The reason why believers receive so little by their attendance on this ordinance is, that they expect so little. They expect to have their affections somewhat stirred, and their faith somewhat strengthened; but they perhaps rarely expect so to receive Christ as to be filled with all the fulness of God. Yet Christ in offering Himself to us in this ordinance, offers us all of God we are capable of receiving.[147]

Nevertheless, as with baptism and the ministry of the Word, the Supper only becomes an effectual means of grace when the Spirit chooses to make it so: "As the Word when attended by the demonstration of the Spirit, becomes the wisdom and power of God unto salvation; so does the sacrament of the Lord's Supper, when thus attended, become a real means of grace."[148]

In his discussions of the "presence" of Christ in the Supper, Hodge distinguishes a number of basic viewpoints. The local-presence theologies of Rome and the Lutheran communion are, of course, rejected.[149] For reasons noted above, Hodge also rejects the Mercersburg notion of a union with the "generic" humanity of Christ. Hodge then distinguishes three theories of the presence of Christ held among the Reformed—the Zwinglian, the Calvinistic, and a mediating viewpoint enshrined in the confessions. Zwinglians, though they viewed the Supper as "food for the soul," were inclined "to make less of the supernatural aspect of the sacraments than their associates did."[150] Calvin, however, affirmed a presence of Christ's humanity, which Hodge characterizes

---

[144]See ibid., III:585.
[145]Ibid., III:579.
[146]See ibid., III:572, 579, 588.
[147]Ibid., III:624.
[148]Ibid., III:622.
[149]See ibid., III:661-692.
[150]Ibid., III:626. See also "Doctrine of the Reformed Church," 231-33.

in the following terms.

> While Calvin denied the real presence of the body and blood of Christ in the eucharist, in the sense in which that presence was asserted by Romanists and Lutherans, yet he affirmed that they were dynamically present...So the body of Christ is in heaven, but from that glorified body there radiates an influence, other than the influence of the Spirit (although through his agency), of which believers in the Lord's Supper are the recipients. In this way they receive the body and blood of Christ, or, their substance, or life-giving power.[151]

Finally, Hodge distinguishes a third category he believed to be a rapprochement of the Zwinglian and Calvinistic viewpoints. Here Hodge placed great emphasis on the Consensus Tigurinus (1549), which he viewed as "the most considered and cautiously worded exposition of the Reformed in relation to the sacraments."[152] This consensus statement, written by Bullinger and Calvin, is to be preferred to the "extreme passages" found in Calvin's *Institutes* and his sacramental treatises,[153] and also to confessions conforming "to the peculiar views of Calvin," such as "the Gallican, the Belgian, and the early Scottish."[154]

---

[151] Hodge, *Systematic Theology*, III:628. See also "Doctrine of the Reformed Church," 233-37.

[152] Hodge, *Systematic Theology*, III:517. See also pp. 580, 631-32; "Doctrine of the Reformed Church," 230-37. An English translation of the Consensus Tigurinus is found in A. A. Hodge, *Outlines of Theology*, 651-56.

[153] Hodge, "Doctrine of the Reformed Church," 234. Hodge's treatment of Calvin in his *Systematic Theology* differs at points from that in his 1848 "Doctrine of the Reformed Church." The earlier article is rather harsh, disparaging the merely "private authority of Calvin" on the issue (p. 251), arguing that Calvin was overly concerned to placate the Lutherans (pp. 229-30, 233, 236), and that Calvin's theory was a "uncongenial foreign element" in conflict with the doctrine of justification by faith (pp. 251-53). In the latter piece, Hodge is more kind to the Reformer. Placing great emphasis on Calvin's teaching that the substance of the sacraments is the same in both Old and New Testament dispensations, and that the grace received in the Supper is also available to faith by the ministry of the Word, Hodge argues (III:647): "Unless we are willing to accuse the illustrious Calvin of inconsistency, his meaning must be made to harmonize with what he says elsewhere...To preserve the consistency of the great Reformer his language must be interpreted so as to harmonize with the two crucial facts for which he so earnestly contends; first, that believers receive elsewhere by faith all they receive at the Lord's table; and secondly, that we Christians receive nothing above or beyond that which was received by the saints under the Old Testament, before the glorified body of Christ had any existence."

[154] Hodge, *Systematic Theology*, III:630. See also "Doctrine of the Reformed Church," 251. As Nevin and others since have pointed out, Hodge's strategy here was to place undue weight on the Consensus Tigurinus, and upon strained readings of the Second Helvetic Confession and the Heidelberg Catechism. In short, Hodge simply selected statements he found congenial without much regard for historical or exegetical

Hodge frequently admits that while there is a "real presence" of Christ's humanity in the Supper, this is to be seen as a presence of "virtue and efficacy." Here the influence of his empiricist epistemology is apparent as he reasons by analogy from the sensory to the spiritual realm.

> Anything is said to be present when it operates duly on our perceiving faculties. A sensible object is present (*prae sensibus*) when it affects the senses. A spiritual object is present when it is intellectually apprehended and when it acts upon the mind...God is present with his people when He controls their thoughts, operates on their hearts, and fills them with the sense of his nearness and love. This presence is not imaginary, it is in the highest sense real and effective. In like manner Christ is present when He thus fills the mind, sheds abroad his love in our hearts by the Holy Ghost given to us; and not only communicates to us the benefits of his suffering and death, that is, the remission of our sins and reconciliation with God, but also infuses his life into us.[155]

This presence of "virtue and efficacy" corresponds closely with Hodge's view of union with Christ and his doctrine of justification. The "presence" of the body and blood ultimately reduces to the forensic benefits of the sacrifice of Christ which are called to mind by the ordinance.

> What is affirmed to be present is not the body and blood of Christ absolutely, but his body as broken, and his blood as shed. It is the sacrifice which He offered that is present and of which the believer partakes. It is present to the mind, not to our bodies. It is perceived and received by faith and not otherwise. He is not present to unbelievers. By presence is meant not local nearness, but intellectual cognition and apprehension, believing appropriation, and spiritual operation. The body and blood are present to us when they fill our thoughts, are apprehended by faith as broken and shed for our salvation, and exert upon us their proper effect.[156]

In light of Hodge's statements regarding the time of justification, and his contention that the sacraments avail to communicate neither regeneration nor justification, one is forced to ask what this presence of "sacrificial efficacy" really is. In the final analysis, Hodge seems to view the sacrament as nothing more than a mental exercise of remembrance and reflection that may be used by the Spirit from time to time to deepen the recipient's faith and commitment.

Hodge's view of the Supper and of the doctrine of union with Christ it implied received a good deal of support within the Reformed community, largely because many orthodox Calvinists apparently saw no real alternative to

---

context. See Nevin, "Doctrine of the Reformed Church," 295-389. See also Nichols, *Romanticism in American Theology*, 88-92.

[155] Hodge, *Systematic Theology*, III:637-38. See also "Doctrine of the Reformed Church," 244-46.

[156] Hodge, *Systematic Theology*, III:641-42. See also "Doctrine of the Reformed Church," 229, 249, 251.

the federal theology which Hodge both defended and further developed. Supporters included the southern Presbyterian theologian Robert L. Dabney (1820-1898), and the Scottish federalist William Cunningham (1805-1861).[157] Hodge encountered opposition, however, from members of the high-Presbyterian wing of the Southern Presbyterian Church—especially John B. Adger (1810-1899) of Columbia Seminary—who took both Hodge and Cunningham to task for their treatment of Calvin's doctrine of the Eucharist and for their own theology of the sacrament.[158]

As we have seen, much of the debates dealt with in this chapter had to do with the soteriological role of the incarnate humanity of Christ. Intriguingly, there is a bit evidence that Hodge had some second thoughts late in his career with regard to this issue. A passage in his *Systematic Theology* suggests a

---

[157] See Cunningham, *Reformers and the Theology of the Reformation*, 240: "We have no fault to find with the substance of Calvin's statements in regard to the sacraments in general, or with respect to baptism; but we cannot deny that he made an effort to bring out something like a real influence exerted by Christ's human nature upon the souls of believers, in connection with the dispensation of the Lord's Supper—an effort which, of course, was altogether unsuccessful, and resulted only in what was about as unintelligible as Luther's consubstantiation. This is, perhaps, the greatest blot in the history of Calvin's labours as a public instructor."

Robert L. Dabney, *Syllabus and Notes of the Course of Systematic and Polemic Theology*, 2nd ed. (St. Louis: Presbyterian Publishing Company of St. Louis, 1878), 811-12, remarks in Common Sense fashion: "We reject the view of Calvin concerning the real presence...first, because it is not only incomprehensible, but impossible...To my mind, therefore, there is as real a violation of my intuitive reason, in this doctrine; as when transubstantiation requires me to believe that the flesh of Christ is present, indivisible and unextended, in each crumb or drop of the elements."

[158] See John B. Adger, "Calvin Defended Against Drs. Cunningham and Hodge," *Southern Presbyterian Review* 27 (1876): 133-66; "Calvin's Doctrine of the Lord's Supper." Adger takes issue with Hodge and Cunningham at three major points. He held that a "vital union" is necessary to the representative relationship involved in justification ("Calvin's Doctrine," 787). Adger also insisted, with Calvin and Nevin, that the Supper involves a real communion with the incarnate humanity of Christ ("Calvin Defended," 146-150). Finally, Adger as a church historian criticized the tendentious reading of the tradition urged by Hodge and Cunningham ("Calvin Defended," 156-166). Adger, "Calvin Defended," 134, also quotes James H. Thornwell (1812-1862) as declaring his agreement with Calvin's view of the Supper.

The eucharistic debates involving Hodge, Nevin, and these southern Presbyterian figures are treated in Holifield, "Mercersburg, Princeton, and the South"; and *Gentlemen Theologians*, 175-185. Holifield, "Mercersburg, Princeton, and the South," 244-45, attributes Hodge's view of the sacrament to a disjunctive christology arising out of his commitment to the philosophical principle of *finitum non capax infiniti*. While agreeing that Hodge did indeed operate with a disjunctive Christology, we have suggested here that his christology and soteriology are better explained by his Scottish-Common-Sense-influenced theological method, and by his federal theology.

personalistic communion of the believer with the incarnate humanity by virtue of its union with the Logos.

> But what is meant by the work Christ when He is said to be thus present with us? It does not mean merely that the Logos, the eternal Son of God, who fills heaven and earth, is present with us as He is with all his creatures; or, simply that He operates in us as He operates throughout the universe. Nor does it mean merely that his Spirit dwells in believers and works in them both to will and to do of his good pleasure. Something more than all this is meant. Christ is a person; a divine person with a human nature; that is with a true body and a reasonable soul. It is that person who is present with us. This again does not mean, that Christ's human nature, his body and soul are ubiquitous; but it does mean that a divine person with human affections and sympathies is near us and within us...If any one asks, How the humanity of Christ, his body and soul in heaven, can sympathize with his people on earth? the answer is, that it is in personal union with the Logos. If this answer be deemed insufficient, then the questioner may be asked, How the dust of which the human body is formed can sympathize with the immortal spirit with which it is united? Whether the mystery of the human sympathy of Christ can be explained or not, it remains a fact both of Scripture and of experience. In this sense, and not in a sense which implies any relation to space, it may be said that wherever the divinity of Christ is, there is his humanity, and as, by common consent, He is present at his table, he is there in the fulness of his human sympathy and love.[159]

Given Hodge's earlier statements, this passage is difficult to explain, focusing as it does on the mediatorial role of the Logos rather than of the Holy Spirit. Note that here Hodge affirms a real presence of Christ's humanity in personalistic terms ("sympathy and love"). Here one senses a softening Hodge's rugged extrinsic piety. He perhaps recognized a genuine and appropriate religious need for a presence of Christ humanity, if not in, at least with the believer.

We have seen that Hodge's defense of the federal trajectory made several important contributions to the discussion of union with Christ. First, he accentuated the tendency toward the extrinsic in the federal doctrine of justification. The moves he made in response to the New England critics of federalism had the paradoxical effect of making federalism even less religiously satisfying and viable. Second, it is during the period of Hodge that a decisive break with Calvin's soteriology and sacramental theology becomes

---

[159]Hodge, *Systematic Theology*, III:638-39. In a footnote to this passage, Hodge wrote: "The late Dr. Cutler, of precious memory, formerly rector of St. Ann's Church, Brooklyn, a short time before his death, met the writer in Chestnut Street, Philadelphia, and, without a word of salutation, said, "Have you ever thought of the difference between communion with God and communion with Christ?" and passed on without adding a word. These were the last words the writer ever heard from lips which the Spirit had often touched with a coal from the altar."

both explicit and programmatic for many in the Reformed tradition. With respect to Hodge, Dabney, and Cunningham, the term "Calvinism" can be used only in an attenuated sense, that is, as a reference to a particular view of divine sovereignty. When the Reformed tradition was defined solely in terms of predestination, and was stripped of its rich ecclesiology and sacramental theology, its decline was doubtless hastened in the American context.

CHAPTER 7

The Later Federal Textbook Tradition: A. A. Hodge and Louis Berkhof

The influence of Charles Hodge on American Presbyterianism is not to be underrated. It is estimated that he trained over three thousand students of theology at Princeton Seminary, and at a time when that institution was generally recognized as the most academically formidable in the country. We now turn to a brief examination of this influence, particularly as it relates to the Reformed textbook tradition.

A. A. Hodge

Archibald Alexander Hodge (1823-1886), the eldest son of Charles Hodge, succeeded his father in the chair of Systematic Theology at Princeton Seminary in 1878.[1] The younger Hodge has been widely regarded as a popularizer of his father's theology rather than a creative theologian in his own right.[2] To be sure,

---

[1] Biographical treatments of A. A. Hodge include Salmond, *Princetoniana*, 53-110; William M. Paxton, *Address Delivered at the Funeral of Archibald Alexander Hodge* (New York: Anson D. F. Randolph, 1886); Francis Landey Patton, *A Discourse in Memory of Archibald Alexander Hodge* (Philadelphia: Times Printing House, 1887); the last was reprinted as "Archibald Alexander Hodge: A Memorial Discourse," in A. A. Hodge, *Evangelical Theology* (see below), ix-xli.

Hodge's theological works include *The Atonement* (Philadelphia: Presbyterian Board of Publication, 1867); *A Commentary on the Confession of Faith* (Philadelphia: Presbyterian Board of Publication, 1869); *Outlines of Theology*, rev. and enlarged ed. (New York: Robert Carter, 1878); *Popular Lectures on Theological Themes* (Philadelphia: Presbyterian Board of Publication, 1887). The last has been reprinted as *Evangelical Theology: Lectures on Doctrine* (Edinburgh: Banner of Truth, 1976). Also of considerable interest is his "The *Ordo Salutis*; or, Relation in the Order of Nature of Holy Character and Divine Favor," *Princeton Review* 54 (1878): 304-321. Excerpts from theological lectures are included in Salmond, *Princetoniana*, 115-239.

[2] For example, note the oft-quoted judgment of W. G. T. Shedd regarding Hodge's "uncommon ability to popularize scientific theology"; quoted in Patton, "Memorial Discourse," in Hodge, *Evangelical Theology*, xxxiii. More recently, Mark A. Noll, *The Princeton Theology* (Grand Rapids: Baker, 1983), 211, writes that "A. A. Hodge was more the popularizer and less the discursive theologian than his father. Yet he was a careful thinker who clarified and advanced Charles Hodge's ideas." We will argue

he closely follows Charles Hodge on many topics, including original sin, the distinction between *reatus culpae* and *reatus poenae*, infant salvation, ecclesiology, and baptism. In certain soteriological matters, however, Hodge the younger shows himself to be an original thinker who displays a measure of independence from his father's legacy, particularly in his doctrines of the *ordo salutis* and justification, and his doctrine of the Lord's Supper.

In his definition of union with Christ, Hodge does not, in the final analysis, surmount the limitations of the federal theology, although he seems to have been aware of some of the difficulties it posed. For example, in contrast to many earlier federal thinkers who blithely bifurcated the *unio Christi* into federal and vital unions, Hodge insists that it is "a single, ineffable, and most intimate union." Nevertheless, he proceeds to define it in rather traditional federal terms as "presenting to our view two different aspects," which are "federal and representative" on the one hand, and "spiritual and vital" on the other.[3]

This bifurcation is also evident in his view of justification and the *ordo salutis*, where the separation of justification from sanctification is even more stark than in the theology of Charles Hodge. Here Hodge the younger presents two fundamental principles of Protestant theology. First, he insists on the "clear distinction between the change of relation signalized by justification, and the change in character signalized by regeneration and sanctification." Second, he radicalizes the distinction between the forensic and the transformatory by arguing that justification must entirely precede the transformation of character: "Remission of punishment must precede the work of the Spirit. We are pardoned in order that we may be good, never made good in order that we may be pardoned."[4] Hodge recognized, however, that this leads to an "apparent circle in the order of grace." Hodge wrote: "The righteousness of Christ is said to be imputed to the *believer*, and justification to be *through faith*. Yet *faith* is an act of a soul already regenerated, and regeneration is possible only to a soul

---

below that the younger Hodge, particularly in his latter works, shows himself to be a more christocentric thinker than his father. Interestingly, he expressed admiration for two christocentric theologians—the New School theologian Henry B. Smith, and John W. Nevin, whom he described as "one of the ablest men America has produced"; quoted in Salmond, *Princetoniana*, 198. See also Patton, "Memorial Discourse," xxv.

[3]Hodge, *Outlines*, 482. See also idem, *Atonement*, 199-211.

[4]Hodge, *Outlines*, 517. See also "Ordo Salutis," 311. While this certainly is consistent with the larger concerns of Charles Hodge, it also involves a different *ordo*, in which justification in some sense precedes even regeneration. On this larger problem, see chapter 2 above.

Citing Albrecht Ritschl, Hodge here introduces the distinction between "analytic" and "synthetic" justification ("Ordo Salutis," 314). He also approvingly quotes I. A. Dorner on justification as a divine forensic act antecedent to faith (ibid., 316): "viewed as an *actus Dei forensis*, there is a necessity that it should be regarded as existing prior to man's consciousness thereof—nay, prior to faith."

to whom God is reconciled by the application of Christ's satisfaction."[5]

Hodge's response was to posit a preliminary forensic act of justification prior to regeneration and the exercise of faith by the believer. This act is rooted in the pretemporal covenant of redemption between the Father and the Son.

> The solution to this problem is to be found in the fact...that Christ by his obedience and suffering impetrated [i.e., procured] for his own people, not only the possibility of salvation, but salvation itself and all it includes, and the certainty and means of its application also. This he did in the execution of the provisions of a covenant engagement with his Father, which provides for the application of the purchased redemption to specific persons at certain times, and under certain conditions, all which conditions are impetrated by Christ, as well as definitely determined by the covenant.[6]

Thus far, the argument closely parallels that of Charles Hodge noted earlier. A new element—a second forensic act of justification—is introduced, however. Although this focus on the pretemporal covenant of redemption could easily have led to a doctrine of justification from eternity, the association of this notion with antinomianism made this unappealing. Instead, he posited a "conditional" or preliminary imputation of righteousness to the elect from birth, this imputation then conditioning the later *ordo* of regeneration, faith, justification, and sanctification.

> Hence the satisfaction and merit of Christ are imputed to the elect man from his birth, so far as they form the basis of the gracious dealing provided for him in preparation for his full possession. When that time has come, they are imputed to him unconditionally to that end, the consequence being that the Spirit, who had previously striven with him, and finally convinced him of sin, now renews his will, and works in him to act faith, whereby he appropriates the offered righteousness of Christ, and actually and consciously is received into the number, and is openly recognized and treated as one entitled to all the privileges, of the children of God. To this consummating and self-prevailing act of God theologians have assigned the title "Justification" in its specific sense.[7]

The results of this elaboration of the *ordo salutis* illustrate the limitations of this mode of thinking. Justification is further abstracted from sanctification and from the ongoing life of faith. Furthermore, the real transition from wrath to grace (so important to many federalists) is softened. It also suggests that

---

[5]Hodge, *Outlines*, 517. See also "Ordo Salutis," 313. In contrast to Charles Hodge, for whom the relationship between regeneration and justification was rather obviously temporal, A. A. Hodge insisted that the relationship is logical rather than temporal: "they take place at the same moment of time." "Ordo Salutis," 314; see also *Outlines*, 517.

[6]Hodge, "Ordo Salutis," 316-17. See also *Outlines*, 517-18.

[7]Hodge, "Ordo Salutis," 317. See also *Outlines*, 518.

Reformed *ordo salutis* thinking, if carried to its natural conclusion, leads not only to the bifurcation of the *unio Christi*, but even to the splintering of justification itself. Thus the unity of salvation is further obscured.

A markedly different tendency is evident, however, in A. A. Hodge's doctrine of the Lord's Supper. Particularly in his posthumously published *Popular Lectures*, Hodge gave expression to a eucharistic piety that went far beyond that of his father. Here one finds a rich theology of the "real presence," in contrast to Charles Hodge, who is perhaps better characterized as teaching the "real absence." In striking fashion for a Reformed theologian (and reminiscent of Nevin in *The Mystical Presence*), Hodge asserts the centrality of the Supper in the life of the Christian and of the church.

> We now enter the innermost Most Holy Place of the Christian temple. We approach the sacred altar on which lies quivering before our eyes the bleeding heart of Christ. We come to the most private and personal meeting-place, appointed rendezvous, between our Lord and his beloved...It marks the central, vital epochs of the believer's life and intercourse with heaven...It is consequently the central ordinance in the whole circle of church life, around which all the other ministries of the Church revolve, and through which we have exhibited to the outward senses the indwelling of God with men, the real presence and objective reality of "the holy catholic Church," and the reality and power of "the communion of saints."[8]

Also distinctive is the view of the presence of Christ in the Supper, and the union with Christ implied therein. Hodge insists that the presence is "objective," and that it is not to be reduced to presence of the Holy Spirit or of the deity of Christ alone. Rather, it must involve the whole Christ, including the incarnate humanity.

> It does not do to say that the presence is only spiritual, because that phrase is ambiguous...Christ as an objective fact is as really present and active in the sacrament as are the bread and wine, or the minister or our fellow-communicants by our side. If it means that Christ is present only as he is represented by the Holy Ghost, it is not wholly true, because Christ is one Person and the Holy Ghost another, and it is Christ who is personally present. The Holy Ghost doubtless is coactive in that presence and in all Christ's mediatorial work, but this leads into depths beyond our possible understanding. It does not do to say that the divinity of Christ is present while his humanity is absent, because it is the entire indivisible divine-human Person of Christ which is present.[9]

In arguing this point, Hodge appeals to the fact of the incarnation. A presence of the humanity is "just as essential as his divinity, otherwise his incarnation

---

[8] Hodge, *Evangelical Theology*, 339. See also p. 362. The difference in eucharistic doctrine is briefly noted by Deifell, "Ecclesiology of Charles Hodge." 225.

[9] Hodge, *Evangelical Theology*, 355.

would not have been a necessity. His sympathy, his love, his special tenderness, are human."[10]

In addition to the focus on the humanity of Christ in the Supper, we find a number of other differences with the elder Hodge. There is, first of all, a remarkable lack of the occasionalism so evident in Charles Hodge's descriptions of the Supper: "Whatever may be our fortune under other conditions and at other times, here and now and in this breaking of bread we have a personal appointment to meet our Lord. And he never disappoints those who thus seek him with faith and love."[11] There is also a concern for the integrity of the divine-human person of Christ, in contrast to the dualistic christology of Hodge the elder. Finally, Hodge repeatedly asserts the mysterious and incomprehensible character of the presence. He insists that the presence of Christ is a matter of "relation" rather than locality, but finally he argues that it cannot be explained: "So we need not speculate how it is that Christ, the whole God-man, body, soul, and divinity, is present in the sacrament, but we are absolutely certain of the fact. He has promised it."[12] In all of this Hodge the younger stood closer to Calvin and Nevin than to his father.

We sense in A. A. Hodge a tension between his *ordo salutis* federalism and his eucharistic piety. In the former, he followed his father closely, and even accentuated the soteriological dualism involved; in the latter (at least late in his life) he charted a different path. It is interesting to speculate as to what the later direction of the Princeton theology would have been if the younger Hodge had not died suddenly at the age of sixty-three.

Louis Berkhof

The twentieth-century federal textbook tradition is doubtless best represented by Louis Berkhof (1873-1957), long-time professor of theology at Calvin Theological Seminary, whose *Systematic Theology* and other compendia continue to be widely used.[13] While Berkhof drew extensively on the late

---

[10]Ibid., 356.

[11]Ibid., 357. See also p. 342. This passage is remarkable, given the occasionalism that characterizes his doctrine of baptism. See *Confession of Faith*, 330, 362-63; *Outlines of Theology*, 592, 596, 627; *Evangelical Theology*, 318.

[12]Hodge, *Evangelical Theology*, 357. See also p. 360.

[13]Berkhof studied at Princeton Seminary from 1902-1904. See Henry Zwaanstra, "Louis Berkhof," in *Reformed Theology in America*, ed. David F. Wells (Grand Rapids: Eerdmans, 1985), 153-169. Berkhof's role in the history of the (Dutch-American) Christian Reformed Church is explored in James D. Bratt, *Dutch Calvinism in Modern America: A History of a Conservative Subculture* (Grand Rapids: Eerdmans, 1984).

Berkhof's theological textbooks include *Reformed Dogmatics*, 2 vols. (Grand Rapids: Eerdmans, 1932 [retitled *Systematic Theology* in 1941]); *Introductory Volume to Reformed Dogmatics* (Grand Rapids: Eerdmans, 1932 [later retitled as *Introductory*

nineteenth-century Dutch federal theology tradition of Abraham Kuyper and Herman Bavinck, the influence of Princeton is evident, both in content and citation. For example, Berkhof follows Charles Hodge in strongly distinguishing, both in hamartiology and soteriology, between *reatus culpae* and *reatus poenae*.[14] In a passage that the elder Hodge himself could have written, Berkhof argued:

> The usual position of Reformed theology, however, is that in justification God indeed removes the guilt, but not the culpability of sin, that is, He removes the sinner's just amenability to punishment, but not the inherent guiltiness of whatever sins he may continue to perform. The latter remains and therefore always produces in believers a feeling of guilt, of separation from God, of sorrow, of repentance, and so on.[15]

With respect to union with Christ, Berkhof again largely follows Old Princeton federalism. Clearly an *ordo salutis* theologian, he follows the Hodges in rooting union with Christ in the eternal covenant of redemption, and in the strict separation of the forensic and transformatory benefits. Thus, Berkhof insists on the necessity to "distinguish between our legal unity with Christ and our spiritual oneness with Him."[16] But this dualistic tendency is eternalized and carried even further, for Berkhof proceeds to bifurcate the eternal union of the believer with Christ in the mind of God into a "federal union" (which is itself a preliminary "imputation" grounding temporal justification) and a "union of life ideally established in the counsel of redemption" (which grounds the "tie of a common life" between Christ and those united with him).[17]

When discussing the believer's experience of union with Christ, Berkhof largely completes the federal dissolution of the theme of union with Christ by insisting that the "mystical union" properly applies only to the "subjective" aspects of salvation, that is, to sanctification and the transformatory benefits of salvation, and not to the forensic at all.

> From the proceeding it appears that the term "mystical union" can be, and often is, used in a broad sense, including the various aspects (legal, objective, subjective)

Volume to Systematic Theology); *Manual of Reformed Doctrine* (Grand Rapids: Eerdmans, 1933); *Principles of Biblical Interpretation* (Grand Rapids: Eerdmans, 1937); *History of Christian Doctrines* (Grand Rapids: Eerdmans, 1937); *Systematic Theology* (Grand Rapids: Eerdmans, 1941); *Textual Aids to Systematic Theology* (Grand Rapids: Eerdmans, 1942).

[14]See Berkhof, *Systematic Theology*, 232, 515. On p. 232, he cites R. L. Dabney on this distinction (who, of course, learned it from Charles Hodge).

[15]Ibid., 515. That Berkhof would cite this novelty as the "usual position of Reformed theology" indicates the extent to which Princeton orthodoxy has defined federal theology for America.

[16]Ibid., 452.

[17]Ibid., 448.

of the union between Christ and believers. Most generally, however, it denotes only the crowning aspect of that union, namely, its subjective realization by the operation of the Holy Spirit, and it is this aspect of it that is naturally in the foreground in soteriology.[18]

In his definition of "mystical union," then, Berkhof excludes the forensic, and his discussion of justification is undertaken with no substantial mention of spiritual union with Christ.

Berkhof's treatment of the sacraments is largely consistent with this. The sacraments, including baptism, are in no way initial agents of grace: "the sacraments do not originate faith but presuppose it, and are administered where faith is assumed."[19] The influence of the Hodges is also evident in the virtualism and occasionalism of Berkhof's treatment of the Lord's Supper. Here the presence of Christ's humanity is viewed in terms of its sacrificial efficacy: "Figuratively speaking, they 'eat the flesh of the Son of Man, and drink His blood,' John 6:53, that is, they symbolically appropriate the benefits secured by the sacrificial death of Christ."[20] Furthermore, the polemic of the elder Hodge against Calvin's view of the Supper continues in Berkhof. Calvin's view of the Supper is regarded as "an obscure point in Calvin's representation," and Berkhof maintained that the Genevan Reformer "seems to place too much emphasis on the literal flesh and blood."[21]

Conclusions Regarding the Princeton Federal Trajectory

Our survey of nineteenth-century American federal theology has shown that its conception of union with Christ was framed in conscious opposition to the revisionist Calvinism of New England on the one hand, and a variety of so-called "realists" on the other, the latter best represented by John W. Nevin of

---

[18] Ibid., 450. Berkhof wrote an appreciative, though somewhat critical, preface to a work by the German Kohlbrüggian federalist, Edward Boehl, for whom even the federal bifurcation of the *unio Christi* was a fatal compromise of justification by faith. Boehl maintained that all of salvation is by imputation, and that there is no change of nature in the inner being of the Christian. See Edward Boehl, *The Reformed Doctrine of Justification*, trans. C. H. Riedesel (Grand Rapids: Eerdmans, 1946), 274-290. In Boehl, imputation has completely effaced impartation.

[19] Berkhof, *Systematic Theology*, 619; cf. 616. Later (p. 642), Berkhof allows that baptism may "serve in some mysterious sense to increase the grace of God in the heart, if present, but may also be instrumental in augmenting faith later on."

[20] Ibid., 650. See also p. 654, where the early A. A. Hodge (*Confession of Faith*) is quoted as to how "the virtues and effects of the sacrifice of the body and blood of Christ are made present and are actually conveyed in the sacrament to the worthy receiver by the power of the Holy Ghost, who uses the sacrament as His instrument according to His sovereign will."

[21] Ibid., 654.

Mercersburg. The key figure in stating the federal alternative was Charles Hodge, whose views on the related issues of original sin, the *ordo salutis*, union with Christ, ecclesiology, and the sacraments were profoundly influential on his successors.

With respect to original sin, the elder Hodge reframed the doctrine in consistently extrinsic and legal terms, so that imputation stood as a reality more or less independent of other factors. In order to do this, "guilt" was defined solely as *reatus poenae*, or "liability to punishment," and inherent moral corruption was viewed as a penal result of that imputation. In Hodge's soteriology one finds a number of important moves. Considerable attention is paid to the *ordo salutis*, with justification carefully abstracted from sanctification in the order (although regeneration does precede justification). Furthermore, justification is framed in what Hodge viewed as purely forensic terms, that is, as the satisfaction of *reatus poenae*, or the legal liability to punishment. For Hodge, the death of Christ does not at all atone for the demerit or *reatus culpae* of sin. Consistent with this, Hodge continues the traditional federal bifurcation of union with Christ into two dissimilar elements—legal/federal and spiritual/vital—which correspond to justification and sanctification. Thus the essential unity of salvation in spiritual union with Christ is effaced. Furthermore, there is a consistent polemic against any notion of real union with the incarnate humanity of Christ, and the humanity of Christ is not a material factor for Hodge in the application of salvation to the Christian.

Hodge's doctrine of the sacraments involves, in addition to the consistent denial of union with the incarnate humanity of Christ, a spiritual occasionalism which tends to undercut any consistent notion of the sacraments as genuine and concrete means of grace. Also, we find here a continued polemic against the eucharistic theology of Calvin, with Hodge even suggesting at times that Calvin had undermined the central doctrine of the Reformation, justification by faith.

In A. A. Hodge, we detect conflicting tendencies. On the one hand, there is further development of the *ordo salutis*, and a further abstracting of justification and sanctification. The younger Hodge posits a second, preliminary divine act of imputation and justification anterior to regeneration, so as to safeguard the complete gratuity of justification. On the other hand, we also find in the later writings of A. A. Hodge a deep eucharistic piety which affirms a real union with the incarnate humanity of Christ.

In the work of Louis Berkhof there is both a further development of the *ordo salutis* and further bifurcation and fragmentation of the *unio Christi*. In contrast to A. A. Hodge, who posited a temporal act of imputation before regeneration and final justification, Berkhof argues for an eternal act of imputation prior to regeneration. Furthermore, he also bifurcates the eternal union in the mind of God into a "federal union" and a "union of life." Even in the mind of God from all eternity past, the forensic and realistic categories must be kept completely separate! Finally, in Berkhof union with Christ has, for all intents and purposes, ceased to function as an umbrella category unifying all of salvation. For Berkhof, the term "mystical union" applies only to sanctification, and not at all to justification.

The federal trajectory reaches its logical conclusion in Berkhof. Justification and sanctification are completely separated from each other, even in the mind of God. The gratuity of justification has been preserved, but at great cost, for the integration of Christian life and experience has been sacrificed. The linchpin of the Christian's relationship with God—justification—has been wholly abstracted from the life of faith and from union with Christ. Second, as the bifurcation of union with Christ became complete, the theme itself also become superfluous as an umbrella concept unifying justification and sanctification. To speak of a federal or legal union with Christ is simply to describe justification without remainder. Likewise, to speak of a vital union is to speak of sanctification. To the extent that the theme of union with Christ remains present in the successors of the Hodges and Berkhof, it is largely vestigial.

The religious implications of this federal trajectory should also be carefully noted. There is, on this soteriological model, no real and complete forgiveness of sins, only an attenuated justification involving the satisfaction of a liability to punishment. The Christian can have no confidence that he or she really enjoys the favor of God, because the culpability and demerit of sin remain. Furthermore, with justification almost completely abstracted from the life of the church and from the ongoing economy of faith, the problem of assurance is only heightened. Finally, the bifurcation of forensic and transformatory categories made it virtually impossible to grasp the essential unity of salvation, and the Christian is left with an unstable dialectic tending toward legalism one moment, and antinomianism the next. Such a soteriology was unlikely to appeal to many, and the eclipse of federal theology in the larger context of American religion in the early twentieth century must be seen in light of these developments.

PART V

EPILOGUE

CHAPTER 8

Subsequent Developments

The theme of union with Christ continued to have an intriguing history during the twentieth century, as a variety of new avenues were explored. The assessment of this later history of the theme of union with Christ will follow two tracks. For a variety of reasons, we distinguish between academic theology, which has had a marked impact on the theology of the so-called "Protestant mainline," and more popular-level presentations that have influenced American Evangelicalism. Very different audiences and institutional constituencies are involved, as are different theological methods. Note that the treatments here will of necessity be more brief than what has preceded, and that the field of examination here extends beyond the American Reformed tradition.

The Academic Tradition

The second third of the nineteenth century saw the fragmentation and virtual collapse of Hegelian and Schellingian idealism in Germany. This development occasioned a return to Kant by theologians such as Albrecht Ritschl (1822-1889) and Wilhelm Herrmann (1846-1922). Herrmann's *The Communion of the Christian with God* was quite influential in the English speaking world, and sheds considerable light on the soteriological viewpoint of the Ritschlian school.[1]

In line with the neo-Kantian tradition, here we find both a rejection of metaphysics and a turn toward the ethical. Gone are metaphysical notions of divine and human "nature" (traditional christology with its "two-natures doctrine" is rejected).[2] This antimetaphysical and ethical bent also issues in attacks on "mysticism" and "pietism," both of which are rejected because they represent a preoccupation with the transcendent, and in so doing they distract from concrete moral endeavor within history. In Herrmann, one also finds a sustained polemic against Protestant orthodoxy, as traditional *ordo salutis*

---

[1] Wilhelm Herrmann, *Der Verkehr des Christens mit Gott*, 4th ed. (Stuttgart: Cotta, 1903); ET: *The Communion of the Christian with God*, trans. J. Sandys Stanyon and R. W. Stewart, ed. Robert T. Voelkel, Lives of Jesus Series (Philadelphia: Fortress Press, 1971). The citations below are from this English edition.

[2] Herrmann, *Communion*, 32-37, 142-184.

conceptions and forensic categories such as imputation and satisfaction are repudiated.³

Herrmann's soteriology was framed in personalistic rather than supernatural and metaphysical categories. Personal Christianity is a matter of "a communion of the soul with the living God through the mediation of Christ."⁴ This personal communion with God, which takes place through the "imagination," is nevertheless an intimate one, though Herrmann rejects notions of a union with the divine substance, for a metaphysics of substance would depersonalize the presence: "A more immediate contact of the soul cannot be conceived or wished for, save by those who do not think of their God as a Personal Spirit but as an impersonal substance."⁵

This mediation of Christ takes place as the morally sublime "inner life" of Christ, as revealed in the Gospel accounts, takes hold of the Christian and evokes the faith and inner freedom necessary to empower moral action and obedience. Herrmann argued that "the Christ of the New Testament shows a firmness of religious conviction, a clearness of moral judgment, and a purity and strength of will, such as are combined in no other figure in history."⁶ He added: "The Christian has a positive vision of God in the personal life of Jesus Christ. This vision of God does actually set us free from the world, because it leads us to deny self, and is grasped and realized only in connection with this moral impulse."⁷

While Herrmann occasionally spoke of being "united to Christ," he overwhelmingly preferred the term "communion with God." To be sure, this communion was through the mediation of the historical Christ, but Herrmann insisted that this mediation occurred through the evocative personal power of the inner life of the historical, earthly Christ. There is no experience of communion with the "exalted Christ."

> We desire to commune with God; the way to that communion is to hold to the Christ of history and live in the confidence that the exalted One is with us…We cannot speak of a communion with the exalted Christ. Nor do we find such a communion spoken of in the New Testament, apart from the visions therein recorded. We can commune with God because he touches us and reveals Himself

---

³See ibid., 129-142. On the notion of a "Plan of Salvation" (*Heilsordnung*), see pp. 41, 134, 359 n. 8. Note also that justification is framed in largely subjective terms as a matter of being convinced of God's forgiveness. See pp. 246-252.

⁴Ibid., 9. See also pp. 14-15.

⁵Ibid., 185.

⁶Ibid., 85.

⁷Ibid., 33. See also pp. 72-73.

Herrmann's emphasis on the "inner life" sounds quite individualistic, but this is balanced somewhat by his insistence that communion with God takes place in the context of the Christian community (pp. 189-195). Thus there is a "moral communion" with other Christians (p. 191) and the church forms a "moral brotherhood" (p. 211).

to us in definite facts whose contents have the power of creating faith in us. God is revealed to us; the risen Christ is hidden from us.[8]

Thus, union and communion with Christ is largely replaced, for Herrmann, by communion with God. The soteriology of German classical liberalism found little room for the notion of a "union with Christ." As was the case with New England Calvinism, a soteriology that begins with the moral and ethical ultimately will have little place for the theme of union with Christ. Nevertheless, the personalism of classical liberalism was profoundly influential, and even those who wished to speak more forthrightly of a "union with Christ" found it increasingly necessary to frame it in personalistic categories.[9] The difficulty here, of course, was that this personalism never really rose above the notion of a "moral union," with its air of externality.[10]

The suffering and moral trauma of the First World War created enormous difficulties for the anthropological optimism of classical German liberalism, however, and so we turn to the Neo-orthodoxy of Herrmann's student Karl Barth (1886-1968). Here we encounter a self-consciously Reformed theologian in dialogue with the tradition, and the motif of union with Christ is somewhat more prominent. The theme is implicitly present near the beginning of Barth's discussion of the doctrine of reconciliation ("The Being of Man in Jesus Christ"),[11] and his views on union with Christ are developed more specifically in the discussion of *vocatio*.[12]

In Barth's soteriology, as elsewhere in his theology, we encounter a striking christocentrism. He insists that reconciliation with God is only "in Christ"; only in Christ is the human being elect, justified, and sanctified, for Christ himself is the elect, the justified, and the obedient one. Yet certain characteristics of

---

[8]Ibid., 291.

[9]See H. R. Mackintosh, "The Unio Mystica as a Theological Conception," *Expositor* 7 (1909): 138-155. Writing from a liberal evangelical Scottish Presbyterian perspective, Mackintosh suggested that the eclipse of the notion of a "mystical union" with Christ had not been advantageous for theology (p. 139). He adds, however, that it must be reframed in modern terms (p. 140): "What we have to do, therefore, in regard to our present subject, is to put aside the category of 'substance,' and try to think out the matter in terms of personality. On the accepted principle of modern philosophy that there are degrees of reality, a personal union must be regarded as infinitely more real than a 'substantial' one."

[10]A problem also noted by Mackintosh, "Unio Mystica," 147. Mackintosh goes on to argue that this personalistic union goes deeper than the moral and ethical, though he has great difficulty explaining how (pp. 146-151). The importance of the *unio Christi* for Mackintosh is noted by Robert R. Redman, Jr., "H. R. Mackintosh's Contribution to Christology and Soteriology in the Twentieth Century," *Scottish Journal of Theology* 41 (1988): 517-534.

[11]Barth, *Church Dogmatics*, IV/1:92-122.

[12]Ibid., IV/3.2:537-554. Cf. Heppe, *Reformed Dogmatics*, 511-12.

Barth's theology define the scope and role of the *unio Christi*. The first is an actualism where the focus is on event, decision, and personal encounter. The second is an objectivism in which the human response of faith and obedience is overshadowed by the work and experience of Christ. Both of these are evident in Barth's soteriology generally, and in his relatively brief explanation of union with Christ.

Like Ritschl and Herrmann, Barth continues the polemic against "mysticism." In fact, Barth prefers the term "fellowship" to "union," and he repeatedly stresses that the relationship of Christ and the Christian is one of "confrontation" and "encounter." It involves no "mysticism" and no confusion or conflation of the individual persons involved. Barth writes:

> Are we not justified in asking whether the word "fellowship" is not too weak to embrace everything that is involved between Jesus Christ and the man called by Him?...Yet this is not the case. From all these different angles the relationship is always one of fellowship because, for all the intimacy and intensity of the connexion between them, there can be no question of an identification of the follower with his preceding leader, the possession with its owner, or the life of the one awakened by the Holy Spirit with the One who gives him this Spirit.[13]

Underscoring the actualistic nature of the relation, Barth maintains that union with Christ does not involve an extension of the incarnation. Rather, it concerns the "extended action in his prophetic work of the one Son of God." In this prophetic call through the Holy Spirit, the Christian is summoned to "believe, obey and confess."[14]

This relationship of fellowship is treated from two directions. The initiative lies with Christ, and the Christian then responds. From the first perspective, Christ is "in the Christian," which means that Christ though the Holy Spirit "speaks, acts and rules" in the "free human heart."[15] From the second perspective, "the Christian is in Christ," by which Barth means an act of gratitude in which the "free human heart and reason and acts are oriented on Him, i.e., on agreement with His being and action."[16] Thus, the Christian's union with Christ consists in this dynamic relationship of call and response, in which the Christian is voluntarily united with Christ in will and action, knows the self to be justified and sanctified in Christ, and awakens to his or her genuine humanity. The term "union with Christ" is not the most natural term

---

[13] Barth, *Church Dogmatics*, IV/3.2:539. On p. 547, Barth writes that in union with Christ "we have an encounter in time between two personal partners who do not lose but keep their identity and particularity in this encounter."

[14] Ibid., IV.3.2:543-44.

[15] Ibid., IV.3.2:547.

[16] Ibid., IV/3.2:548. On this Barthian actualism, see Lewis B. Smedes, *All Things Made New: A Theology of Man's Union with Christ* (Grand Rapids: Eerdmans, 1970), 87-90.

for Barth's functional conception here, and his discomfort with it is apparent.

Another factor tending to displace the union with Christ motif is Barth's objectivism—his insistence that Christ not only fulfilled the divine initiative toward fallen humanity, but also fulfills the human requirement of response in faith and conversion. Thus, all of salvation—redemption accomplished and applied—is objectively comprehended in Christ. The difference, therefore, between the Christian and the non-Christian is not that the non-Christian is outside Christ, but that he or she lacks the knowledge of reconciliation in Christ, and the obedience that flows from it.

> But Christians know and can declare what it is that belongs to them and all other men in Jesus Christ...That is something we cannot say of others. It is not that they lack Jesus Christ and in Him the being of man reconciled to God. What they lack is obedience to His Holy Spirit, eyes and ears and hearts which are open to Him, experience and knowledge of the conversion of man to God which took place in Him.[17]

This soteriological objectivism flows from several factors: a justified reaction against the subjectivism of the Ritschlian tradition and of Rudolf Bultmann, a concern to exalt the grace of God in Christ, and a desire to highlight the universal significance of the Christ event. But this objectivism also runs the risk of obviating the need for a human response.[18] Furthermore, by highlighting the importance of individual involvement in Christ, the union with Christ motif has traditionally had an air of soteriological particularity about it. This also in part explains the lack of prominence given to the theme of union with Christ by Barth.

We may conclude by saying that for Barth's view of the *unio Christi*, act has replaced state and condition, reconciliation accomplished has to a considerable degree overshadowed redemption applied, and the *extra nos* has eclipsed the *intra nos*. In short, "union with Christ" (in the sense of traditional Reformed dogmatics) has been largely replaced by "reconciliation already in Christ."

Despite the powerful influence of Barth, the theme of union with Christ has retained considerable prominence and vitality in twentieth-century Scottish

---

[17] Barth, *Church Dogmatics*, IV/1:92-93. On p. 103, Barth adds: "The love of God in Jesus Christ is decisively, fundamentally and comprehensively His coming together with all men and their coming together with Him...It embraces *realiter* both the world and the community, non-Christians and Christians. But the knowledge and proclamation of it is a matter only for the Christian community. Those who know it are marked off from all other men as Christians."

[18] On this point, see Donald G. Bloesch, *The Christian Life and Salvation* (Grand Rapids: Eerdmans, 1967), 24-25, 60. See also, G. C. Berkouwer, *The Triumph of Grace in the Theology of Karl Barth*, trans. Harry R. Boer (Grand Rapids: Eerdmans, 1956), 262-296; G. W. Bromiley, "Karl Barth," in *Creative Minds in Contemporary Theology*, ed. Philip Edgcumbe Hughes (Grand Rapids: Eerdmans, 1966), 54-55.

Reformed theology. This is due in considerable measure to the rich tradition of "high Calvinism" in Scottish Presbyterianism, where the theme of union with Christ and notions of sacramental efficacy have a long and honorable history. Of major importance here has been the work of Thomas F. Torrance (1913-2007), who combined a strong Barthian influence with a variety of other influences and concerns.[19]

With Torrance, the objectivism of Barth continues to some degree. The theanthropic Christ is the mediator of divine revelation and reconciliation on the one hand, and also of the human response to divine grace on the other.[20] Here the saving incarnational union of Christ with humanity as a whole is emphasized: "There is a sense, therefore, in which we must speak of all men as ingrafted into Christ in virtue of His incarnational and atoning work."[21] But Torrance also departs from Barth, at least in emphasis, in a number of important ways. Here there is a vigorous emphasis, not merely on reconciliation through Christ, but on union with Christ, and particularly on the subjective application of that union through the means of grace. Echoing Calvin, Torrance insists that it "is through partaking of Christ Himself that we partake of His benefits and blessings,"[22] and he maintains that the church is not externally related to Christ—though there is an "objective union" through the incarnation, that union must be "subjectively actualised in us through his indwelling Spirit."[23]

In distinction from Barth, there is considerably more emphasis on the

---

[19] See Thomas F. Torrance, *School of Faith*, xi-cxxvi; *Theology in Reconstruction* (Grand Rapids: Eerdmans, 1965); *Theology in Reconciliation* (Grand Rapids: Eerdmans, 1975); *Space, Time, and Resurrection* (Grand Rapids: Eerdmans, 1976); *The Mediation of Christ* (Exeter: Paternoster Press, 1983).

[20] See Torrance, *Mediation*, 83-108.

[21] Torrance, *School of Faith*, cxvii. A Scottish theologian of an earlier generation, H. R. Mackintosh, "Unio Mystica," 151-52, decried what he took to be an undue emphasis on the incarnational "union" to the exclusion of vital or spiritual union: "It is of no slight importance to bring out clearly the fact that the Union we are speaking of is…a Union between Christ *and His people.* For various writers, like Erskine of Linlathen and Maurice in a past generation, and Dr. Moberly in our own, have asserted rather a Union between Christ and the race…But…to say that the race is in Christ is to say something that has no relation to experience. One can understand what is meant by a Christ who is vitally one with believers; for this is interpreted to us by first-hand acquaintance with the Christian life, and the psychological coefficients involved in it can be pointed out. But if we refuse to depersonalize Christ, or to think away the ethical qualities revealed in His career on earth, the statement that He is vitally one with all men, even a Caesar Borgia, becomes, I submit, quite unintelligible. The tendency of such a view, in short, is to bring salvation down to the level of a natural process. We are in Christ just as our bodies are in the atmosphere, and in either case we may undergo the specific effects of the encompassing medium without knowing it."

[22] Torrance, *School of Faith*, cx.

[23] Torrance, *Mediation*, 77.

humanity of Christ as a factor in the application of salvation, something Torrance regards as a distinctive characteristic of the Scottish Reformation.[24] In fact, Torrance's writings are replete with references to the "mediatorial humanity" and the "vicarious humanity" of Christ, and union with Christ is framed primarily in terms of this union with the incarnate humanity: "it is in and through our sharing in that human and creaturely being, sanctified and blessed in him, that we share in the life of God."[25] The humanity of Christ is not merely individual, but it has a corporate dimension as well.[26] Furthermore, the Holy Spirit does not replace the presence of the divine-human Christ, but rather mediates that presence.[27] Through spiritual union with Christ's incarnate humanity, the believer is united with Christ in his saving activities in such a way that the believer's actions before God are accepted "in Christ." Torrance writes:

> In the activity of the Spirit...God unites us with Christ in such a way that his human agency in vicarious response to the Father, overlaps with our response, gathers it up in its embrace, sanctifying, affirming and upholding it in himself, so that it is established in spite of all our frailty as our free and faithful response to the Father in him.[28]

Torrance also repeatedly insists that the humanity assumed by the Logos in the incarnation was a fallen humanity: "the Incarnation is to be understood as the coming of God to take upon himself our fallen human nature, our actual human existence laden with sin and guilt, our humanity diseased in mind and soul in its estrangement or alienation from the Creator."[29] In its assumption by the Logos, this fallen humanity was then progressively sanctified, humanized, and brought into a proper relationship of responsiveness to God.[30] This process of elevation and transformation reached its climax in the resurrection and ascension of Christ. Christ's humanity has become "spiritual," for "by the Spirit physical existence is redeemed from all that corrupts and undermines it, and

---

[24]See Torrance, *Theology in Reconstruction*, 151. See also *School of Faith*, lxxxii.
Torrance also takes firm exception with the later Scottish federal tradition on this point: "It is however right here that we are faced with the deepest *scandalon*, that by His human nature Christ exerts saving influence on us This was the very point in Calvin's teaching so strenuously rejected by some of the greatest champions of the Westminster Theology, such as William Cunningham." Torrance, *School of Faith*, lxxxii.
[25]Torrance, *Space, Time, and Resurrection*, 136.
[26]Torrance, *Theology in Reconstruction*, 200, writes: "His being was not only individual but also corporate, recapitulating in himself the chosen people and the messianic seed, and embodying in himself also the new humanity of the future."
[27]Torrance, *Theology in Reconstruction*, 204-5.
[28]Torrance, *Theology in Reconciliation*, 103.
[29]Torrance, *Mediation*, 48-49. See also *School of Faith*, lxxxv.
[30]See Torrance, *Mediation*, 81-82.

from all or any privation of being."[31]

In marked contrast to Barth, Torrance lays great emphasis on the sacraments and the sacramental life of the church.

> Certainly the living Lord continues to heal and forgive sins in the midst of his Church, and that is no less a miraculous activity than what he manifested before his ascension, but now in on-going history his healing and forgiving work is normally mediated through the Holy Sacraments which are given to the historical church to accompany the proclamation of the Gospel and to seal its enactment in the lives of the faithful.[32]

Baptism is the once-for-all sacrament of incorporation into Christ, and Torrance terms it the "Sacrament of Justification." The Lord's Supper is the sacrament of "continuous participation in Christ and may be spoken of as the Sacrament of Sanctification."[33] The presence of Christ in the Supper is a "real presence" of Christ's body and blood, and of the "whole Christ" through the power of the Holy Spirit.[34]

In all of this, Torrance has moved well beyond the actualism of Barth toward a sort of philosophical realism. The emphasis here is less on act and function and more on being and ontology. Thus Torrance speaks of "the ontological reality of the Church concorporate with Christ himself."[35] This realism should not, however, be dismissed as naive, for Torrance has given considerable thought to the matter. His soteriological realism must be viewed in light of his polemic against "dualism," and his call for an "onto-relational" mode of thought. The old causal and ontological categories inherited from Aristotelian and Newtonian science, Torrance argues, tend to separate God from the world and to cause one to see disjunction where essential unity and continuity exist. In place of such "dualism," Torrance invokes the findings of contemporary theoretical physics, and he calls for an "onto-relational" mode of thought in which matter and energy, time and space are viewed in relational rather than absolute terms.[36] "Here," he argues, "we have an integrative rather than an analytical way of thinking in which the concept of the continuous indivisible field of relations can be employed to express the interpenetration of the order of creation and the order of redemption."[37]

In the final analysis, however, this call for "onto-relational" thinking functions more to deter potential objections than to explain the realism in

---

[31]Torrance, *Space, Time and Resurrection*, 141. See also pp. 139-142.

[32]Ibid., 149. See also p. 65; *Theology in Reconstruction*, 152.

[33]Torrance, *Space, Time and Resurrection*, 150. On baptism and the Lord's Supper, see also *Theology in Reconciliation*, 82-138.

[34]See Torrance, *Theology in Reconciliation*, 110-12, 119-121; *Mediation*, 99-102.

[35]Torrance, *Mediation of Christ*, 78. See also *Theology in Reconstruction*, 201.

[36]See Torrance, *Space, Time and Resurrection*, 186-88; *Mediation*, 58-62.

[37]Torrance, *Theology in Reconciliation*, 13. See also pp. 8-14.

question, for when all is said and done Torrance must still appeal to the mysterious work of the Holy Spirit, and he also recognizes an eschatological dimension. While believers still live in the context of the "old structures" of the present age, through the sacraments Christians "participate in the time of the new creation through the Spirit of the risen Christ."[38] For these reasons, the ontology behind this soteriological realism finally remains inexplicable.[39] One also senses a tension in Torrance's thought between his heavy emphasis on the objective incarnational union with all humanity (a legacy, perhaps, of Barth's objectivism) and the subjective spiritual union with Christ established in the context of the church and sacraments. Nevertheless, in the work of Torrance we find a striking integration of classical Reformed and modern influences in which the theme of union with Christ plays a central role.[40]

Yet another approach is evident in those who construe the theme of union with Christ in social-psychological terms, using the notion of "corporate personality." This concept, which arose out of the context of early twentieth-century Old Testament studies, has been utilized by some to explain both human solidarity in sin with Adam and solidarity in salvation with Christ. A key figure here is British Old Testament scholar H. Wheeler Robinson (1872-1945),[41] who argued that within the Hebrew Bible one finds a striking sense of corporate responsibility, as families and whole nations are held responsible for the deeds of an individual (e.g., the stoning of Achan's family in Joshua 7:22-26).[42] Building on the anthropological work of Lucien Lévy-Bruhl and Emile

---

[38] Torrance, *Space, Time and Resurrection*, 103.

[39] See Torrance, *Theology in Reconciliation*, 121: "it is impossible for us to construe the real presence of Christ in the Eucharist in terms of anything we can analyse naturally in this world." See also *Mediation*, 61-62.

[40] While to this writer's knowledge Torrance never cites John W. Nevin, the parallels between the two are nevertheless remarkable. Both oppose dualistic, disjunctive modes of thought. Both stress the theme of union with Christ, the assumption by the Logos of a fallen humanity, and the sacraments as real means of grace. Both operate with corporate conceptions of Christ's humanity, and both are philosophical realists. Both also tend to conflate justification and sanctification. For Torrance, *Space, Time and Resurrection*, 62, "Justification is not only a declaratory act, but an actualization of what is declared." See also *Theology in Reconstruction*, 153-161.

[41] See H. Wheeler Robinson, *Corporate Personality in Ancient Israel*, rev. ed. (Philadelphia: Fortress Press, 1980). This volume consists of two essays by Robinson: "The Hebrew Conception of Corporate Personality" (1936), and "The Group and the Individual in Israel" (1937).

This concept is used in programmatic fashion in a study of solidarity in sin and salvation by Russell Phillip Shedd, *Man in Community: A Study of St. Paul's Application of Old Testament and Early Jewish Conceptions of Human Solidarity* (Grand Rapids: Eerdmans, 1964). For a survey of use and criticism of the notion of corporate personality in the field of New Testament studies, see Gaffin, *Resurrection and Redemption*, 55-58.

[42] Robinson, *Corporate Personality*, 25-27.

Durkheim, Robinson argued that this corporate legal aspect is rooted in the social psychology of primitive peoples, where a "prelogical mentality" prevails. Here a distinction between subject and object is not yet made, and this permits a "quasi-mystical" identification of the individual and the group. Robinson also argued that this notion of solidarity is a form of "realism," and is not to be confused with mere personification or with notions of legal solidarity through a social contract.[43]

The attractiveness of this theory for framing the theme of union with Christ is doubtless apparent. Justification in Christ is explained in terms of the legal aspect of corporate personality, while sanctification is explained in terms of the social-psychological dimension. Thus, R. P. Shedd writes:

> The frame of reference in which the Pauline doctrine of the transferred merit of Christ is cast is familiar from the Old Testament and Early Jewish conceptions of solidarity. It is no more than the re-application of the conception of corporate personality which conceived of the guilt or blessing of the one involving the group in his own representative acts...From a human standpoint it [the church] is the corporate Society which by ensphering itself in Christ produces the extension of the personality of Christ upon the earth.[44]

Both the coherence and the adequacy of the notion of "corporate personality" have been severely challenged in recent years. The adequacy of "corporate personality" as an explanation of ancient Hebrew legal practices has been challenged by J. R. Porter, and J. W. Rogerson has shown that Robinson's notion of "corporate personality" involves two distinct ideas—corporate responsibility and psychical unity—and that the relationship between the two is both ambiguous and highly problematic.[45] R. C. Tannehill has observed that corporate personality cannot account for the differences between solidarity with Adam and solidarity with Christ that are evident in the Pauline writings.[46] G. C. Berkouwer has noted that the idea of causality is alien to "corporate personality," the implication being that the concept has little explanatory

---

[43]Ibid., 29-32. See also Shedd, *Man in Community*, 3-41.

[44]Shedd, *Man in Community*, 152, 156. See also pp. 179, 181, 190, 194-199.

[45]See J. R. Porter, "The Legal Aspects of the Concept of 'Corporate Personality' in the Old Testament," *Vetus Testamentum* 15 (1965): 361-380; J. W. Rogerson, "The Hebrew Conception of Corporate Personality: A Re-examination," *Journal of Theological Studies* NS 21 (1970): 1-16. Rogerson also notes that the notion of a "primitive mentality," on which the theory is largely dependent, is dubious. Porter and Rogerson are cited and discussed in the brief but helpful summary of critical responses to the notion of corporate personality found in Gene M. Tucker, "Introduction," in H. Wheeler Robinson, *Corporate Personality in Ancient Israel* (Philadelphia: Fortress Press, 1980), 7-13.

[46]Robert C. Tannehill, *Dying and Rising with Christ: A Study in Pauline Theology* (Berlin: Verlag Alfred Töpelmann, 1967), 28-29.

value.[47] Despite these problems, the idea of "corporate personality" has been remarkably attractive, an appeal noted by R. B. Gaffin when he observed that the concept of corporate personality has been used in rather vague fashion "to brush aside...the problematics of the 'realist-federal' debate which has structured to such a great extent traditional Reformed interpretations of Paul's conceptions of solidarity."[48] It thus appears that the theme of union with Christ can no longer be explained simply in terms of a social psychology utilizing the notion of "corporate personality."

A final approach to the theme of union with Christ has been suggested by the Dutch-American Reformed theologian Lewis B. Smedes, who specifically proposes an alternative to the ontological approach of sacramental theology and to the actualism of Barth. Influenced in part by the so-called "Biblical Theology Movement" and also by Dutch thinkers such as Herman Ridderbos and G. C. Berkouwer, Smedes construes the theme of union with Christ in terms of "redemptive history."[49] To be "in Christ" is to be brought within the context of a new historical "situation." Regarding this "situational Christology," Smedes writes:

> For the most part, situationists do not much care to use the word "mystical" for our life in Christ. They prefer to talk about being involved in a new historical order, a new movement, a new epoch, or, as we have called it, a new situation. We are bound to Christ by the present reality of His lordship. We live and move and have our being in a situation where the Spirit is closer to us than we can possibly realize. But the upshot is not that we are infused with life, but we are incorporated into the new situation under Christ.[50]

This new "situation," with which Christians identify themselves by faith, is characterized by the work of the Holy Spirit, with whom Christ is redemptive-historically and functionally identified: "Being in the Spirit means being in the new situation, created by Christ and dominated by his Spirit. Within the new order, the Spirit represents, indeed is, Christ."[51]

---

[47]G. C. Berkouwer, *Sin*, trans. Phillip C. Holtrop (Grand Rapids: Eerdmans, 1971), 515-16. This is also apparent in the fact that those who stress the theme of corporate personality in soteriology have to supplement it with references to the work of the Holy Spirit, etc. See, e.g., Shedd, *Man in Community*, 152-56.

[48]Gaffin, *Resurrection and Redemption*, 56.

[49]See Lewis B. Smedes, *All Things Made New: A Theology of Man's Union with Christ* (Grand Rapids: Eerdmans, 1970); an abridged and revised version was published as *Union with Christ: A Biblical View of the New Life in Jesus Christ* (Grand Rapids: Eerdmans, 1983).

[50]Smedes, *Union with Christ*, 66.

[51]Ibid., 48. Smedes insists that this relationship of Christ and the Spirit is only one of functional identity—the Spirit does Christ's work on earth. In this sense, the Spirit is the redemptive-historical replacement of an absent Christ: "As the concrete individual named Jesus, He is "out there," away from us in time and in the mode of His present

Consistent with this approach, Smedes treats applied soteriology in situational and environmental terms. To be "in Christ" is to be brought within the bounds of the new creation where the "reconciliation of Christ is preached and lived."[52] Through the work of Christ on the cross, "sin has been condemned in the flesh" and through the work of the Spirit Christ "enables us to 'fulfill the just requirements of the law' even as He liberates us from the 'condemnation' of the law and sin."[53] Traditional forensic categories have little place in this situational approach, and Smedes says rather little about justification.[54]

The sacraments too are interpreted in terms of this situational approach. This new historical situation into which the believer is introduced is, by definition, a corporate one that involves the church as a whole.[55] Just as in the Exodus from Egypt when Israel was "baptized into Moses" (i.e., was introduced into the new historical situation effected through Moses), so in Christian baptism the human being is incorporated into a new situation effected by the work of Christ.[56] Likewise, in the Lord's Supper, the presence of Christ is framed in terms of history and situation. Smedes writes:

> In the bread we share in the *significance* of what Jesus did bodily. Jesus is always Jesus in His *significance* for the community. And the significance of what He did lies in the creation of a new community within history which is the seedbed of a whole new historical order—indeed, of a whole new creation..."Body" is a liturgically telescoped reference to all that Jesus accomplished in history and for history, all that had begun to take effect in Christ's community.[57]

Clearly, the category of "history" is required to carry a great deal of theological freight in Smedes' revisioning of union with Christ. Because of this, human solidarity in sin and salvation is cast in largely extrinsic and rather abstract terms. Thus the problem of sin is viewed as external to the individual—the favored analogy here is of the inhabitants of a slum who are oppressed by their social and political situation.[58] Similarly, as has been noted

---

existence. But as Lord, He is at work bringing into the reality of life here and now the new reality of his salvation." *Union with Christ*, 132.

[52] Smedes, *Union with Christ*, 76.

[53] Ibid., 80.

[54] Smedes, *Union with Christ*, 81-82, writes: "Surely the theology of Christ 'for us' cannot be in tension with the theology of existence 'in Christ'...Only if we let ourselves think of Christ 'for us' is a purely personal and juridical way and then let ourselves think of being in Christ in a purely personal and mystical way, only if we let them be at odds will they be at odds at all."

[55] See ibid., 76.

[56] See ibid., 99-107.

[57] Ibid., 182.

[58] See ibid., 15-17. On p. 96, Smedes adds: "A strange way to talk about sin! We are hard put to think of sin as a force or power outside of us, a power that can make a

above, solidarity with Christ in salvation is framed in extrinsic terms. The Christian is "with Christ" in the same sense that the American citizen is "with George Washington" at Valley Forge. Smedes writes:

> As an American I can hardly think of Valley Forge and the battle of Gettysburg without identifying myself with them. For I am a member of a community which owes its existence and continuity to the Revolutionary and Civil wars. I was given my political existence by Washington's army at Valley Forge. Insofar as they created a new nation, they created me. And in that sense, I was at Valley Forge.[59]

In this focus on history and situation, a number of important questions are pushed to the side.[60] To say that the parallel between Adam and Christ is found in the fact that both introduced new historical situation is not, in the final analysis, to say very much. As with the corporate personality proposal, part of the appeal of Smedes' suggestion lies in the fact that it seems at first glance to move beyond the traditional Reformed polarity of the federal and legal on the one hand, and the transformatory on the other. But in the end, the critical questions of responsibility and causality are not answered.

As we have seen, most modern Protestant academic approaches to the theme of union with Christ have eschewed realism and ontology. Instead, there have been various attempts to frame it in terms of personalism (Ritschl, Herrmann, Mackintosh), function and act (Barth), social psychology (Shedd), and history (Smedes). None of these can be said without reservation to have been satisfactory.

In addition to the problem of articulation, other difficulties are present as well. The acids of historical criticism have created doubts on the part of many about the reliability of the New Testament accounts about Jesus.[61] Also, the notion of a union with Christ suggests a soteriological particularity and exclusivism that does not mesh with an age concerned with questions of

---

prisoner of man. But Paul talks about Jesus dying to sin the same way he speaks of Christ dying to death, to the world, and to the law."

In fairness to Smedes, we must note that he does view the sinful situation as one with which individuals have personally identified themselves, but the overwhelming emphasis is placed on sin as an external, historical situation.

[59]Ibid., 105-6.

[60]We should also note that the exegetical case for this reduction to the historical depends, in large measure, on a questionable distinction between Hebrew thought (thought to be dynamic, historical, and concrete) and Greek thought (thought to be static, abstract, and concerned with ontology rather than history). See Smedes, *Union with Christ*, 162-63; *All Things Made New*, 220-222. For telling criticism of this alleged distinction between Hebrew and Greek thought, see James Barr, *The Semantics of Biblical Language* (London: Oxford University Press, 1961), 35-36; Moises Silva, *Biblical Words and Their Meaning* (Grand Rapids: Zondervan, 1983), 13-22.

[61]A point noted by J. K. S. Reid, *Our Life in Christ* (Philadelphia: Westminster, 1963), 57-70.

interreligious dialogue and the problem of religious intolerance (i.e., some are "in Christ" while others ostensibly are not). For these reasons, the theme of union with Christ has not been prominent in mainline American Protestant theology in recent years, and it is unlikely to play a significant role in mainline Protestant theology in coming years. This eclipse is quite evident in the United Presbyterian "Confession of 1967." Here the theme of "reconciliation" predominates while "union with Christ" is largely absent.[62]

Evangelical Theology

In twentieth-century evangelical theology, the situation is somewhat different, for the theme of union with Christ retains some prominence in evangelical life and piety. Nevertheless, certain factors, when combined with the federal bifurcation, caused justification and sanctification to become further abstracted from one another. The first factor was a new interest in sanctification. As George Marsden has shown, the second half of the nineteenth century saw a remarkable resurgence of interest in sanctification or "holiness," and in the work of the Holy Spirit. Furthermore, many of the influential "holiness" writers had theological backgrounds in the Reformed tradition.[63] Even as the theme of union with Christ was being eclipsed as a material theological factor in the federal theology of orthodox Calvinism, it was being appropriated by pietist groups in Britain and America (generally those with a Calvinist background) for which the notion of an experiential and spiritual "union and communion" with Christ was a powerful religious motif.[64] Central here was the conviction that sanctification is a "second work of grace," and that this change of life occurs through an act of faith and surrender subsequent to conversion. A person may be justified, but that individual will remain a "carnal Christian" unless he or she proceeds to "total surrender" to Christ. Only then will he or she be "filled with the Spirit" and empowered for obedience and service. Here there is a further modification of the *ordo salutis*: regeneration and justification as punctiliar acts are then perhaps followed later by a punctiliar act of surrender and sanctification. The important point here, for the purposes of this study, is

---

[62]See *The Book of Confessions* (New York: Office of the General Assembly, 1983), 9.01-9.56.

[63]See George M. Marsden, *Fundamentalism and American Culture: The Shaping of Twentieth-Century Evangelicalism, 1870-1925* (New York: Oxford University Press, 1980), 72-101.

[64]See, e.g., Andrew Murray, *The Master's Indwelling* (New York: Fleming H. Revell, 1896); *Abide in Christ: Thoughts on the Blessed Life of Fellowship with the Son of God* (New York: Grosset & Dunlap, n.d.); J. Hudson Taylor, *Union and Communion, or Thoughts on the Song of Solomon* (London: China Inland Mission, 1914); Arthur T. Pierson, *Shall We Continue in Sin: A Vital Question for Believer Answered in the Word of God* (New York: Baker and Taylor, 1897), later reprinted as *Vital Union with Christ* (Grand Rapids: Zondervan, 1961).

that the disjunction of justification and sanctification, implicit in the federal bifurcation of union with Christ, was now augmented by a pietist Evangelical modification of the *ordo salutis* which separated the two even more starkly.[65]

The vocabulary of Reformed federal theology itself provided a vehicle for this further separation and fragmentation. American Presbyterian holiness writer Arthur T. Pierson (1837-1911), for example, distinguished in not too careful fashion between seven aspects of union with Christ: "Judicial, Vital, Practical, Actual, Marital, Spiritual, and Eternal."[66] Though certain vestiges of the older Reformed piety are still present, Pierson's major theme is that the Christian, who has been justified or judicially united with Christ, should then move on to the level of "spiritual union," that is, to the point "where the Spirit of God becomes to him a living, present indwelling and inworking Spirit of power and holiness."[67] In order that this second blessing might be effected, Pierson calls on the Christian to exercise faith in the Holy Spirit in addition to faith in Christ: "Faith in Christ's work is indispensable to salvation; faith in the Spirit's work is as indispensable to sanctification—to holiness."[68] For Pierson, as for others of his ilk such as Andrew Murray, justification is an initial step that may or may not be followed by real ongoing transformation of life. Imputation and impartation are further separated, and union with Christ is further fragmented. It was this perspective that largely informed the soteriology of American evangelicalism as it developed during the twentieth century.

The second and closely related factor leading to the further separation and abstraction of imputation and impartation was the rise of dispensationalism as a defining force in evangelical theology. This movement had its origins in the thought of John Nelson Darby (1800-1882), an Irish Anglican priest who was instrumental in the formation of the Plymouth Brethren.[69] Deeply concerned about what he perceived as legalism in the established church, Darby saw a need completely to separate law and grace. If salvation is by grace alone, and the Christian is to have assurance of having attained to that salvation, then the law, obedience, and sanctification can have no bearing whatsoever on one's justification and ultimate salvation. This separation of law and grace issued in a hermeneutic whereby stark divisions were drawn between God's dealings with humanity in successive "dispensations."

---

[65]Previous Reformed theology had maintained that sanctification was a process begun at conversion and continuing throughout the lifetime of the Christian. On this shift, see Marsden, *Fundamentalism*, 74.

[66]Pierson, *Vital Union*, 9.

[67]Ibid., 90.

[68]Ibid., 99.

[69]On Darby, see W. G. Turner, *John Nelson Darby* (London: C. A. Hammond, 1951); Robert H. Krapohl, "A Search for Purity: The Controversial Life of John Nelson Darby," (Ph.D. diss., Baylor University, 1980); Larry Vance Crutchfield, "The Doctrine of Ages and Dispensations as Found in the Published Works of John Nelson Darby (1800-1882)," (Ph.D. diss., Drew University, 1985).

The strongest "dispensational" distinction is that drawn between Israel and the Christian church. Salvation in the dispensation of the Mosaic law was by obedience to that law, while salvation for the Christian church is solely by grace through faith. In order to keep law and grace completely separate from one another, Darby argued that there are two peoples of God—an earthly people (the Jewish people) and a heavenly people (the church)—and that these two peoples are forever separate in the divine plan. Darby's distinctive view of prophecy and eschatology flows from this stark distinction between Israel and the church. Emphasizing the need for "literal" interpretation, Darby argued that the Old Testament prophetic materials say nothing about the church, but solely concern national Israel. Jesus came to offer Israel an earthly millennial kingdom, but this offer was rejected by the Jewish people, and so the predominantly Gentile church was formed. The "church age," which is viewed as an unforeseen "parenthesis" in redemptive history, will come to an end with the secret "rapture" of the church as Christ calls the church to heaven. Then the "Great Tribulation" will occur, at the end of which Christ will return in glory to establish a "millennial" or thousand-year reign over a Jewish kingdom on earth.[70]

This "dispensational evangelicalism," as popularized by *The Scofield Reference Bible* (1909), was extraordinarily influential in America.[71] Among the Reformed churches, it found vigorous defenders within the northern wing of American Presbyterianism in figures such as James H. Brooks, A. T. Pierson, and William J. Erdman.[72] Furthermore, as dispensationalists played an

---

[70] While Darby's distinctive eschatology was shaped in part by his desire to separate law and gospel, it was formulated in the context of the wave of intense eschatological interest and speculation that swept Europe and America in the wake of the French Revolution and the Napoleonic wars. See Ernest R. Sandeen, *The Roots of Fundamentalism: British and American Millenarianism, 1800-1930* (Chicago: University of Chicago Press, 1970), 3-41; Clarke Garrett, *Respectable Folly* (Baltimore: Johns Hopkins University Press, 1975).

The influence of dispensational premillennialism on American fundamentalism and evangelicalism is explored in Sandeen, *Roots of Fundamentalism*; and Timothy P. Weber, *Living in the Shadow of the Second Coming: American Premillennialism, 1875-1982*, enlarged ed. (Grand Rapids: Zondervan, 1983).

[71] On the popular level, dispensational theology was codified for many by *The Scofield Reference Bible* (New York: Oxford University Press, 1909 [the second and definitive edition was published in 1917]). On the more academic level, see Lewis Sperry Chafer, *Systematic Theology*, 8 vols. (Dallas: Dallas Seminary Press, 1948).

[72] See Marsden, *Fundamentalism*, 43-71; John H. Gerstner, *Wrongly Dividing the Word of Truth* (Brentwood, Tenn.: Wolgemuth & Hyatt, 1991), 57-72. Marsden, p. 46, notes: "In fact the millenarian (or dispensational premillennial) movement had strong Calvinistic ties in its American origins...[I]n most respects Darby was himself an unrelenting Calvinist. His interpretation of the Bible and of history rested firmly on the massive pillar of divine sovereignty, placing as little value as possible on human ability."

increasingly prominent role in the early twentieth-century battles against Modernism in the larger denominations, so Evangelicalism itself came to be increasingly identified with dispensational distinctives. It is also important to note that at least in its earlier years, dispensationalism identified itself with the Reformed tradition and considered itself to be a form of mild Calvinism. It is not at all surprising, therefore, that dispensational writers used the conceptual structure and some of the terminology of federal theology to describe union with Christ—the federal bifurcation of a federal and a spiritual union fit well with the dispensational separation of law and grace.[73] But this separation and abstraction of the forensic and the transformatory (characteristic, to be sure, of federal theology) was exacerbated within evangelicalism by the new approaches to sanctification and by dispensationalism.

That the unity of salvation and the relationship between justification and sanctification are a problem for evangelical theology has become increasingly evident, particularly in the late twentieth-century "Lordship Salvation" controversy within popular evangelicalism.[74] This episode has illustrated the limitations of the federal paradigm and its bifurcation of union with Christ. An opening salvo came from a group of dispensationalists convinced that American evangelicalism was moving away from a strict separation of law and grace. Zane Hodges contended that any tendency to view obedience as "necessary" for salvation will inevitably compromise the gratuitous character of forensic justification.[75] Noting the close connection between justification and assurance of salvation, Hodges argued that because the obedience of the Christian is at best incomplete, the need for assurance of salvation demands a complete separation of the forensic and the transformatory. He contends that "saving faith" does not necessarily issue in obedience at all, and that a person may cease to believe entirely and still be saved.[76]

Reacting against this stark separation of justification and sanctification, other evangelicals such as James M. Boice, John MacArthur, and John H. Gerstner have argued that salvation involves an acceptance of Jesus as "Lord of

---

[73] See, e.g., Pierson, *Vital Union with Christ*. Chafer, *Systematic Theology*, IV:100, makes a programmatic distinction between a forensic "in Christ" and a transformatory "Christ in us." See also ibid., III:72-76.

[74] On this controversy, see Brian Bird, "Old Debate Finds New Life," *Christianity Today*, March 17, 1989, 38-40; S. Lewis Johnson, "How Faith Works," *Christianity Today*, September 22, 1989, 21-25.

[75] Zane C. Hodges, *The Gospel Under Siege* (Dallas: Redención Viva, 1981); *Absolutely Free: A Biblical Reply to Lordship Salvation* (Dallas: Redención Viva, 1989). See also Charles C. Ryrie, *So Great Salvation* (Wheaton, Ill.: Victor Books, 1989).

[76] Hodges, *Gospel Under Siege*, 9-33. This point is echoed by Ryrie, *So Great Salvation*, 137-144, and decried from the opposing side by Gerstner, *Wrongly Dividing the Word of Truth*, 221, 225-230.

one's life" as well as "Savior."[77] These writers contend that the call to faith is at the same time a call to discipleship. They argue that faith properly includes the idea of repentance, and that obedience will inevitably flow from true faith and repentance. From this they concluded that obedience may be viewed as a necessary and inevitable concomitant of justification, although not as the meritorious ground of justification. In this sense, then, the life of obedience is "necessary" for salvation. And because it is inevitably concomitant with conversion and justification, great emphasis is placed on the "practical syllogism," that is, on attaining assurance by discerning the marks of grace in one's life.[78]

Both sides in this dispute can claim support for their views from within the Reformed tradition. Like Calvin, Hodges is suspicious of grounding assurance in one's good works, and for largely the same reasons—it can be deadly to assurance, and it implicitly undermines justification by faith.[79] In insisting on the inseparability of justification and sanctification, Boice, MacArthur, and Gerstner clearly have the weight of the Reformed tradition on their side. But in the virtual absence of any third element such as union with Christ, the dangers of antinomianism and legalism are real. In this sense, the squabbles between conservative "Reformed" and "Dispensational" thinkers have been a family dispute. These debates have largely recapitulated earlier debates between Antinomian and Neonomian elements within the Reformed tradition from the seventeenth century onward.

It is apparent, then, that American evangelical theology has had significant difficulty viewing salvation as a unity in Christ. This difficulty stems in large measure from the influence of Reformed federal theology, with its bipolar soteriology. If evangelical theology is to advance beyond this impasse—which has existed in Reformed theology generally since the rise of *ordo salutis* thinking and the federal bifurcation of union with Christ—then a soteriological "paradigm shift" is called for. The next chapter will suggest that such a shift will involve, among other things, a recovery of the theme of union with Christ.

---

[77]See James M. Boice, *Christ's Call to Discipleship* (Chicago: Moody Press, 1986); John F. MacArthur, Jr., *The Gospel According to Jesus* (Grand Rapids: Zondervan, 1988); Gerstner, *Wrongly Dividing the Word of Truth*.

[78]MacArthur, *Gospel According to Jesus*, 23, writes: "The Bible clearly teaches that the evidence of God's work in a life is the inevitable fruit of transformed behavior (1 John 3:10). Faith that does not result in righteous living is dead and cannot save (James 2:14-17). Professing Christians utterly lacking in the fruit of true righteousness will find no biblical basis for assurance they are saved (1 John 2:4)."

Sometimes the notion of faith is expanded to include works of evangelical obedience. Gerstner, *Wrongly Dividing the Word of Truth*, 257, writes: "Lordship teaching does not 'add works,' as if faith were not sufficient. The 'works' are part of the definition of faith."

[79]See Calvin, *Inst.* III.13.3-5.

CHAPTER 9

Retrospect and Prospect

We have seen that the theme of "union with Christ," though ostensibly central to the Reformed tradition, undergoes striking shifts in both formulation and emphasis from Calvin through the nineteenth century, and even into the present period. In this chapter, certain observations arising out of the historical findings will be made, and, finally, some prospective avenues for further reflection will be suggested.

Retrospective Observations

First of all, Calvin's attempt to frame all of applied soteriology in terms of union with Christ was extraordinarily influential, at least on the formal level. For centuries thereafter, Reformed thinkers reflexively viewed salvation in terms of "union with Christ." But they also deemed it necessary to reconceptualize the nature of union with Christ so as to respond to new religious challenges and new winds of thought. Thus, while one may speak of the "centrality" of union with Christ for Reformed theology, this is at best a formal statement. There is no single "Reformed doctrine of union with Christ." In the context of nineteenth-century American Reformed theology, one must distinguish the "federal union" of Hodge, the "organic union" of Nevin, and the "moral union" of New England Calvinism.

Second, we discern in these three American Reformed views the three major possibilities of soteriological approach that have prevailed among Reformed Christians generally. One may, like Charles Hodge of Princeton and many before him, begin with the forensic by speaking of a "federal" or "legal union" with Christ. The problem here, however, is that with this single-minded focus on the forensic, justification is then abstracted from the life of faith and obedience, and the unity of salvation in Christ is imperiled. One may, with the later stages of New England Calvinism, begin with the moral and ethical by framing union with Christ in terms of a "moral union." But here the danger is that religion will be reduced to the moral or the subjective or personalistic. A third position, evident in both Calvin and Mercersburg, is to overcome this dualism of the forensic and ethical by grounding both in a third factor—union with the incarnate Christ by the power of the Holy Spirit. But here the problem is one of intelligibility. Both Calvin and Nevin found it necessary to frame the *unio Christi* in realistic terms, but such formulations run the risk of being tied to the ontology of a particular period, and of becoming unintelligible or at least implausible to a later generation. Furthermore, there is the problem of relating various conceptualities together. How do realistic and ontological ways of thinking relate to the forensic on the one hand, and the ethical on the other?

Third, there is often an obvious connection between theological methodology on the one hand and views of union with Christ on the other. The integrative tendency implicit in both the idealist philosophical commitments and general methodological orientations of Jonathan Edwards and John W. Nevin is reflected in their respective soteriologies and in their conceptions of union with Christ. Likewise, the disjunctive and dualistic tendencies inherent in the Scottish Common Sense Realism embraced by Charles Hodge are apparent in his soteriology as well. In point of fact, the federal theology drew most of its defenders in nineteenth-century America from among the devotees of Scottish Realism.

Fourth, there is a strong historical connection between notions of human solidarity in sin and in salvation. While the parallel between hamartiological and soteriological soteriology is most complete in Charles Hodge, it is nevertheless present in New England Calvinism and in the Mercersburg theology of John W. Nevin. That is to say, soteriological solidarity is rarely discussed in a vacuum, and we have seen how in these nineteenth-century discussions hamartiology and soteriology tended to influence each other.

Finally, we must note the persistent problem for Reformed thinkers of what might be termed "structural soteriology," that is, the relationship of the various elements of salvation to one another and to union with Christ. In Calvin one finds a structure in which justification and sanctification are both grounded in a third element, the deeper reality of spiritual union with the incarnate Christ. Later, however, there was a shift toward a bipolar soteriology in which justification and sanctification are related more directly. In this context, it was all but inevitable that one and then the other would dominate, leading to the oscillation of the tradition between legalism and antinomianism. Furthermore, this shift to a bipolar soteriology made the theme of union with Christ in large measure superfluous. This eclipse is for all intents and purposes complete in later New England Calvinism, and is well on the way in Princeton orthodoxy. As a consequence, Augustus H. Strong could write around the turn of the century that the theme of union with Christ "receives little of formal recognition, either in dogmatic treatises or in common religious experience."[1]

---

[1] Augustus H. Strong, *Systematic Theology: A Compendium Designed for the Use of Theological Students* (Valley Forge, Pa.: Judson Press, 1907), 795. Strong adds: "The majority of printed systems of doctrine, however, contain no chapter or section on Union with Christ, and the majority of Christians much more frequently think of Christ as a Savior outside of them, than as a Savior who dwells within."

Prospect

This work has been in large measure an attempt to understand the historical development of Reformed soteriology, particularly as it has informed the theological tradition we call "American Evangelicalism." A subtheme of this work has been a recognition that, while the motif of union with Christ has been used by Reformed thinkers as a unifying theme for all of soteriology, this unity has nevertheless been difficult to identify and achieve. This, to be sure, is a problem that also affects the larger Christian community. The increasingly deep split between so-called "liberal" and "evangelical" elements within the Reformed branches of American Christianity can be viewed through this interpretive lens. In many churches, for example, this split takes the form of a tension between a concern for "evangelism" (where the focus is on justification before God) and "social action" (corporate sanctification or "social righteousness").[2] In this one can perhaps see a legacy of the earlier Reformed split between the forensic and the transformatory.

A major problem for both Evangelicalism and the liberal or "modernist" mainline has been a lack of soteriological integration. The mainline churches have been stronger on corporate social action and concern for the marginalized and oppressed, while evangelicals have historically been stronger on individual theocentric piety. But even these strengths have been compromised. The Protestant mainline has tended to neglect individual sanctification, faith development, spirituality, and the like, and its ecclesiology is sometimes reduced to that of a voluntary society meeting to achieve shared social aims. On the other hand, evangelical piety sometimes betrays an arid legalism, and its ecclesiology is often reduced to a voluntary society of those who share a particular private experience of grace. Both, we would argue, have an incomplete soteriology. The completeness and unity of salvation is a problem for both.

We would contend that the two poles of traditional Reformed soteriology (the forensic and the transformatory) represent religiously legitimate concerns that, furthermore, are amply reflected in the Biblical witness. But these concerns are subverted by bipolar approaches that attempt to relate both by starting with one or the other. There is a need, for example, to retain a doctrine of justification that is forensic and synthetic. The essential Reformation insight of Luther and Calvin—that the freedom and joy of the Christian is at stake here—is a valid one. But attempts to begin with the forensic, to make the forensic decree of imputation "stand on its own" have led, not only to an inability to relate the ongoing economy of faith and obedience to the doctrine of justification, but also to the rather severe attenuation of the forensic dimension itself (if, as Hodge thought, justification removes only the liability to punishment but not demerit, then the problem of *reatus culpae* remains

---

[2] See Thomas W. Gillespie, "Evangelism and Social Witness: Recovering the Full Presbyterian Tradition," *Princeton Seminary Bulletin*, n.s. 12 (1991): 231-235.

untouched by the work of Christ). Here the wisdom of Calvin's insight—that "as long as Christ remains outside of us, and we are separated from him, all that he has suffered and done for the salvation of the human race remains useless and of no value for us"—is confirmed.[3]

Conversely, many recent approaches seek to start with elements that roughly correspond to the transformatory pole (the "moral union" of New England Calvinism, the personalism of Herrmann, the actualism of Barth, the corporate personality of Shedd). But these have difficulty integrating the forensic—it is often reduced to a rather general and abstract notion of "reconciliation," usually framed in terms of the divine forgiveness and goodwill toward all, or to the subjective consciousness of forgiveness.

There is clearly a need to reorient and revision Reformed soteriology in a way that avoids these problems and aporias, and we may at this point ask what such a reformulation might look like. Although little more than brief suggestions may be offered in this context, the building blocks for such a revisioning are already present within the Reformed tradition itself. The shape and history of the tradition also provide certain parameters for the further development of an enriched yet authentically Reformed soteriology. In broad terms, such a soteriology would preserve the centrality of union with Christ as a theme comprehensive of all applied soteriology. It would preserve the integrity and necessity of both justification and sanctification, and avoid the imbalances of both antinomianism and legalism. Furthermore, it would avoid any hint of a "mystical" unmediated union with the divine.

A Spiritual and Eschatological Realism

If a bipolar soteriology is problematic, and if soteriological reflection cannot begin from either the forensic or the transformatory alone without incurring difficulties (as the history of the tradition suggests), then how can it be articulated? We have already suggested that the three-element soteriology of Calvin offers a significant and positive alternative to the bipolar approach of *ordo salutis* federal theology. We would also cautiously suggest that the tendency of other approaches to reduce union with Christ to either the forensic or the transformatory gives some reason for re-examining the "realist" option, and more specifically, a spiritual and eschatological realism. It is intriguing to note that those who use union with Christ as a crucial third element (Calvin, Nevin, and Torrance) turn to realistic formulations of the relationship, and that all three focus particularly on the incarnate humanity or "flesh" of Christ as the key. This is not, however, a mysticism in any technical sense of the term (e.g., an unmediated union with the divine). Here one is reminded of the emphasis, evident in several strains of New Testament tradition, on the union of the Christian with the incarnate humanity of Christ—a theme evident both in

---

[3]Calvin, *Inst*. III.1.1.

Johannine discourses (e.g., John 6:53-58) and in Pauline eucharistic language (1 Cor. 11:27-29). The value of this, as some in the Reformed tradition have intuitively realized, is that it constitutes a third element that is not reducible to either the forensic or the transformatory poles of soteriology. This theme was strongly stressed, as we have seen, by Calvin, Nevin, and Torrance (it also finds a legitimate and even prominent place in the confessional documents of the Reformed tradition[4]). All were convinced that it is difficult to reduce this biblical and confessional language to "virtual" categories.

The problem of ontology raises its head at this point, however. In an antimetaphysical atmosphere, how can this be formulated? Can a realistic approach be framed so that it is neither unintelligible nor in bondage to what Charles Hodge disparaged as "philosophy"? The answer here may lie not so much in "philosophy" as in the language and imagery of the New Testament, which calls our attention to the identity and work of Christ as the second Adam and root of the new humanity (Rom. 5:12-21; 1 Cor. 15:45, 49; Col. 1:18),[5] to the relationship of the resurrected Christ and the Holy Spirit (1 Cor. 15:45; 2 Cor. 3:17-18; 1 Tim. 3:16), and to the believer's participation in the new creation through union with Christ (2 Cor. 5:17). Here we are concerned particularly with Paul's understanding of the eschatological transformation of the humanity of Christ by the Holy Spirit at Christ's resurrection in anticipation of the general resurrection (1 Cor. 15:20-22). Only as Christ's humanity has been transformed by the Spirit is it spiritually accessible and "life-giving" (1 Corinthians 15:42-45).[6] In the resurrection, one encounters the nexus of the old and the new creations, and it is precisely here that all "philosophy" fails. Any attempt to frame the matter in terms of a philosophical ontology is to confuse

---

[4]See Westminster Confession of Faith, 29.7, Heidelberg Catechism, Q. 79, Belgic Confession, Art. 35, Scots Confession, Ch. 21. Note also that the Westminster Standards were written prior to the point when the language of an extrinsic "legal union" emerges in Reformed thought. See, e.g., Westminster Larger Catechism, Q. 66.

[5]On the pervasive character and importance of the "second-Adam" christology in Paul, see Matthew Black, "The Pauline Doctrine of the Second Adam," *Scottish Journal of Theology* 7 (1954): 170-179.

[6]This essential insight was grasped to a great extent by Nevin, but by few others in the classical Reformed tradition. Twentieth-century biblical studies has paid more attention to this, however. See Geerhardus Vos, "The Eschatological Aspect of the Pauline Conception of the Spirit," in *Redemptive History and Biblical Interpretation: The Shorter Writings of Geerhardus Vos*, ed. Richard B. Gaffin, Jr. (Phillipsburg, N.J.: Presbyterian and Reformed Publishing, 1980), 91-125; Eduard Schweizer, "*pneuma, pneumatikos*," in *Theological Dictionary of the New Testament*, ed. Gerhard Kittel and Gerhard Friedrich, trans. Geoffrey W. Bromiley (Grand Rapids: Eerdmans, 1964-76), VI:416-422; Neill Q. Hamilton, *The Holy Spirit and Eschatology in Paul* (Edinburgh: Oliver and Boyd, 1957), 12-15; Robin Scroggs, *The Last Adam* (Philadelphia: Fortress Press, 1966), 92-112; Murray J. Harris, *Raised Immortal* (London: Marshall, Morgan and Scott, 1983), 53-57, 94-97.

the old and new creations.

But our historical survey revealed a further problem here. Both Nevin and Calvin had difficulty integrating forensic and realistic categories (e.g., "imputation" and "substance"). Here the basic problem is the relationship of Christ's person and work. How do the forensic benefits of Christ's work so inhere in his person that to be united with the person is to receive the benefits of the work? Calvin's failure to explain this set the stage for federal theology, and Nevin sometimes falls into an analytic conception of forensic justification.

A Concrete and Christocentric Soteriology

It is here that a concrete soteriological approach is called for. In contrast to the abstractions of the *ordo salutis* framework, in which justification and sanctification are not "in Christ" but rather occur somehow "on the basis of what Christ did," there is a need to reflect more deeply on the relationship of the person and work of Christ. Once again, the Pauline materials provide food for thought. R. B. Gaffin has argued that for St. Paul, all of the traditional loci of Reformed soteriology—justification, sanctification, adoption, and glorification—are comprehended in the experience of Christ as the resurrected second Adam.[7] Furthermore, the Pauline perspective here is that the redemptive

---

[7]See Gaffin, *Resurrection and Redemption*, 114-127. Of particular interest here is the presence of both forensic and transformatory poles in the redemptive experience of Christ. The most direct textual support for the notion of a "justification" of Christ is found in 1 Tim. 3:16, which states that Christ was *edikaiōthē en pneumati* (ἐδικαιώθη ἐν πνεύματι). While there are many interpretive questions relating to this hymn, the following points are crucial in this context. The humiliation-exaltation pattern in this verse strongly suggests that the resurrection is in view here. While the phrase in question is often rendered "vindicated in the Spirit," there is little reason to deny the forensic sense that *dikaiein* generally has in the Pauline trajectory. Regarding the larger question of Christ's resurrection justification, the justification of the Christian and the resurrection of Christ are closely associated in Pauline materials (Rom. 4:25; 8:34; 1 Cor. 15:17). In addition, note the intriguing Pauline connection between adoption (a forensic category) and the believer's resurrection in Rom. 8:23. On these points see especially Gaffin, *Resurrection and Redemption*, 119-124; Geerhardus Vos, *The Pauline Eschatology* (Princeton, N.J.: Princeton University Press, 1930), 149-153. See also Eduard Schweizer, *Lordship and Discipleship* (London: SCM Press, 1960), 64-66.

References to the transformatory dimension of Christ's experience are evident in both Paul and the Epistle to the Hebrews. In Rom. 6:6-10, Paul connects the sanctification of the believer with his or her union with Christ in Christ's own "death to sin," the presupposition being that Christ's own relationship to sin and death is decisively changed by the cross and resurrection. See Gaffin, *Resurrection and Redemption*, 124-126. The author of Hebrews, while affirming the sinlessness of Christ (Heb. 4:15), nevertheless maintains that the "pioneer" (*archegos*) of salvation was made "perfect through sufferings" (Heb. 2:10; cf. 12:2), and that Christ "learned obedience through what he suffered" (Heb. 5:8).

experience of Christ is not only paradigmatic for the Christian, but also is constitutive of the believer's experience (the believer will not be merely raised *like* Christ, but is crucified and raised *with* and *in* Christ, Rom. 6:4-10; Eph. 2:4-7).[8] If these insights are to be utilized in Reformed dogmatics, then all of salvation is in a sense "participatory," that is, a participation in the redemptive experience of Christ. All is to be found, as T. F. Torrance rightly suggests, in the "vicarious humanity of Christ."

A decisive break with the *ordo salutis* thinking that has vitiated Reformed thought since the early seventeenth century is clearly implied here. This historical record shows that as long as justification is viewed as taking place at a specific point in time (either in eternity or upon the exercise of faith) it is nearly impossible to find a meaningful relationship between justification and the economy of faith (the ongoing life of faith and obedience). Only when the traditional *ordo salutis* is eschewed can a truly forensic and synthetic doctrine of justification that is at the same time relational and dynamic be articulated.

Here the earlier Reformed notion of the resurrection justification of Christ opens up new possibilities, for it now becomes possible to move beyond the aporias of *ordo salutis* thinking. No longer is justification viewed as an abstract punctiliar decree in eternity or when a person believes. Rather, justification inheres once for all in the person of Christ, the resurrected and justified one. The believer's justification, then, is viewed as a continual and ongoing participation in the one divine forensic decree of justification—the resurrection justification of Christ. Such a decree of justification is both analytic (in the case of Christ) and synthetic (for the believer).[9] Its dynamic and relational character is evident both in the time of justification and in the mode of imputation. As to the time of justification, to speak theologically, the Christian's justification is intended in the eternal purposes of God; it is objectively declared at the resurrection of Christ; it is subjectively realized in the ongoing union with Christ by faith and the Holy Spirit; and it is conclusively ratified at the eschaton. The mode of imputation is to be framed neither in terms of immediate imputation (if this is taken to mean a merely extrinsic, legal union) nor in terms of a mediate imputation grounded in a participation in the moral condition of Christ (though such a participation certainly exists). Rather, justification is viewed as a participation in Christ's justified life and thereby in the forensic decree declared at the resurrection.

Similarly, the transformatory pole of salvation is not simply "on the basis of" Christ's work, which somehow results in the sanctifying work of the Spirit, but is rooted in baptismal union with the one who "died to sin, once for all" (Rom. 6:10 RSV), and in the concrete working out of Christ's obedient life in the life of the Christian. Only as one is in union with Christ does his personal

---

[8] See William B. Evans, "Union with the Second Adam," (Th.M. thesis, Westminster Theological Seminary, 1986), 133-146.

[9] See Gaffin, *Resurrection and Redemption*, 123.

triumph over temptation become the Christian's. Furthermore, the process of sanctification is integrally related to justification, not directly (as its analytic ground), but indirectly through the crucial third element—union with Christ. Obedience is necessary to the ongoing life of faith, and therefore to union with Christ and, by extension, to the believer's ongoing participation in the justification of Christ.

Benefits of a Revisioned Reformed Soteriology

We will also recall that union with Christ is, for St. Paul and for Calvin, an integrative theme; here justification and sanctification, faith and experience, the vertical and the horizontal, come together. If a major problem for both "conservative" and "liberal" Christians has been the integration of a holistic soteriology, then the theme of union with Christ may well have contributions to make.

A concretely christocentric soteriology offers, first of all, a means of moving beyond the merely extrinsic and legal. As long as the critical point of one's relationship with God (i.e., justification) is viewed in completely extrinsic terms, the religious relationship will almost inevitably suffer, and antinomianism or legalism will result.[10] Only as the concrete person of Christ is seen as the realization and source of all the benefits of salvation will the devotional and the dogmatic come together.

Second, there is the potential for the meaningful integration of justification and the life of faith. If justification is viewed as an ongoing participation, through faith and the Spirit, in Christ's justification, then the importance of the life of faith and all that relates to it is heightened, and it becomes possible to move beyond a preoccupation with the punctiliar. What is important is not so much the initial act of faith, but the life of faith in Christ. The Christian life is no longer seen as a series of isolated events but as a pilgrimage, and a genuine *theologia viatorum*, or "pilgrim theology," emerges.

Third, a new and concrete ecclesiology unfolds as we recognize that the pilgrimage of the individual Christian is ineluctably connected with the pilgrimage of other Christians through union together with the life of Christ. If spiritual union with Christ and incorporation thereby into the body of Christ is the starting point for soteriological reflection, then the corporate, as Nevin cogently argued, logically precedes the individual in ecclesiology. In a contemporary context increasingly dominated by a therapeutic individualism (both on the "right" and the "left") a renewed emphasis on the corporate dimensions of union with Christ will be salutary.[11] Here an ecclesial theology

---

[10] Or both at the same time, since the history of American dispensational fundamentalism suggests that theoretical antinomianism often issues a practical legalism.

[11] On the contemporary therapeutic mindset and its impact on the churches, see

of the sacraments, of the means of grace, and a healthy evangelical "spirituality" (as opposed to the current therapeutic preoccupations) becomes possible.

Fourth, the theme of union with Christ provides a basis for the renewal of Reformed worship. In an age of worship "styles" driven by "church growth" goals and a pragmatic desire to appeal at all costs to the therapeutically defined "felt needs" of the "unchurched," there is a real danger that the church will discard as so much excess baggage its fundamental identity as the body of Christ and people of God. But when worship is viewed as a corporate endeavor of God's people throughout the ages in union with Christ, as the expression of those joined with Christ in the offering of praise, prayer, worship, and supplication to God for the needs of fellow human beings, then liturgical expression congruent with that theology will be demanded. It then becomes possible to appropriate the richness of the worship traditions of the ancient, medieval, Reformation, and modern church as Calvin's *sursum corda* is heeded and God's people "lift up their hearts" in union with Christ in heaven.[12]

Finally, a theology of union with Christ provides a concrete basis for Christian activity within the larger society. A persistent danger in twentieth-century America has been the tendency of Christian social action activities to become unhinged from both christology and ecclesiology. This phenomenon is unfortunately apparent on both the "right" and the "left" sides of the religious and political spectrum. A theology of *imitatio Christi* that does not move deeper to a *unio cum Christo* will almost inevitably remain superficial, and risks an extrinsic legalism as well. Only when the Christian views himself or herself as truly united with the Christ who both came "to proclaim liberty to the captives" (Isaiah 61:1 RSV; cf. Matt. 11:5) and "to serve, and to give his life as a ransom for many" (Mark 10:45 RSV) will social action be placed on a consistently christological basis.

In short, the theme of union with Christ provides a basis for a theology that is, to use a time-worn phrase, truly "evangelical, catholic, and Reformed." It is this vision for theology that, we believe, lay at the heart of the soteriology of John Calvin, and it is a vision that has a good deal to offer the church of today.

Edward Farley, "The Modernist Element in Protestantism," *Theology Today* 47 (1990): 135-36; David Wells, *No Place for Truth, Or, Whatever Happened to Evangelical Theology* (Grand Rapids: Eerdmans, 1993), 137-186.

[12]On the connection between union with Christ and worship, see Torrance, *Theology in Reconciliation*, 139-214; Douglas F. Kelly, "Prayer and Union with Christ," *Scottish Bulletin of Evangelical Theology* 8 (1990): 109-127.

Bibliography

Books

Althaus, Paul. *The Theology of Martin Luther*. Translated by Robert C. Schultz. Philadelphia: Fortress Press, 1966.

Ames, William. *The Marrow of Theology*. Translated by John D. Eusden. Boston: Pilgrim Press, 1968.

Appel, Theodore. *The Life and Work of John Williamson Nevin*. Philadelphia: Reformed Church Publication House, 1889.

Armstrong, Brian G. *Calvinism and the Amyraut Heresy*. Madison, Wis.: University of Wisconsin Press, 1969.

Aulén, Gustav. *Christus Victor*. Translated by A. G. Hebert. New York: Macmillan, 1969.

Augustine. *On the Trinity*. In *Nicene and Post-Nicene Fathers*, 1st series, 14 vols., ed. Philip Schaff, III:15-228. New York: Christian Literature Co., 1886.

Baird, Samuel J. *The First Adam and the Second: The Elohim Revealed in the Creation and Redemption of Man*. Philadelphia: Lindsay & Blakiston, 1860.

Baker, J. Wayne. *Heinrich Bullinger and the Covenant: The Other Reformed Tradition*. Athens, Oh.: Ohio University Press, 1980.

Baker, J. Wayne and Charles S. McCoy. *Fountainhead of Federalism: Heinrich Bullinger and the Covenantal Tradition*. Louisville: Westminster/John Knox, 1991.

Barr, James. *The Semantics of Biblical Language*. London: Oxford University Press, 1961.

Barth, Karl. *Church Dogmatics*. 4 vols. Edited by G. W. Bromiley and T. F. Torrance. Edinburgh: T. & T. Clark, 1936-1969.

_____. *Protestant Theology in the Nineteenth Century*. Valley Forge: Judson Press, 1973.

Bauke, Hermann. *Die Problem der Theologie Calvins*. Leipzig: J. C. Hinrich'scher Buchhandlung, 1922.

Beeke, Joel R. *Assurance of Faith: Calvin, English Calvinism, and the Dutch Second Reformation*. New York: Peter Lang, 1991.

Bell, M. Charles. *Calvin and Scottish Theology: The Doctrine of Assurance*. Edinburgh: Handsel Press, 1985.

Berk, Stephen E. *Calvinism vs. Democracy: Timothy Dwight and the Origins of American Evangelical Orthodoxy*. Hamden, Ct.: Archon Books, 1974.

Berkhof, Louis. *History of Christian Doctrines*. Grand Rapids: Eerdmans, 1937.

_____. *Introductory Volume to Reformed Dogmatics*. Grand Rapids: Eerdmans, 1932. [later retitled as *Introductory Volume to Systematic Theology*)

_____. *Manual of Reformed Doctrine*. Grand Rapids: Eerdmans, 1933.

_____. *Principles of Biblical Interpretation*. Grand Rapids: Eerdmans, 1937.

_____. *Reformed Dogmatics*. 2 vols. Grand Rapids: Eerdmans, 1932.

_____. *Systematic Theology*. Grand Rapids: Eerdmans, 1941.

_____. *Textual Aids to Systematic Theology*. Grand Rapids: Eerdmans, 1942.

Berkouwer, G. C. *Faith and Justification*. Translated by Lewis B. Smedes. Grand Rapids: Eerdmans, 1954.
_____. *The Sacraments*. Translated by Hugo Bekker. Grand Rapids: Eerdmans, 1969.
_____. *Sin*. Translated by Phillip C. Holtrop. Grand Rapids: Eerdmans, 1971.
_____. *The Triumph of Grace in the Theology of Karl Barth*. Translated by Harry R. Boer. Grand Rapids: Eerdmans, 1956.
Biblical Repertory and Princeton Review: Index Volume from 1825 to 1868. Philadelphia: Peter Walker, 1871.
Binkley, Luther J. *The Mercersburg Theology*. Lancaster, Pa.: Franklin and Marshall College, 1953.
Bloesch, Donald G. *The Christian Life and Salvation*. Grand Rapids: Eerdmans, 1967.
Boehl, Edward. *The Reformed Doctrine of Justification*. Translated by C. H. Riedesel. Grand Rapids: Eerdmans, 1946.
Boice, James M. *Christ's Call to Discipleship*. Chicago: Moody Press, 1986.
Bogue, Carl W. *Jonathan Edwards and the Covenant of Grace*. Cherry Hill: Mack, 1975.
The Book of Confessions. New York: Office of the General Assembly, 1983.
Boston, Thomas. *The Complete Works of the Late Rev. Thomas Boston*. Edited by Samuel M'Millan. 12 vols. London: W. Tegg & Co., 1853.
_____. *Human Nature in Its Fourfold State*. Edinburgh: Banner of Truth, 1964 [reprint ed.].
Bozeman, Theodore Dwight. *Protestants in an Age of Science: The Baconian Ideal and Antebellum Religious Thought*. Chapel Hill, N.C.: University of North Carolina Press, 1977.
Bratt, James D. *Dutch Calvinism in Modern America: A History of a Conservative Subculture*. Grand Rapids: Eerdmans, 1984.
Bratt, John H., ed. *The Rise and Development of Calvinism*. Grand Rapids: Eerdmans, 1959.
Briggs, Charles Augustus. *Theological Symbolics*. New York: Charles Scribner's Sons, 1914.
Bruce, Robert. *The Mystery of the Lord's Supper*. Edited by Thomas F. Torrance. London: James Clarke, 1958.
Brunner, Emil. *Vom Werk des Heiligen Geistes*. Zurich: Zwingli Verlag, 1935.
Calhoun, David B. *Princeton Seminary (1812-1862): Faith and Learning*. Carlisle, Pa.: Banner of Truth, 1995.
Calvin, John. *Calvin's New Testament Commentaries*. Edited by D. W. Torrance and T. F. Torrance. 12 vols. Edinburgh: Oliver and Boyd, 1959-72.
_____. *The Commentaries of John Calvin*. Edinburgh: Calvin Translation Society, 1844-1856; reprint, Grand Rapids: Eerdmans, 1948-1950.
_____. *Institutes of the Christian Religion*. Edited by John T. McNeill. Translated by Ford Lewis Battles. 2 vols. Philadelphia: Westminster Press, 1960.
_____. *Ioannis Calvini Opera quae supersunt Omnia*. Edited by G. Baum, E. Cunitz, E. Ruess. 59 vols. *Corpus Reformatorum*. Vols. 29-87. Brunsvigae: Schwetschke, 1863-1900.
_____. *Theological Treatises*. Edited and Translated by J. K. S. Reid. Philadelphia: Westminster, 1954.

_____. *Tracts and Treatises*. Translated by Henry Beveridge. 3 vols. Grand Rapids: Eerdmans, 1958.

Chafer, Lewis Sperry. *Systematic Theology*. 8 vols. Dallas: Dallas Seminary Press, 1948.

Cherry, Conrad. *The Theology of Jonathan Edwards: A Reappraisal*. Garden City, N.Y.: Anchor Books, 1966.

Cohen, Charles Lloyd. *God's Caress: The Psychology of Puritan Religious Experience*. New York: Oxford, 1986.

Collins, Joseph B. *Christian Mysticism in the Elizabethan Age with Its Background in Mystical Methodology*. Baltimore: Johns Hopkins Press, 1940.

Conforti, Joseph A. *Samuel Hopkins and the New Divinity Movement*. Grand Rapids: Christian University Press, 1981.

Conser, Walter H., Jr. *Church and Confession: Conservative Theologians in Germany, England, and America, 1815-1866*. Macon, Ga.: Mercer University Press, 1984.

Copleston, Frederick C. *Aquinas*. New York: Penguin Books, 1955.

_____. *A History of Philosophy*. Vol. 6, *Fichte to Nietzsche*. London: Burns and Oates, 1965.

Cragg, Gerald R. *The Church and the Age of Reason: 1648-1789*. Grand Rapids: Eerdmans, 1964.

Cuningham, Charles E. *Timothy Dwight, 1752-1817*. New York: Macmillan, 1942.

Cunningham, William. *The Reformers and the Theology of the Reformation*. Edinburgh: T. & T. Clark, 1866.

Dabney, Robert L. *Syllabus and Notes of the Course of Systematic and Polemic Theology*. 2nd ed. St. Louis: Presbyterian Publishing Company of St. Louis, 1878.

Danhof, Ralph J. *Charles Hodge as a Dogmatician*. Goes, the Netherlands: Oosterbaan & le Cointre, 1929.

Dee, Simon Pieter. *Het Geloofsbegrip van Calvijn*. Kampen: J. H. Kok, 1918.

DeJong, Peter Y. *The Covenant Idea in New England Theology: 1620-1847*. Grand Rapids: Eerdmans, 1945.

Donnelly, John Patrick. *Calvinism and Scholasticism in Vermigli's Doctrine of Man and Grace*. Leiden: Brill, 1976.

Dorner, I. A. *The Liturgical Conflict in the Reformed Church of North America, with Special Reference to Fundamental Evangelical Doctrines*. Philadelphia: Loag, 1868. [Also published in *The Reformed Church Monthly* I (1868): 327-381]

_____. *A System of Christian Doctrine*. Translated by Alfred Cave and J. S. Banks. 4 vols. Edinburgh: T. & T. Clark, 1882.

Doumergue, Êmil. *Jean Calvin, les hommes et les choses de son temps*. 7 vols. Lausanne: Georges Bridel, 1899-1928.

Dwight, Timothy. *Theology; Explained and Defended, in a Series of Sermons*. 11th ed. 4 vols. New Haven: T. Dwight & Sons, 1843.

Ebrard, August. *Das Dogma vom heiligen Abendmahl und seine Geschichte*. 2 vols. Frankfurt am Main: Zimmer, 1845-46.

Edwards, Jonathan. *A Careful and Strict Inquiry into the Prevailing Notions of the Freedom of the Will*. In *The Works of President Edwards*, 4 vols., II:1-182. New York: Robert Carter and Brothers, 1868.

_____. *Concerning Efficacious Grace*. In *The Works of President Edwards*, 4 vols., II:547-597. New York: Robert Carter and Brothers, 1868.

_____. *Concerning the Perseverance of Saints*. In *The Works of President Edwards*, 4 vols., III:509-532. New York: Robert Carter and Brothers, 1868.

---. *A Dissertation on the Nature of True Virtue.* In *The Works of President Edwards*, 4 vols., II:261-304. New York: Robert Carter and Brothers, 1868.

---. *A Divine and Supernatural Light, Immediately Imparted to the Soul by the Spirit of God, Shown To Be Both a Rational and Scriptural Doctrine.* In *The Works of President Edwards*, 4 vols., IV:438-450. New York: Robert Carter and Brothers, 1868.

---. *An Essay on the Trinity.* In *Treatise on Grace and Other Posthumously Published Writings*, ed. Paul Helm, 99-131. London: James Clarke, 1971.

---. *Ethical Writings.* Edited by Paul Ramsey. *The Works of Jonathan Edwards*, vol. 8. New Haven: Yale University Press, 1989.

---. *The Excellency of Christ.* In *The Works of President Edwards*, 4 vols., IV:179-201. New York: Robert Carter and Brothers, 1868.

---. *Freedom of the Will.* Edited by Paul Ramsey. *The Works of Jonathan Edwards*, vol. 1. New Haven: Yale University Press, 1957.

---. *The Great Christian Doctrine of Original Sin Defended.* In *The Works of President Edwards*, 4 vols., II:305-510. New York: Robert Carter and Brothers, 1868.

---. *An Humble Inquiry into the Rules of the Word of God, Concerning the Qualifications Requisite to a Complete Standing and Full Communion in the Visible Christian Church.* In *The Works of President Edwards*, 4 vols., I:83-192. New York: Robert Carter and Brothers, 1868.

---. *Justification by Faith Alone.* In *The Works of President Edwards*, 4 vols., IV:64-132. New York: Robert Carter and Brothers, 1868.

---. *Observations Concerning Faith.* In *The Works of President Edwards*, 4 vols., II:601-641. New York: Robert Carter and Brothers, 1868.

---. *Religious Affections.* Edited by John E. Smith. *The Works of Jonathan Edwards*, vol. 2. New Haven: Yale University Press, 1959.

---. *Scientific and Philosophical Writings.* Edited by Wallace E. Anderson. *The Works of Jonathan Edwards*, vol. 6. New Haven: Yale University Press, 1980.

---. *A Treatise Concerning Religious Affections.* In *The Works of President Edwards*, 4 vols., III:1-228. New York: Robert Carter and Brothers, 1868.

---. *Treatise on Grace and Other Posthumously Published Writings.* Edited by Paul Helm. London: James Clark, 1971.

---. *The Works of President Edwards.* 4 vols. New York: Robert Carter, 1868.

Edwards, Jonathan, Jr. *The Faithful Ministration of the Truth, the Proper and Immediate End of Preaching the Gospel. A Sermon Delivered November 5, 1783, at the Ordination of the Reverend Timothy Dwight, to the Pastoral Office over the Church in Greenfield.* New Haven: Thomas and Samuel Green, 1783.

Elert, Werner. *The Structure of Lutheranism.* Translated by Walter A. Hansen. St. Louis: Concordia Publishing House, 1962.

Erb, William H., ed. *Dr. Nevin's Theology: Based on Manuscript Class-Room Lectures.* Reading, Pa.: I. M. Beaver, 1913.

Fackenheim, Emil. *The Religious Dimension of Hegel's Thought.* Bloomington: Indiana University Press, 1967.

Fiering, Norman. *Jonathan Edwards's Moral Thought and Its British Context.* Chapel Hill: University of North Carolina Press, 1981.

Fitzmier, *John R. New England's Moral Legislator: Timothy Dwight, 1752-1817.* Bloomington, Ind.: Indiana University Press, 1998.

Foster, Charles I. *An Errand of Mercy: The Evangelical United Front, 1790-1837*. Chapel Hill: University of North Carolina Press, 1960.
Foster, Frank Hugh. *A Genetic History of the New England Theology*. Chicago: University of Chicago Press, 1907.
Gaffin, Richard B., Jr. *Resurrection and Redemption: A Study in Paul's Soteriology*. Phillipsburg, N.J.: Presbyterian and Reformed, 1987.
Ganoczy, Alexandre. *Calvin, Théologien de l'eglise et du ministère*. Unam Sanctum XLVIII. Paris: Editions du Cerf, 1964.
_____. *The Young Calvin*. Translated by David Foxgrover and Wade Provo. Philadelphia: Westminster, 1987.
Garrett, Clarke. *Respectable Folly*. Baltimore: Johns Hopkins University Press, 1975.
Gerrish, Brian A. *Grace and Gratitude: The Eucharistic Theology of John Calvin*. Minneapolis: Fortress Press, 1993.
_____. *Tradition and the Modern World: Reformed Theology in the Nineteenth Century*. Chicago: University of Chicago Press, 1978.
Gerstner, John H. *Wrongly Dividing the Word of Truth*. Brentwood, Tenn.: Wolgemuth & Hyatt, 1991.
Göhler, Alfred. *Calvin's Lehre von der Heiligung*. Munich: Chr. Kaiser Verlag, 1934.
Goen, Clarence C. *Revivalism and Separatism in New England, 1740-1800: Strict Congregationalists and Separate Baptists in the Great Awakening*. New Haven: Yale University Press, 1962.
Gollwitzer, Helmut. *Coena Domini*. Munich: Chr. Kaiser Verlag, 1937.
Goodwin, Thomas. *The Works of Thomas Goodwin, D.D*. 12 vols. Edinburgh: James Nichol, 1861.
Grave, S. A. *The Scottish Philosophy of Common Sense*. Oxford: Clarendon Press, 1960.
Greaves, Richard L. *Theology and Revolution in the Scottish Reformation: Studies in the Thought of John Knox*. Grand Rapids: Christian University Press, 1980.
Grotius, Hugo. *A Defense of the Catholic Faith concerning the Satisfaction of Christ, against Faustus Socinus*. Translated by Frank Hugh Foster. Andover, Mass.: W. F. Draper, 1889.
Gründler, Otto. *Die Gotteslehre Girolami Zanchis und ihre bedeutung für seine Lehre von der Prädestination*. Neukirchen: Neukirchener Verlag, 1965.
Gunton, Colin E. *Yesterday and Today: A Study of Continuities in Christology*.Grand Rapids: Eerdmans, 1983.
Guthrie, William. *The Christian's Great Interest*. Edinburgh: Banner of Truth, 1969 [orig. 1658].
Hall, David D. *The Antinomian Controversy, 1636-1638*. 2nd ed. Durham, N.C.: Duke University Press, 1990.
Hambrick-Stowe, Charles E. *The Practice of Piety: Puritan Devotional Disciplines in Seventeenth-Century New England*. Chapel Hill: University of North Carolina Press, 1982.
Hamilton, Neill Q. *The Holy Spirit and Eschatology in Paul*. Edinburgh: Oliver and Boyd, 1957.
Haroutunian, Joseph. *Piety Versus Moralism: The Passing of the New England Theology*. New York: Henry Holt and Company, 1932.
Harris, Murray J. *Raised Immortal*. London: Marshall, Morgan and Scott, 1983.
Hart, D. G. *John Williamson Nevin: High Church Calvinist*. Phillipsburg, N.J.: Presbyterian & Reformed, 2005.

Hayner, Paul Collins. *Reason and Existence: Schelling's Philosophy of History*. Leiden: E. J. Brill, 1967.
Helfenstein, Jacob. *A Perverted Gospel; or, The Romanizing Tendency of the Mercersburg Theology*. Philadelphia: William S. Young, 1853.
Heppe, Heinrich. *Reformed Dogmatics*. Edited by. Ernst Bizer. Translated by G. T. Thomson. London: Allen & Unwin, 1950.
Herrmann, Wilhelm. *The Communion of the Christian with God*. Translated by J. Sandys Stanyon and R. W. Stewart. Edited by Robert T. Voelkel. Lives of Jesus Series. Philadelphia: Fortress Press, 1971.
_____. *Der Verkehr des Christens mit Gott, im Anschluss an Luther dargestellt*. 4 aufl. Stuttgart: J. G. Cotta, 1903.
Hewitt, Glenn A. *Regeneration and Morality: A Study of Charles Finney, Charles Hodge, John W. Nevin, and Horace Bushnell*. Brooklyn, N.Y.: Carlson Publishing, 1991.
Hodge, A. A. *The Atonement*. Philadelphia: Presbyterian Board of Publication, 1867.
_____. *A Commentary on the Confession of Faith*. Philadelphia: Presbyterian Board of Publication, 1869.
_____. *Evangelical Theology: Lectures on Doctrine*. Edinburgh: Banner of Truth, 1976. [Reprint of *Popular Lectures on Theological Themes* (see below)]
_____. *Life of Charles Hodge*. New York: Charles Scribner's Sons, 1880.
_____. *Outlines of Theology*. Rev. and enlarged ed. New York: Robert Carter, 1878.
_____. *Popular Lectures on Theological Themes*. Philadelphia: Presbyterian Board of Publication, 1887.
Hodge, Charles. *The Church and Its Polity*. Edited by William Durant. London: Thomas Nelson, 1879.
_____. *Conference Papers*. New York: Charles Scribner's Sons, 1879.
_____. *The Constitutional History of the Presbyterian Church in the United States of America*. 2 vols. Philadelphia: William S. Martien, 1839-40.
_____. *Systematic Theology*. 3 vols. New York: Charles Scribner's Sons, 1872-1873.
_____. *The Way of Life*. Philadelphia: American Sunday School Union, 1841.
_____. *What Is Darwinism?* New York: Scribners, Armstrong, and Co., 1874.
Hodges, Zane C. *Absolutely Free: A Biblical Reply to Lordship Salvation*. Dallas: Redención Viva, 1989.
_____. *The Gospel Under Siege*. Dallas: Redención Viva, 1981.
Hoekema, Anthony A. *Saved by Grace*. Grand Rapids: Eerdmans, 1989.
Hoffecker, W. Andrew. *Piety and the Princeton Theologians*. Phillipsburg, N.J.: Presbyterian and Reformed, 1981.
Holifield, E. Brooks. *The Covenant Sealed: The Development of Puritan Sacramental Theology in Old and New England, 1570-1720*. New Haven: Yale University Press, 1974.
_____. *The Gentlemen Theologians: American Theology in Southern Culture, 1795-1860*. Durham, N.C.: Duke University Press, 1978.
Holte, Ragnar. *Die Vermittlungstheologie. Ihre theologischen Grundbriffe, kritisch untersucht*. Uppsala: Almquist & Wiksell, 1965.
Hopkins, Samuel. *An Inquiry Concerning the Promises of the Gospel*. Boston: W. M'Alpine and J. Fleeming, 1765.
_____. *An Inquiry into the Nature of True Holiness*. Newport: Solomon Southwick, 1773.

_____. *Sin, thro' Divine Interposition, an Advantage to the Universe.* Boston: Daniel and John Kneeland, 1759.

_____. *The System of Doctrines, Contained in Divine Revelation, Explained and Defended.* 2 vols. 2nd ed. Boston: Lincoln and Edmands, 1811.

Howell, Wilbur S. *Logic and Rhetoric in England, 1500-1700.* Princeton, N.J.: Princeton University Press, 1956.

Huntington, Joseph. *Calvinism Improved: or, the Gospel Illustrated as a System of Real Grace, Issuing in the Salvation of All Men.* New London: Samuel Green, 1796.

Hutchinson, George P. *The Problem of Original Sin in American Presbyterian Theology.* Philadelphia: Presbyterian and Reformed, 1972.

Irving, Edward. *The Orthodox and Catholic Doctrine of Our Lord's Human Nature.* London: Baldwin and Cradock, 1830.

Jones, James William. *The Shattered Synthesis: New England Puritanism Before the Great Awakening.* New Haven: Yale University Press, 1973.

Kendall, R. T. *Calvin and English Calvinism to 1649.* New York: Oxford University Press, 1979.

Kickel, Walter. *Vernunft und Offenbarung bei Theodor Beza.* Neukirchen-Vluyn: Neukirchener Verlag, 1967.

Kolfhaus, Wilhelm. *Christusgemeinschaft bei Johannes Calvin.* Neukirchen: Kreis Moers, 1939.

_____. *Vom Christlichen Leben Nach Johannes Calvin.* Neukirchen: Kreis Moers, 1949.

Krusche, Werner. *Das Wirken des Heiligen Geistes nach Calvin.* Göttingen: Vandenhoeck & Ruprecht, 1957.

Kuklick, Bruce. *Churchmen and Philosophers: From Jonathan Edwards to John Dewey.* New Haven: Yale University Press, 1985.

Lachman, David C. *The Marrow Controversy, 1718-1723: An Historical and Theological Analysis.* Rutherford Studies in Historical Theology. Edinburgh: Rutherford House, 1988.

Landis, Robert W. *The Doctrine of Original Sin as Received and Taught by the Churches of the Reformation.* Richmond, Va.: Whittet & Shepperson, 1884.

Lee, Sang Hyun. *The Philosophical Theology of Jonathan Edwards.* Princeton: Princeton University Press, 1988.

Leith, John H. *John Calvin's Doctrine of the Christian Life.* Louisville: Westminster/John Knox, 1989.

Loeb, Louis E. *From Descartes to Hume: Continental Metaphysics and the Development of Modern Philosophy.* Ithaca: Cornel University Press, 1981.

Loetscher, Lefferts A. *Facing the Enlightenment and Pietism: Archibald Alexander and the Founding of Princeton Theological Seminary.* Westport, Conn.: Greenwood Press, 1983.

Lumsden, John. *The Covenants of Scotland.* Paisley: A. Gardner, 1914.

Lüttge, Willy. *Die Rechtfertigungslehre Calvins und ihre Bedeutung für seine Frömmigkeit.* Berlin: Reuther & Reichard, 1909.

MacArthur, John F., Jr. *The Gospel According to Jesus.* Grand Rapids: Zondervan, 1988.

Macleod, John. *Scottish Theology: In Relation to Church History Since the Reformation.* 2nd ed. Edinburgh: Publications Committee of the Free Church of Scotland, 1946.

Mackintosh, H. R. *The Doctrine of the Person of Christ.* New York: Charles Scribner's Sons, 1912.

Marsden, George M. *The Evangelical Mind and the New School Presbyterian Experience.* New Haven: Yale University Press, 1970.

———. *Fundamentalism and American Culture: The Shaping of Twentieth-Century Evangelicalism, 1870-1925.* New York: Oxford University Press, 1980.

———. *Reforming Fundamentalism: Fuller Seminary and the New Evangelicalism.* Grand Rapids: Eerdmans, 1987.

Maxwell, Jack Martin. *Worship and Reformed Theology: The Liturgical Lessons of Mercersburg.* Pittsburgh: Pickwick Press, 1976.

May, Henry. *The Enlightenment in America.* New York: Oxford University Press, 1976.

McCormack, Bruce L. *For Us and Our Salvation: Incarnation and Atonement in the Reformed Tradition.* Studies in Reformed Theology and History, I:2. Princeton, N.J.: Princeton Theological Seminary, 1993.

McCosh, James. *The Scottish Philosophy.* New York: R. Carter, 1874.

McDonnell, Kilian. *John Calvin, the Church, and the Eucharist.* Princeton: Princeton University Press, 1967.

McEwen, James S. *The Faith of John Knox.* Richmond: John Knox, 1961.

McGiffert, Michael, ed. *God's Plot: the Paradoxes of Puritan Piety, Being the Autobiography & Journal of Thomas Shepard.* Amherst: University of Massachusetts Press, 1972.

McGrath, Alister E. *Iustitia Dei: A History of the Christian Doctrine of Justification.* 2 vols. Cambridge: Cambridge University Press, 1986.

McKim, Donald K. *Ramism in William Perkins' Theology.* New York: Peter Lang, 1987.

McLaughlin, William G. *Isaac Backus and the American Pietistic Tradition.* Boston: Little, Brown and Co., 1967.

McLelland, J. C. and G. E. Duffield, eds. *The Life, Early Letters and Eucharistic Writings of Peter Martyr.* The Courtenay Library of Reformation Classics, 5. Abingdon, England: Sutton Courtenay Press, 1989.

McNeill, John T. *The History and Character of Calvinism.* New York: Oxford University Press, 1954.

Mead, Sidney Earl. *Nathaniel William Taylor, 1768-1858: A Connecticut Liberal.* Chicago: University of Chicago Press, 1942.

Miller, Perry. *Errand Into the Wilderness.* Cambridge, Mass.: Harvard University Press, 1956.

———. *Jonathan Edwards.* New York: William Sloane, 1949.

———. *The New England Mind: The Seventeenth Century.* Cambridge, Mass.: Harvard University Press, 1939.

Miller, Russell E. *The Larger Hope: The First Century of the Universalist Church in America, 1770-1870.* Boston: Unitarian Universalist Association, 1979.

Milner, Joseph. *History of the Church of Christ.* 2nd ed. 5 vols. Boston: St. Armstrong and Crocker & Brewster, 1822.

Morgan, Edmund S. *Visible Saints: the History of a Puritan Idea.* Ithaca: Cornell University Press, 1965.

Morris, William Sparkes. *The Young Jonathan Edwards: A Reconstruction.* Chicago Studies in the History of American Religion, 14. New York: Carlson Publishing, 1991.

Mosheim, Johann Lorenz. *Ecclesiastical History, Ancient and Modern, From the Birth of Christ to the Beginning of the Present Century.* 6 vols. Translated by Archibald Maclaine. Charlestown, Mass.: Samuel Etheridge, 1810-11.

Müller, Julius. *The Christian Doctrine of Sin.* 2 vols. Translated by WilliamUrwick. Edinburgh: T. & T. Clark, 1868.

Muller, Richard A. *Dictionary of Latin and Greek Theological Terms.* Grand Rapids: Baker, 1985.

_____. *God, Creation, and Providence in the Thought of Jacob Arminius.* Grand Rapids: Baker, 1991.

_____. *Post-Reformation Reformed Dogmatics.* 4 vols. 2nd ed. Grand Rapids: Baker, 2003.

Murray, Andrew. *Abide in Christ: Thoughts on the Blessed Life of Fellowship with the Son of God.* New York: Grosset & Dunlap, n.d.

_____. *The Master's Indwelling.* New York: Fleming H. Revell, 1896.

Murray, John. *Universalism Vindicated: Being the Substance of Some Observations on the Revelation of the Unbounded Love of God.* Charlestown, Mass.: J. Lamson, 1798.

Murray, John. *The Imputation of Adam's Sin.* Grand Rapids: Eerdmans, 1959.

Nevin, John W. *The Anxious Bench.* 2nd ed. Chambersburg, Pa.: Publication Office of the German Reformed Church, 1844.

_____. *Catholic and Reformed: Selected Theological Writings of John Williamson Nevin.* Edited by Charles Yrigoyen, Jr. and George H. Bricker. Pittsburgh: Pickwick Press, 1978.

_____. *Human Freedom and A Plea for Philosophy: Two Essays.* Mercersburg, Pa.: P. A. Rice, 1850.

_____. *My Own Life: The Earlier Years.* Lancaster, Pa.: Historical Society of the Evangelical and Reformed Church, 1964. [Initially published in serial form in the *Reformed Church Messenger* (March 2-June 22, 1870)]

_____. *The Mystical Presence: A Vindication of the Reformed or Calvinistic Doctrine of the Holy Eucharist.* Philadelphia: J. B. Lippincott, 1846.

_____. *The Mystical Presence and Other Writings on the Eucharist.* Edited by Bard Thompson and George H. Bricker. Lancaster Series on the Mercersburg Theology, 4 Boston: United Church Press, 1966.

_____. *A Summary of Biblical Antiquities; for the Use of Schools, Bible-Classes and Families.* Philadelphia: American Sunday-School Union, 1849.

Nichols, James Hastings, ed. *The Mercersburg Theology.* New York: Oxford University Press, 1966.

_____. *Romanticism in American Theology: Nevin and Schaff at Mercersburg.* Chicago: University of Chicago Press, 1961.

Niebuhr, Richard R. *Schleiermacher on Christ and Religion.* New York: Charles Scribner's Sons, 1964.

Niesel, Wilhelm. *The Theology of Calvin.* Translated by Harold Knight. Philadelphia: Westminster, 1956.

Noll, Mark A. *America's God: From Jonathan Edwards to Abraham Lincoln.* New York: Oxford University Press, 2002.

_____., ed. *The Princeton Theology.* Grand Rapids: Baker Book House, 1983.

Nuttall, Geoffrey Fillingham. *The Holy Spirit in Puritan Faith and Experience.* Oxford: Oxford University Press, 1946.

Ong, Walter J. *Ramus: Method, and the Decay of Dialogue.* Cambridge, Mass.: Harvard University Press, 1958.

Orr, James. *The Progress of Dogma.* Grand Rapids: Eerdmans, 1952.

Owen, John. *The Works of John Owen.* Edited by William H. Goold. 16 vols. Philadelphia: The Leighton Publications, 1862-1871.

Park, Edwards Amasa, ed. *The Atonement: Discourses and Treatises.* Boston: Congregational Board of Publication, 1859.

Park, Edwards Amasa. *Memoir of the Life and Character of Samuel Hopkins, D.D.* Boston: Doctrinal Tract and Book Society, 1854.

Partee, Charles. *Calvin and Classical Philosophy.* Leiden: E. J. Brill, 1977.

Patton, Francis Landey. *A Discourse in Memory of Archibald Alexander Hodge.* Philadelphia: Times Printing House, 1887.

Paxton, William M. *Address Delivered at the Funeral of Archibald Alexander Hodge.* New York: Anson D. F. Randolph, 1886.

Pettit, Norman. *The Heart Prepared.* New Haven: Yale University Press, 1966.

Pfleiderer, Otto. *The Development of Theology in Germany Since Kant: and Its Progress in Great Britain Since 1825.* Translated by J. Frederick Smith. New York: Macmillan, 1893.

Pierson, Arthur T. *Shall We Continue in Sin: A Vital Question for Believers Answered in the Word of God.* New York: Baker and Taylor, 1897.

_____. *Vital Union with Christ.* Grand Rapids: Zondervan, 1961. [A later edition of *Shall We Continue in Sin* (see above)]

Platt, John. *Reformed Thought and Scholasticism.* Leiden: E. J. Brill, 1982.

Post, Stephen Garrard. *Christian Love and Self-Denial: An Historical and Normative Study of Jonathan Edwards, Samuel Hopkins, and American Theological Ethics.* Lanham, Md.: University Press of America, 1987.

Prestige, G.L. *Fathers and Heretics.* London: SPCK, 1958.

Prestwich, Menna, ed. *International Calvinism, 1541-1715.* New York: Oxford University Press, 1985.

Rauch, Frederick A. *Psychology: Or, A View of the Human Soul: Including Anthropology, Adapted for the Use of Colleges.* 2nd ed. New York: M. W. Dodd, 1841.

Raitt, Jill. *The Eucharistic Theology of Theodore Beza: Development of the Reformed Doctrine.* AAR Studies in Religion, 4. Atlanta: Scholars Press, 1972.

Reid, J. K. S. *Our Life in Christ.* Philadelphia: Westminster Press, 1963.

Reid, W. Stanford, ed. *John Calvin: His Influence on the Western World.* Grand Rapids: Zondervan, 1982.

Relly, James. *Union: or, A Treatise on the Consanguinity and Affinity between Christ and His Church.* Boston: White and Adams, 1779.

Riley, Woodbridge. *American Thought: From Puritanism to Pragmatism and Beyond.* New York: Henry Holt, 1915.

Ritschl, Albrecht. *A Critical History of the Christian Doctrine of Justification and Reconciliation.* Translated by John S. Black. Edinburgh: Edmonston and Douglas, 1872.

Robinson, H. Wheeler. *Corporate Personality in Ancient Israel.* Rev. ed. Philadelphia: Fortress Press, 1980.

Rohr, John von. *The Covenant of Grace in Puritan Thought.* Atlanta: Scholars Press, 1986.

Rudisill, Dorus Paul. *The Doctrine of the Atonement in Jonathan Edwards and His Successors*. New York: Poseidon Books, 1971.
Rutherford, Samuel. *The Covenant of Life Opened: Or A Treatise of the Covenant of Grace*. Edinburgh, 1655.
Ryrie, Charles. *So Great Salvation*. Wheaton, Ill.: Victor Books, 1989.
Salmond, C. A. *Princetoniana: Charles and A. A. Hodge, with Class and Table Talk of Hodge the Younger*. New York: Scribner & Welford, n.d.
Sandeen, Ernest R. *The Roots of Fundamentalism: British and American Millenarianism, 1800-1930*. Chicago: University of Chicago Press, 1970.
Schaff, Philip, ed., *The Creeds of Christendom*, 3 vols. 6th ed. New York: Harper and Brothers, 1931.
_____. *Germany: Its Universities, Theology, and Religion*. Philadelphia: Lindsay and Blakiston, 1857.
_____. *The Moral Character of Christ, or the Perfection of Christ's Humanity a Proof of His Divinity*. Chambersburg, Pa.: M. Kieffer, 1861.
Schleiermacher, Friedrich. *The Christian Faith*. Edited by H. R. Mackintosh and J. S. Stewart. Edinburgh: T. & T. Clark, 1928.
Schmid, Heinrich. *The Doctrinal Theology of the Evangelical Lutheran Church*. 3rd ed. rev. Translated by Charles A. Hay and Henry E. Jacobs. Minneapolis: Augsburg Publishing House, 1961.
Schneckenburger, M. *Vergleichende Darstellung des lutherischen und reformirten Lehrbegriffs*. 2 vols. Stuttgart: J. B. Metzler, 1855.
Schweizer, Eduard. *Lordship and Discipleship*. London: SCM Press, 1960.
Scofield, C. I., ed. *The Scofield Reference Bible*. New York: Oxford University Press, 1909.
Scroggs, Robin. *The Last Adam*. Philadelphia: Fortress Press, 1966.
Selden, William K. *Princeton Theological Seminary: A Narrative History, 1812-1992*. Princeton, N.J.: Princeton University Press, 1992.
Shedd, Russell Phillip. *Man in Community: A Study of St. Paul's Application of Old Testament and Early Jewish Conceptions of Human Solidarity*. Grand Rapids: Eerdmans, 1964.
Shedd, William G. T. *Dogmatic Theology*. 3 vols. New York: Charles Scribner's Sons, 1891.
_____. *A History of Christian Doctrine*. 2 vols. 14th ed. New York: Charles Scribner's Sons, 1902.
Sibbes, Richard. *The Complete Works of Richard Sibbes, D.D.* Edited by Alexander B. Grosart. 7 vols. Edinburgh: James Nichol, 1864.
Silva, Moises. *Biblical Words and Their Meaning*. Grand Rapids: Zondervan, 1983.
Smedes, Lewis B. *All Things Made New: A Theology of Man's Union with Christ*. Grand Rapids: Eerdmans, 1970.
_____. *Union with Christ: A Biblical View of the New Life in Jesus Christ*. Grand Rapids: Eerdmans, 1983.
Smith, H. Shelton. *Changing Conceptions of Original Sin*. New York: Charles Scribner's Sons, 1955.
Sprunger, Keith L. *Dutch Puritanism: A History of English and Scottish Churches of the Netherlands in the Sixteenth and Seventeenth Centuries*. Leiden: E.J. Brill, 1982.
_____. *The Learned Doctor Ames: Dutch Backgrounds of English and American Puritanism*. Chicago: University of Illinois Press, 1972.

Stadtland, Tjarko. *Rechtfertigung und Heiligung bei Calvin*. Neukirchen-Vluyn, Neukirchener Verlag, 1972.

Stoeffler, F. Ernest. *The Rise of Evangelical Pietism*. Leiden: E.J. Brill, 1965.

Stoever, William K. B. *'A Faire and Easie Way to Heaven': Covenant Theology and Antinomianism in Early Massachusetts*. Middletown, Conn.: Wesleyan University Press, 1978.

Storms, C. Samuel. *Tragedy in Eden: Original Sin in the Theology of Jonathan Edwards*. Lanham, Md.: University Press of America, 1983.

Strehle, Stephen. *Calvinism, Federalism, and Scholasticism: A Study in the Reformed Doctrine of Covenant*. New York: Peter Lang, 1988.

Stromberg, Roland N. *Religious Liberalism in Eighteenth-Century England*. London: Oxford University Press, 1954.

Strong, Augustus H. *Systematic Theology: A Compendium Designed for the Use of Theological Students*. Valley Forge, Pa.: Judson Press, 1907.

Stuermann, Walter E. *A Critical Study of Calvin's Concept of Faith*. Tulsa: Privately printed, 1952.

Sweeney, Douglas A. *Nathaniel Taylor, New Haven Theology, and the Legacy of Jonathan Edwards*. New York: Oxford University Press, 2003.

Tamburello, Dennis E. *Union with Christ: John Calvin and the Mysticism of St. Bernard*. Louisville: Westminster/John Knox Press, 1994.

Tannehill, Robert C. *Dying and Rising with Christ: A Study in Pauline Theology*. Berlin: Verlag Alfred Töpelmann, 1967.

Taylor, J. Hudson. *Union and Communion, or Thoughts on the Song of Solomon*. London: China Inland Mission, 1914.

Taylor, Nathaniel W. *Essays, Lectures, Etc. Upon Select Topics in Revealed Theology*. New York: Clark, Austin & Smith, 1859.

TeSelle, Eugene. *Christ in Context: Divine Purpose and Human Possibility*. Philadelphia: Fortress Press, 1975.

Thomas Aquinas. *Basic Writings of St. Thomas Aquinas*. 2 vols. Edited by Anton C. Pegis. New York: Random House, 1945.

Thompson, Bard, ed. *Liturgies of the Western Church*. Philadelphia: Fortress Press, 1961.

Tillich, Paul. *A History of Christian Thought*. Edited by Carl E. Braaten. New York: Simon and Schuster 1972.

Torrance, Thomas F. *The Mediation of Christ*. Exeter: Paternoster Press, 1983.

————. *The School of Faith: The Catechisms of the Reformed Church*. London: James Clark, 1959.

————. *Space, Time, and Resurrection*. Grand Rapids: Eerdmans, 1976.

————. *Theology in Reconciliation*. Grand Rapids: Eerdmans, 1966.

————. *Theology in Reconstruction*. Grand Rapids: Eerdmans, 1965.

Turner, W. G. *John Nelson Darby*. London: C. A. Hammond, 1951.

Turretin, Francis. *Institutes of Elenctic Theology*. Translated by George Musgrave Giger. Edited by James T. Dennison, Jr. Phillipsburg, N.J.: Presbyterian and Reformed, 1992-97. [Translation of *Institutio Theologicae Elencticae*, 4 vols. Edinburgh: John D. Lowe, 1847 (orig. 1679-1685)].

Ullmann, Carl. *The Sinlessness of Christ: An Evidence for Christianity*. Translated by Sophia Taylor. Edinburgh: T. & T. Clark, 1882.

_____. *Die Sundlosigkeit Jesu: eine apologetische Betrachtung*. 7 Aufl. Gotha: Friedrich Andreas Perthes, 1863.
Van Buren, Paul. *Christ in Our Place*. Grand Rapids: Eerdmans, 1957.
Van Til, Cornelius. *The Defense of the Faith*. 3rd ed. Philadelphia: Presbyterian & Reformed, 1967.
Vander Stelt, John C. *Philosophy and Scripture: A Study in Old Princeton and Westminster Theology*. Marlton, N.J.: Mack, 1978.
Vos, Geerhardus. *The Pauline Eschatology*. Princeton, N.J.: Princeton University Press, 1930.
Wakefield, Gordon Stevens. *Puritan Devotion: Its Place in the Development of Christian Piety*. London: Epworth Press, 1957.
Wallace, R. S. *Calvin's Doctrine of the Christian Life*. Edinburgh: Oliver and Boyd, 1959.
_____. *Calvin's Doctrine of Word and Sacrament*. Grand Rapids: Eerdmans, 1957.
Warfield, Benjamin Breckinridge. *Calvin and Augustine*. Philadelphia: Presbyterian and Reformed, 1956.
_____. *Two Studies in the History of Doctrine*. New York: Christian Literature, 1897.
Weber, Otto. *Foundations of Dogmatics*. 2 vols. Translated by Darrell L. Guder. Grand Rapids: Eerdmans, 1981.
Weber, Timothy P. *Living in the Shadow of the Second Coming: American Premillennialism, 1875-1982*. Enlarged ed. Grand Rapids: Zondervan, 1983.
Welch, Claude, ed. *God and Incarnation in Mid-Nineteenth Century German Theology*. New York: Oxford University Press, 1965.
_____. *Protestant Thought in the Nineteenth Century*. 2 vols. New Haven: Yale University Press, 1972, 1985.
Wells, David. *No Place for Truth, Or, Whatever Happened to Evangelical Theology*. Grand Rapids: Eerdmans, 1993.
Wendel, François. *Calvin: Origins and Development of His Religious Thought*. Translated by. Philip Mairet. New York: Harper and Row, 1963.
Wenzke, Annabelle S. *Timothy Dwight (1752-1817)*. Lewiston, N.Y.: Edwin Mellen Press, 1989.
West, Stephen, ed. *Sketches of the Life of the Late Rev. Samuel Hopkins, D.D., Pastor of the First Congregational Church in Newport, Written by Himself; Interspersed with Marginal Notes Extracted from His Private Diary*. Hartford, Conn.: Hudson and Goodwin, 1805.
White, John. *New England's Lamentations*. Boston: T. Fleet, 1734.
Willis, E. David. *Calvin's Catholic Christology*. Leiden: Brill, 1966.
Wilson Robert J., III. *The Benevolent Deity: Ebenezer Gay and the Rise of Rational Religion in New England, 1696-1787*. Philadelphia: University of Pennsylvania Press, 1984.
Witsius, Herman. *The Economy of the Covenants between God and Man: Comprehending a Complete Body of Divinity*. 2 vols. Translated by William Crookshank. London: R. Baynes, 1822.
Wollebius, Johannes. *Compendium Theologiae Christianae*. In *Reformed Dogmatics: J. Wollebius, G. Voetius, F. Turretin*, ed. and trans. John W. Beardslee III, 29-262. New York: Oxford University Press, 1965.

Wright, Conrad. *The Beginnings of Unitarianism in America*. Boston: Starr King Press, 1955.
Zaret, David. *The Heavenly Contract: Ideology and Organization in Pre-Revolutionary Puritanism*. Chicago: University of Chicago Press, 1985.
Ziegler, H. J. B. *Frederick Augustus Rauch: American Hegelian*. Lancaster, Pa.: Franklin and Marshall College, 1953.

Articles, Papers, etc.

Adger, John B. "Calvin Defended Against Drs. Cunningham and Hodge." *Southern Presbyterian Review* 27 (1876): 133-66.
_____. "Calvin's Doctrine of the Lord's Supper." *Southern Presbyterian Review* 35 (1885): 785-800.
Ahlstrom, Sydney E. "The Scottish Philosophy and American Theology." *Church History* 24 (1955): 257-272.
Alexander, Archibald. "The Early History of Pelagianism," *The Biblical Repertory and Princeton Review* 2 (1830): 77-113.
Anderson, Marvin W. "Peter Martyr on Romans." *Scottish Journal of Theology* 26 (1973): 401-420.
Anderson, Wallace E. "Editor's Introduction." In *Jonathan Edwards: Scientific and Philosophical Writings*, ed. Wallace E. Anderson, 1-143. *The Works of Jonathan Edwards*, vol. 6. New Haven: Yale University Press, 1980.
Beeke, Joel R. "The Dutch Second Reformation (Nadere Reformatie)." *Calvin Theological Journal* 28 (1993): 298-327.
Benrath, Gustav Adolf. "Evangelische und katholische Kirchenhistorie im Zeichen der Aufklärung und der Romantik," *Zeitschrift für Kirchengeschichte* 82 (1971): 203-217.
Bierma, Lyle D. "Federal Theology in the Sixteenth Century: Two Traditions?" *Westminster Theological Journal* 45 (1983): 304-321.
Bird, Brian. "Old Debate Finds New Life." *Christianity Today*, 17 March 1989, 38-40.
Black, Matthew. "The Pauline Doctrine of the Second Adam." *Scottish Journal of Theology* 7 (1954): 170-179.
Brauer, Jerald C. "Types of Puritan Piety." *Church History* 56 (1987): 39-58.
Breitenbach, William K. "The Consistent Calvinism of the New Divinity Movement." *William and Mary Quarterly* 41 (1984): 241-264.
_____. "Piety and Moralism: Edwards and the New Divinity." In *Jonathan Edwards and the American Experience*, ed. Nathan O. Hatch and Harry S. Stout, 177-204. New York: Oxford University Press, 1988.
_____. "Unregenerate Doings: Selflessness and Selfishness in New Divinity Theology." *American Quarterly* 34 (1982): 479-502.
Bromiley, G. W. "Karl Barth." In *Creative Minds in Contemporary Theology*, ed. Philip Edgcumbe Hughes, 27-62. Grand Rapids: Eerdmans, 1966.
Brown, William Adams. "Covenant Theology." In *Encyclopaedia of Religion and Ethics*, 13 vols., ed. James Hastings, 4:216-224. New York: Charles Scribner's Sons, 1924-27.
Bruce, F. F. "The Humanity of Jesus Christ." In *A Mind for What Matters: Collected Essays of F. F. Bruce*, 248-258. Grand Rapids: Eerdmans, 1990.

Burrell, S. A. "The Covenant Idea as a Revolutionary Symbol: Scotland, 1596-1637." *Church History* 27 (1958): 338-350

Cashdollar, Charles D. "The Pursuit of Piety: Charles Hodge's Diary, 1819-1820." *Journal of Presbyterian History* 55 (1977): 267-283.

Cherry, Conrad. "The Puritan Notion of the Covenant in Jonathan Edwards' Doctrine of Faith." *Church History* 34 (1965): 328-341.

Christie, Francis Albert. "The Beginnings of Arminianism in New England." *Papers of the American Society of Church History*, 2nd ser. 3 (1912): 153-172.

Conforti, Joseph A. "Antebellum Evangelicals and the Cultural Revival of Jonathan Edwards." *American Presbyterians* 64 (1986): 227-241.

_____. "Samuel Hopkins and the New Divinity: Theology, Ethics, and Social Reform in Eighteenth-Century New England." *William and Mary Quarterly* 34 (1977): 572-589.

DiPuccio, William. "Nevin's Idealistic Philosophy." In *Reformed Confessionalism in Nineteenth-Century America*, ed. by Sam Hamstra and Arie J. Griffioen, 43-67. Lanham, Md.: Scarecrow Press, 1995.

Donnelly, John Patrick. "Calvinist Thomism." *Viator: Medieval and Renaissance Studies* 7 (1976): 441-455.

Dorner, I. A. "On the Proper Version of the Dogmatic Concept of the Immutability of God." In *God and Incarnation in Mid-Nineteenth Century German Theology*, ed. and trans. by Claude Welch, 115-180. New York: Oxford University Press, 1965.

Edwards, Jonathan. "Unpublished Letter on Assurance and Participation in the Divine Nature." In Jonathan Edwards, *Ethical Writings*, ed. Paul Ramsey, 636-640. *The Works of Jonathan Edwards*, vol. 8. New Haven: Yale University Press, 1989.

Edwards, Jonathan, Jr. "Three Sermons on the Necessity of Atonement, and the Consistency between That and Free Grace in Forgiveness." In *The Atonement: Discourses and Treatises*, ed. Edwards A. Park, 1-42. Boston: Congregational Board of Publication, 1859.

Eenigenburg, Elton M. "The Place of the Covenant in Calvin's Thinking." *Reformed Review* 10 (1957): 1-22.

Emerson, Everett H. "Calvin and Covenant Theology." *Church History* 25 (1956): 136-44.

Evans, William B. "'Really Exhibited and Conferred . . . in His Appointed Time': Baptism and the New Reformed Sacramentalism." *Presbyterion: Covenant Seminary Review* 31/2 (2005): 72-88.

Fackenheim, Emil L. "Immanuel Kant." In *Nineteenth Century Religious Thought in the West*, ed. by Ninian Smart and others, 3 vols., I:17-40. New York: Cambridge University Press, 1985.

Farley, Edward. "The Modernist Element in Protestantism." *Theology Today* 47 (1990): 131-144.

Fiering, Norman. "The Rationalist Foundations of Edward's Metaphysics" In *Jonathan Edwards and the American Experience*, ed. Nathan O. Hatch and Harry S. Stout, 73-101. New York: Oxford, 1988.

Fisher, George Park. "The Augustinian and Federal Theories of Original Sin Compared." In *Discussions in History and Theology*, 355-409. New York: Charles Scribner's Sons, 1880.

_____. "Channing as a Philosopher and Theologian." In *Discussions in History and Theology*, 253-284. New York: Charles Scribner's Sons, 1880).

_____. "Original Sin: The State of the Question." *The New Englander* 18 (1860): 694-710.

_____. "The Philosophy of Jonathan Edwards." In *Discussions in History and Theology*, 227-252. New York: Charles Scribner's Sons, 1880.

Frei, Hans W. "Niebuhr's Theological Background," In *Faith and Ethics: The Theology of H. Richard Niebuhr*, ed. Paul Ramsey, 9-64. New York: Harper & Brothers, 1957.

Fulcher, J. Rodney "Puritans and the Passions: The Faculty Psychology in American Puritanism." *Journal of the History of the Behavioral Sciences* 9 (1973): 123-39.

Ganoczy, Alexandre. "Observations on Calvin's Trinitarian Doctrine of Grace." In *Probing the Reformed Tradition: Historical Studies in Honor of Edward A. Dowey, Jr.*, ed. Elsie Anne McKee and Brian G. Armstrong, 96-107. Louisville: Westminster/John Knox, 1989.

Gerrish, Brian A. "Charles Hodge and the Europeans." In *Charles Hodge Revisited: A Critical Appraisal of His Life and Work*, ed. John W. Stewart and James H. Moorhead, 129-158. Grand Rapids: Eerdmans, 2002.

_____. "Friedrich Schleiermacher." In *Nineteenth Century Religious Thought in the West*, 3 vols., ed. by Ninian Smart and others, I:123-156. New York: Cambridge University Press, 1985.

_____. "Sign and Reality: The Lord's Supper in the Reformed Confessions." In *The Old Protestantism and the New*, 118-130. Edinburgh: T. & T. Clark, 1982.

_____. "Theology Within the Limits of Piety Alone: Schleiermacher and Calvin's Notion of God." In *The Old Protestantism and the New: Essays on the Reformation Heritage*, 196-207. Edinburgh: T. & T. Clark, 1982.

Gillespie, Thomas W. "Evangelism and Social Witness: Recovering the Full Presbyterian Tradition." *Princeton Seminary Bulletin*, n.s. 12 (1991): 231-235.

Gilpin, W. Clark. "The Doctrine of the Church in the Thought of Alexander Campbell and John Nevin." *Mid-Stream* 19 (1980): 417-427.

Godfrey, W. Robert. "Reformed Thought on the Extent of the Atonement to 1618." *Westminster Theological Journal* 37 (1974-75): 133-71.

Grafland, C. "Hat Calvin einen ordo salutis gelehrt." In *Calvinus Ecclesiae Genevensis Custos*, ed. Wilhelm H. Neuser, 221-244. Frankfurt am Main: Verlag Peter Lang, 1984.

Griffin, Edward D. "An Humble Attempt to Reconcile the Differences of Christians Respecting the Extent of the Atonement." In *The Atonement: Discourses and Treatises*, ed. Edwards A. Park, 137-427. Boston: Congregational Board of Publication, 1859.

Guelzo, Allen C. "Jonathan Edwards and the New Divinity: Change and Continuity in New England Calvinism, 1758-1858." In *Pressing Toward the Mark: Essays Commemorating Fifty Years of the Orthodox Presbyterian Church*, ed. Charles G. Dennison and Richard C. Gamble, 147-167. Philadelphia: The Committee for the Historian of the Orthodox Presbyterian Church, 1986.

Helm, Paul. "Calvin and the Covenant: Unity and Continuity." *The Evangelical Quarterly* 55 (1983): 73.

Henderson, George D. "The Idea of the Covenant in Scotland," *Evangelical Quarterly* 27 (1955): 2-14.

Hodge, A. A. "The *Ordo Salutis*; Or, Relation in the Order of Nature of Holy Character and Divine Favor." *The Princeton Review* 54 (1878): 304-321.

Hodge, Charles. "Beecher's Great Conflict." *The Biblical Repertory and Princeton Review* 26 (1854): 96-138.

———. "Beman on the Atonement." *The Biblical Repertory and Princeton Review* 17 (1845): 84-138.

———. "Bishop McIlvaine on the Church." *The Biblical Repertory and Princeton Review* 27 (1855): 350-59.

———. "Bushnell on Christian Nurture." *The Biblical Repertory and Princeton Review* 19 (1847): 502-539.

———. "Bushnell on Vicarious Sacrifice." *The Biblical Repertory and Princeton Review* 38 (1866): 161-194.

———. "The Church—Its Perpetuity." *The Biblical Repertory and Princeton Review* 28 (1856): 689-715.

———. "The Church Membership of Infants." *The Biblical Repertory and Princeton Review* 30 (1858): 347-389.

———. "The Doctrine of Imputation," in *Princeton Theological Essays*, ed. Patrick Fairbairn, 144-167. Edinburgh: T. & T. Clark, 1856.

———. "Doctrine of the Reformed Church on the Lord's Supper." *The Biblical Repertory and Princeton Review* 20 (1848): 227-278.

———. "The First and Second Adam." *The Biblical Repertory and Princeton Review* 32 (1860): 335-376.

———. "The General Assembly." *The Biblical Repertory and Princeton Review* 17 (1845): 428-471.

———. "The Idea of the Church." *The Biblical Repertory and Princeton Review* 25 (1853): 249-290, 339-389.

———. "Inquiries Respecting the Doctrine of Imputation." *The Biblical Repertory and Princeton Review* 2 (1830): 425-472.

———. "Is the Church of Rome a Part of the Visible Church." *The Biblical Repertory and Princeton Review* 18 (1846): 320-344.

———. "Nature of Man." *The Biblical Repertory and Princeton Review* 37 (1865): 111-135.

———. "Neander's History." *The Biblical Repertory and Princeton Review* 16 (1844): 155-183.

———. "The New Divinity Tried." *The Biblical Repertory and Princeton Review* 4 (1832): 278-304.

———. "Presbyterianism." *The Biblical Repertory and Princeton Review* 32 (1860): 546-67.

———. "Regeneration, and the Manner of Its Occurrence." *The Biblical Repertory and Princeton Review* 2 (1830): 250-297.

———. "Testimonies on the Doctrine of Imputation." *The Biblical Repertory and Princeton Review* 11 (1839): 553-579.

———. "Theories of the Church." *The Biblical Repertory and Princeton Review* 18 (1846): 137-158.

———. "Visibility of the Church." *The Biblical Repertory and Princeton Review* 25 (1853): 670-685.

———. "What Is Christianity." *The Biblical Repertory and Princeton Review* 32 (1860): 118-161.

Hodgson, Peter C. "Georg Wilhelm Friedrich Hegel." In *Nineteenth Century Religious Thought in the West*, 3 vols., ed. Ninian Smart and others, I:81-119. New York: Cambridge University Press, 1985.

Hoekema, Anthony A. "The Covenant of Grace in Calvin's Teaching." *Calvin Theological Journal* 2 (1967): 133-161.

Holbrook, Clyde A. "Original Sin and the Enlightenment." In *The Heritage of Christian Thought: Essays in Honor of Robert Lowry Calhoun*, ed. Robert E. Cushman and Egil Grislis, 142-165. New York: Harper & Row, 1965.

Holifield, E. Brooks. "Mercersburg, Princeton, and the South: The Sacramental Controversy in the Nineteenth Century." *Journal of Presbyterian History* 54 (1976): 238-257.

_____. "The Renaissance of Sacramental Piety in Colonial New England," *The William and Mary Quarterly* 29 (1972): 33-48

Howe, Daniel Walker. "The Decline of Calvinism: An Approach to Its Study." *Comparative Studies in Society and History* 14 (1972): 306-327.

Johnson, S. Lewis. "How Faith Works." *Christianity Today*, 22 September 1989, 21-25.

Jones, R. Tudur. "Union with Christ: The Existential Nerve of Puritan Piety." *Tyndale Bulletin* 41 (1990): 186-208.

Kelly, Douglas F. "Prayer and Union with Christ." *Scottish Bulletin of Evangelical Theology* 8 (1990): 109-127.

Kennedy, Earl William. "Authors of Articles in *The Biblical Repertory and Princeton Review*." Typescript, Speer Library, Princeton Theological Seminary, 1963.

_____. "Writings about Charles Hodge and His Works, Principally as Found in Periodicals Contained in the Speer Library, Princeton Theological Seminary, for the Years 1830-1880." Typescript, Speer Library, Princeton Theological Seminary, 1963.

Klempa, William. "The Concept of the Covenant in Sixteenth- and Seventeenth-Century Continental and British Reformed Theology." In *Major Themes in the Reformed Tradition*, ed. Donald K. McKim, 94-107. Grand Rapids: Eerdmans, 1992.

Landis, Robert W. "The Gratuitous Imputation of Sin." *Southern Presbyterian Review* 27 (1876): 318-353.

_____. "Imputation, Part I." *The Danville Quarterly Review* 1 (1861): 390-427.

_____. "Imputation, Part II: Antecedent Imputation and Supralapsarianism." *The Danville Quarterly Review* 1 (1861): 553-613;

_____. "Imputation, Part III: Imputation and Original Sin." *The Danville Quarterly Review* 2 (1862): 58-111, 248-282, 514-578.

_____. "Unthinkable Propositions and Original Sin." *Southern Presbyterian Review* 26 (April 1875): 298-315.

Lane, A. N. S. "Calvin's Doctrine of Assurance." *Vox Evangelica* 11 (1979): 32-54.

_____. "The Quest for the Historical Calvin." *Evangelical Quarterly* 55 (1983): 95-113.

Lewis, Tayler. "The Mercersburg School," *Literary World* Nos. 114, 115 (April 7, 14, 1849): 311-313, 331-333.

Lindsay, T. M. "The Covenant Theology," *British and Foreign Evangelical Review* 28 (1879): 521-537.

Logan, Samuel T., Jr. "The Doctrine of Justification in the Theology of Jonathan Edwards." *Westminster Theological Journal* 46 (1984): 26-52.

Lovejoy, David S. "Samuel Hopkins: Religion, Slavery and the Revolution." *New England Quarterly* 40 (1967): 227-243.

Mackintosh, H. R. "The Unio Mystica as a Theological Conception." *Expositor* 7 (1909): 138-155.

Marsden, George M. "Perry Miller's Rehabilitation of The Puritans: A Critique." *Church History* 39 (1970): 91-105.

May, Henry F. "Jonathan Edwards and America." In *Jonathan Edwards and the American Experience*, ed. by Nathan O. Hatch and Harry S. Stout, 19-33. New York: Oxford University Press, 1988.

McGiffert, Michael. "The Problem of the Covenant in Puritan Thought: Peter Bulkeley's Gospel-Covenant." *New England Historical and Genealogical Register* 130 (1976): 107-129.

Moffatt, James Clement. "Popular Education." *The Biblical Repertory and Princeton Review* 29 (1857): 609-635.

Møller, Jens Glebe. "The Beginnings of Puritan Covenant Theology." *Journal of Ecclesiastical History* 14 (1963): 46-67.

Moore, Walter L. "Schleiermacher as a Calvinist: A Comparison of Calvin and Schleiermacher on Providence and Predestination." *Scottish Journal of Theology* 24 (1971): 167-183.

Morris, William Sparkes. "The Genius of Jonathan Edwards." In *Reinterpretation in American Church History*, ed. Jerald C. Brauer, 29-65. Chicago: University of Chicago Press, 1968.

Muller, Richard A. "Emanuel V. Gerhart on the "Christ Idea" as Fundamental Principle." *Westminster Theological Journal* 48 (1986): 97-117.

_____. "Perkins' *A Golden Chaine*: Predestinarian System or Schematized *Ordo Salutis*?" *Sixteenth Century Journal* 9 (1978): 69-81.

Murray, John. "Covenant Theology." *The Encyclopedia of Christianity*, ed. Philip E. Hughes, III:199-216. Marshalltown, Del.: National Foundation for Christian Education, 1972.

Nelson, John Oliver. "Charles Hodge: Nestor of Orthodoxy." In *The Lives of Eighteen from Princeton*, ed. Willard Thorp, 192-211. Princeton, N.J.: Princeton University Press, 1946.

Nevin, John W. "The Anglican Crisis." *Mercersburg Review* 3 (1851): 359-398.

_____. "Answer to Professor Dorner." *Mercersburg Review* 15 (1868): 532-646.

_____. "The Apostles' Creed." *Mercersburg Review* 1 (1849): 105-127, 201-221, 313-347.

_____. "Catholic Unity." In *The Mercersburg Theology*, ed. James Hastings Nichols, 33-55. New York: Oxford University Press, 1966.

_____. "Catholicism." *Mercersburg Review* 3 (1851): 1-26.

_____. "The Church." In *The Mercersburg Theology*, ed. James Hastings Nichols, 56-76. New York: Oxford University Press, 1966. [Originally published in pamphlet form as *The Church: A Sermon Preached at the Opening of the Synod of the German Reformed Church at Carlisle, October 1846*. Chambersburg: German Reformed Church Publishing House, 1847.]

_____. "Cur Deus Homo." *Mercersburg Review* 3 (1851): 220-238.

———. "Doctrine of the Reformed Church on the Lord's Supper." In John W. Nevin, *The Mystical Presence and Other Writings on the Eucharist*, ed. Bard Thompson and George H. Bricker, 267-401. Lancaster Series on the Mercersburg Theology, 4. Philadelphia: United Church Press, 1966. [Originally appeared in *Mercersburg Review* 2 (1850): 421-548.]

———. "Hodge on the Ephesians." *Mercersburg Review* 9 (1857): 46-83, 192-245.

———. "Jesus and the Resurrection." *Mercersburg Review* 13 (1861): 169-190.

———. "Liebner's Christology." *Mercersburg Review* 3 (1851): 55-73.

———. "The New Creation in Christ." *Mercersburg Review* 2 (1850): 1-11.

———. "Noel on Baptism." *Mercersburg Review* 2 (1850): 231-265.

———. "Our Relations to Germany." *Mercersburg Review* 14 (1867): 627-633.

———. "Puritanism and the Creed," *Mercersburg Review* 1 (1849): 585-607.

———. Review of *God in Christ*, by Horace Bushnell. *Mercersburg Review* 1 (1849): 311-312.

———. "The Sect System." In *Catholic and Reformed: Selected Theological Writings of John Williamson Nevin*, ed. Charles Yrigoyen, Jr. and George H. Bricker, 127-173. Pittsburgh: Pickwick Press, 1978. [Originally appeared in *Mercersburg Review* 1 (1849):482-507; 521-539.]

———. "Schleiermachers Verhältnis zur reformierten Tradition." *Zwischen den Zeiten* 8 (1930): 511-525.

Noll, Mark A. "Charles Hodge as an Expositor of the Christian Life." In *Charles Hodge Revisited: A Critical Appraisal of His Life and Work*, ed. John W. Stewart and James H. Moorhead, 181-216. Grand Rapids: Eerdmans, 2002.

———. "Common Sense Traditions and American Evangelical Thought." *American Quarterly* 37 (1985): 216-238.

———. "Introduction." In *The Princeton Theology, 1812-1921*, ed. Mark A. Noll, 11-48. Grand Rapids: Baker, 1983.

———. "Jonathan Edwards and Nineteenth-Century Theology." In *Jonathan Edwards and the American Experience*, ed. Nathan O. Hatch and Harry S. Stout, 260-287. New York: Oxford University Press, 1988.

———. "The Princeton Review." *Westminster Theological Journal* 50 (1988): 283-304.

Otto, Randall E. "Justification and Justice: An Edwardsean Proposal." *Evangelical Quarterly* 65 (1993): 131-145.

———. "The Solidarity of Mankind in Jonathan Edwards' Doctrine of Original Sin." *Evangelical Quarterly* 62 (1990): 205-221.

The Oxford English Dictionary. 1971. S.v. "Surety."

Park, Edwards Amasa. "Introductory Essay." In *The Atonement: Discourses and Treatises*, ed. Edwards Amasa Park, vii-lxxx. Boston: Congregational Board of Publication, 1859).

Partee, Charles Partee. "Calvin's Central Dogma Again." *The Sixteenth Century Journal* 18 (1987): 191-199.

Patton, Francis Landey, "Archibald Alexander Hodge: A Memorial Discourse." In A. A. Hodge, *Evangelical Theology: Lectures on Doctrine*, ix-xli. Edinburgh: Banner of Truth, 1976.

Payne, John B. "Schaff and Nevin, Colleagues at Mercersburg: The Church Question." *Church History* 61 (1992): 169-190.

Porter, J. R. "The Legal Aspects of the Concept of 'Corporate Personality' in the Old Testament." *Vetus Testamentum* 15 (1965): 361-380.
Raitt, Jill. "Calvin's Use of *Persona*." In *Calvinus Ecclesiae Genevensis Custos*, ed. Wilhelm H. Neuser, 273-287. Frankfurt am Main: Peter Lang, 1984.
Ramsey, Paul. "Infused Virtues in Edwardsean and Calvinistic Context." In Jonathan Edwards, *Ethical Writings*, ed. Paul Ramsey, 739-750. *The Works of Jonathan Edwards*, vol. 8. New Haven: Yale University Press, 1989.
Redman, Robert R. Jr. "H. R. Mackintosh's Contribution to Christology and Soteriology in the Twentieth Century." *Scottish Journal of Theology* 41 (1988): 517-534.
Reily, William M. "Schleiermacher and the Theology of the Mercersburg Review." *Mercersburg Review* 18 (1871): 165-182.
Richards, George Warren. "The Mercersburg Theology, Historically Considered." *Papers of the American Society of Church History*, second series, 3 (1912): 119-149
_____. "The Mercersburg Theology: Its Purpose and Principles." *Church History* 20 (1951): 42-55.
Rogerson, J. W. "The Hebrew Conception of Corporate Personality: A Re-examination." *Journal of Theological Studies* n.s. 21 (1970): 1-16.
Rohr, John von. "Covenant and Assurance in Early English Puritanism." *Church History* 34 (1965): 195-203.
Rolston, Holmes III. "Responsible Man in Reformed Theology: Calvin versus the Westminster Confession." *Scottish Journal of Theology* 23 (1970): 129-156.
Rupp, George. "The 'Idealism' of Jonathan Edwards." *Harvard Theological Review* 62 (1969): 209-226.
Schafer, Thomas A. "Jonathan Edwards and Justification by Faith," *Church History* 20 (1951): 55-67.
Schaff, Philip. "Additions" in J. P. Lange and F. R. Fay, *The Epistle of Paul to the Romans*. Translated by J. F. Hurst. New York: Charles Scribner, 1869.
Scheick, William J. "Introduction." In *Critical Essays on Jonathan Edwards*, ed. William J. Scheick, ix-xxv. Boston: G.K. Hall, 1980.
Schmidt, Leigh Eric. "'A Second and Glorious Reformation': The New Light Extremism of Andrew Croswell." *William and Mary Quarterly* 43 (1986): 214-244.
Schweizer, Eduard. "*pneuma, pneumatikos*." In *Theological Dictionary of the New Testament*, ed. Gerhard Kittel and Gerhard Friedrich, trans. Geoffrey W. Bromiley, VI:332-455. Grand Rapids: Eerdmans, 1964-76.
_____. "Zanchius on Saving Faith." *Westminster Theological Journal* 36 (1973-74): 31-47.
Shriver, George H. "Passages in Friendship: John W. Nevin to Charles Hodge, 1872." *Journal of Presbyterian History* 58 (1980): 116-122.
Smalley, John. "Justification Through Christ, An Act of Free Grace." In *The Atonement: Discourses and Treatises*, ed. Edwards A. Park, 43-64. Boston: Congregational Board of Publication, 1859.
Spijker, Willem van't. "'*Extra Nos*' and '*In Nobis*' by Calvin in a Pneumatological Light." In *Calvin and the Holy Spirit*, ed. Peter De Klerk, 39-62. Grand Rapids: Calvin Studies Society, 1989.
Stein, Stephen J. "Stuart and Hodge on Romans 5:12-21: An Exegetical Controversy about Original Sin." *Journal of Presbyterian History* 47 (1969): 340-358.
Stoever, William K. B. "Nature, Grace and John Cotton: The Theological Dimension in the New England Antinomian Controversy." *Church History* 44 (1975): 22-33.

Swift, David E. "Samuel Hopkins: Calvinist Social Concern in Eighteenth-Century New England." *Journal of Presbyterian History* 47 (1969): 31-54.

Thompson, D. Bard. "The Mercersburg Divines." Unpublished paper read before the Avon Literary Club, May 4, 1962.

Torrance, James B. "Calvin and Puritanism in England and Scotland—Some Basic Concepts in the Development of 'Federal Theology.'" In *Calvinus Reformator: His Contribution to Theology, Church, and Society*, 264-287. Potchefstroom, S.A.: Potchefstroom University, 1982.

_____. "The Covenant Concept in Scottish Theology and Politics and Its Legacy." *Scottish Journal of Theology* 34 (1981): 225-243.

_____. "Covenant or Contract?: A Study of the Theological Background of Worship in Seventeenth-Century Scotland." *Scottish Journal of Theology* 23 (1970): 51-76.

_____. "The Incarnation and Limited Atonement." *Evangelical Quarterly* 15 (1983): 83-94.

Tracy, David W. "The Catholic Analogical Imagination," *Proceedings of the Catholic Theological Society of America* (1977): 234-244.

Trinterud, Leonard J. "The Origins of Puritanism." *Church History* 20 (1951): 37-57.

Tucker, Gene M. "Introduction." In H. Wheeler Robinson, *Corporate Personality in Ancient Israel*, 7-13. Philadelphia: Fortress Press, 1980.

Tylenda, Joseph. "Calvin and Christ's Presence in the Supper—True or Real?" *Scottish Journal of Theology* 27 (1974): 65-75.

Ullmann, Carl. "Preliminary Essay," in *The Mystical Presence: A Vindication of the Reformed or Calvinistic Doctrine of the Holy Eucharist*, by John W. Nevin (Philadelphia: J. B. Lippincott, 1846), 13-47. [A loose translation of Ullmann's "Das Wesen des Christentums," *Studien und Kritiken* (1845)]

Vos, Geerhardus. "Doctrine of the Covenant in Reformed Theology." In *Redemptive History and Biblical Interpretation: The Shorter Writings of Geerhardus Vos*, ed. by Richard B. Gaffin, Jr., 234-267. Phillipsburg, N.J.: Presbyterian and Reformed, 1980.

_____. "The Eschatological Aspect of the Pauline Conception of the Spirit." In *Redemptive History and Biblical Interpretation: The Shorter Writings of Geerhardus Vos*, ed. Richard B. Gaffin, Jr., 91-125. Phillipsburg, N.J.: Presbyterian and Reformed, 1980.

Walker, Williston. "The Sandemanians of New England." *Annual Report of the American Historical Association for the Year 1901* 1 (1902): 133-162.

Warfield, Benjamin B. "Imputation." In *Biblical and Theological Studies*, ed. Samuel G. Craig, 262-269. Philadelphia: Presbyterian and Reformed, 1968.

_____. "On the Literary History of Calvin's Institutes." In *Institutes of the Christian Religion by John Calvin*, 2 vols., trans. by John Allen, I:v-lvi. Philadelphia: Presbyterian Board of Christian Education, 1936.

Wells, David F. "Charles Hodge." In *Reformed Theology in America: A History of Its Modern Development*, ed. David F. Wells, 36-59. Grand Rapids: Eerdmans, 1985.

Williams, Stanley, ed. "Six Letters of Jonathan Edwards to Joseph Bellamy." *New England Quarterly* 1 (1928): 226-242.

Willis, David. "Calvin's Use of Substantia." In *Calvinus Ecclesiae Genevensis Custos*, ed. Wilhelm H. Neuser, 289-301. New York: Peter Lang, 1984.

Wolverton, John F. "John Williamson Nevin and the Episcopalians: The Debate on the 'Church Question,' 1851-1874." *Historical Magazine of the Protestant Episcopal Church* 49 (1980): 361-387.

Yoder, Don. "The Bench vs. the Catechism: Revivalism and Pennsylvania's Lutheran and Reformed Churches." *Pennsylvania Folklife* 10 (Fall 1959): 14-23.
Yrigoyen, Charles. "Mercersburg's Quarrel with Methodism." *Methodist History* 22 (1983): 3-19.
Zwaanstra, Henry. "Louis Berkhof." In *Reformed Theology in America*, ed. David F. Wells, 153-169. Grand Rapids: Eerdmans, 1985.

Theses and Dissertations

Breitenbach, William K. "The New Divinity and the Era of Moral Accountability." Ph.D. diss., Yale University, 1978.
Carlough, William L. "A Historical Comparison of the Theology of John Williamson Nevin and Contemporary Protestant Sacramentalism." Ph.D. diss., New York University, 1961.
Crutchfield, Larry Vance. "The Doctrine of Ages and Dispensations as Found in the Published Writings of John Nelson Darby (1800-1882)." Ph.D. diss., Drew University, 1985.
DeBie, Linden Jay. "German Idealism in Protestant Orthodoxy: The Mercersburg Movement, 1840-1860." Ph.D. diss., McGill University, 1987.
Deifell, John Jey, Jr. "The Ecclesiology of Charles Hodge." Ph.D. diss., University of Edinburgh, 1969.
Evans, William B. "Union with the Second Adam." Th.M. thesis, Westminster Theological Seminary, 1986.
Fitzmier, John R. "The Godly Federalism of Timothy Dwight, 1752-1817: Society, Doctrine, and Religion in the Life of New England's "Moral Legislator."" Ph.D. diss., Princeton University, 1986.
Kennedy, Earl William. "A Historical Analysis of Charles Hodge's Doctrines of Sin and Particular Grace." Th.D. diss., Princeton Theological Seminary, 1968.
Krapohl, Robert H. "A Search for Purity: The Controversial Life of John Nelson Darby." Ph.D. diss., Baylor University, 1980.
McAllister, James L. Jr. "The Nature of Religious Knowledge in the Theology of Charles Hodge. Ph.D. diss., Duke University, 1957.
Murchie, David Neil. "Morality and Social Ethics in the Thought of Charles Hodge." Ph.D. diss., Drew University, 1980.
Plummer, Kenneth Moses. "The Theology of John Williamson Nevin in the Mercersburg Period, 1840-1852." Ph.D. diss., University of Chicago, 1958.
Tyner, Wayne C. "The Theology of Timothy Dwight in Historical Perspective." Ph.D. diss., University of North Carolina at Chapel Hill, 1971.
Venema, Cornelis P. "The Twofold Nature of the Gospel in Calvin's Theology: The *duplex gratia dei* and the Interpretation of Calvin's Theology." Ph.D. diss.: Princeton Theological Seminary, 1985.
Won, Jonathan Jong-Chun. "Communion with Christ: An Exposition and Comparison of the Doctrine of Union and Communion with Christ in Calvin and the English Puritans." Ph.D. diss., Westminster Theological Seminary, 1989.

General Index

Adger, J.B. 181, 216, 225
Agricola, R. 45
Ahlstrom, S. 191
Alexander, Archibald 187
Ames, William 56-57, 71
Anderson, W.E. 90-91
Antinomian Controversy 50-51
antinomianism 94, 159
Aristotelianism 46-52
Arminianism 92-94
Armstrong, B.G. 31, 43
assurance 16, 125-126, 137
atonement 64-65, 101, 117-122, 163, 173-175, 204
Augustine 58, 65, 70-71, 91, 98, 182
Baird, Samuel J. 201
Baker, J.W. 61
baptism 17-18, 127-128, 177-178, 220-222
Barr, James 253
Barth, Karl 55, 243-246
Bauke, H. 13
Baxter, Richard 117
Beecher, Edward 196
Bell, M.C. 64-65, 68-69
Bellamy, Joseph 113
Berkeley, George 89-90
Berkhof, Louis 52, 233-235
Berkouwer, G.C. 9, 55, 250-251
Beza, Theodore 26, 43, 67
Bierma, Lyle 61
Bloesch, D.G. 245
Boehl, E. 235
Boston, Thomas 66, 69-70
Bozeman, T.D. 192
Bratt, J.D. 233
Brauer, Jerald 77
Breitenbach, W. 111-112, 114
Briggs, C.A. 53-54
Bruce, F.F. 167
Bruce, Robert 65
Brunner, Emil 1

Bullinger, H. 7, 60-61
Bushnell, H. 173
Calvin, John 1, 7-41, 46- 47, 63, 66-67, 88, 204, 223, 262, 267
Cashdollar, C.D. 188
Chafer, L.S. 256
Chauncy, Charles 94
Cherry, C. 89, 100
church 126-128, 163-164, 215-219
conditionality of covenant 60-65
Conforti, J. 114
Consensus Tigurinus 23-24, 26, 223
corporate personality 249-251
Cotton, John 50-51
Cunningham, W. 47, 106-107, 225
Dabney, R.L. 47, 225, 234
Darby, J.N. 255-256
Dee, S.P. 12
Deifell, J.J. 215-216, 232
DeJong, P.Y. 88
Descartes, R. 89
Dick, John 155
disinterested benevolence 115-116, 132
Dispensationalism 255-257
Donnelly, J.P. 49
Dordt, Synod of 51, 93
Dorner, I.A. 153-154, 182-183
Doumergue, E. 11-12, 34
Dwight, Timothy 107, 130-136, 178
Ebrard, A. 179
Edwards, Jonathan 87-113, 115, 122-125, 178
Edwards Jr., Jonathan 113, 118
Elert, W. 54-55
Emmons, Nathanael 113
Erb, W.H. 146
Evans, W.B. 18, 265
faculty psychology 47, 96, 117, 162
faith 15-16, 96-97, 135, 164-165, 203
federal theology 57-75, 94-95, 104, 111, 120, 174, 181, 187-237, 257
Fiering, N. 90

filioque 168
Finney, C.G. 137, 143, 194
Fisher, G. P. 90, 197
Fitzmier, J. 130-131
Formula Consensus Helvetica 72-73
Foster, F.H. 107, 113, 131
Gaffin, R.B. 54-55, 57, 264
Ganoczy, A. 13-14, 37
Garrett, C. 256
Gay, Ebenezer 94
generic humanity 161-163
Gerrish, B.A. 19, 45, 155, 220
Gerstner, J. 256-258
Gillespie, T.W. 261
Godfrey, W.R. 65
Goodwin, T. 77-78
governmental atonement 117-122
Griffin, E.D. 137
Grotius, Hugo 117
Guelzo, A. 114
Gunton, C.E. 82
Guthrie, William 69
habitus 47-48, 50-51, 98-99
Half-Way Covenant 80, 112, 132
Hambrick-Stowe, C. 77
Hamilton, N.Q. 263
Haroutunian, J. 113
Harris, M.J. 263
Hegel, G.W.F. 148-149, 153-154
Helfenstein, Jacob 182
Heppe, H. 1, 56
Herrmann, W. 241-243
Heshusius, T. 20, 23
Hobbes, Thomas 89
Hodge, A.A. 187, 210, 229-233, 235
Hodge, Charles 1, 47, 107, 142, 144, 167, 178, 182, 187-227, 231, 234
Hodges, Z. 257
Hoekema, A.A. 55
Hoffecker, W.A. 194
Holifield, E.B. 78-80, 225
Holy Spirit 14-15, 33-34, 97-98, 124, 165-168
Hopkins, Samuel 113-130
Howe, D.W. 94
humanity of Christ 19-22, 23-29, 39-40, 159-168, 180, 205-208, 213, 247, 262-265

Hume, David 190
Hutchinson, G.P. 35, 71-72, 198
idealism 89-92, 148-149, 156-158
imputation 34-38, 72-75, 102, 104-106, 126, 170-171, 195-208
infant salvation 199-200
Irenaeus 58, 163
Irving, Edward 167
Jones, R. T. 77
justification 1, 9, 30-38, 101-103, 107-111, 169-175, 211-215, 265
Kant, I. 148
Kennedy, E.W. 189, 200
Knox, John 65
Kolfhaus, W. 12
Krusche, W. 16
Kuklick, B. 91-92, 147
Lachman, D. 70
Landis, R.W. 201-202
Lee, S.H. 87
Lewis, Tayler 182
loci method 45-46
Loeb, L.E. 89
Logan, S. 89
Lord's Supper 19-23, 112, 127, 158, 178-180, 222-227, 232-233
Luther, Martin 19, 48
Lutheran Orthodoxy 54-55
Lüttge, W. 10
MacArthur, J. 257-259
Mackintosh, H.R. 151, 243, 246
Marsden, G.M. 137, 256
Mayhew, J. 94
McCormack, B.L. 167
McDonnell, K. 17, 28
McGiffert, M. 60
McGrath, A. 35, 39, 47
McNeill, J. T. 24
Mead, S. 113
mediate imputation 72-75, 170-171
Mediating Theologians 152-155
Miller, Perry 45, 48, 59-60, 87-88, 90
Moffatt, J.C. 192
moral union 123-124, 134-135, 158
Morris, W.S. 88
Müller, Julius 154
Muller, R.A. 43, 46, 49, 199
Murchie, D.N. 219

Murray, A. 255
Murray, J. 107
Murray, John 62, 107
mysticism 77, 99-100
Neander, J.A.G. 142-143, 152-153
Neoplatonism 99-100
Nettleton, A. 137, 142
Nevin, J.W. 1, 141-183, 249
New Divinity 113-131
New School Presbyterianism 137
Nichols, J.H. 155
Noll, M.A. 2, 113, 214, 229
nominalism 38, 48, 58, 70-71, 193, 202
Nuttall, G. 78
Olevianus, C. 56
ordo salutis 37, 40, 52-57, 81-82, 107-108, 111, 124-125, 175, 208-211, 230-232
original sin 34-35, 70-75, 104-107, 196-202
Orr, J. 54
Osiander, A. 24-26, 31
Owen, John 79-80
Park, E.A. 101-102
Partee, C. 8, 28
participation 28, 100
Payne, J.B. 155
Pettit, N. 60
Pierson, A.T. 255
pietism 75-81
Placaeus, J. 34, 72-75
Platonism 28
Plummer, K.M. 155
Porter, J.R. 250
Princeton Seminary 142, 188
Prynne, W. 80
Puritanism 75-81, 145-146
Raitt, J. 26
Ramus, Peter 45-46
Rauch, F.A. 143, 164
reatus culpae/reatus poenae 199, 213, 234, 236
Reformed Orthodoxy 43-83, 195
regeneration 29, 53-54, 208-210, 220, 230-231
Reid, J.K.S. 253
Reid, Thomas 190-191
Relly, J. 120

resurrection justification 55-57, 103, 263-266
Ritschl, A. 11, 57, 230
Rivet, A. 72
Robinson, H.W. 249-250
Rogerson, J.W. 250
Rohr, J. von 60, 78
Rollock, Robert 66
Rutherford, Samuel 65, 68-70, 75
Ryrie, C. 257
sacraments 17, 78-81, 175-180, 219-227
sanctification 29-30, 107-111, 168-169
Sandeen, E.R. 256
Schafer, T.A. 88-89, 112
Schaff, P. 143, 145, 153
Schleiermacher, F. 148, 150-155, 173
Schneckenburger, M. 1, 9
Schweizer, E. 263-264
scientia media 173
Scottish Common Sense 121-122, 189-193, 205
Scroggs, Robin 263
Shedd, R.P. 249-250
Shedd, W.G.T. 201, 210, 229
Shriver, G.H. 206
Sibbes, R. 77
Silva, Moises 253
Smedes, L.B. 251-253
Solemn League and Covenant 66
Song of Solomon 77
Stoever, W.K.B. 50-51, 53, 60
Strong, A.H. 260
Stuart, M. 200
Stuermann, W.E. 10
substantia 23-29
sursum corda 23
Sweeney, D. 114, 130-131
Tamburello, D. 41
Tannehill, R.C. 250
Taylor, John 93
Taylor, N.W. 107, 135, 137
Thomas Aquinas 47-49
Thornwell, J.H. 216
Tillich, Paul 44
Torrance, J.B. 63-65
Torrance, T.F. 62-63, 167, 246-249
Tracy, D.W. 176
Trinterud, L. 60

Turretin, F. 68, 71, 73-74, 187
Tylenda, J. 19, 22
Ullmann, C. 153-154
universalism 120-121
Ursinus, Z. 56
Venema, C. 9, 11-13, 29, 34
Vermigli, Peter Martyr 7, 40, 49
virtual communion 81
Vos, G. 263-264
Wallace, R.S. 20
Warfield, B.B. 8, 52, 187
Weber, O.
Weber, T.P.
Wells, D.F. 200
Wendel, F. 12, 23, 26, 29
Whitby, Daniel 93
White, J. 93
Willis, E.D. 14, 20, 23, 27-28, 79
Witherspoon, John 191
Witsius, H. 54, 56
Wollebius, J. 53, 71
Won, J. 76-78
Zanchi, J. 49-50
Zaret, D. 60, 67
Zwingli, H. 19-20, 22, 60, 204